ECONOMIC AND BUSINESS ETHICS

Practical and Professional Ethics Series

Vol. 1: The Primer of Applied Ethics
Vol. 2: Environmental Ethics
Vol. 3: Bio-Medical Ethics
Vol. 4: Educational Ethics
Vol. 5: Economic and Business Ethics
Vol. 6: Socio-Political Ethics

About the Author

Dr. Debashis Guha, teaches Ethics, and Phenomenology and Existentialism in the Post Graduate Department of Philosophy, Ranchi University, Ranchi. After doing masters course in Philosophy from Delhi University in 1980, he was conferred the Ph.D. degree of Jadavpur University in 1988. Dr. Guha takes interest in Philosophy of Religion, Social and Political Philosophy, Philosophy of Science and Analytic Philosophy. He taught at the undergraduate level in a constituent college of Ranchi University from 1981 to 1989 and was then asked to serve the Post Graduate Department. Dr. Guha is teaching Ethics for twenty-four years. He was awarded the Visiting Associateship of the U.G.C. (1994-96) in Jadavpur University, Calcutta, where he worked out *An Inquiry into the cases of Pain and Suffering,* which awaits publication. He was further awarded U.G.C.'s Major Research Project (1997-2000) on *Applied Ethics in Indian Context,* which has been now shaped in Six volumes, of which the present work is the fifth one under the series: **Practical and Professional Ethics**. Dr. Guha has fifteen papers to his credit. He has presented philosophical papers in different Seminars, Symposia and Congress, two of them were presented in International Congress; one in the Platinum Jubilee Celebrations of the Indian Philosophical Congress, 2000-01, and the other in the XVth International Congress of Aesthetics in Tokyo, Japan in 2001. During his Major Research Project work, Dr. Guha has talked to many people from different walks of life, interviewed them and also arranged ethical dialogues leading to resolution of value-laden practical problems of urgency. Dr. Guha envisions people's participation in Practical and Professional Ethics.

Practical and Professional Ethics

Volume - Five

Economic and Business Ethics

DEBASHIS GUHA

CONCEPT PUBLISHING COMPANY, NEW DELHI-110059

Cataloging in Publication Data—DK
Courtesy: D.K. Agencies (P) Ltd. <docinfo@dkagencies.com>

Guha, Debashis.
Practical and professional ethics / Debashis Guha.
v. 5 cm.
Includes bibliographical references.
Includes indexes.
Contents: v. 5. Economic and business ethics.
ISBN 13: 9788180693144 (set)
ISBN 10: 8180693147 (set)
ISBN 13: 9788180694899 (v. 5)
ISBN 10: 81806934895 (v. 5)
ISBN 13: 9788180694905 (pbk.) (v. 5)
ISBN 10: 81806934909 (pbk.)(v. 5)

1. Applied ethics. 2. Professional ethics. 3. Environmental ethics. 4. Bioethics. 5. Medical ethics. 6. Moral education. 7. Business ethics. I. Title.

DDC 170 22

ISBN-13: 978-81-8069-314-4 (Series) ISBN-10: 81-8069-314-7 (Series)
ISBN-13: 978-81-8069-489-9 (H.B.) ISBN-10: 81-8069-489-5 (H.B.)
ISBN-13: 978-81-8069-490-5 (P.B.) ISBN-10: 81-8069-490-9 (P.B.)

First Published 2008

Published and Printed by
Ashok Kumar Mittal
Concept Publishing Company
A/15-16, Commercial Block, Mohan Garden
New Delhi-110059 (INDIA)

Phones : 25351460, 25351794
Fax : 091-11-25357103
Email : publishing@conceptpub.com

My Sisters and Brothers:
Phalguni, Banasree, Rupasree, Prashanta
Sujit, Abhijit and Subhashis
—The sources of my inspiration

Dr. Sarveshwar Pd. Mishra
Professor
University Dept. of Economics
Dean, Faculty of Social Sciences
Ranchi University, Ranchi - 834 008
Phone: 0651-2233885

Res.: H1/111
Harmu Housing Colony
Ranchi - 834 012
Phone : 0651 - 2243563

Foreword

Economics begins with historical records of human society where economic problems have been faced by the people. There were philosophers, scribes, prophets and statesmen to ponder these problems and to comment on them. The emphasis of Aristotle (384–322 BC) on the ethical values paved the way of economic and political thinkers, at that time, in analysing the economic events. It was Aristotle effect that economists realized the importance of 'just price'; "to sell a thing for more than its worth and to buy it for less than its worth is in itself unjust and unlawful". Kautilya in his 'Arthasastra' combined Ethics and Economics, which guided the people, policy makers and politicians of that period.

Thus ever since Political Economics took its rise, economists tried to incorporate ethical values in economic decisions. Most of the economists of these days also accepted the normative character of economics and it has been realised that the good of human welfare cannot be achieved if one ignores the ethical values and moral judgement in economic and business, policy decisions.

Economists of these days are putting their attractions on Humanistic Economics in which human beings have been given the central place in economic affairs. These economists tried to show that Economics combined with Ethics will help to achieve the dignity and ultimate worth of all human beings. They advocated reconstructing an economic theory based on Kantian ethics which is more faithful to the authentic nature of mankind and which requires the affirmation of 'a person as a person'.

Recently, the policy makers and academicians of our country have realized that the study of the Economics and Business problems should be integrated with Ethics. The Gandhian Economics is a guide for them. The book *Economic and Business Ethics* written by Dr. Debashis Guha, which is 5th volume of the series *Practical and Professional Ethics*, is helpful for the students of this field. The author tried to emphasize the value-related issues in Economics. The writer has exercised the ethical values of the new economic policy and its impact on the present and future generations.

The Author, apart from other philosophical interests, specializes in Practical and Professional Ethics, a branch of Ethics that is evolving in India in the present time.

The Series and this work in particular, is unique effort by an Indian scholar. The work *Economic and Business Ethics* contributes to the growth of our knowledge in the field of value-related issues in Economics, Business, Administration and Management with special reference to India.

The work is focused in three major ways: It takes on the analytic task of nature analysis and justification of Economic, Business, Administrative and Management Ethics; considers time tormenting value crises in India in particular (and in the global scenario in general) such as: globalization, liberalization, free trade and privatization; computerization and modernization of industries; marketing and advertisement and taxation; and finally, takes up the issue of methodology of teaching ethics and economic, business and management ethics in our educational institutions.

The most absorbing and novel aspect of the book is the establishment of the methodology of "people's participation" in the resolution of value-crises in economics, business and so on, which the author calls, "intersubjective corroboration". This is best exemplified in the 5th Chapter of the book where the author considers the ethically charged issues of globalism, privatization, and free trade and so on and attempts at resolving them through people's participation. He further analyses the ethical features of the ethical dialogues to show how application of ethics also has an analytic task to perform.

It is heart-rending to find that the author has faced so many ethical issues in Indian economy and business with a number of people having professions and occupations.

The bibliography of the work is extensive and rich. The fluidity and force of language of the work need special mention.

Dr. Sarveshwar Pd. Mishra

Preface

During the formative stages of the research work on "Applied Ethics In Indian Context", which was subsequently supported with the Major Research Project Award of the U.G.C. (1997-2000), I frequented the National Library in Calcutta. I also had a chance to work in the library of the Indian Council of Philosophical Research in Lucknow. Nearly eight to ten months were devoted to shape the research project covering a wide range of value-laden issues awaiting moral resolution in our society. It is during this stage that I was acquainted with the phenomenal growth of knowledge of practical and professional ethics across the globe; the U.S.A., the U.K., Australia and Canada leading way for us to follow. However, in India, passionate philosophers never tire boasting about the practical concerns of Indian philosophy and Indian ethics. My awe was about the range of ethics, the way the subject has crossed the hackneyed frontiers of the first and the second order tasks, and about the pile of information printed in books and journals in this field. Most interesting is that the story of the growth of practical and professional ethics, as we know it now, is not too old, the real spurt being the post-Vietnam catastrophe. I thought that our libraries of esteem, particularly those having the credential of housing good books on philosophy, were flooded with books on practical and professional ethics. Nevertheless, after going deeper into the realms of ethics, I find that we are not really flooded with latest information; rather we have a good collection. Yet, at the formative stage, I wondered mostly about economic and business ethics in particular, and to some extent about social and political ethics, though for me environmental, medical and educational ethics were not of much wonder. There are reasons for wondering about the global rise of economic and business ethics in particular. First reason is that many people around me, philosophers and non-philosophers alike said that where money matters, there is no ethics, that is, ethical churnings about economic and business matters are sheer nonsense. Harsher assertion is: "There is no ethics in business". Second is that I had little or no idea that business ethics has so many titles, enormous research articles devoted to it and even an encyclopaedia has come up! A cursory glance through these works compelled me to believe that either something must be substantive in these works or what some people said must be true. It is during this period that I had an opportunity to face an interview followed after presentation of a paper in the Indian Institute of Management in Calcutta for the post of professor in the department of Human Values and Ethics. Here I had some experience about what a modern business school really means when it comes to teaching ethics, business ethics, and managerial ethics and so on. All this was a good exposure for me who was still indecisive about incorporating economic and business ethics in his scheme of things. While I write this book, I neither have doubt nor regret about considering economic and business ethics in my scheme of things, this comes not as a matter of personal favour rather well thought out justification, which forms a major part of the book. The work, therefore, tries its best to show the ethically relevant ways in which economics and business should be discussed. It also tries to come out of the growing stagnation and orthodoxy that has undesirably crept in a number of works in this field by means of the theory-laden approach, which is, championing standard ethical theories or norms in dealing with the questions of value in economics and business.

To complete any work, many good souls need to be disturbed, which I have done at liberty, which no one objects to. I thank a number of people who supported me in many ways. The economists, businessmen, managers, technocrats, teachers, lawyers and students helped me enormously to complete the work of value-resolution through moral debates. My heartfelt gratitude to the staff and officers of the National Library and the ICPR library, Lucknow. I thank Mr. G. Kumarappa of the National Library for his support. I am thankful to Mr. Sanjay Singh for carefully typing the manuscript and the family of Concept Publishing Company for publishing the work.

Contents

Introduction

Some confusions should be dispelled before we proceed to discuss in details about economic and business ethics. First and foremost is that we fail to understand what economic and business ethics is, that is, what exactly we understand by economic ethics and business ethics. In one way, we are asking about the nature and meaning of economic and business ethics. This takes us to the deconstruction of th enature of ethics in relation to economics and business, two fields alien to ethics. Another confusion is about the justification, that is, we have to find out the reasons behind ethical considerations in the fields of economics, business, and management and so on. But that is a different story, first we have to know what exactly we mean by ethical interest in economics and business. More confusions about economic ethics lies in the apparent vagueness of the notion of "economic ethics" because considering the case of business, which is closely related to economic affairs and economic theories and issues do not allow us to speak separately of economic ethics. Similar confusion is about business ethics because careful consideration about economic ethical issues is thought to be sufficient to cover business ethical issues. Other confusions about business ethics are no less peculiar, we wonder whether managerial ethics makes a separate case of study or is it well within business ethics. Hence, we are at hand good ethically relevant issues to discuss what economic, business and managerial ethics mean and in what ways are they different as well as related. We are here asserting the relevance of philosophical study of morality or what is moral philosophy in the context of some other fields, which are in essence different from moral philosophy. We are here asserting the relevance of philosophical morality in economic and business studies, which despite ambiguities cover the study of management of business enterprises. Certainly, in some way or the other we are asserting the relevance of relating philosophical morality in "money matters". The point is crucial because nothing in philosophical study is wayward or without definite reasons. Philosophical morality striving to mingle in the realms of economic and business studies must have definite reasons, which should be stated unambiguously because a number of philosophers and non-philosophers have a good habit to catch hold of people doing irrational things in the name of growth of knowledge. Hence, a group of people cannot suddenly jump in enthusiasm to carry ethics to alien fields and demand that something great has been done. It is thus just to be reasonably sceptical to accept any relation between ethics and economics or ethics and management. This work considers the successful prevention of sceptical ways to trash economic and business ethics as main issues. The work does not, therefore, abruptly try to resolve so-called ethical problems in economics and business by virtue of enlisting and applying a number of academic normative theses. Rather, it focuses to show that for such and such strong grounds or reasons, ethical study of economic and business affairs holds good. In doing so the work tries to establish that the touted task of value resolution of economic and business matters does not in anyway beg normative thesis popular in academic ethics, rather, doing so is testimony to a wrong notion of what economic and business ethics is. It is expected, therefore, that in this work we shall come to the task of value resolution of worth considering issues through defeating sceptical challenge and thus justifying the value of economic and business ethics. Nevertheless, issues awaiting value resolution are plenty and for all practical purposes I shall limit myself in presenting some such issues as they appear in the Indian context, the value elements that incite us for more care and the way in which I have faced them for resolution through moral debates and the subsequent analysis of normative elements that emerged in the debates and the prescriptions that ensued from the dialogue. This I have done keeping in view the basic conception of economic and business ethics, which is unjustifiable on pure normative basis, and I believe this must be a shock for a number of ardent believers of theoreticism in applying ethics in fields like economics and business. Shocks are reserved for those who have carved out ethico-religious or ethico-spiritual basis to business and economic affairs including resolution of value-crises in these fields because these are theory-laden and wrongly conceived. I must say that readers should be ready for a philosophically relevant study of economics and business, which clearly sidesteps the false gimmicks of amateurish non-philosophical orientation of economic and business ethics more popular among its many passionate followers. These harsh acts were needed because drawing a line between muddled ethical interceptions in economics and business and proper ethical interceptions in these fields becomes more important for me.

In Chapters 1 and 2, nature analysis and justification of economic as well as business ethics becomes vital for knowing that they are not synonymous and that management ethics cannot be simply equated to business ethics. In Chapter 3, I have considered the task of nature analysis and justification of managerial ethics in details. The two subsequent Chapters deal in major value crises in economics, business and management in India and the method I deem to be necessary for their resolution. The last chapter deals with methods of teaching economic business ethics in the Indian business and management schools in particular.

1

Economic Ethics: Nature, Justification and Issues

Philosophers involv,ed in the analysis of the nature of ethics or any branch therein as well as the analysis of the logic of accepting ethics or any of its branch should as a golden rule avoid to provide cut and dried definition of ethics or any of its branch as well as avoid pseudo-rational or pseudo-logical grounds to establish ethics or any branch therein. More often than not philosophers of our time do not hesitate in doing both, that is, discovering and suggesting a satisfactory definition of ethics or economic ethics and enforcing so-called formal or informal grounds for accepting ethics or economic ethics as sensible studies, which are nevertheless, not shade better than personal wishful imaginations. What is expected of philosophers is to deconstruct what ethics or economic ethics is, and for that, it is important to know, as in case of economic ethics, the meaning of "economics" and "ethics", which in turn asks for what are done or undertaken in these studies or branches of knowledge. It is an assertion with some welcome risk to say that for economists and philosophers alike, deconstruction or analysis of meaning of "economics" does not necessarily beg a satisfactory cut and dried definition. In fact, in ethics and economics, a range of definitions was of no use, they turned out to be trouble-shooters in clarity of understanding of these subjects. Something like this must have been in the mind of Professor Jacob Viner when he argued that "economics" should be better understood in terms of what is "done" or what is its subject matter or better said, what its tasks are. The same is in my mind when I have argued in *The Primer* (volume 1) that ethics should be understood as what it does or what are its tasks. And then as an expected course of simplicity, "economic ethics" should reveal its tasks and its meaning, therefore, though its tasks are neither similar to economics nor ethics, but related to both. Hence, the complex notion of "economic ethics" does not unfold its nature and meaning with all clarity on the basis of either analysis of "economics" or "ethics" because the significance of components has no logical bearing on the significance of the complex though the complex includes the significant elements of both the components. Hence, mere statement of the tasks of ethics and economics cannot be juxtaposed in an accidental relation to form the task of "economic ethics" and for that matter to form the meaning of the same. It takes further logical acumen on our part, which is contributory to a synthetic statement of what economic ethics is when we know well what economics and ethics are like. We shall, therefore, take on our analytic task of discovering the tasks of economics and ethics and then applying our logical acumen to synthesise what economic ethics amounts to. In fact, we are in the queer realm of analysis and synthesis because we deconstruct the significance of the components of the complex first and then discover the significance of the complex by added logic of construction, which is true of nature analysis of almost all *interdisciplinary studies* like this.

A few words are needed to clarify why the expression "economic ethics" has been favoured. The expression at its face value sounds peculiar (not as peculiar as "economical ethics" though), because we are not sure about "economic" in the said expression. Can it not be "ethical economics" or, "ethic of economics" or, "ethics and economics"? Well, it can be but these need equal amount of effort for meaning clarification as others because we are not sure what it amounts to when economics is "ethical", or when we have an ethic of "economics". "Ethics and economics", like all "X and Y" assertions do not really bring out the sense of "economic ethics" or "ethical economics" rather mentions that both economics and ethics are different though some relation may be noticed. Economic ethics really does not merely try to tell us those different things like economics and ethics are related, it goes beyond to show what it amounts to when they are related and why they are related, that is, by which the relation holds good and makes any sense. This must be vital for many writers who have a title like *Ethics and Economics* and *On Ethics and Economics* because these writers, I am sure, never tried to make us any wiser by telling us what the components are and how they are related and why at all the relation holds good. Hence, excuses for using any expression mentioned above that juxtaposes ethics and economics are needed, and when excuses are so important, we can have them for our usage of "economic ethics". Precisely, in "economic ethics", ethics is not the least "economic", if that ethics is not the least "beneficial for our material good". "Economic" here signifies nothing but "what pertains to economics or to economical affairs". Using "ethics" signifies nothing but "what pertains to ethics or ethical matters". Hence, "economic ethics" is not ambiguous, it states that something pertaining to economics or economic affairs are related to something that pertains to ethical matters. Precisely but crudely, money-matters involve ethical matters, but we have to be clearer, we should know 'what pertains to economics', 'what pertains to ethics' and 'what pertains to economic ethics'. This is nothing but inviting us to take on our analytic-cum-synthetic task.

To clarify the tasks of economics one has to take some risk to be simplistic because the field has grown so phenomenally that a satisfactory statement in terms of all the tasks is never a matter of absolute satisfaction. To my mind, the glimpse of tasks of economics can be obtained from its root. Economics like "ecology" and other *ecumenical* terms, that is, those derived from the root "oikos" suggests that they have something to do with the "household" or "the place where we live", though where people live (or household) cannot be limited to "world" in an old-fashioned way because we have flown to the strata beyond the so-called household, the "world". We thus reach, interact and use as much portions of the cosmos as we can, not only because we have been perennially inquiring people rather we have been basically suckers in existence knowing well that nectar is good though limited. Yet, we cannot stop our inexhaustible existential demands to live as best as we can, sometimes completely unaware of the future and the future progeny. Hence, economics like ecology takes on humans as existing in relation to a number of beings and things in a vast household and trying to do a number of things that might either sustain or deplete the household itself, the micro-household, the world, is already facing depletion at the hands of wise people. In any case economics, unlike ecology, is not a science of the nature and structure of the household itself, rather a science of the human activities in relation to beings and things or *resources* of the household both at the levels of *positive* study of 'what is' and *normative* study of 'what should be'. But these statements about economics are far too satisfactory because we need a lot of clarification on how human interactions with the vast existential resources may be studied in the constant flux of use, development, depletion and restoration.

Economists generally believe that economics undertakes to collect a number of relevant facts about particular issues related to an economy, advances simple explanations of the workings and the important aspects of the economic system, and strives to explain the causes and significance of facts collected about particular issues related to an economy and to test the explanations of the workings of the economic system. It is convenient to explain these tasks of economics as the *description* of economically relevant topics, the *theoretical* task of analysis of an economic system and the *applied* task of proving the different thesis advanced about an economic system. Given the complexity of the world where we live and interact, it is very difficult to collect *all* relevant facts about particular issue related to an economy and to establish an economic theory, which tries to or even boasts of explicating *all* the complexities involved in an economy. Hence, the descriptive and the theoretic tasks of economics have their own limits, but that is not a great disadvantage because no science should attempt to be absolute in terms of performing its allotted tasks and to discover truth.

In performing the theoretical task of economics, we need to assume about conditions in the economy under our analytic consideration. These assumptions are of general nature and are mostly concerned with the ways in which we act in given physical environment and the social and economic institutions. Further, we derive necessary inferences from these general assumptions or hypothesis. Economists conceive of three broad assumptions while considering the analytic task. First is that economic activities in complex world are undertaken by two groups of people, in one group are those who have certain demands or wishes to be fulfilled at some cost, in the other group are those who fulfil these wishes of people at some cost. The first group belongs to the consumers, whereas the second belongs to the entrepreneurs. Economists assume that the consumers and the entrepreneurs should behave rationally, that is, the consumers should not only strive to fulfil their reasonable wishes they should do so most of the time, their preferences remaining fairly the same. On the part of the entrepreneurs, it is assumed that they will be reasonably profit oriented in fulfilling the demands of others. Economists assume that consumers should reasonably try to derive best value out of their money, which is so needed for desire satisfaction. Hence, they would never prefer money spent without a purpose and without a comparatively greatest return. Similarly, rational entrepreneurs would never prefer resources and money spent without a comparatively greater return of profit. However, for the entrepreneurs maximisation of profit is a complex affair. In any case, what entrepreneurs and consumers do are said to be "economic rationality". *Per se,* there is no question of unethicality here, but we have to peruse into the matter more carefully. Equally true is, economists assume that where consumers and entrepreneurs are in free play, the society should have a stable polity, a more or less civil state having a government and where important economic institutions and market mechanisms run as expected, that is, as stable systems. Another important theoretic assumption in economics is that the nature and structure of the 'household', our world to be precise (broadly the universe), is such that though what we demand for our satisfaction are unlimited, our ability to fulfil them are limited, the major reason for which is the *scarcity* of resources needed for our desire satisfaction. In some cases, if we have a large amount of resource, it may not be practically possible to use them given our state of progress. Nevertheless, 'scarcity' in economics mainly refers to the limit at the natural plane, which has to be shared judiciously among all those who have legible claim over it. The truth of scarcity of economic goods and the need for just sharing principles call for ethical attention. Theoretical economics mainly depends on this necessary assumption and economists often stress the point that without this assumption it is difficult to conceive of economic system and economics. Economics thus deals with the important theoretical task of finding out the way an economic system runs given the tension of wants and scarcity.

The economic consideration of need satisfaction and the factors related to it are classified for a clear and deeper study by the economists under the broad field of theoretical or analytic economics, which for its success depends on descriptions of relevant economic facts. In any case, use of resources by entrepreneurs and their distribution becomes an extremely important realm of study in economics in the basic economic thesis of scarcity of resources and their distribution. We find the economists performing this analytic task under what we popularly know as *micro* and *macro* economics. Hence, there are a number of micro and macro economic analytic thesis of the way economies or economic systems function notwithstanding the elements of wants and scarcity. We believe that economics (micro and macro) provides us analysis of the following issues: First, given the scanty resources in an economy, which goods are in the asking for production by the productive bodies and what quantity needs to be produced. Second, what are the desirable methods to produce the needed goods and services? Third, given an amount of goods and services produced in economy, what should be judicious ways to distribute them? Fourth, to consider whether the economic efficiency of the use of productive resources in a society has been fully utilised or some are still unutilized. Finally, whether there are signs of decline or *status quo* or increment in the productive capacity of an economy over a period. Interestingly analysis of the above issues in theoretical economics are not monolithic because we may have at least two reactions, one being the *capitalist* theoretical analysis, and the other being the *non-capitalist* analysis. The former is often taken as "mainstream" analysis assuming "free market economy" as the holy grail of economics, whereas the others are breakaway or iconoclastic or even arrogant (rogue!) analysis. Well, profusion of ethical interceptions are expected at almost every important points of mainstream and breakaway analysis of those issues because for many analysts, the assumption of free market and the capitalists' ploy of answering each issue in a unique way is ethically repugnant, whereas for those in the mainstream, economic theories make sense only in the context of a mainstream assumption. Whatever the case may be, ethical repercussions at both ends suggests that theoretical economics cannot be value-neutral, where "value" does not amount to economic or material value rather, *ethical value*. Hence, *normativity* creeps in economic theories, making it far from being value-neutral or starkly oriented to consider what "is" the case. In fact, many economists believe that though many stark truths underline the holy-grail of economics, it is worth considering to find out what "ought" to be or what "should" be the case.

It is important for us to find out what exactly are undertaken in analytic economics when it comes to answering the important issues mentioned above. The first issue under the micro-economic consideration is the issue of *allocation* of scanty resources available in an economy. It is a question of contesting choice and thus decision-making to produce something at the cost of refraining from producing some other things out of an available resource because certain things are imagined as alternatively more useful than other things in the main context of scarcity of the resource. In the mainstream explanation laced with the holy-grail of the capitalists, the issue of allocation should be settled by some *impersonal* considerations of demand and supply, and profit than any personal considerations. This takes us to the micro-economic task of constructing a *price theory* in the context of resource allocation. Moving further to the role of choice and decision-making, we comc to the micro-economic task of choosing and deciding in favour of a *production method* over any other as the most profitable way to produce goods in demand. This takes us to choose resources for that purpose. Again, we undertake the use of the most effective ways to use scarce resources involving technological interference whether it is labour intensive or capital intensive or both. This task is to construct a *theory of production* which gives way to a *theory of economic growth*, the former mostly considering the 'cost aspect' of production, whereas the later the 'surplus aspect' as source of further investment. Micro-economics further considers the task of resolving the problem of *distribution* of *national product*, a problem of *sharing* the national product among the individuals and classes in the society. This in turn takes us to the problem of meeting social justice or equity; the important parties demanding it are the capitalists who are believed to be producers in mainstream theories and those who are the consumers of the products. In this scenario emerges the issue of who is entitled to what has been produced. In the mainstream philosophy of economics, greater income implies greater entitlement for goods and services or simply the products, whereas lesser income amounts to less entitlement of the same. Naturally, the iconoclasts might urge for equality of income owing to equality in entitlement of products by the parity of reasoning. Hence, in a given economy, *equal income distribution* is linked to equal distribution of national product. This is exactly the task of constructing a *theory of distribution* in micro-economics, which is again a lucrative field for ethical interception. Just distribution and entitlement have emerged as pet issues for ethical queries particularly when we keep in mind the fact of effect of distribution of ownership property on the personal distribution of income granting the truism in capitalist free market thesis that unequal ownership of property is linked to inequality in income. Furthermore, in micro-economics we consider the issue of *economic efficiency* particularly in the view of scant resources. Hence, most efficient ways of producing and distributing national products becomes important in economics. The production is most efficient if the scarce resources cannot be better used by an alternative way to reallocating the resources. The distribution is most efficient if it is impossible to make through any redistribution of goods some individuals better off without making other worse off. Micro-economics does not mess up such economic efficiency with technical efficiency because the former is not in consideration of technological interventions best suited for production of goods. In economic efficiency, we consider how fully and efficiently a society is using available resources to produce goods and services that people want to buy with their available incomes. In this case, the high technological efficiency of a society does not necessarily suggest its economic efficiency, though economic efficiency apart from other things does not imply technological efficiency. This is clearer when we realise that economic efficiency depends on the efficient distribution of goods and services among individuals in a society. It is extremely interesting to find out whether both technological and economic efficiency *should* be blind to ethical efficiency of civil states, that is, whether a state having little or no regard for ethical choice of means and be called efficient both technologically and economically.

Something different from what has been said thus far are consideration of the issues of *full employment of available resources* in an economy and the issue of *increment of the productive capacity* of an economy. The former is put under macro-economic consideration and the latter under the economics of growth and development. The macro-economic consideration of the full employment of available resources is in reality related to the issue of intensive use of the workplace on whom optimum use of scarce resources is related to the issue of *aggregate effective demand* for goods and services. Nevertheless, there has been a phenomenal change in perception of this issue beyond Keynes and the issue has grown extremely wide and complex. The issue of economic growth as taken up in development economy is one of increase of productive capacity of an economy. It is expected that with the growth of the productive capacity of an economy there is progression in production of goods and services and thus the uplift of the standard of living of people or the aggregate. To study the nature, causes and components of such increase is the study of economic growth. Nevertheless, through the modern times we have come to realise that mere talk of economic growth in terms of material well being of people at an epoch is not sufficient for a sensible development economics because proper consideration of the natural or environmental well being, the good for future humans and sustainable development are needed if truly economy strives to develop. These are all related closely to the ethical concerns of modern man, which we now find in other ecumenical sciences like ecology. But that is a different story to be narrated shortly. Before that, readers are reminded of another task of economics, called the 'applied' task. Applied economists are involved in the task of justification of theories studying statistical and other evidences. This task has been aptly undertaken in the recent times by what we call *econometrics*, which unlike any normative encouragements in economics takes the world as it is, or "positively" to show why particular economic theories may be justified and others not to be justified. We can say that econometrics deals with measurement of economic relationships. The field of study is a queer amalgam of economic theory, mathematical economics and statistics, but completely different from these branches. This amalgam amounts to provide us with numerical values for the measurement of economic relationships and verifying economic theories. In this sense econometrics has an *analytic* task of testing economic theories, the task of *policy making* as well as *decision making* through the supply of numerical information needed for the measurement of economic relationships and *forecasting* the future values of economic ramifications based on the above numerical estimates. Econometrics has two distinct branches, the theoretical and the applied, the former considers developing proper methods for the measurement of economic relationships which are indeterminate; the latter includes application of methods in econometrics to particular branches of economic theory.

Nothing is perhaps complete about explanation of nature of economics in terms of its tasks unless we now come to the *normative* task of economics. First, we should know why this task is worth considering. Economists hold that it is not always desirable to explain how the economy in general or in particular actually operates rather it is desirable at times to state as a matter of norm, how economy *should* operate or what is *desirable* in economy, where 'should' and 'desirable' bear moral or ethical significance. Many things are non-morally desirable in economics, at least economists of orthodox tradition think like that. They believe that what is right, just and desirable economically speaking is starkly physical or material, that is, not beyond pertinent objectively valid natural explanation because the science as such involves itself with what things and facts are in nature not in the way of describing how, what and why they are rather in what ways they come to human manipulations for human well-being keeping in mind that such material well-being is a natural demand on the part of humans which they must attain at some cost and for that, definite mechanisms needs to be discovered. This does not call for any interception of the non-natural, for instance, the ethical elements such as asking for the ethical relevance (or right, good, just and so on) of deciding to exploit some natural scant resources for human good at the present time overlooking the good of future humans to infest the world, or, the nature which has been exploited without any sustenance for its good. Economists, of late, reacted strongly to morally or normatively neutral attitude of those who think of any economic good of human race by any means. Economists think that when we are concerned with the national economy it is more often than not a hackneyed irrational objective or positivist stand of economics to interfere with serious questions of ethical right, good and just, which calls for bases of ethics and not a naturalistic science. For the economists this became so natural later on that one wonders what was right below our nose could not be found. We find as a matter of practical truth that very ordinary people as well as the economists try to find out whether such and such economic decisions were at all ethically just to take notwithstanding a number of objective grounds have been provided by the economists to do so. Naturally, therefore, it becomes a prerogative on the part of sane people to question whether what government or other agencies have done with regard to economic good of the citizens were at all ethically good. Every sane individual will think twice to attack a country to establish a puppet government to get uninterrupted supply of sufficient oil at standard price for the good of the people of their country. It is not always that what is good for us economically speaking is good for others economically and ethically speaking. Hence, the need of normative judgements of economic affairs was included as task of economics. It is perhaps due to *moral evolution* of man, which always faces regress that Robbins' scarcity conception and subsequent thesis that followed for human good in terms of material good at any cost seemed to be without a human face, and for that matter, normative elements in economics were deemed to be essential. People following Robbins could not follow that human well-being or welfare becomes an important aspect of economics provided that well-being is not merely becoming monetarily or otherwise rich because these may not be paradigms of social welfare, which Marshall came to realise and acted accordingly. Keeping this high ideal or *end* in mind, economists faced the tough task of ascertaining the *means* which are humane or ethically desirable for attaining the end. The tension between the ends in view was owing to the added conception of economic growth because foolhardy people argue that bereft of such growth we can be well off truly speaking. Given the needs, aspirations and wants, the scarcity of resources notwithstanding, the clarion call for just means for well being becomes all the more crucial. We shall see many things about the normativity of economics but we have to be careful to find out the basic features of the discipline that considers normative statements about human acts as most important. Let us now speak of ethics as a normatively conscious discipline.

It has become a prerogative on my part to write about the tasks of ethics because every volume of this series demands an explanation about this matter. As we now stand in this work, it is important to make a statement about the tasks of ethics briefly because clarity of its nature further enables us to understand the way ethics comes to be related to economics to constitute economic ethics. Ethics, like economics should not be defined in haste though a number of definitions of ethics through the ages have tried to make us wise. Greatest problem with these definitions of ethics is that they attempt to touch one or two or some tasks of ethics like blind men who described an elephant differently. However, a wise choice was open to us to explain the different tasks and then provide a normative definition if needed, that is, a definition which tries to unravel how ethics should be explained if some people demand clarity for knowing its nature. In any case, what precedes normative definition is analysis of the tasks of ethics. The first task of ethics or rather the first order ethics is known as *normative* ethics. Sometimes, we call it substantive ethics because it gives us the bases or grounds for a range of moral evaluations common in moral discourses. This may be thus called evaluative function of ethics meaning thereby not merely to evaluate but to provide grounds of evaluation. We should readily accept that without any norm or criterion of evaluation, it becomes subjective determination having no strong logic in its favour that may be presented during the course of contesting theoretical disagreements. Hence, normative ethics provides us with grounds or norms for evaluating voluntary human actions having a purpose, done by choosing definite means and which comes under the purview of ethical scrutiny or ethical discussion. The last part is important to follow because not all human voluntary and purposeful actions need to be evaluated on the basis of normative thesis for their ethical value. My choice of a blue fine-tipped ball pen cannot be judged for moral value on the basis of teleological norms available to us because the choice does not call for any such evaluation rather different sets of evaluation on different grounds, for instance, the choice may be evaluated as *non-morally good* because the said brand is cheap but writes well or that it is too costly at my standard of living though does not write extremely well. Nevertheless, in both cases, I may not be branded as either ethical or unethical person, but I may be judged as economic-fool head or impractical or economically wise and practical and so on. Hence, normative ethics does not take into its purview some such topics for moral discussion, which in reality has nothing to do with such discussion. Many people were of the opinion that any interception of ethics in fields other than it is completely undesirable or unfounded because ethics deals with normative issues or value issues whereas non-normative disciplines like biology, ecology, economics and many others do not deal with such issues rather they are concerned with issues completely unrelated to normative evaluation or does not depend on any normative basis for judgement of ethical goodness or rightness. However, these people failed to realise that though biology, ecology, economics, etc. essentially belongs to factual studies, they have elements, which are not beyond normative scrutiny. We have seen in the volumes 2 and 3 of this series that human concerns with the environment and biomedical matters are never starkly factual, they involve us in ethical evaluation because some of our *voluntary purposeful actions* affect the components of our environment as well as the individuals and animals awaiting their biological and medical well-being which obviously are not judged for value on factual grounds or scientific grounds rather on ethical or what we now call, normative grounds. Hence, a number of fields other than ethics come under ethical discussion, something like an interdisciplinary inquiry to evaluate the ethical value of voluntary actions that bear ethical significance, that is, have value-elements in them calling for careful normative judgement. We have seen above that of late economists felt that a number of economic policies, decisions, functions and even theories attract us for ethical evaluation based on ethical norms. Hence, normative ethics should be understood as understanding an evaluative function on normative grounds unique to ethics that happily assimilate a number of positive sciences, social sciences and sciences having both positive and normative character.

Nevertheless, we must not forget that the normative thesis are not sacrosanct, they fight each other for validity and absolute authority on moral matters because they are essentially monolithic norms always imposing on us a truth that all moral judgements beg such norms. If relativism has any truth in it, the absoluteness of norms or the objectivity of norms cannot be accepted, this is particularly true when we come down to real life moral disagreements about moral value of decisions and actions. Hence, moral norms cannot be accepted without scrutinising the strength of the logic of establishing the norms and the ability to withstand the counter justifications of contesting norms. It becomes the task of metaethics to find out the ways in which norms are justified, that is, the logic behind their acceptance overruling other thesis. Metaethics is thus the study that goes beyond (meta), the consideration of normative ethics, which is believed to be first order or basic or said to be substantive. In this sense, meta-ethics is *second order* ethics or its tasks are second order, including the task of justification of norms. Another task of justification considered in meta-ethics is with regard to the language of ethics. Linguistic justification in ethics is of extreme importance. In recent times ethicists consider it central to ethics because bereft of justification of ethical language, any ethical talk becomes meaningless. This task is also called the "analytic" task of ethics because we take up analysis of meaning and truth of ethical language as most important. It is important to clarify that ethical language is not another type of language; rather the constituents of the language with the necessary elements of grammar vary greatly depending on the users of that language. It may thus be expressed in English, Spanish, and Hindi and so on but the constancy in nature is that they express *something pertaining to ethical evaluation*. Hence, ethical judgements or statements (in any living language of the world) bear uniform significance of expressing something regarding morality, moral values, virtues, norms, decisions, intentions, actions and so on. Clearly, as we have seen before, non-moral judgements of value or virtue, duty, obligation and so on, do not come under the purview of analytic inquiry. Hence, we might ask for the justification of meaning and truth of the assertion: "Voluntary euthanasia is desirable or just", we should not ask to justify the assertion "Voluntary euthanasia is best served with a lethal injection" because the former is a statement of morally justifiable value of intentional human act, whereas the latter is not. For the justification of meaning and truth of the latter assertion, we need *non-moral grounds* such as the test of lethal injections on non-human mammals for its killer effectiveness, whereas the same is not needed in case of justification of the former assertion. Yet, meaning and truth of ethically relevant assertions is extremely important because we cannot take the risk of expressing a moral statement or a value assertion bereft of its truth and meaning. The grounds of truth and meaning of such assertions are not one, they are many. Probably, we speak of *cognitive* and *non-cognitive* justifications each having different thesis to establish. One way is to assert that ethical statements are known to be true and meaningful by virtue of sense experience or intuitive experience, whereas another way is to say that such statements are true and meaningful because they express the feelings, emotions, attitudes, and tastes, towards human decisions and actions.

Ethics has grown phenomenally in the recent times banking on its practical or applied task, which faced initial protests from the orthodox philosophers of the older analytic tradition, i.e., from the applied ethical sceptics or the nihilists because philosophy and any branch therein, such as ethics was believed to have no relation whatsoever with application, the main reason being ignorance of nature and method of application. People have a conception (wrong perhaps) that application of ethics is to apply any one or more normative theories like deontology or teleology in value-laden practical cases like euthanasia by the ethicists so that we find pertinent resolution of these cases. Application of ethics thus becomes an artificial misadventure on the part of the ethicists because ethical theories cannot be fit into crises situations to resolve them satisfactorily by an expert. Hence, many people argued that application of ethics is none of the business of ethics. It is rather an inquiry into several theoretical issues like nature analysis and justification of applicative aspect of ethics and the models of application, as well as real life participation in value-resolution of ethical crises of people having various occupations and professions through what I call intersubjective corroboration or involvement of concerned parties, including ethicists, to debate on moral issues to resolve them and thus come to a consensus. This is further backed up by an analytic task, that is, the analysis of moral opinions and decisions to find out the dynamics of standard normative theories, which is, post-corroboration analytic task of the trained ethicists.

It is important to note that ethics includes in its task the aspects of occupational and professional forms of life which need ethically oriented inquiries, which takes us to occupational ethics, for instance, business ethics; professional ethics, for example, health care ethics; and sub-professional ethics, such as nursing ethics. These fields of inquiry further have two important features, one being theoretical and the other being the applied. The theoretical queries are concerned mainly with nature analysis and justification of these fields of study as well as nature analysis and related questions involved in a number of value-laden issues. Applied part deals with the resolution of these issues, which is related to the justification and application of a method of resolution. When we come to the applied task of occupational and professional ethics, we realise that though these fields have their own identities and problems, they are closely related to applied ethics. The same is the case when we come to environmental ethics, which is another way in which ethics gets involved in matters transcending it. Environmental ethics cannot be said as a part of either occupational or professional ethics though it is closely related to occupational and professional life forms. Similarly, environmental ethics is not a branch of applied ethics owing to its own identity and have distinct set of problems; it is nevertheless, related closely applied ethics. Environmental ethics consists of a distinguished set of theoretical issues and practical functions. It is only when we come to consider its practical task; we realise that environmental concerns of ethics cannot be met without involving the ethical rights, duties, obligations and good of people having various occupations and professions. For instance, we cannot overlook the ethic of lay involvement in environmental crises management as well as the ethics of eco-friendly biological materials management.

In the recent times, there is a marked enthusiasm of virtue and value related tasks of ethics, much hyped as *virtue ethics*. The prodigal children of ethics have suddenly realised that not everything is fine with the lofty ethical theories, language analysis and applying theories in practical life to resolve crises. Rather, we have forgotten the root of ethical inquiry, the urge to make us good or to enable us to be people of noble character. Hence, the clarion call for becoming virtuous, takes ethics to the task of character shaping. This is the crux of virtue ethics, which again has a predominant theoretical aspect, namely, analysis of nature of virtue and value, their kinds and justification of moral evolution through embedding virtue and values, and the practical aspect, namely applying monistic, pluralistic, agent centred, agent based, agent focused and a number of virtue theories in practical cases of resolution of crises in virtues and values. In any case, the growing interest of ethicists in empirical matters and the freedom of taking social-scientific methods in its practical affairs have enabled us to imagine the empirical tasks of ethics, thus coming out of the bindings of a branch of philosophy, which erstwhile was cursed to be language analysis. Ethics as we get is right, is not merely a theoretical enterprise within philosophy, it has deep practical interests whether that is value-resolution or making us good people. The concern of ethics in matters of values and virtues takes it closer to different disciplines wherein questions of values and virtues emerge constantly. Ethics thus gets closely related to environmental, biomedical, educational, business, economic, managerial, technological, administrative, nursing, engineering, mass communication, journalism and numerous studies. Let us now find out the way ethics gets related to economic and business studies, the latter taken in its wider sense includes studies in administration and management, and both include some studies in the advances in technology and its various use.

While discussing about economic and business ethics, as I have said earlier juxtaposing what we have seen about nature of economics (extremely scrappily but good enough for my purpose) and ethics (again too unsatisfactory but useful), will not be sufficient because economic ethics taken on the whole is something more and different from economics and ethics taken separately as parts of the whole. Moreover, the nature analysis of the whole of economic ethics is closely related to justification of the same, which is needed in order to find out the ways in which both economics and ethics are sensibly related or that ethics as an alien field of inquiry places itself in economic inquiry. This is important because philosophers and many others demand (rightly) that interdisciplinary inquiries should be well grounded on reason otherwise it will be difficult to find out why ethics should not interfere in fields of inquiries which have little or no ethical relevance. It is, therefore, important to find out why economic ethics makes great sense but ethic of calculus (integral and differential) makes no sense. Hence, keeping away from some hopeless inquiries, we concentrate further in economic ethics—its nature and justification, a part of which has been undertaken by means of analysing what roughly economics and ethics amounts to do. Ethically relevant inquiries of economic matters or tasks of economics are not one but many. We had a rough idea of some of these ethically relevant inquiries while going through the tasks of economics but we must be clearer on this account. Nevertheless, what appeared from the discussion is that almost on all accounts of economic discourses, whether theoretical or applied, there are many issues which raises serious questions of moral or ethical right, good, just etc., that is, questions of moral value as distinct from non-moral value. The questions of moral value are not as rudimentary as asking what people think or believe to be right and just or what has been traditionally or customarily believed to be right and just about economic affairs because moral or ethical value questions are not equivalent to questions of traditional morality or habits or customs of people. All these things are transcended by *personal and collective* analysis of what is right and just irrespective of tradition, custom, beliefs and dogmas. Something that is well acceptable on universal or general basis irrespective of the dogmas of the class and nations, though not overlooking the unique settings of nations, time and flux of social and political changes. In a major part of this work, I would like to argue that such personal and collective analysis of the morally right and the just bear strong *normative* character which is essentially dynamic for value resolution, but that does not in any way beg the standard normative theory—cooption expected mostly of an intellectual enterprise. Rather, such analysis depends greatly on our empirical status, that is, on our experiences of the right and the just on moral grounds, be it performance of duty or achievement of pleasure, which we all have by virtue of our interaction in this "household".

The experiences in our "household" are of great importance, therefore, both economists and ethicists will not disagree, and we are also reminded of the truth that both ethics and economics have deep concerns about the humans thriving in this household because ethics on the one hand is predominantly a study of the *moral worth* of human intentional decisions and actions apart from concerns of moral language, that humans use; economics on the other hand is predominantly a study of the *economic worth* of some human intentional decisions and actions, which despite being a non-moral study, is not unrelated to moral probing. Hence, both "human oriented and human based" studies have something to do in association, that is, an ethical study of economical probing of unique human enterprises. The simple nature of economic ethics thus reveals that a number of human related queries that are *economic* in nature, call for ethical queries as well; that is, call for queries that are about *right and just of human decisions and actions which have specific economic bearings* in this vast 'household'. Now we have to clarify which economically relevant studies of human enterprises call for moral probing and be thus included in economic ethical study. This takes us through the *justification* of economic ethics as a sensible study *within ethics* (and not economics), which is a good way to understand further what exactly are the *tasks* of economic ethics and then the nature of the subject. Readers should be careful to notice here that the task of justification of economic ethics includes the justification of the same under ethics and not economics, which raises fresh set of questions. It is also important to note that justification of economic ethics (and clarification of nature thereby), is not only possible by showing which economic decisions and actions raise questions of right and just, rather, which theoretical and applied aspects of the subject call for close ethical scrutiny on grounds available to ethics. In addition to this, justification of economic ethics is also possible by showing the ways in which different tasks of ethics such as the metaethical and the normative are related to economics. Hence, the justification is two pronged: to justify that aspects of economics call for ethical probing and to justify that aspects of ethics relates to economics, and most interestingly perhaps, both justifies that economic ethics as interwoven body of ethical and economic interests is "within ethics". However, our enthusiasm may be soon damned by *sceptics* who forcefully argue against any possibility of economic ethics. If we are true to our task of justification, we should not shy away from the sceptical arguments. So let us first consider the arguments against economic ethics. Most forceful arguments against the possibility of economic ethics are attributed to L. C. Robbins in *An Essay on the Nature and Significance of Economic Science* (1935). Robbins thinks that economics and ethics are categorically different because they are different on account of what they do or what their nature is. Economics in the main considers factual study as its subject matter, whereas ethics considers non-factual evaluative study to be most important. Hence, with respect to their basic interests, they are categorically different, and therefore, unlikely to be related and shaped as economic ethics or ethic of economics. The gist of Robbins' argument amounts to a fixity of notion of tasks of economics by virtue of an old-fashioned *positivist* conception of economics gifted by Max Weber. Consequently, as its logical corollary ethics has been conceived as normative study much to the liking of the positivists, who have an old habit (bad perhaps) to categorise some sciences as "positive" and other arts as "normative", and tragically the positive and the normative have logical grounds to be different but never to be in *relation* because by that (poor) logic, 'things of different categories implies logical non-relation'. And the (poor) logic that if 'things of different categories are related they must be equivalent by simple logical implication'. In that case, if Robbins lived in an age of biomedical engineering the idea would be repugnant to him for logical fallacies of relating and thus equating some such things which are categorically different for what subjects they took for consideration. However, Robbins must be worried in case of economic ethics because for him facts and values are too difficult to hold together; who knows he must have read the famous "fact-value" debate popular much before he wrote the essay, and he was scared of committing the "naturalistic fallacy", which could not be committed by Robbins or any other who thought concerns of facts involve or relates to concerns of value because involvement or relation is neither equation nor implication by virtue of simple logic. In fact, much misconception about the divorced status of ethics and economics originated from the stipulation on his part about what economics is or what is its *definition*. For him, 'economics is a relationship between *ends* and *scarce resources* which have alternative uses' (my italics). The definition really limits at the first instance the very "science" Robbins dealt with, which tragically took the normative character out of it because he was happy with the positivists' conception of "science" as dealing with facts, which in turn amounts to just two things, the conceptions of end and means, the first being human *wants* and the second, essential scarcity of the means (the resources) that enable humans to meet their ends or to satisfy their 'wants'. We have seen while going through the nature analysis of economics that Robbins' conception of economics as dealing with ways in which humans meet their basic wants has far-reaching ramifications. We cannot doubt that science truly takes on such factual studies to be extremely important but the suspended elements of ethicality in the soup were too difficult for Robbins to spot (!) This is mind boggling for us who thought that Robbins was preceded by one Mr. Aristotle and his grand *guru* Mr. Socrates and Mr. Adam Smith, whom he could not forget so unmindfully. Professor Amartya Sen in his work—*On Ethics and Economics* remarks that when Robbins argued that ethics and economics are logically incompatible studies and thus unrelated, "He (Robbins) was taking a position that was quite unfashionable then though extremely fashionable now"[1]. And then writes (in footnotes): "Robbins was, of course, well aware that he was contradicting a widely held view"[2]. For clarity, Sen says that the widely held view being the "ethical character" of economics gifted through Socrates to economists of our times. Hence, Robbins must be consistently putting a veil of ignorance to conceal this "ethical character" though it was equally difficult to digest the idea that economics is an offshoot of ethics or moral philosophy (as thought Adam Smith). What Robbins tried to conceal was not as grave as concealing the truth that though humans have wants, which needs to be satisfied amongst scare resources, and nothing is unnatural and unethical in it, nevertheless, humans more often than not, *unnaturally and undesirably* produce huge satisfactory commodities for use that remain unused for that much can never be used for various reasons. This must be shocking concealment on the part of a trained economist to forget the times of feudal, capitalist, Marxist and mixed economy states when most wanted things were produced mindlessly by depleting the natural resources and exploiting the labour, but were never used for they could not be used by various reasons. Hence, satisfaction of *desired desires* of humans at any cost cannot be a *desirable* end of life because that basically evades the Socratic question: After all, how should we behave or live life? How should we behave in the midst of scarcity and tension of wants is crucial to humans in this household, and this crucial study of the 'household' is what economics *should* take up. Hence, what economics takes up in terms of "what is" must be conjoined with "what should be", the latter giving a hand to the former positivist inquiry for a normative character. Hence, economics and ethics come closer, and Robbins' scepticism subsequently must be defeated. It is extremely interesting to note that though Robbins did not assert clearly, what is the end of human life so far as economic enterprises are concerned, we read between the lines to find that he was not averse of advocating human want-satisfaction to its optimum. It is not clear whether he meant to be a good follower of Cārvāka materialist overlooking all references to quality of the desired objects, he must not be apathetic to obtain means that are most amenable to satisfaction through having objects, which in any case might be as liberal as obtaining otherwise gross means. Now, this choice of the so-called *gross* means like optimum exploitation of the natural resources and the ideal of want-fulfilment through such choice is testimony to his concealed ethical interests, it is difficult now to know whether Robbins pretended to be against ethical interceptions in economics when he knew very well that he was encouraging an ethical theory or an ideal to be followed in our economic life of need-satisfaction to the optimum at the cost of not so-sacrosanct means. It does not matter much in ethics whether you advocate a rogue end or means or both because the subject in its normative garb has no apathy to discuss any such rogue thesis or a relatively sacred one because it has to be secular in approach to counter any defect remnant in any thesis. We must assure Robbins that he was not a shade uninterested about the ethical scrutiny of "what should be done while we make an economic choice". Only point is that he might have advocated an end-means thesis repugnant to us, but he nevertheless, had an ethical interest. The sceptic he appeared to be was replaced by the *egoistic gross hedonist* in reality may be an interesting idea to ponder about, but is that in any way against economic ethics? Perhaps, it is difficult to say that Robbins was against economic ethics if we think carefully. However, what he has said further about end and means is worth analysing. Robbins thinks that it is pointless to speak about economic and uneconomic end though to speak about economic and uneconomic means is sensible. In this case Robbins should accept any evil end like ruthless exploitation of natural resources overlooking the welfare of the future generation for maximisation of pleasure of individuals of the present generation irrespective of the quality of the pleasure. However, the means, which the science of economics provides with care for its proper evaluation, should be good and not evil so far as the economic goodness of the same is concerned. We may disagree with Robbins on both points—we may argue that the choice of an end for economists should not be value-free, whether that means economic value of the end or the ethical value of the end. Similarly, we may argue that the choice of means should not be value-free on account of economic value or ethical value, the latter neglected by Robbins. Still, a careful look at Robbins' position reveals that the he was unclear about any ethical value-considerations regarding 'means' or 'end', the ethical considerations are very much in the asking. Hence, ethical and economical inquiries might go hand-in-hand. This becomes all the more important when the question of choosing among alternative means and ends comes to the fore. What would Robbins prefer than the choice on purely economic grounds the maximisation of "benefit" (at any cost)? It is again interesting to notice that the basis of choice of most 'economic means' rather uneconomic means, that is, valuable not a disvalue comes to the known "ethical" basis of 'benefit maximisation' (of individuals or the collective). Hence, whether Robbins preferred or not, desired or not, concealed or not, he did show signs of an ethical involvement, a strongly normative one when it comes to value-choice in economic matters like choice of means. Had Robbins cared for the value-elements in matters like choice of ends, the story would have been the same, I am sure, but strangely he did not do so, or, he did so, but camouflaged in his so-called value-free end thesis. The positivist in Robbins was thus squarely defeated in his own hands whenever he tended to deal with the science a little too far to consider questions of value or when he gave a name to the means and the end of economic enterprise. In fact, people after Robbins were extremely appreciative about the "maximisation" theory of economics. No one really contests that economics should be concerned with satisfaction of our wants—the most ethical issue is, which wants needs to be satisfied at what costs and why? Economists really do not shy away from these questions any more because the positive science has concerns with questions of ethical value for it deals with humans in the household as beings having a humane face. Humans *qua* humans stand for close ethical query for their economic acts.

Nevertheless, economists have been active against the hackneyed conception of economics as dealing with human want satisfaction to the very best because the inner core contending an ethical thesis most famously touted as "utility" thesis (in reality, pleasure satisfaction if we go by the ethical texts), has not been liked by many. Hence, quite different from Robbins, many economists advocated the idea that to be sceptical about the very conception of economics having the said inner ethical core is to enter into an ethical scrutiny. Such scepticism about the basic content of the positive science is welcome particularly when it leads to an optimistic ethical theory of altruism without an individualistic reference. This is welcome because the conception of maximisation of expected utility has somehow come to be attracted to egoistic theory. Hence, the content of economics turned out to be closer to maximisation of expected egoistic satisfaction of wants with an inner core of ethical thesis advocating *egoistic hedonism* rather than "altruistic" in the ethical parlance. This is tragic that economics should be seen as individual centred enterprise in which ego satisfaction of wants turns out to be the only important thing giving a wrong impression of the concept of "utility", therefor. Whatever the case may be, the very conception of economics is again a testimony to ethical involvement. We surely want to scrutinise whether the inner core of economics emanating ethical thesis does any good to it. Or, is it true that an ethical critique of the same that takes us to the ethics of transcending self-interests to enter to others-interests is any better. Surely, individuals have liking for self-abnegation even in economic matters. This is, however, not a ground to be sceptical about economic ethics but one way to see the way in which moving on opposite directions, economics and ethics still goes together in theoretical analysis of their contents.

We shall return to the questions of self-interest, altruism and welfare at proper places but for now let us find out what W. S. Vickrey's sceptical arguments amounts to[3]. Vickrey's paper is a good ground to find out the way in which "applied economics" much to the dislike of some economists have close relationship with ethics rather than showing that there is no such relationship. Vickrey thinks that economic theory should be seen as a body of logical construction devoid of ethical content just like geometrical constructions of Euclid. For Vickrey applied economics is also like this because without any ethical resources, this is likely to have practical applications. Yet, a careful analysis of the nature and tasks of applied economics reveals that it is not to the least devoid of ethical content when it comes to the real aspect of application than abstract thinking. An instance of such ethical involvement could be seen in the context of the judgements to be made on the basis of available relevant information of present market prices to develop a pricing system justifiable on ethical grounds for well-being of the future generations. This is all the more clear with regard to pricing of non-renewable resources, which has far-reaching effect on future life as well as on the environment in which we live. It is a matter of value-orientedness in applying a method of pricing such resources based on the present data and the subsequent decisions to exploit the resources for the present at some price though the future well-being is always looming large in our minds. The same is the case when we consider questions of economic preferences of people and market value of the preferred objects. Peter Groenewegen in a compact introduction to his work *Economics and Ethics* argues that "In 'applied economics', the ethical considerations tend to enter more directly. Take an example from tax economics. For tax economists, the criteria explicitly include the ethical one of 'fairness' (equity) as well as 'efficiency', 'neutrality' and 'simplicity' with their seemingly greater economic content. The last invariably entail ethical judgements[4]. Groenewegen clarifies that though the demand for 'neutrality' in taxation is attributed to the preservation of market values not maligned by any tax 'distortions', the market valuations in any case gets flawed or maligned owing to types of preferences in the market and the conjoined ethical assumptions. Further, Groenewegen argues that the conception of 'efficiency' in taxation is close to the concept of ethical values owing to the good or the worthwhileness of interference and/or non-interference in private sector involvement in such matters. Similarly, the questions of individual taxpayers' conception about the stringency in tax compliance and interpersonal comparisons becomes loaded with ethical questions when any enforced taxation system is touted as 'simple' by the responsible authorities. Gunnar Myrdal, says Groenewegen, "has so clearly demonstrated, once communal or social values arise, pure economics has less and less to offer and the ideal of *Westofreiheit* disappears under the weight of the various pleas for 'just', or 'fair', or 'equitable' taxation in reform programmes involving the financing of the state".[5]

Not exactly in course of economic ethical scepticism should we speak about the primitive conceptions of Adam Smith regarding relation between economics and ethics, but the views closely ended up to such thing by virtue of the over-simplistic justification of economic ethics in terms of a fortuitous conjunction of economics and ethics. Such an explanation in reality tends to be sceptical about the possibility of economic ethics on logically stronger grounds than being fortuitous. However, it is worth noting that the oversimplicism charged on Adam Smith was himself a professor of moral philosophy in Glasgow where in popular perception economics was a branch of ethics. Anyway, Adam Smith and De Mandeville argued that market systems of social interaction is a realm free of ethical values because in a human form of life consisting of active market exchanges no ethical probing are needed for a desirable result. In fact, the conceptions of moral values, moral desirability, just and the right including those of human well-being pops up as fortuitous results of the form of life infested with number of amoral and immoral behaviour. Hence, the relationship that emerges between ethics and economics is completely non-academic or non-theoretical because no amount of normative deliberation ever causes such close relation. This oversimplicism in terms of fortuitous relation of the two fields has been thoroughly criticised (and rightly so in my mind), because it seriously tends to encourage scepticism of one type in which moral agents partaking in complex and dynamic socia' interactions including those of market interactions are ordinary components of an intricate mechanical system who do not probe morally on economic matters rather morality comes to them even if they are amoral or immoral, as if the mechanical conception is sufficient for conceiving a economic ethics. Taking a deeper look into what Smith assumes to be so mechanical and fortuitous in the market, we find that the imagined by-product of morality out of immorality in the market is possible if and only if several undesirable conjectures of market system are taken to be valid without any logic. The imagined immorality leading to accidental moral growth in man, mainly through perfect competitions in the world markets, is a misconception because world markets are not perfectly competitive. Moreover, in perfect markets we assume (wrongly) that outcomes are efficient if there are free exchanges for gain. In reality, in markets the assets brought by the individuals for distribution are grossly unequal. A number of unlucky people do not bring enough assets to bargain with and for that reason are unequal in terms of free exchanges. Hence, even if there is free change at competitive prices, the market cannot be termed "efficient". Or, if still on unequal grounds, we do say that the market functions efficiently because some participants gain well in free exchange, the ethical problem is whether such efficient market is ethically desirable or good? Hence, morality among us does not come accidentally when in the free markets we act immorally rather when we probe on matters of the nature and functions of such efficient market on ethical grounds. To be clearer, A. Buchnan writes: "Ethical reasoning is needed to determine whether, or under what conditions, undeserved differences in initial endowments are unjust; and if so, what means of correcting or preventing them are permissible".[6]

In order to find out the different aspects of modern economics that waits ethical probing and thereby justify economic ethics we have to consider the economic analysis of markets. More often than not economists assume that moral agents act in a typical self-interested way in an atmosphere of rules of exchange in which contesting agents strive for their *own* benefits which conflicts with each other in stiff competition among the agents. The economists come to probe ethically whether the assumption of self-interest is at all viable. This is not to say that the ethical theory of egoistic hedonism or *egotism* is a gross one as compared to altruism, which of late the economists rightly preferred. In fact, nothing has been cursed by ethics as grossly unethical, it leaves a lot of room for us to find out whether in market order, the ethic of self-interest and altruism has something to contribute and thereby justify economic ethics as a sensible study. It is interesting to notice in this regard that many economists such as F. A. Hayek and P. S. Dasgupta have strongly argued against the thesis of pure self-interest as necessary for explaining the market order, which however, does not necessarily amount to the acceptance of *pure altruism* as it is clear in the case of Hayek, though Dasgupta works out an altruistic alternative for the same. The effect of such ethical probing of market order is very deep as in many cases, it leads to champion government interference in the operation of the market because altruistic and welfare considerations are supreme, whereas in other cases, it leads to champion a more liberal thesis that abstains from government interceptions, though that does not amount to the same as egotism, but cares for diversity of moral goals of the population thriving in a market economy who would otherwise be subjected to ruthless government constraints. The perceptions of economic welfare in the context of individuals and society at large, is thus affected by the ethico-economic inquiries we have just seen. This is one way to justify why ethics has a role in economic considerations or why economic ethics holds well.

Coming back to the market society again, we find that a survey of ethical foundations of such society has been a popular theme of many economists. J. P. Platteau, for instance, has provided a good account of the survey in his paper "Behind the Market Stage Where Real Societies Exist, I and II" (*Journal of Development Studies*, 30 (3) and 30 (4), 1994). Again, this does not amount to say that economists laud an ethically based market society and curse the unethical ones. Rather, there is a lot of scope to find out whether ethical basis of market society is worth discussing, and if it is worthwhile, there is no way to avoid the probability of ethical consideration of economics or what is economic ethics. The debate dates back to Karl Marx, who has been linked to the legacy of many classical economists like Adam Smith on this matter. These thinkers argue that social agents as participators of market come in relationships only through the commodities in exchange. Hence, their relationship is completely accidental, impersonal and thus anonymous. Participating people are thus not in any social bond such as camaraderie, friendship and so on. As such, the participants in the market are not governed by moral responsibilities or moral theories of personal nature. From this, it is argued that the market society requires generalisable or universalisable ethical principles if the said society has to sustain for a longer time without getting disturbed through unlawful and unworthy methods of transactions of good. The principles of honesty, lawfulness, just in exchanges naturally come in the economic parlance, which is a testimony to its growing interest in ethical matters. It is believed that ethics with its abstract principles provide grounds for the economists to find out which principles regulates or should regulate the anonymous market relationships with the phenomenal changes in the traditional society and its market system and the evolution of the modern market system where numerous complexities of division of labour and exchange of commodities are unique in their own ways. The growing anonymity and impersonality in market transactions thus asks for sea change in moral probing, the change from individual oriented moral thinking to a general or universal moral thinking. In any case, market transactions does call for the right, just, good, responsibility and duty of the anonymous persons participating in the market order. It is interesting in economic ethics to study the classical theory of the rise of morality in most fortuitous manner, we have already seen because all self-interested parties in small group interactions exchanged commodities caring for basic honesty because none wanted to lose their commercial good-boy features. We have seen that the *a priori* conception of a market order that itself gave ethicality to people is fraught with problems, but that is exactly what is expected of an ethical probing of economic issues. It is all the more important to see that when *a priori* history of primitive market systems gives way to a realistic picture of present markets of complexity, the older notion of ethicality as by-product of market behaviour is seriously challenged. We now feel strongly that there are different ways in which ethical evalution of market behaviours may bc initiated. This is further scope of an economic ethics to grow. A proof of this is the said survey of Plateau in which he comes to conclude that if the contemporary complex market orders are really anonymous to some extent, there is an urgent need for *moral interventions* at the organised level, that is, through cducation rather than expect any fortuitous moral evolution. But the thesis does not remain uncontested (which is a good sign with any ethical query that enters subject's alien to it). M. Moore, for instance, in the *Journal of Development Studies*, 30 (4), 1994 argues in his paper, "How Difficult is it to Construct Market Relation? A Commentary on Plateau" that even in the contemporary world, markets is placed in an intricate mesh of social relations, which evolves moral values and moral thesis from *within*, that is, they are *internal* to the system and not exogenous or external to the system. The main reason is that the modern markets are no receptacles of anonymous relations in cases of exchanges of commodities. Rather, the firms and the buyers are well related, well known and acquainted of their shares to care for basic morality. The credit must go to information surges, and for that matter, moral *gurus* and their sacred commandments need not be learnt through value-added organised teachings. Nevertheless, these thinkers cannot disregard the role of ethical probing within complex market systems. A return to classical ethics with self-interest overtones is a good case of moral debates about economic issues constantly hitting and moving as billiard balls. The concerns of ethicality in market orders are further extended to the moral limits put to an internal order by virtue of emotive reasons such as nationalism. A good moral debate crops up when internal moral order is countered by universal moral order in the age of global market and global citizenship. Can nationalism, glory of national market flourishing be shelved at the cost of a broader and more glorified universality? Who has to take up such trifling issue than economic ethics? Take this observation by Robert Rowthorn: "ethics and morality matter in economic life, and that their influence is largely ignored by the modern economic profession.... This undermines the moral commitment of the people to the institutions in which they operate, causing them to behave in the fashion assumed by the theory.... Even normal market transactions, where self-interest is most prevalent, have their own moral codes, which are not observed simply out of fear of retribution. The common failure of professional economists to take these into account is a serious intellectual weakness".[7]

It appears that the nature, structure and functions of the modern markets pose important questions, some of which are *internal* to economics as a positive science and others are *external* to it but unavoidable nevertheless, when economics takes on the ethical reflections as valuable because it cannot on the one hand completely hide its normative nature or normative tasks and on the other hand hide the truth that perennially it has a close bond with normative ethics which comes to the fore when normative tasks are performed seriously. In this sense, the study of markets reveals that as an internal study largely neutral to ethical perceptions, it has its own goals—it has own standards of efficiency and goodness and own values that a more or less economically sane-head would agree. Yet, ethical perceptions are differently poised, markets are seen to promote greater values—sane-head people are labelled like that on different grounds, which comes to a new set of evaluation of right, good and just when it comes to the goals of the market and players in it. A good case of study that transcends the internal inquiries to the external or the ethical critiques is that of economic growth with associated references to market. Paul Ormerod in his work *The Death of Economics* (1994) argues that the internal ways of measuring economic growth in terms of monetary transactions are believed to be value-neutral, which it is not. Moreover, it is myopic on the part of the measure of GNP as the criterion of the growth of an economy. A wider perspective of discussion questions these criteria on ethical grounds and ushers new concepts for market and growth, especially when questions of environmental depletion and ransack pollution are put to the fore. The moot point in these scathing critiques of market and growth puts material well-being in the straight jacket for a thorough ethical scrutiny which well-being is doubted for its varied value-neutrality. Hence, ethics-talk in economic matters like these encourages a discipline like economic ethics for serious study.

It is exactly in this regard that the ethic of free market economy is important, which we shall consider in a separate chapter. However, it is important to note that many disputes about market economy, which is value-laden, have been extremely interesting in economic ethical arena owing to the socialist and the capitalist contestants—both parties ready to spat on the basis of unethicality drawn from the vast body of normative thesis. The moot point is whether centrally planned economy is any better than a competitive market economy in being humane as well as eco-friendly. The questions of "success" that is often crafted by economists on 'internal' grounds thus gives way to external evaluations of the same because more often than not something does succeed better than falsely conceived success. Hence, the questions of 'success' in terms of pure profits by virtue of liberal entrepreneurial drives in a capitalist system opens the can of worms for the socialists to evaluate the guise of success that exploits a number of things—people, non-human animals, rivers, air and many more, most likely, freedom of speech. Alternately, the capitalists would like to show the ethic of profit oriented liberal entrepreneurial drives and thereby bring out the inhuman rogue in the humane-guise that exploits masses, environment and freedom as well. The traditional belligerence of the parties in economical thinking, who, nevertheless, bring in ethical queries are encouraged to discuss the issue of "living standards" of people of any part of the world, which is closely related to the questions of their 'well-being'. However, such well-being covers the individuals, nations and households. Economists generally study and evaluate standard of living or well-being on the basis of desire satisfaction, or the satisfaction of *desired desires* that amounts to pleasure of body and mind though mostly through the material or physical sources. Naturally, evaluation of these means or sources on economic grounds of usefulness determines the good for man. However, the ethical critique of this conception of good for man has been vigorously taken up by a number of ethicists such as Amartya Sen and Bernard Williams who urges to move 'beyond' utilitarian well-being on various ethical reasons which is another testimony to economic ethics. The basic assumption in the idea of utility that a man is happy when his desired desires are fulfilled either to the optimum or to the minimum stands for an ethical scrutiny because often-happy people are so even when their cherished desires are unfulfilled. Moreover, people are happy for different reasons, not necessarily and sufficiently when their desired desires are fulfilled or their life style is good, rather, when their social conditions mould them in a fashion to be happy with whatever they have. Ethical critiques of utility theory may be on the grounds of fictitious choice of the good means and ends as well as on the ground of possessing the undesirable in undesirable ways and proportions. It is exactly in this context that Sen speaks of the ethic of *capabilities and functioning* that give a different dimension to an economic way of interpreting living standards of men on earth. Surely, this is one way in which economic ethics comes to be sensible. Nevertheless, we should not understand from this that an economic ethics always need to curse utility thesis and speak of metaphysical, religious and qualitative ways of life that stands as the good for man. Economists taking great interest in ethical scrutiny of human good need not agree to a queer entity for overall good. If economists do not lose their good habit, their ethical query of human good should still be anchored to a calculus of the material ways in which human good is possible, says many. With this must be added concerns for humane ways to care for *self and others* when it comes to live a good life however, materially anchored it may be. Still more, economic ethics might strangely be sceptical about the calculus of standard of living as ethical basis to evaluate our well-being or better said, sceptical about standard of living as an ethical basis of human good. Hence, it should be remembered that economic ethics is not monolithic; it does not demand to take it for granted that non-physical theories of human good are the only concern of an ethical study of economic matters. Many people strangely look at philosophers as Godly freaks, and to satisfy them, often they are forced to mention the non-physical or the metaphysical so that the freaks do not start jumping on their heads. In fact, economic ethics by any extension is not metaphysical economic ethics. I do not find any encouragement in shaping economic ethics as a Hindu or a Christian or a Moslem economic ethics either. Well, for that matter, the cursed old "utility" thesis needs repeated reading and evaluation, too.

It is interesting to note with some welcome risk of repetition that economists' concern with ethics always tries to justify that some matters of fact though different from matters of value, are nevertheless, related to shape something different from both economics that deals with the former and ethics that deals with the latter. Geoffrey Brenan calls it a testimony to "take feasibility seriously".[8] He argues that the issue of "feasibility" which is "internal" to economics as issue of fact, should be considered *de novo* in the perspective of "desirability" or the issue of ethical value. Hence, "the conceptualization of practical ethics as a kind of confrontation of the feasible with the desirable remains consistent.... And what the economist sees himself or herself as distinctively providing in that confrontation is an analysis that takes "feasibility seriously".[9] Brennan argues that welfare economics is one good instance of showing why serious economics comes to be so good, but surely (for us), within economic ethics. Brennan gives five instances of welfare economics, which testifies "serious economics". First is the attempt to replace the traditional utilitarianism by Robbins as an 'informationally infeasible' thesis. Second in the 'market failure' literature during 1950s to the 1980s that deal with the 'feasibility of equilibria' under market organisation. Third is to analyse the 'feasibility of set of equilibria' within democratic political systems in the special context of 'public choice response' to the market failure during the above period. Fourth is to be concerned with the feasibility of deriving 'aggregative orderings' from 'individual orderings' over social outcomes which are apparently desirable. Finally, the feasibility of 'supply of virtue' on the part of the morally constrained humans so without their intentional good motivations at least good results are guaranteed, nevertheless[10]. However, Brennan comments that a lot of energy that has been devoted in early welfare economics to justify that many concerns in feasibility or factual considerations in economics are of great ethical worth, really does not touch the core of 'desirability considerations' in economics, which is core in ethical inquiries about economics. Brennan also comments (rightly as I think) that the artificiality of differentiating feasibility and desirability calls for artificiality in making a division of labour, the former going to economists, the latter to the ethicists. This is crucial in an understanding of economic ethics, which hardly amounts to accept any such division of labour. Nevertheless, Friedman and other economists of a relatively older notion believes that any question of feasibility is basic to policy decision, and therefore, basic to economics and economists. They argue that though desirability concerns may be of some value, an ethicist 'who has to take up the questions of desirability (by virtue of division of labour), should be careful about the feasibility aspects or else mistaken ethical evaluations ensue, which is unacceptable. Brennan fills up the gap by mentioning that though foolproof care for feasibility questions are good on part of the economists (by virtue of division of labour), any mistake on account of the desirability aspects does the same damage as seen before. Crucial for economic ethics is that both aspects have been cared for. This demands a good concern for both aspects on parties interested in such studies. Brennan reminds the economists that most of the time downplaying the desirability analysis of economic issues in the face of an orthodox notion of the economists that such and such are set of feasible thesis and others are infeasible might be wrong themselves, which does great harm to the desirability-inquiry. Hence, orthodoxy of economists themselves might be detrimental to value inquiry even if they are expected to experts of that field. In fact, in economic ethics, when we turn to the feasible for finding out the desirable in it, each case of finding out the feasible as distinct from infeasible is itself a matter of categorisation that calls for desirability analysis. Hence, finding out the feasible involves the desirable, and thereafter, the distinct inquiry into the desirable aspects of the feasible comes natural to us. Conclusively, economic ethics cares for inquiry into the *nature* of the 'feasible' on grounds of desirable. Hence, economics and ethics go hand-in-hand together. Brennan says, "The feasibility analysis cannot be pursued, even provisionally, in isolation from desirability considerations except in (unusual) deterministic cases".[11] Brennan takes lessons from both minimisation of ethics as well as maximisation of the same by staunch orthodox economists and ethicists respectively to justify that economic issues can be neither minimalised nor maximised.

Both Brennan and Buchanan argue strongly in favour of economic ethics wherein distinct role of the economists and ethicists are intact in the face of a joint effort, but Brennan and many others are obliged to a survey conducted by Hansman and McPherson (1993) that elaborates the seriousness of a 'serious economics' which is in reality ethical scrutiny of economics.[12] The main theme of Hansman's and McPherson's justification of economic ethics is that the intentional acts of moral agents are influenced by their moral opinions and probing. The shift from traditional utilitarianism to welfare economics have strong ethical grounds, and the moral opinions and probing underlying public policy is basic to shape public policy advices. Based on the writings of Samuelson many economists argued that positive and normative economics cannot be separated, they mingle in the science itself. We have seen a majority of these justifications by this time. However, other authors such as Amartya Sen (cf. *On Ethics and Economics*, 1990) and K. W. Rothschild (cf. *Ethics and Economic Theory Ideas—Models—Dilemmas*, 1993) gives us important intuitions towards justifying ethical involvement in economic matters. Yet, as I have said before, economic ethics should not be taken as a body of literature in which a number of economists and ethicists argue in favour of possibility of ethical queries on economic matters on the grounds stated here rather, it is also a body of literature that contests the idea that the stated grounds of ethical study of economics is sound enough. In fact, scepticism in this field is a welcome idea. An instance of such scepticism (others we have seen), comes from the paper of Flora Gill "On Ethics and Economic Science".[13] The author is particular about refuting some points made by Brennan, Buchanan, Hansman and McPherson based on the idea that enthusiasts in economic ethics make an intellectual journey forgetting the *analytical limits* imposed by virtue of the basic methodology of mainstream economics. Hence, ignorance or deliberate concealment of the core methodological limits set by economics does not allow us to justify economic ethics properly. Flora Gill thinks that there are 'five fundamental features of economic science and its core methodology', which seriously limits its desired invitation of an ethical inquiry. "There are:

(1) the state frame of analysis,
(2) the commitment to methodological individualism,

(3) the radical assumptions about the extent to which the economic is separable from the non-economic,
(4) the strong grip of consequentialism with its emphasis on ends even to the exclusion of concern about means, and
(5) the adherence to a particular philosophy of science which posts extreme forms of independence between fact and theory, the objective and subjective".[14]

Gill tries to show that Brennan and Buchanan in particular overstretches economic framework to accommodate ethics. One overstretching is to adopt the "constitutionalist political economists" framework of the Buchanan School. For Gill, such a framework is neither necessary nor sufficient or both for the economic science to adopt just because it has to prove its value-interests. In fact, such shared view of economic theory does not justify that such views are shared about the world by us. The scepticism of Gill, nevertheless, addresses to the Brennan, Buchanan and other such schools of thought that forget the intrinsic constraints of economics and shape it as they want to because the normativity lurking in the science is far too important for them to project. Gill does not deny that there are important perceptions in the survey of Hansman, McPherson, Sen, Brennan and Buchanan and for that matter she really does not try to refute economic ethics, she tries to impress us by a simple truth that economics cannot invite ethics by distorting itself or overstretching itself or alternately by fitting suitable norms of ethics in economic matters (thus limiting it unnecessarily as in case of consequentialism). If we remember constraints and limits of the science and its opening up for ethical queries, we should be rightly sceptical to economic ethical justifications, which are subjective, because subjectivism is in bad taste in justification for its obvious irrational clinging to arbitrary dogmas. If economics is Stalinized in definite form, it does not do much good in coming closer to ethics. For me, the greater value of such sceptical writings in economic ethics is that despite its inherent flaws that may be debated at length by economists on technical grounds, surely, it warns us of a danger, that is, not all justifications showing economics opening up for ethics is acceptable even on ethical grounds.

Remembering the constraints of economics, I would still hover in the field of economics opening up for ethical interceptions to justify economic ethics, though ethics opening up for economics will still remain a far cry. This is needed because we have not seen some strong arguments that comes from Amartya Sen in his book *On Ethics and Economics*, which truly J. M. Letiche in his Foreword commends the work as a "treasure-chest for economic philosophers." By far, Sen has not transgressed the limits of economics in this regard; his dealing with 'welfarism' will be visited squarely at a proper place.

Sen justifies an ethically relevant study of economics by first arguing about the origin of the science of economics from more basic disciplines—politics and ethics. He says that the history of western ethics wherein concerns about economic matters could be traced, owes to Aristotle. He draws instances from Aristotle's *The Nicomachean Ethics*, to argue that it is Aristotle who made us believe that politics as 'the master art' includes concerns about wealth as we find in the science of economics, whereas both in turn are concerned about the 'good for man', a concern of *ethics*. Aristotle made us believe that any talk about wealth involves talk about more higher human ethical pursuits and therefore, does not end up in seeking "wealth" because it is not the "chief good" for man, it is rather one of the higher goods for man, the "chief good" being, *well-being* or *flourishing* (i.e., *eudemonia*), and any talk about such higher end in relation to the lower ones is a talk about the inseparable relation of economic science and ethics. Hence, economics opens up for ethical study in so far as it relates to the study of a higher desirable end of life. This point has been clarified in Aristotle's *Politics* as well. Sen further shows the way in which economics opens up for ethical study as we find in Aristotle's conception of the chief good in relation to the relativistic scheme of the good (or rather, goods for man) which holds good not in the context of individual agents rather, the society at large. Thus, human goods as means to chief good make ethical sense not only in the context of individuals but in the context of the state. Economics as a study of wealth thus stands for an ethical critique either when it aims at good for an individual or for *city-states*. The economic goodness cannot be perceived as an ethical goodness when it is merely "efficient" for an individual rather when it broadens to cover social achievements. The broader view of the economic good is basic to *welfare economics*, says Sen. Modern economics thus cannot be neutral to the Aristotelian legacy of ethical orientation or evaluation of economic pursuits at the individual and the social levels. Equally true is that it cannot be neutral to the Socratic ethical legacy questioning the goodness of human ways of life that includes various economic pursuits. Tragically, some economists argue that ethical approach to economics has weakened the positive science about which we have seen something. It is important here to mention that economists of the *logistic* legacy or what Sen calls, the *engineering* legacy, has a lot to offer to economics, and hopefully not beyond the scope of ethical scrutiny. The restrictions we should impose on ethical query of economics should not be forgotten; nevertheless, there is no point in putting a veil on our effort to find out how logistic legacy has to open to ethics. Sen illustrates this with the help of example of problem of hunger and famine, which does not merely depend on economic causal analysis and subsequent measures. In fact, we should delve deeper into different levels of analysis that cuts through the ethical currents in connection with the causal analysis.

Sen further argues that the economists' perception of human nature which is so important in economic enterprises turn out to be vital for an ethical inquiry. The 'economic man' is supposed to be universally selfish, that is, striving for the safeguard of own interests. This has become a 'standard assumption' of economics, so natural to accept that despite call for ethical inquiry into such analysis of human nature inherent in it, economists try to camouflage it with several intricate justifications that transcend the psycho-physical justification needed for that purposes. He refers to economist G. J. Stigler's work *Economics or Ethics* (1981) in this matter. Not only did Stigler assume psycho-physical humans as essentially self-interested when they come to be engaged in economic pursuits, Stigler thinks that the desirable way of life of economic agents should be "self-interest". Hence, nothing like ethicality is expected of economic man. Hence, economic dealing with such men need not be unnecessarily concerned with ethicality. This is a real tragedy on the part of the economists to forget that such conception of human nature itself calls for an ethical scrutiny, and no stranger is that ethical egotism and egoism both contributes to the economic conceptions of man, thus standing for thorough criticism. If economic ethics does not take up the issue of critique of such conception, it will be undesirable of it. Sen writes that economic affluence of Japan with a remarkable shift from the self-interested attitude is empirical proof against the conception of economic man. Sen further argues that Adam Smith's conception of self-interested men and Edgeworth's conception of utilitarianism as economic calculus as distinct from ethical principle of utility both calls for some care in economic ethical consideration rather than neglecting it. For me it is as simple as neglecting what was evidently clear in economics, that is, analysis of human nature. The psycho-physical basic interests influenced the economists to shape a conception of man, nevertheless, was completely overlooked for an ethical study by many economists though their thesis testified that far from being ignorant they were more or less closer to the realisation of an ethic of economic conception of psycho-physical existential humans.

It is here that Sen realises the value of discussing welfare economical theory or simply welfarism, which is a strong case of ethical involvement in matters of economics; though he feels that welfare economics has been "impoverished" owing to the growing distance between ethics and economics. Sen argues that a number of "evaluative criteria" used in modern welfare economics have been particularly "inadequate", for instance, the specific interpersonal comparisons of utility, Pareto optimality and the interpretation of 'well-being' in.terms of 'that utility provides'. For Sen, one instance of the ethical distancing is that we have been conditioned to evaluate the welfare or well-being of moral agents on the basis of happiness or fulfilment of desired desires. This is not to say that the bad idea to conceive human nature as pleasure seeking and thus the imposing thesis of hedonism in its gross form have influenced Sen to find out flaws in the modern conception of well-being. He wants to stress that the hedonic conception of end of human life completely neglects the empirical justification of non-hedonic desirable ends in life. The fact that a poor man gets pleasure out of a small pittance eked out by a well-off person does not justify that the poor man's welfare has been taken care of. The desire-fulfilment of the poor beggar at any instance will similarly not justify the welfare of the beggar. The call for transcendence of the ethical philosophy of hedonism thus brings an advantage to economics to come closer to other ethically meaningful scrutiny. Nevertheless, even if Sen did not tell us about the telling defects of a specific analysis of human nature and the hedonic thesis, he should be assured of the economic ethical analysis because the critique of the above conceptions and the subsequent justification of welfarism by transcending the theses is a testimony to ethical interests of economists. Hence, defects of older versions of welfarism and any other thesis does not justify that economics was any less closer to ethical inquiry. Another sense in which Sen thinks that economics comes closer to ethics is the discussion of *benefits* or *advantages* of moral agents if that is at least one important end of human life, though it is difficult to limit it to pleasure or any absolute non-hedonic end. However, the interpretation of benefit of moral agents in terms of welfare cannot be ruled out or rather should not be ruled out. Nevertheless, what amounts to "welfare" that further gives us the desirable advantage, is again a matter of evaluation, which the economists need not do on their terms alone. Hence, the entry into the fields other than it becomes natural. For Sen, the entry is through the cluster-concepts like 'rights, liberties, freedom and real opportunities' which appears in the realm of ethical enterprise. In any case, the evaluation of welfare as an advantage to humans is based on the ethical cluster-concepts. Sen writes: "advantage may be better represented by the freedom that the person achieves—in well-being or in terms of agency—on the basis of that freedom. This type of consideration will take us in the direction of rights, liberties and real opportunities".[15] Taking a cue from what has been said in the ethical analysis of freedom, rights and opportunities, Sen argues that the transcending status of welfare economics, which is a transcendence from predictive economics, engineering aspects of economics and the older version of welfarism as well as hedonism should happily take on ethical considerations *de novo* because welfare economical considerations are related directly to the considerations of what is *desirable on the* part of moral agents *qua* moral beings. Welfare considerations expectedly have positive impact on humans *qua* humans thinking, rationalising, deciding and acting proactively for human good at least and this is a strong point to remember why such considerations takes us to the heart of ethical-talk. Hence, the welfare economics as we get, is based on a critique of or logically grounded transcendence from a myopic ethical theory which moves surely to the real level of human intentionality to strive for holistic human good on several non-hedonic grounds, but that is not tantamount to metaphysical good or any other good which non-hedonists fashionably support. Nevertheless, Sen reminds us that the justification of economic ethics, is not possible only by showing the ways in which issues and conceptions in economics comes closer to ethics for a unique probing. In fact, the story after the discovery of ethics of welfarism is different; it is a discovery of ethics throwing its generous wisdom on economic considerations. It is due to this that the normative ethical probing led us to discover the inherent flaws underlying the economic conceptions of human nature, hedonic calculus, utilitarian thesis and naïve welfarism. Hence, *economic ethics do not follow one way justification that is, from economics to ethics, it moves the other way as well.* This is what I was commenting at times when it is evident that economic ethical justifications do not merely depend on dragging economical discussions rather the ways in which ethical reflections help in economical evaluations. We have been largely involved in this chapter to show the ways in which economical considerations open up for ethical considerations, but that did not hide (nor should it), the truism that ethical thinking helps economics. However, I have to add to what Sen thinks in this regard. First, ethics does not help economics by extending its normative reflections only but it extends its metaethical, virtue ethical and practical wisdoms to justify why economic ethics makes great sense. This is clearer while we take up the justification of economic ethics on the above mentioned grounds.

Before moving to justification of economic ethics by showing the opening up of academic ethics to economics, we have to find out the ways in which *market economy* and *financial* concerns in economics are important grounds to know why economic ethics holds well because these concerns in economics have ample opportunities for ethical problems. The touted 'market economy' in our times have created great ripples in the global conception of human society and values therein. Hence, fundamental presuppositions and mechanisms in market economy open the wide entry of ethical or value inquiries, thus justifying economic ethics. In the popular parlance, the value inquiry begins with the idea that though market economy is necessary for economic dynamism, growth and material well-being of some humans, it is nevertheless, susceptible to the growth of a peculiar 'market society' having intrinsic values and motivations replacing other human and social values and attitudes which are at loggerheads with the domineering values. Hence, we are at the moral crossroads to consider the market values involved in market economy because we may not prefer living in market society bereft of several desirable human values and ethical values. Some economists like Raymond Plant and Michael Walzer thus argues that the inherent moral values of markets and the moral consequences of the markets are grounds for justifying why the talk of market economy involves the talk of ethics and values.[16] Plant, for instance, argues that though the study of market mechanisms in a market economy is a testimony to unlimited self gratification of the players therein, there are nevertheless, "moral underpinnings". He clarifies: "In talking of moral underpinnings of markets, I have in mind the idea that in order to work effectively the market requires certain moral attitudes on the part of those involved, and that there is some danger of these moral underpinnings being disturbed by markets themselves, thereby striking at the roots of their own effectiveness and efficiency".[17] Plant thinks that the ethic of civility cannot be overlooked at the face of the glorious market growth and flourish. Several civil virtues do not amount to optimization of self-gratification that is basic to market economic ethos. Hence, we have to consider (within economic ethics) a moral critique of market ethos that tends to jeopardise basic civil virtues and values. This is a testimony to the way in which some economical rumblings involving markets opens for ethical analysis. Further, Plant and Walzer argue that market economical ethos have an inherent bulldozing spirit, that is, to dominate with all might entire distributive process, thus transforming various social good to mere commodity value, which is a kind of "imperialism". Plant quotes Walzer from *Spheres of Justice* (1983): "A radically *laissez faire* economy would be like a totalitarian state, involving every other sphere, dominating every other distributive process. It would transform every social good into a commodity. This is market imperialism".[18] Plant and Walzer thinks that such lurking danger posed by market imperialism needs serious value-based inquiry, which is the point much needed for us to show why questions of economics opens up for ethical inquiries. Plant argues in his essay that under the ethical inquiry we need to find out why some *limit* has to be imposed on the bulldozing market spirit of material growth at some cost. The spirit to contractual buying and selling, profiteering cannot be extended to anything and be seen as commodities, which people in accidental or contractual association buy and sell for instance, kidneys of humans, and sexual and human relations. Can everything around us be treated as commodities? Is a moot ethical question. Therefore—"We should not be surprised that the growing extension of the market order will have an impact on how we conceive value in other aspects of our lives".[19] In the same spirit of Walzer, Plant further argues that market economic perceptions are followed by their natural outcomes or consequences, which needs ethical scrutiny and thereby call of economic ethical enterprise. The questions of social justice and ethical justice are thus intertwined with the natural consequences of market economy to create huge fissures in the power structures in society. The questions of inequalities in power and distribution thus open for ethical query. However, Plant takes up the important counter-arguments ensued by the free market economists to justify that the consequences of markets are not amenable to a 'moral critique' because market consequences are owing to individual's act of free exchange, such consequences are unintended and we do not have any agreeable basis for distributive justice to say that market creates unjust conditions. Whatever Plant says in refuting these sceptical arguments, we find more interest in asserting the point that the arguments and counter-arguments in the context of market ethos, we are at hand stimulating discussions within ethics, which for its unique features of economics is happily under economic ethics.

A careful study of market economy opens up new vistas for ethical critique. We may have a glimpse of it though much has to be analysed if we need to be clearer on these accounts. One important aspect in market operations is the role of the entrepreneurs in the market. This is important in so far as entrepreneurs as moral agents decide and act intentionally with definite ends in life led as a unique form in markets. Such intentional acts are thus amenable to judgement for moral value. It is interesting to note that in the entrepreneurial atmosphere in the markets, value judgements are passed not only by the associates of the entrepreneurs but by the market consumers as well. In fact, moral value judgments of entrepreneurial decisions and acts are done mainly by the consumers because it is they who are directly influenced either positively or negatively by such decisions and acts. The meaningfulness of entrepreneurial acts largely depends on how the consumers react, response and evaluate. Many economists believe that in the realm of economics it becomes extremely important to find out whether market entrepreneurship should be solely guided by the profit motives of the entrepreneurs, that is, the motive underlines self-interest and nothing else. It is a different matter whether market entrepreneurs are *in fact* self-interested people, ethical interception calls for the desirability of the motive. It is interesting to notice that self-interestedness is not equivalent to hedone-centredness because being 'self-interested' does not necessarily and sufficiently call for gratification of the hedonic self. Like egoists, self-interested people may be speaking about the maximisation of good of the self but that is not tantamount to hedonic good of the self. These are interesting moral questions, which in the backdrop of economic matter should be included in economic ethics. Further, economists encouraging ethical inquiries believe that the motive of gain through competition may be ethically good if minimal hedonic gain is necessary and desirable for the existence of the self, the questions of minimal moral expectations to put *internal* sanctions as well as to allow *external* sanctions on the entrepreneurs comes within stimulating ethical discussion. This is also related to the ethical query of market societies, that is, the query about the desirability of self-oriented or hedon-oriented society keeping in view the minimal respect for self and the society. We have seen something about this in the earlier discussion. Economists like Patrick Shaw and Toby Lowe[20] share serious moral concern about the impact of market entrepreneurship laced with the basic egoistic and/or hedonic motives on the community, who have more or less uniform form of life aspirations and evaluative patterns. The moral question of desirability centres on the market relations that tend to spread throughout the community with its ethos and motives. The questions of human values and virtues along with market values and virtues permeates the community as such, nothing can be really out of it. Hence, the question of devaluation and immoralisation of the community through market entrepreneurs and market morality become important in economic ethics.

Market economy comes closer to ethics not only on the grounds mentioned above, new vistas of relationship are opened when the role of the *consumers* in market are considered seriously because the realistic market situations and functions cannot overlook the importance of the consumers, and more often than not economists and ethicists raise questions about the ethically desirable motives, decisions and acts of the consumers for the greater good of the entrepreneurs, market and the society at large. The problem is that not only the entrepreneurs, the consumers are believed to be sufficiently egoistic and egotistic, which is however, not unethical in the face value because buyers of goods cannot be wholly foolhardy and saints, they can neither deceive their corporeal self to buy undesirable things at any price and remain nagging or bluff themselves as saints, who consumes without any subsequent satisfaction. Desirelessness is not a needed property of a consumer. Can it be an ethical property in the real sense of the term? No one thinks that consumers should be aggressively self-gratifying, that too at low expenses, neither should they be irresponsible towards the social beings. In fact, the ethic of power to consume at greater liberty obtained by virtue of power to purchase, the money-power so to say has been a perennial question in ethics. Aristotle has nicely portrayed such unethical prodigal persons in his *Nicomachean Ethics*. Can consumers be ugly while they spend? Yes, they can be so but should they be so ethically vulgar? Is it desirable to either purchase or consume all good things with money-power or to purchase and hoard all good things with the same power? Who is thus an "ethical consumer" is a moot question in economic ethics when it comes to market behaviours in particular. The ethical interceptions in such matters are in the contexts of dilemmas regarding sovereignty, liberation and desirability. The issues of rights of under and unprivileged people in a liberal market, their sovereignty to buy but the hindrance caused by lack of money, global justice and environmental concerns all come to create an atmosphere for market economy to open up for ethical debates. Ethical issues in consumerism may thus indulge us into a critique of market perceptions of the wealthy and those of the poor. It may deal with the critique of hopeless cry of the economically handicapped to jeopardise liberal economy by forcing reformism and the critique of the prodigal who do not reform their attitudes of gratification.

Another area in which economics opens up for ethics and thus shape economic ethics is *financial ethics* or ethical discussions pertaining to financial matters. However, many people are not sceptical about the relevance of such study in economic ethics because they think that neither financial issue ever make a case for ethical query nor are we sure about the subject matter of such alien query. Nevertheless, many economists, the experts of finance and ethicists have now come together to justify why ethical discussion regarding finance makes a good case under economic ethics. A critical survey of financial ethics is provided by John R. Boatright in his work *Ethics in Finance* (1999). To start with we can say that financial affairs are bulk of economic activities undertaken by professional people in which financial assets are handled with great degree of "integrity" to extend "welfare" of masses but it invited a number of irresponsibility, callousness and intentional acts of damage and malice to the money earned by the masses, thus calling for ethical checks. This brings in the ethical critiques of the financial custodians in so far as their rights, duties, obligations and responsibilities are considered in the context of dealing with money earned by people other than the financial experts. Boatright puts it as this: "finance concerns other people's money (OPM), and OPM invites misconduct. Professionals in the financial services industry… have a responsibility to the clients they serve…. Everyone else involved in finance, from financial analysis to market regulators, fill position of trust that carry certain duties".[21] It is clear that the experts in finance deal with a number of people having occupations and professions, whose hard-earned honest money needs to be handled properly by the said financial professionals. Equally true is that among people having occupations, businessmen are of great importance, who earn with risky investment of money, the handling of their money needs a lot of care and integrity. Boatright rightly thinks that finance related ethical concerns cover the fields of business and professional ethics because ultimately such concerns boils down to the ethic of financial profession in the context of a number of occupations and obligations, desires and the claim to the safe keep of what has been earned by them, though that may amount to a bad and good in money earned by these people. The 'badness' and the 'goodness' is not value-judgements on purely economic grounds or on grounds of criminality *vis-à-vis* honesty, it takes us to the *ways* in which people have earned money that need external interceptions for an ethical value-judgement on the basis of available standards.

Financial profession in itself has a few problems with regard to clarity of meanings. Like other professions such as teaching and occupations such as business, finance is not easily conceivable as a profession or an occupation because like teaching or other professions, it does not have a well-defined field of activity and a service based ideal, and like business occupation, it does not have a well-defined field of activity with profiteering ideal. The central problem with finance is thus defining its field of activity. People trained in financial practices take up a wide range of activities. It is interesting to contrast here the case of 'accounting profession', which although being concerned with definite financial practice, unlike financial practice has a well-defined field of action and ideal. Accountants thus take up specific account-keeping functions at the public and private institutions and organisations involving subsidiary practices like auditing, which calls for serious ethical queries and ethical codes. Accounting ethics is one possibility within professional ethics, which is nevertheless, different from financial ethics, which may not be so easily put under professional ethics. It is due to this that though it is relatively easy to find out the ethically relevant issues in education, business and accounting, it is equally difficult to find out ethical issues in finance. The wideness of financial practices is really problems for us in limiting and shaping the ethical issues in finance to know exactly what is financial ethics. Naturally, what are ethically relevant in financial advices may be different financial services or financial decisions regarding investment. Equally true is that the ethical codes for each defined financial practices may be different. There is no conceivable uniformity in either ethical theorising or ethical codifications in finance. Boatright successfully argues in his book that finance related experts are not concerned with the good of a particular group of people, like students or the teachers or sick persons or the doctors. In one sense, the clients or the stakeholders or professionals other than the financial experts are well-defined. Hence, ethical issues in education, medicine and business emerge mainly in the simple nexus of relations among stake and stockholders in professions and occupations other than financial expertise. Naturally, some care should be taken to find the range of persons, groups of people, financial markets and institutions with which the financial experts are related and work for their good, and thus a range of ethical issues crop-up in such an atmosphere. The whole atmosphere of the financial practices and ethical queries therein is thus un-uniform and complex. It may be largely due to such uneven complex terrains that the vistas of financial ethics have been relatively uneventful through the years of ethical journey. However, things are changing rapidly with growing contributions in the field. It is due to this that interested parties have been attracted to as diverse issues as finance in trading practices, business enterprises, corporate sectors and public sectors. In each of these fields, financial experts are involved with the ethical dilemmas of persons, groups of people and the corporate.

Strong justification of economic ethics comes from the need of ethical inquiry in financial markets, financial service industry and people in organisation dealing in finance. For every market, we presuppose some financial transactions among the stake and stockholders. It is expected that these parties follow basic moral discipline so that there is neither anarchy nor crunch in the market, because both cases lead to its gradual decay. It is expected that parties in the market avoid gross fraudulent acts, bluffs, deceit and manipulations injurious to the public life and the growth of the market as an institution. The basic principle that ought to be followed in the market is the principle of "fairness" in *playing* in the market that is, transacting or dealing in the market with various means or goods or commodities in an intricate relation with the public who are the consumers of the said goods or utilities. However, by virtue of the *undesirable* intentions and decisions of the players in the market the playing atmosphere is ruined, it becomes polluted by virtue of inequality in information, lack of bargaining power, possibly in the face of monopolistic pressures on consumers and the intended or planned scarcity of resources. The market is not merely a place of exchanging goods among people at some cost, wherein parties have accidental relation; it is also a place where long-term contracts among parties could be seen. The basic ethic of contract demands that the consumers and the producers do not violate the boundaries of desirable conducts, that is, mainly they do not try to overpower each other for gains by becoming too opportunistic and cunning. Hence, the players in the market are expected to enjoy certain moral rights, notwithstanding mutual obligations and duties because people in the market, someway or the other belong to a community expecting minimum humanly acceptable attitudes and behaviour so that the community life is not jeopardised. If the world community is equally important, any relation or contract among players belonging to different countries is equally bound by certain ethical practices—some moral duties and obligations. Equally true is that in any community a member cannot be purely a consumer or a producer, each of us are consumers with powers to contribute as producers as well (whether we really are contributors, depends on several factors). Hence, none of us is expected to be ethically so unwise to act undesirably as producers. People need to remember their complex duties and obligations as consumers and producers. In the common parlance, intentional decisions and actions are said to involve the moral agent and a number of people though at times it appears only one or some moral agent or agents are affected by our decisions and acts. In this climate of intricacy of effects of intentional acts, we are remembered of the intentional decision and actions in the market, which naturally affects a number of people, even those who were visibly unrelated to the players in the market. The financial institutions cannot forget that their decision and actions should be ethically conscious about "other parties" or the "third parties" who are not visibly in direct contractual relation. The financial market ethics is thus needed for the basic social responsibility of decision makers in the market. The justification of ethical interest in the field of finance is noticed in the atmosphere of providing *services* to the common people of our societies. It is ethically important to take care of the question of obligations, duties and responsibilities of the financial service producers to provide things that people need and to sell them effectively though non-deceitfully and in non-coercive ways. It is expected in the typical atmosphere of financial service production that the seller does not perceive the buyers as the one who depends on him or her and that the depending persons need to be fully expected for gains. The "seller", ethically speaking, should not be ethically myopic about moral agents as "buyers". Their perception should not be morally neutral, inhuman and without any care for the good of the buyer. The ethical question of sellers being desirably good counsellors and honest in explaining the "risk" elements in any transactions for the overall financial good of the buyers is of great concern. These issues thus become important in economic ethics. The greatest concern in financial service ethics is thus the ethical integrity in an atmosphere of competency in selling and gains, the integrity largely depends on the vision of the seller about good for fellow people, the buyers, to avoid conflicts in interests and to perform as competent as a seller. Ethical concerns in finance are also marked in the professional ideals and involvement of the financial professionals. It is difficult to imagine a serious financial expert or professional having no care for a number of professional markets. Value-neutrality is supposed to be an ethically challenging issue in financial expertise. It is in this dilemmatic situation that many financial professionals in an organisation or corporation are cross-fingered about becoming whistleblowers, that is, to point out the gross institutional, legal and ethical violations. It is important to find out as professionals whether ethical demands for human good can at all outwit institutional good and/or personal good. Indians are no less acquainted with these in financial services because a number of such situations rise when financial experts are coerced, allured and clinched to think of profiteering at any cost, even at the cost of killing what some say the 'moral conscience'.

Keeping the above justifications of ethical interceptions in finance and thus the meaningfulness of putting it in economic ethics, one imagines that when we turn mainly to the ground reality or the practical aspects of finance, only then ethics becomes important. This amounts to the propagation of a sceptical view that financial theory has nothing to offer for an ethical study. The reason being the one we have seen earlier that financial theories come under positive science, dealing what are the cases with regard to financial markets, institutions, organisation, that is, what are their nature, functioning and the status of the several means that make up effective financial functioning. Such positive science, therefore, is believed to be value-free, their assertions, assumptions and justifications all being basically observable or empirical in nature. Hence, there should be no scope left for the normative study of ethics in such theoretical enterprises. Most interesting feature is that ethics is believed to be a discipline concerned with the end of human enterprises whereas financial theory with the means. Nevertheless, the said positivism and means-end divergence is repugnant. Financial experts in reality deal with means and end as well as with values in financial decisions, management and actions. Financial theory does not merely analyse what are the cases, they tell us what *should* be done or should not be done. It tells what should be done or what is ethically desirable on the part of the financial experts, when it comes to their rights, duties, obligations and responsibilities towards the public, the consumers and the nation and the international community as such. The norms of duties and obligations are thus basic to financial theory; most of them are *prescriptive* in nature not stating what the case is but what is desirable when something is the case. Naturally, financial theory is a gamut of ethically meaningful query. This is another way to justify economic ethics through the meaningfulness of the ethic of financial theory.

We have seen that the diversity of financial activities pose problems for us to identify one or two activity or activities which open up for ethical inquiry. Nevertheless, most economists believe that financial market transactions and financial contracting are most important activities that come under the ethical scanner. When we come to the ethical issues in financial transactions, the issue of fairness or equity becomes most important. On the other hand, when we come to financial contracting, major ethical issue is about the duties and obligations of financial agents or fiduciaries. Hence, it may be said that financial study opens for ethical intervention on two grounds, the first being the ground of *fairness* in financial exchanges and the second being the *duties* of financial agents. It is believed that though it is expected of the financial markets to be efficient, it should be nevertheless, fair. The principle of fairness in trade-offs thus opens new vistas for ethics and in one way shows how economic ethics is important. It is equally important to note that efficiency in market exchanges also becomes an ethically relevant query because we might always ask, whether inefficiency is at all desirable in exchanges, but we can add to ask whether the desirable efficiency should make fairness its scapegoat. The question takes us to the ethical conception of general welfare through the touted efficiency in market transactions, where the element of fairness can never be ruled out. The ethical query regarding this matter turns out to be extremely important when we consider the means-end issue, that is, whether 'fairness' be viewed as purely a means or an end, or should it be seen as valuable both as means and end. Generally, in economic exchanges, fairness in trade-offs is seen valuable as means because in financial markets, only through fairness do participants become so dynamic to achieve the end of efficient transactions and thus welfare. However, one cannot overlook the truth that fairness *in-itself* or as *end-in-itself* is so valuable that only owing to it, do players participate in transactions leading to efficiency and welfare. Hence, the intrinsic worth or worth as end of fairness cannot be ruled out. It is much like Plato answering our perennial question whether 'justice' is good as means or end or both. In any case, there is a perennial dilemma to find the worth of fairness or equity *vis-à-vis* efficiency in trade offs. Hence, we have for us in ethics the issue of equity/efficiency trade off. It is exactly in this context that in financial ethics we discuss the questions of *institutional harms*, *infringement of financial laws* and *denial of claim rights* in financial markets. The questions of frauds and manipulations, equality in information and equality in bargaining power are discussed. Despite its importance, financial market transactions are not only important for ethical inquiries. The questions of duties of persons in relation in financial activities are important. The perennial ethical questions in this regard is whether the buyer and the seller in financial activities are doing what is expected of them to do, that is, among other things whether the exchange is 'fair'. Once we come to the ethic of such relation, by virtue of contact among the clients and the sellers, we expect something that has been mutually agreed upon is respected. Bequeathing becomes an important contractual virtue, which transcends the market rules, though any breach of trust or contract does transcend ethicality to enter into legality. However, legality cannot suffice the needs of market transaction respectability because it is something closer to human dignity to make vows, entitle rights to parties and abide by it owing to the respectability of the duties that the parties enjoy. Naturally, we imagine certain duties bestowed on the fiduciaries or the agents, which we call *fiduciary duties* and the duties of the professionals or *professional duties*. The former duties are of the moral agents who are bound by contractual bequeathing to act mostly *altruistically* notwithstanding the expected respectable gains as claim rights. The duty to enjoy a right to gain becomes correlative to the contractual duty to be performed without any gain by deceit, and therefore, to be performed altruistically. It is an important issue for ethical reflection to find out whether moral agents in financial contracts needs to act as *trustees*, the buyer is trustee to what gains one owes to him after supply, whereas the seller is trustee to what gains one owes to him by virtue of a supply or transactions; both parties thus become duty bound to act for the interest of the other party though their interests are taken care of by those whose interests are taken of by the other parties. It is another important ethical matter to inspect on the aspect of *choice of means* to fulfil the altruistic duties of trustees in a financial relation. Professional duties on the other hand are those specialised service ideal based duties enjoyed by experts in finance bestowed by institutions, agencies, organisations or by one that calls for taking care of the claim rights enjoyed by people in financial contract. The financial planners, chartered consultants and accountants are those bound by certain service ideal based duties that protect the rights of clients in contractual relations. Certain ethically important features of such duties are to face and resolve the dilemmas in case of conflict of interests and to find out the latitudes of confidentiality. Somewhat different from the fiduciary duties, wherein one party is believed to be acting for another's interest altruistically (in the main), we conceive *agency-duties*, that is, those duties expected of agents of clients in contract to give some vowed benefit to the clients with overriding conception of personal benefits. Agency duties thus presuppose typical give and take relations among the clients and the experts, wherein experts maximize their own benefits not committed legally to maximize clients' benefits. When such relations and duties are ethically viable; it becomes important to scan the opportunism and greed of the receivers of benefits from these agents as well as the greed of the agents being parasitic to clients.

Much has been said in the way of justifying economic ethics based on financial ethics or the ways in which finance comes closer to ethical inquiries. We have still not seen the ways in which ethics comes closer to economics or for that matter to financial discipline. We will now take care of this aspect to justify economic ethics. The justification of economic ethics based on the instances of ethics taking an advantage from economics is queer because in reality none of the two disciplines is logically dependent, none has grown with the help of crutches. These independent fields have their own features, scope and methods, but two independent fields may be nevertheless, closely related, and relations are not necessarily logically contingent relations which is true about ethics and economics. We have seen thus far that economics consists of a number of perspectives or dimensions which leaps its field to cross over to yet another field like ethics because economics draws ethical attraction for being value-loaded, there are distinct questions of good, desirable, right, just, obligatory, duty and virtues. Hence, economics itself shows signs of becoming amenable to inquiries beyond its positivistic inquiries. Now, we come to know that though ethics is essentially or categorically different from such positivistic study, it bears on some non-ethical inquiries to show that what it does (its tasks so to say), makes perfect sense even when it leaps the limits set to philosophical inquiries of morality to enter non-philosophical disciplines such as economics. Hence, ethical disposition to come to non-philosophical grounds in one way shows how ethics as normative, metaethical, virtue-ethical and practical inquiries are perfectly meaningful even when it embraces fields like economics. This further shows why economic ethics is something sensible within ethics in two ways: When ethical dynamics are visible in the field of economics and when economical tasks are visible in the field of ethics. We have seen that many things done under economics appear to be sensible in one important way, that is, in the way of opening up for a normative or value-oriented study. It is time that the other side of the coin reveals itself though on face value it appears that the normative and metaethical tasks of ethics have no opening when we consider the field of economics. This is based mainly on the orthodox notion that normative ethics is talk of norms that makes sense in ethics and nowhere else—metaethics is talk of language of morals that makes no sense in economics—practical ethics is talk of resolution of ethical problems in practical life and not in economic life and virtue and value-talks make sense in ethics but not in economics. This is, in one sense, *ethical scepticism* with regard to ethical dispositions to leap its framed limits to show that it is sensible in many ways, not in one way. To shed off such scepticism is to move away from hopeless limitations put by ethicists on ethics to remain cursed as an isolated enterprise when it bears signs of an interdisciplinary enterprise. It is extremely important to note that sceptical arguments against ethics opening up for economics and its critique is nevertheless, an interesting account of *metaethical* task. Whether or not sceptics succeed is a different matter because history of ethics that has widened to include economic ethics has not been defeated till date, nor have the sceptics given up completely. We still have sceptical arguments and their refutations making a continuous debate to prove or to disprove any non-philosophical entry of moral philosophy. Who wins is a matter perhaps not to be seen so easily, but without any doubt metaethics wins because it goes on with its basic task to inquiry into the logic of establishing economic ethics through ethical openings for economics or to destabilise the whole effort. We must find out whether the same metaethical zeal is seen when the concepts and language of economics bearing value-character are analysed for their truth and meaning, and whether normative judgements of value in economics as based on ethical first principles such as utilitarianism and Kantianism are logically sound. Hence, it is important to take up the most trifling task of justifying metaethical opportunities in the field of economics.

Ethical sceptics are extremely orthodox about metaethical opportunities in economics because they believe that the language of economics with major concepts therein has nothing for metaethical inquiry of truth and meaning because the language in essence is non-moral or non-ethical language. We can say that the language of economics in essence is ethical-value-free. Hence, the problem of the truth and meaning of the *so-called* ethical language is misconception. It is useless to conceive economics as a body of value-assertions, therefore, and to inquire about the truth and meaning of such assertions. This is much in tune with the basic orthodox conception of Max Weber and David Hume that positive sciences like economics are "value free"; its language can bear no value, therefore. Concluding it, we can say that economics being value-free does not leave any room for ethics because ethics is where questions of ethical value are. However, this does not mean that the language of economics being value-free is not true and meaningful, rather, we have different non-ethical or positivistic grounds to justify the language are true and meaningful. We have to remember as said Hume, that the truth-value of descriptive value assertions (as we find in economics), cannot be logically derived from non-descriptive assertions of value, as we find in ethics. Thus the descriptive assertions of ethics bear no ethical significance, no ethical value so to say, and for that matter metaethical inquiry of the truth and meaning of the *touted* value assertions in economics make no sense. This brings before us the core issue, of complete value freedom of economic statements, which becomes doubly interesting for us when we are reminded of one Mr. C. L. Stevenson (*Ethics and Language*, 1944), who argued strongly that it was grossly mistaken to imagine that ethics was a body of value-language or assertion of moral value and nothing else, though it reveals the *descriptive* features equally prominently because a statement of ethical value cannot be completely divorced from correlative descriptive elements. The point is whether the language of economics is wholly positivistic or descriptive, bereft of value elements. If we can show that the basic misconception of the Weberian-Humean analysis of language of economics lies here, that is, the unwanted divorcing of value-elements from the descriptive elements, we can retort to justify that it is not always that ethics or rather metaethics should keep off from analysis of meaningfulness of economic language. This may be further true of any scientific language lest elements of value are clearly noticed. In any case, our metaethical discovery does not least bother the value-free aspects of economic language because no one is really trying to justify that economic language *necessarily* and *sufficiently* imply value-judgements. Hence, by virtue of our metaethical discovery we are least worried about proving that the nature of economics is such that it consists of language, which are value-loaded, and nothing more than that. Infact, we forget an important metaethical finding by Austin and many others that the value-loaded aspects of economic language does not either drop from the blue or is fortuitous to the sciences itself because no language is fortuitous or *ex-nihilo* occurrence, they emerge as a body of assertions of different people needing them as means for communicating ideas important for the clarification of various aspects of that science. Hence, we do not claim that economics does not have value-free language as well because we know well that science like economics cannot and need not necessarily *use* value-loaded language for each and every purpose. We are also aware as metaethicists that the value-loaded feature of language of economics is not by virtue of *propagandists* in economics, that is, it is not owing to the economists' reactions, counter-reactions and persuasions regarding a number of public policies. It may well be that propagandists in economics deliberately use value-charged language while commenting on economic policies to mislead or incite public sentiments at any cost. But these tactics on the part of the economists that gives us a unique value-charged language, is not the one we are trying to inspect for truth and meaning as metaethicists. Metaethical inquiries about economic language or value-loaded economic language are a *methodological* query having little or nothing to do with the query of propagandist language of economists. This is clearly explained by A. W. Coats in his paper: "Value Judgements in Economics" in the

Yorkshire Bulletin of Economic and Social Research (Vol. 16, 1964, pp. 53-67). In addition to this, we have an excellent work by Gunnar Myrdal titled: *Value in Social Theory* (1958), who advances four important arguments to justify that a metaethical venture in economic language is sensible on the main ground that such language is value-loaded not value-free. These views have been nicely explained in Kurt Kalpholz's essay in *The Encyclopaedia of Philosophy* (vol. 2, 1972). However, Kurt Kalpholz himself do not fully adhere to what Myrdal argues, but that is least in refuting metaethical ventures in economics on the ground that economics is value-free. Myrdal argues that the science of economics cannot be value-free and thus not beyond the search for truth and meaningfulness of its value judgements because the economists cannot remain value-neutral when they construct any theory or provide an answer to economic issues. Similarly, they are influenced by *ideologies* which is clear in leftist and rightist ideologists to counter economic questions. Moreover, the values economists nurture in any society shapes their practical or policy aims, they are thus influenced to shape or construct practical policies based on definite values. These things show that economics is a body of assertions, notions and judgements, which are value-loaded, and a metaethical study for their meaning makes great sense. Nevertheless, Kalpholz points out that though economists have values that influence their ways of thinking, solving and constructing theories and policies that do not logically go on to prove that therefore, economics is value-loaded. However, Kalpholz suggests reinterpretations of this problem as provided by F. Croner (1964) and I. M. D. Little (1957) to justify that what Myrdal holds is good enough provided we accept the truth that he was in fact trying to say that descriptive assertions in economics are not without a reason, and the reason cannot be purely descriptively based either because some necessary value-premises percolates in such reasons. Further, what Myrdal wanted to say is that economic judgements cannot be value-free despite its descriptive status because they are *persuasive* in nature, which is specific of a value judgement. Nevertheless, despite all reinterpretations Kalpholz thinks that there are gaps. First, the percolating value in a descriptive assertion is subjective explanation, what Fregé calls, "psychologically infected" (cf. Kalpholz). Second, descriptive statements in economics need not be value-loaded just by virtue of being "persuasive". There is in fact no logical relation between value-loadedness of assertions and persuasiveness as its property. Otherwise, we have to accept that all value assertions need to be persuasive, which it is not. Kalpholz remarks in his work *Critique of Welfare Economics* (1957), that Little agrees to all value judgements being not necessarily persuasive. Hence, Kalpholz comes to conclude that as metaethicists Myrdal's first justification of economics as a value-charged body of persuasive language and for that matter opens for an ethical scrutiny, is not sound. We may have different reasons to show that metaethics makes sense in economics provided it is value-loaded language though not necessarily persuasive. Interesting is to notice that even if economics was bereft of such language, metaethicists still make a good case for them because value-bereft feature of economics still remains to be logically proved—it cannot be corrupted psychologically.

Another argument is based on the *emotive* nature of economic language, which is not awkward for any ethicist who has read Ayer's and Stevenson's works. Ethicists are well aware of the fact that many moral statements have strong emotive function, which becomes the basis for calling them meaningful. However, for the ethicists we now have the idea that a number of economic statements are evaluative in nature in so far as they express emotions, that is, such statements are emotive exhortations of the users of that language. Hence, economic language bears the characteristics of a value-loaded language, which opens for metaethical inquiry of meaningfulness on emotive terms. Kalpholz does not disagree that economic language does have emotive, suggestive, prescriptive and persuasive functions, but a careful look at these 'functions' or the dynamics of such language in the actual context of the positive scientific discourse reveals that they are nothing better than descriptions of state of affairs, which has no logical connection with the aforementioned psychological functions. The *non-moral use* of the descriptive language happens to suggest, exhort emotions, incite emotions, prescribes a course of action and so on, which does not prove that therefore, the descriptive language is also evaluative in nature. However, Kalpholz forgets that in economic judgements such as "Universal welfare and not pleasure through the supply of utilities are good" is not a bare description of a state of affair, it is essentially evaluative in nature. Truly, such assertion cannot be said to be meaningful because they *describe speaker's state of mind* (subjectivism of Hume) or *pure emotive exhortations without descriptive anchor* (Ayer's emotivism) or causes emotions in hearers that speakers have (Stevenson). Kalpholz should have kept in mind a range of economic assertions, which are barely descriptive state of affair, rather, which are value judgements about ends and means in economic enterprises, sometimes appearing as overreaching norms. Truly, when economists say that "Aggressive tax collection is good for exchequer", it is a statement of fact which nevertheless, expresses emotions and prescriptions in the use of "good", but it is non-moral use of the term which shows why the expression is essentially non-moral in nature and emotive aspects are matters of interest for psychologists. However, Kalpholz skips the truth that not all assertions in economics are barely descriptive; many of them are evaluative statements having some descriptive anchor, which is but natural to it. Why should emotive-prescriptive functions be completely absent in descriptively anchored economic language is not shown by Kalpholz. What Kalpholz misses while pointing out the defects of Myrdal is that value-loaded and descriptively anchored economic language is not inherent to economics or that it is accidental rather, the *use* of the language in different contexts and for various purposes evolves the peculiar nature that it *acquires*. To this we may add that Myrdal's first argument may be revised exactly on this line to justify that economic language *per se* is not purely descriptive or descriptive-evaluative or whatever; hence, it is *not* one of the inherent *dispositions* of the language that evokes emotions and things like that owing to assumed causes that Myrdal conceives (and Kalpholz rightly refutes), it is rather the typical *evaluative functions* that the economic language performs in economic contexts that shows its evaluative nature. To this, we finally, add that the value-loaded nature of the language has by this time in our metaethical discourse become an important point of discussion for truth and meaning, we cannot be robbed off this ethical enterprise by a positivistic economic hegemony.

Another attack on the ethical sceptics is that they confine economists to some such functions that it is undesirable of them to pass any *value-imperative* in the form of economic prescriptions because as economists they cannot logically deduce any prescriptive statement from bare descriptions of facts. This is again stipulation of the tasks of economists and the utter confusion that without making any logical deduction from statements of facts, we can comfortably pass value-imperatives based on matters of fact. There is perhaps no logical fallacy when there is no logical deduction from facts to value, and those statements of value, as imperatives need not necessarily and sufficiently presuppose as per division of labour of economists, a party fit for these things, namely, the ethicists but not economists.

Anyway Myrdal refutes the idea of the orthodox sceptics that economists can give prescriptions, which are *non-moral* in character because they are based on the scientific conceptions of ends and means. Hence, for an economist given as non-moral end, they can pass imperatives as means without any added value assumptions. But Myrdal argues that this will at least demand a distinction between economic ends and means, which is impossible practically and without a value assertion. In fact, there are many gaps in the assumption of a totally value-free economic advice regarding means; the gap is whether such advice is at all ethically desirable. Let us assume that economists by virtue of their scientific duty prescribes of a mega power project for which a mega dam needs to be built assuming on purely scientific grounds that the project will last for 60 odd years and give such and such physical benefits to a generation or more but not all may be benefited for associated problems of displacement. The end being still not in sight of the scientific planner, the prescription of means on scientific grounds can be easily value-free as it is often the case. Myrdal need not hopelessly contest this, what he contested is that it may be argued on ethical grounds that such plans bereft of any care for value questions, for instance, the desirability of the plan for the welfare of the future generation or the tribes or the displaced poor or the ecological community, is itself unethical. Hence, the questions of ethical value cannot be kept aside in the course of economic prescriptions or imperatives. This shows the value-loaded nature of economic decision-making and planning which is expressed typically in the imperative language of economics, which is a matter for ethical scrutiny. The crux of the argument again focuses a confusion that what is ethically desirable of the economists on certain normative grounds like ecological welfare or human welfare, goes on to show the value-loaded feature of economics. It will be again an assumption on the part of Myrdal to say that economic language is value-loaded because economists *in reality* passes value-loaded imperatives and that they *should in reality* beg a norm to be so ethical to do this. What is important for the metaethicists is not to lose the sight of the *function of the imperatives* in economics though they are about facts. Whether the economists desire or not, whether they should follow a norm or not, it is imperative on them to see the truth that their counsels are expressed in unique fashions to serve a linguistic purpose which is not what they believe to be starkly descriptive and thus non-moral, these imperatives in many cases functions as moral orders, suggestions and persuasive exhortations in an economic atmosphere of decision-making, debates and closure of debates after stiff moral agreements and disagreements. The imperative language of economics thus becomes important for ethics to enquire into by virtue of its metaethical wisdom.

The value-free nature of economic assertions has been proposed by L. C. Robbins as well when he argues that value-free advices are possible about human welfare, which is touted to be an ethically desirable end. Hence, scientific advices about social welfare have nothing to do with ethical values even if the end is an ethical one. Robbins further argues that the conception that 'a relatively better equality in income distribution amounts to social welfare' demanded an economic advice of *interpersonal comparison of utility*, which is, has clearly nothing to do with value-judgements. Kalpholz counters this by reminding us that though such scientific advices are unverifiable, why they should be value-free is not known to us because the demand itself carries question of ethical desirability and rights on the part of humans who expect equality in the distribution of utilities. Hence, Kalpholz concludes saying, "Both value judgements and synthetic statements are inextricably involved in discussions of economic policy. Yet, it has often been suggested that economists, as economists, must refrain from uttering value-judgements. This suggestion seems to have arisen from a confusion between problems of valid inference and the question of demarcating what economists may properly say but that attempt to restrict the scope of argument in this way can only have stultifying consequences".[22] Still it remains to be noticed by Kalpholz that the metaethicists' basic argument transcends the imputation of values by economists or any other party, metaethicists are more interested in finding out the ways in which economic language functions to call it value-loaded.

It is time now that we move to the justification of ethics by virtue of its normative tasks. It is in these contexts that metaethical justification of one norm as compared to others becomes important; we shall try to find out this as well. To start with, we would like to see what Amartya Sen thinks about ethics opening out for economics. He writes, "I have... been more concerned with what ethics can do for economics than with its converse. I have tried to argue that distancing of economics from ethics has impoverished welfare economics and also weakened the basis of a good deal of descriptive and predicative economics".[23] I quote this passage to remind our readers that what we have seen before in Sen's work (*On Ethics and Economics*) is an account of the way in which welfare economic conceptions opens new vistas for ethical interception, which is to my mind, not what Sen thinks, that is, he was justifying 'what ethics can do for economics', notwithstanding the fact that ethics for him has been largely conceived as a body of norms that awaits logical scrutiny for validity in the field of economics, especially welfare economics. What I found here is that Sen was extremely successful in showing how economics as a science having positive and normative character performs some such tasks (which we have seen in the first part of our discussion), for instance, the task of finding out what is good economically speaking for humans, does not close eyes from what is morally desirable as well. Hence, an inter-relation between economics and ethics is seen clearly, when we come to the normative judgements of economic good for man. Now that we have seen what the tasks of ethics are (in the early part of our discussion), for instance, the normative and the metaethical tasks, we have surely not done as ethicists are expected to do in ethics *vis-à-vis* economics which Sen presumes has been done. A glimpse of what it means to ethics opening up for economics is seen in the just concluded metaethical discussion that takes care of economic language. What exactly does it mean when normative ethics opens up for economics should be seen in Sen's work in case repeated references to egoistic hedonism, theory of self-interest or egoism, utilitarianism (of Bentham and Mill), deontology of Kant and the thesis of moving beyond utilitarianism (cf. Bernard Williams) as normative thesis, which Sen thinks should be taken care of for close scrutiny in the broader context of economical enterprises, but misses to mention clearly that he is in fact, trying to justify economic ethics as meaningful enterprise in two ways: Economics helping ethics to apply its wisdom and ethics helping economics to apply its wisdom. We believe that the way normative ethics helps economics to incite its wisdom to find out that it is not a drab positive science about money matters should be seen more clearly. This comes out clearly and nicely at the fag end of Sen's work when he discusses that though in the economic literature moral agents are typically seen as self-loving people tending to maximize their own benefits, which may be put under "self-interested behaviour" which in turn consists of self-centredness of welfare, self-centredness of life goals, welfare in the main and the correlative self-centred choice for meeting the said goal of personal welfare, it is important that ethical normativism lends cues of ethically desirable goals of life and correlative choice, which is certainly not the same 'self-centredness' or what is ethically known as *egoism* and mixed with hedonic flavour is, *egotism*. Both these theories of ethics give Sen enough insight to argue that, therefore, better options in normative ethics is open for us when it comes to the desirability of choice of life goals and means when we are placed typically as economic-humans. It is due to this that ethics has given us the insight to refute the assumptions that economic-man should depend only on 'own consumption' for his or her welfare, that person's goal should be something more than own consumption and that rational choice of persons loving their self need not be merely own consumption. For Sen, ethical considerations (or normative ethical cues), "might suggest maximizing some objectives other than one's welfare; and can also induce responses that make personal welfare rest on a base wider than one's own consumption. The implications of different ethical considerations on these distinct features incorporated in self-interested behaviour can be systematically worked out".[24] There is no doubt that Sen knows well that ethical normativism has many things to offer than the drab egoism and egotism, it has altruism and altruistic hedonism or utilitarianism to offer which is however, transcended by the questions of "quality" and care for the ecological community by Mill in his *Utilitarianism*, and then by the *welfarists* of the new generation. The transcendence is well shaped in the critique of consequentialism, whether act or rule, but that does not end up in the normative thesis of act or rule deontology or contractarianism either. In any case, knowledge of the *first order ethics* or what is ethical normativism turns out to be good for evaluation of the most popular conception of human good when humans are seen as economic beings. It will be sufficient here to notice that Sen and many other critiques of normativism did not play with human sentiments and emotions to justify ethical welfarism over and above other normative thesis because they have depended heavily on a number of *rational arguments* that shows the inherent defects of several contesting normative thesis that turns out to be injurious to economical thinking about good for man. Such arguments and critiques, therefore, amounts to justification of *normative thesis* as applied in economics which is a metaethical inquiry.

Almost all discussions about the norms of ethics, which finds application in economic affairs, boil down to utilitarianism and Kantian deontology. Some people like Sen speak of welfarism and consequentialism along with egoism and egotism (we have seen this), and some others speak about virtue ethics. First, we have to clarify that though there are less confusions about egoism and egotism in relation to economic affairs, there are some confusions about utilitarianism, consequentialism, and deontology and virtue ethics in relation to economic issues. First is that utilitarianism cannot be a Type of welfarism or the *vice versa* if welfarism as a normative ethical theory (and not merely an economic theory), has any independent existence and value. Second, deontology does not end up in Kant; there are other deontologists of repute owing to their independent original thinking, which finds some role at least in economic matters. We can easily consider that cases of Ross and Carrit when we are dealing in its types called, rule and act deontology. Next, some thinkers like John Rawls support major aspects of normative deontology though they are also contractarians having unique ways to support and assimilate both types of thesis. Further, consequentialism need not be given an independent normative status along with a number of *teleological theories* like egoism, egotism, varieties of altruism covering utilitarianism and welfarism and contractarianism as well. Many thinkers interested in normativism in economics have a peculiar tendency to forget or overlook a simple classification of normative ethical theories that is, to classify them as teleology and deontological and find out the cluster of theories according to their family resemblance knowing well what teleology and deontology amounts to. To my mind, egoism need not be classified under a separate normative category because its teleological character is extremely clear; it stresses the value of the *teleos* of the ego as intrinsic and supreme. Further, the *teleos* of the ego may be seen separately as fulfilling the needs like 'pleasure' or *hedone*. Hence, hedonic egoism or egotism and those not valuing hedone prefer some non-hedonic ends like liberation of the self or self-satisfaction or self-fulfilment and so on because for the ego (or self), it is important to consider the question of kind or quality of the *teleos*. These features of egoism within teleological normativism is extremely important in economic writings because economists take *teleos* of economic planning, decisions and subsequent actions and the calculus of the consequence as extremely important in the distributive sense, that is, when moral agents or individuals are taken to be important and their good in terms of either pleasure satisfaction or non-hedonic satisfactions or both becomes stiff questions for comparative value judgement. In fact, the whole of teleological thesis becomes vital in norm-oriented economic thinking. Hence, normative ethics has many things to contribute to economic value judgements. It is really challenging to value right, good, just and desirable of our intentional economic decisions and actions when 'purpose' becomes basic to judgement, whether of one's own self or other selves. When we come to others, we find that *altruism* within teleology may be either hedonic or non-hedonic. When we speak of pleasure satisfaction or maximisation of pleasure for maximum people, which may or may not include the question of the individuals or self because pure altruism will consider *hedonic* and *non-hedonic teleos* as supreme though *self-abnegation* or *self-sacrifice* cannot be ruled out. Or, in a more *moderate* form, altruism would happily include one's own benefits among others, whether the benefits are either hedonic or non-hedonic. Though pure altruism is difficult to digest in economics, it cannot be completely ruled out in contemporary world that economic decisions are thought (wrongly as I believe) to be 'purely for other', wherein a *veil of ignorance* is needed for the decision-maker or policy-maker to achieve the desirable altruistic end. It is difficult to see how such veil can be imposed on us as decision-makers and actors though each of us have economic goals, aspirations, satisfaction levels, needs, rights and so on, all of them extremely important for a respectable human life. Self-abnegation or even putting the self at last does not seem to be ethically acceptable either with its counterpart but contrary thesis of 'pure egoism'. We shall come to see later on in this work how without putting any veil on self-satisfaction, we can still *socialize* in the course of moral debates and consensus regarding economic decision-making and acting. Pure altruism, like pure egoism provides challenges for economists, therefore, to find out the model of economic planning and decision-making which is nevertheless, ethical by virtue of being *social* neither anti-social nor a-social. Quite often when I speak on these issues, particularly to the audience of welfare economics, I tell them 'The parable of the sympathetic writer' by Mr. Lu Sun. The sympathetic writer cannot be a fool to give away even his undergarments to the poor beggar and think that in that way he did an economically wise and ethical act. I am also fond of quoting our famous philosopher Cārvāka who finds greatness in grabbing everything for one's own self. Socialization must, therefore, be a cue or signpost to ethical decision-making, and we have to take the help of ethics to find out what it can offer in terms of the theories that it has, to make us more oriented to co-operative living with rightful wants and their satisfaction. Altruism nevertheless, might appear in "non-hedonic" form, which is again extremely important for the economists because we ought to think *de novo* amidst the atmosphere of pleasure-satisfaction, what else can be valuable for us as *teleos*. The thought had its germ in the Aristotelian thinking (in *Nicomachean Ethics*) when he proposed *eudemonia* as the *chief good* for man though many other goods in a hierarchy of values for man may be conceived as important which includes pleasure and happiness (though these are not the same things). The talk of happiness and the talk of eudemonia or *welfare* of man brought the elements of 'non-hedonic' altruistic thinking notwithstanding the care for self. These things appear clearly in Aristotle's analysis of *distributive justice*, which makes great importance in economic affairs. The balancing act among egoism, egotism and welfare is well seen in the Aristotelian explanation, which still remains open for further study and criticism in our dealings with equitable distribution of goods and services in economics. The care for "quality" of pleasure and widening of human pleasure through the ecologically conscious acts that cares for pleasures for other beings gives the post-Mill ethicists enough grounds to shape altruism as a non-hedonic theory in terms of liberation of the mankind. Holistic human welfare that cares well-being of other beings becomes extremely alluring for the contemporary economists who deal with questions of economic decision-making, planning distribution and finance. It is interesting to note that the so-called "welfare" of man need not necessarily be an amalgam of hedonic thinking within altruism, not the 'pure' one to be sure. Hence, welfarism as an overreaching moral theory or the first principle of morality cannot be explained as a theory in which basic features of egoism, egotism and utilitarianism are rolled into one. Welfarism cannot be an ethical principle that is guided by either physicalism or metaphysicalism. It cannot be inspired by economics and/or metaphysics or a combination of the two. Most interesting is to imagine that it is an amalgam of consequentialism, utilitarianism and deontology. For this, let us now come to utilitarianism briefly. The touted universalism of human pleasures and happiness has in the recent times changed phenomenally with the growing discontent with pleasure for all as the valuable end of life. We have seen that Mill was discontented with it and so were the *ideal* utilitarians like Sidgwick, Moore and Rashdall, who stressed on the non-hedonic aspect of 'utility' which erstwhile was a strong hedonic thesis advanced by Hume and encouraged by Bentham. The physical aspects of utilitarianism was no less haunting for the economists who would not leave its roots because many ethicists and economists thought that 'quality of pleasure', 'happiness', 'bliss', 'beauty', 'knowledge' and a number of ideals that replaces or adds up with the erstwhile holy grail called "pleasure" was a corruption of the basic ethical thesis under teleology. Simply, utilitarianism cannot be a non-hedonic theory. If it is so, it is not utilitarianism to the least. The economists must be continuing with this (poor) idea because for them an economic explanation of "good" (for man) in terms of "utilities", that is, physical amenities for pleasure-satisfaction is a must. In fact, these things enable economists to find out able calculus for quantitative measures to evaluate the pleasure level of humans, which is the desired end. These ideas remain under the shadows of Benthamite calculus and positivistic leanings extremely haunting till date, and we are still at the end of ethics ready to open for economic inquiry and critique of such old but lucrative ideas. Why should the scientific leanings of economists mould utilitarianism and thus a number of teleological theses like "self-interest" and "hedonic self-interest"? These first principles of teleology remain anchored to ethics perennially and should not be corrupted by any replacement of physical and quantitative concepts by the economists if we come to realise well that ethics *per se* did not stick to the quantitative conception of these teleological theories. History of ethics shows paradigm shifts in our understanding of many teleological theories, particularly utilitarianism. There is no doubt, however, that utilitarianism and other hedonic theories are naturalistic theories which does not guarantee a positivistic status to it by any amount of reasoning, nor is physicalism a natural result to follow. However, we cannot doubt the teleologists, particularly the utilitarians are *consequentialists*, and that calculus of the consequences be an important aspect lest we remember that not all consequences are physically measurable. We also know that utilitarians are propagators of a theory of "benefit", which again raises questions of calculus lest we remember that not all benefits are matters of calculus. Utilitarianism is beneficialism but *not* physical beneficialism *sufficiently* that is measurable or at all pose problems like that necessarily. Utilitarianism is consequentialism because it speaks of maximisation of benefits for man in the major, which is not possible without seeing the consequences of intentional decisions and actions. Utilitarianism does not necessarily and sufficiently speak of physical benefits for which seeing physically appearing consequences are must and the maximisation of such benefits are of only importance. Hence, there is no point in a physical or positivistic economic analysis of the conceptions of "utility", "benefit", "maximisation principle", "consequences" and so on which are important in utilitarianism. The point is that when grounded firmly to perennial ethical philosophy, utilitarianism or any consequentialist hedonic thesis opens new vistas of inquiry for economists. The economists, therefore, should not assume a prerogative to put on a coloured glass of cost-benefit and physical measures of consequences through which the world of normative teleology has to be perceived and understood. This may be good enough to change economic perceptions about utilitarianism and consequentialism. For one thing, both theses are not equivalent because we need to remember that not all consequentialists are utilitarians though utilitarians are consequentialists with a qualification that consequence, is not necessarily and sufficiently a physical or quantitative or scientific conception. I believe that many economists must be reeling under the conception that consequences are *results* (which it is not), and which is quantitatively measurable or is in principle cognized through senses. Many benefits, consequences and the like may not be matters of sense-cognition and measurement. The same must be true of many other benefits that of late, transcended pleasure and happiness. The consequences of human actions that are calculated for their benefits or utility thus remain an open question for economists to pick up from ethics, particularly when many consequences remain unforeseen and unforeseeable. Utilitarianism for the economists must be thus an open-ended option for understanding, criticism and application. The same must be true of consequentialism and welfarism.

Coming to welfarism as a normative ethical theory we must be careful at the outset to dispel any orthodoxy in shaping at our economic whim to call it utilitarianism, egoism and consequentialism in one package. In fact, right from the Aristotelian conception of eudemonia, we had problems of understanding. Many European scholars after Aristotle were equally bewildered to find out fitting synonym in English language, because it was difficult. Yet, most of them as a matter of convenience and parsimony of thought (or wrong thought) called it "happiness", which was strangely not the case because *Nicomachean Ethics* deals at length about pleasure and happiness but not eudemonia as happiness rather, to be sarcastic, eudemonia as eudemonia is not happiness or bliss if by that pleasure is transmitted to a higher status. In any case, many people called it the conception of 'well-being' or 'welfare' or 'flourishing'. The conception of being well or flourishing is not equivalent to doing well in terms of benefits or gains or utilities. It may rather come closer to a state of being or existing under the incessant *imperatives* of the *practical wisdom* as trained by the *philosophical wisdom* and doing without a holiday that elevates our self (not the metaphysical self) to its *fullest*, that is, flourishes it. Such is the conception of *self-fulfilment* (for some, self-realisation) in Aristotle's ethics of welfare. The conception is universal, covering the individuals. Despite the hodgepodge of verbal tricks, the flourishing of the self is possible when one lives with all care for his or her environment in which are other beings and things, and acts and reacts with full intention most *rationally* keeping mind the desirable, the just and the right, which is by virtue of the philosophical wisdom of the person. Such rationality among many things presupposes the economic rationality to do the desirable, the right and the just. Hence, economic rightness is an aspect of being well or flourishing. But this is not everything. It will be far too optimistic to think therefore, that welfare is an economic conception, a conception rolling in it utilitarianism, consequentialism and so on, the one that is, measurable or quantifiable necessarily and sufficiently. To my mind, normative ethical wisdom of welfarism from Aristotle to our times cannot be confined to economic conception—this is one way in which ethics might help economists to read, revaluate and re-examine welfarism or the ideal of human well-being. Surely in doing so, utilitarians remain no more utilitarians and consequentialists because transmutation of both in welfarism is a natural outcome. For a welfarist, therefore, keeping an eye on the consequences of following the imperatives of the *praktike* (practical wisdom) and doing what is desirable, that is, *dein* (duty) is key to find its benefits. Nevertheless for in the economic measurements of benefits these things are not necessary and sufficient.

It is nearly astounding to find that Aristotle's welfarism has been carefully crafted to be non-duty based conception. This takes us to interesting perceptions about deontology, which is another ethical helping hand to economical thinking. David Gauthier finds at least one hundred and seven occurrences of the term *dein* or duty in *Nicomachean Ethics*, which is otherwise believed to be non-Aristotelian as well as post-Greek ethical conception. Most interesting is the occurrence of the notion of 'imperatives' of rational self, which was more closer to Kant and Ross though Kant gave it a turn by virtue of introducing the conception of 'will' or rather, free and autonomous will which is good as well—'good beyond the world' so to say because nothing less than Holy Will can be better than that. Despite Aristotle's legacy, many of us hesitate to give any credit to the person while Kant formulated his famous deontic normative thesis. In any case, Aristotle must have a greater wisdom to my mind to realise that teleologists need not be unnecessarily anti-deontologists though non-deontic good are of much value for them. The person must have outwitted the wisdom of Platonic teleology and Thrasymachus' hedonic (sophistical) teleology when they hopelessly argued about supremacy of value of altruistic non-hedonism and egoistic hedonism respectively. Aristotle rightly saw the flaw in these monolithic thinking and tried to find out the way a teleologist (by virtue of being a eudemonist or welfarist) can perceive the value of duty or intrinsicness of the value of obeying the imperatives of the rational self provided the person has the 'philosophical wisdom' or is a *phronimos*. In fact, greater wisdom lies in the truth that it is a duty or intrinsicness of the value to do something is the *teleos* that underlines a teleological thinking, whereas acting in view of a *teleos* should be seen as the duty. In any case, Kant added many things to this, one important aspect being the *maxims* of morality, which becomes important in the field of economics. The universalisation of these maxims and their direct impact on economic decision-making is now well debated in economic ethics. Of late, Rawls took a cue from Kant with regard to his theory of distributive justice, which he owes to both contractarianism and Kantian deontology. However, it is important again to notice here that deontology cannot be manipulated to suit the scientific and quantitative ways of thinking about value or worth of intentional economic decisions and actions. What best deontic ethics does is to provide ample opportunities to find out the intrinsic worth of certain economic decisions irrespective of the necessity of calculus of consequences with which they are at times over-enthusiastic and obsessed. An interesting question is, 'Can economists transcend consequential calculus when they meet the critiques of both deontology and teleology?'

Ms. G. E. M. Anscombe found that though Socrates, Plato and Aristotle have given us an ethic of virtue, we forget it completely; hence, we need to go back to our roots. Soon the valueless era (as if) caught the last straws of virtue as value from getting completely drowned. The vices of modern human life owed much to economics because it has given us the myopic vision of an economic man bereft of finer human values and virtues. It has given us greed, need, pleasure and so on, which are so bad. Therefore, it is time now that we turn to great virtues of humans because we now want to be good guys first and then follow courses of teleological and deontic ways of life. Ms. Anscombe was visibly attracted to what the great Greeks said in terms of being virtuous men, that is, to inculcate in us a number of virtues, some of them being *cardinal*. Well, everything is fine but the said Greeks were undoubtedly teleologists and not to the least virtue ethicists who do not need these overreaching theories. In fact, these Greeks never established a normative virtue ethical theory, which as first principles of morality like teleology and deontology was basis of moral evaluation of economic and many such acts. Hence, an *anti-theory* movement took place, though arguments in favour of *return to theoreticism* without any neglect to the system of virtue were heard. Whatever may have caused this theory—anti-theory debate, it was rightly noticed by W. K. Frankena and others that knowing about a virtue or a virtuous character for sure begs a normative theory that is beyond virtues. For instance, how do I know that, "honesty" is a virtue and not vice until I argue that "honesty" is either beneficial to me or is intrinsically good in the capacity of my duty? Equally true is that my knowledge of benefit or duty as good is based on the acceptance that beneficence and dutifulness are intrinsic virtues and not vices or that they are worthwhile or good. In any case, what virtue ethics tells us in principle is to 'be good' when we strive to inculcate in us by sheer thought and effort many worthwhile properties like honesty, diligence, truthfulness, fearlessness, justice, temperance and so on. The point is what can economics derive from such wisdom even if the normativism debate is shelved for the time being? In the recent writings in economics and management, some contributors are keen about value and virtue inculcation in economists, planners, managers and so on. Virtues in market transactions, finance and accounting could be easily seen in these writings. Long lists of virtues to be inculcated jumble the writings. Again, it is a matter of re-reading and revaluation in economics when virtue ethics enters its foray. Hence, virtue ethics provides important normative cues in economic ethics.

We may now come to *practical* ethics and *professional* ethics and their contribution to economics. Important things have been said in this regard while we were clarifying the practical and profession related tasks of ethics. Much will be said in this regard in some of the forthcoming chapters. For now, we need to see that practical ethics as we have understood in the course of our analysis of tasks of ethics in this chapter amounts to either normative ethical engineering or inter-subjective corroboration and post-corroboration analysis. Without indulging into the defects of engineering method of application of ethics, we open the case for a critical appreciation for our economists, who on their part find such ethical suggestions as helpful in the construction of economic ethics. It is to be appreciated by the economists whether the value-laden problems, that is, the problem raising distinct questions of ethical good, right, just, duty, obligation and so on in the field of economics with which the professionals and the persons having occupations are related in the economic enterprises, needs to be resolved because the moral dilemmas about ethical values among the professionals cannot remain as they are. Economists, ethicists and any other conscious civil citizens cannot overlook the ethical dilemmas in economic enterprises because that is a sign of moral apathy as well as uncivilized nature of moral agents, which is itself unethical. Now the problem is whether ethicists or moral experts, like able engineers be allowed to resolve these dilemmas by studying the nature of the ethico-economic trifles all by themselves by virtue of their knowledge of normative principles, which are believed to be basis of evaluating what is ethically good, right and just. The question is whether such moral engineers are allowed to apply their technical principlistic know-how because only they have the moral authority to do so? Further question is if our economists and others accept moral experts' authority in such matters, which moral principle is best chosen for resolving numerous ethico-economic impasses? The other side of the imbroglio is why ethicists should apply principles to resolve ethico-economic crises when economists consisting of a group of professionals and occupations and other people who are affected by economic decision-making and actions are equally well placed in resolving these issues. What is great and beneficial in principlism and moral chauvinism? Should we replace it with another humane model that cares for major parties in the resolution of these crises through *moral debates* and further analyse the debates to see which principles were *in fact dynamic* in the actual course of application of our common *ethical knowledge* of right, good and just sidestepping theory or principle cooption? We think that economic ethics as a meaningful enterprise should thus consider these stiff questions that emerge out of practical and professional ethical methodologies. This is one way therefore, to justify economic ethics in the way of the opening up of practical and professional ethics for economics.

I believe we had much about nature and justification of economic ethics, which may be further enriched as we proceed in the next chapter dealing with the nature and justification of business ethics. We must not have any ambiguity about the fact that business has a strong economic aspect or activity but it is just not the same as economics or what is undertaken in terms of economic enterprises.

NOTES

1. Sen, Amartya, *On Ethics and Economics*, O.U.P., India, 1990, p. 2.
2. *Ibid*, p. 2.
3. Readers may refer to W. S. Vickrey's essay "An Exchange of Questions between Economics and Philosophy" edited in *Economic Justice* by E. S. Phelps, Penguin Books, Harmondsworth, 1953, pp. 35-62.
4. Groenewegen, Peter (ed.), *Economics and Ethics?* Routledge, London, 1996, p. 4.
5. *Ibid.*
6. Buchnan, A., "Economics and Ethics" in Werhane, P. H. and Freeman, R. E. (eds.), *The Blackwell Encyclopaedic Dictionary of Business Ethics*, Blackwell, 1997, p. 187.
7. Rowthorn, Robert, "Ethics And Economics: An Economist's View" in Groenewegen, Peter (ed.), *Economics and Ethics?* Routledge, London, 1996, pp. 30-31.
8. Brennan, G., "The Economists' Approach to Ethics: A Late Twentieth Century View", in Groenewegen, Peter (ed.), *Economics and Ethics? Ibid*, p. 127.
9. *Ibid*, p. 127.
10. *Ibid*, pp. 127-128.
11. *Ibid*, p. 134.
12. Hansman, D. M. and McPherson, M. S., "Taking Ethics Seriously: Economics and Contemporary Moral Philosophy", *Journal of Economic Literature*, 31 (2), 1993, pp. 671-731.
13. Gill, Flora, "On Ethics and Economic Science", in Groenewegen, Peter (ed.), *Economics and Ethics?* 1996, Op. Cit., pp. 138-156.
14. *Ibid*, p. 143.

15. Sen, Amartya, *On Ethics and Economics*, Op. Cit., p. 47.
16. Readers may go through Michael Walzer's work *Spheres of Justice, Blackwell*, Oxford, 1983 and Raymond Plant's paper "The Moral Boundaries of Market", in Norman Richard (ed) *Ethics and Market*, Ashgate, Aldershot, 1999, pp. 9-25.
17. Plant, Raymond, "The Moral Boundaries of Markets", *Ibid*, p. 10.
18. *Ibid*, p. 14.
19. *Ibid*, p. 19.
20. Essays by Patrick Shaw: "Markets and Moral Normativism" and Toby Lowe: "The Communitarian Critique of Market" in Norman, Richard (ed.) *Ethics and the Market*, Op. Cit., pp 26-35 and 63-94 are worth reading.
21. Boatright, John R., *Ethics in Finance*, Blackwell, Oxford, 1999, p. 3.
22. Klapholz, Kurt, "Economics and Ethical Neutrality" in Edwards, Paul (ed.), *Encyclopaedia of Philosophy*, Vol. 2, McMillan Publishing Co. & The Free Press, NY, 1972, p. 454.
23. Sen, Amartya, *On Ethics and Economics*, Op. Cit., p. 78.
24. *Ibid*, p. 81.

2

The Nature and Justification of Business Ethics

We have seen that ethical issues in economics are numerous, the most important being the metaethical and in some sense metaeconomic issues of nature analysis and justification of economic ethics, which is nevertheless, extremely important in so far as we want to face successfully the onslaughts of economic ethical nihilism or scepticism. In order to do so we found that ethicists and economists alike, who are interested in justifying economic ethical enterprise, had two ways in this regard. One way is to show that economics makes ample room for ethical or value inquiry and the other way is to show that ethics has ample grounds to allow economics to find out what is relevant to them. Hence, economic ethics was justified, as we believe, beyond doubt. However, we have not clarified the nature of some of the most important economic ethical dilemmas and resolved them because we have a separate chapter on that. It is important now to follow the suit while we consider the nature analysis and justification of business ethics, which comes naturally to us because one important aspect of economic ethics is to take care of many ethically relevant discussions about business as an economic enterprise. Business is a natural ally of economic enterprise because business is basically an enterprise that involves apart from other things, economic concerns about market, marketing, production, distribution, sales and purchase, finance, accounting, profits and loss, demand and supply and many such things, wherein distinct questions of ethical value becomes relevant and important. We may say that though all economic enterprises are not business enterprises, business enterprises are under the broad head of economic enterprise. Hence, business as a natural ally of economic activities raise value-questions for inquiry but in the context of business we need to orient our discussion to a professional/occupational group or groups which is not necessary in economics because we need not forget that discourses in business and business ethics mainly revolves round stake and stockholders—the party who needs something at some cost and thus holds certain rights (also obligations) and the party who supplies needed things at some cost and thus holds certain rights (and obligations). Hence, even if business involves economical insights, may be business ethics need economic ethical insights as well, both cannot be one and the same. The way ethical issues in market and finance is discussed in the economic ethics owing to distinct features of markets and financial talks in the *economic parlance* which need not necessarily and sufficiently be the same as and grounded on the features of such talks in *business parlance*. We need business ethical discussions grounded on business-talks. Nevertheless, many economic talks about market include business talk, and thus broadly ethical concerns in the former happily include the latter. Yet, our knowledge is widening and heightening in business realms as well as in business ethics, which naturally by virtue of the contemporary zeal for deeper specialized discussion calls for separate attention to business and business ethics. Though the unique features of business ethics comes out sharply from the economic ethical contours for business and economic ethical concerns are different in some sense; they need separate care for analysis. We are thus poised to venture into the realm of the nature analysis and justification of business ethics which, as we now understand, will automatically drag us to an analysis of "business" as an enterprise broadly within economical enterprise for bearing family resemblance but the member of the family, that is, business has distinct features for some properties unique to it which is vital to note. Let us, therefore, start with the nature analysis of business ethics and we find out what made it develop within a short span.

Business, as we now understand it today, had some of its elements in the early form of the occupation. The element of a division of labour in terms of providing goods and services to those who need them and have the purchase power for their goods, in a space imagined as market assembling is still present in business today. Nevertheless, there are remarkable changes in the conception of the market and the imaginary places where anonymous people meet for need satisfaction. The change has been gradual, mainly due to the phenomenal rise of the industries and bulk production of commodities for sale and purchase. Mechanisation in production and distribution of goods is a remarkable feature as well. Computerisation and quantum leaps in information systems have also contributed phenomenally in this regard. Moreover, the changes in the social and political structures throughout the world during and after the Great Wars contributed to the remarkable changes in business. The quantum change in the perception of business as an occupation is owing to the limits set by the interfering agencies in business practices, the most important agency being the government. Since the seventeenth century there has been a tension among the individuals or groups of individuals or organisations who did business on the one hand and the government agencies that interfered in business enterprises for what they thought justified grounds for interference. The businessmen wanted more dynamicity, freedom and unlimited movement at the levels of production, sale and profits, whereas those responsible for social cohesion, social good and benefit of the purchasers wanted to curb unlimited dynamicity, freedom and profits. Hence, business and businessmen were put to checks under ethical scanner to some extent at least whether that was liked by them or not. The new wave of putting business practices in the ethical scanner was to follow when social pressures grew greater. Naturally, with the growth of education, businessmen were seen to put some *internal checks* on them as well because it was a matter of simple realisation that as social beings one cannot just remain as parties who do business and needs nothing from other parties. They started realising that as nationalists they too have some duties and obligations. Hence, business as an occupation has at least two important features, if not more, one is the increment of personal good and the other is the care for others' good, to some extent at least. Nevertheless, the basic inner tone to extract greater good in the bargain at the cost of some loss to the customers cannot be completely evaded in the modern times despite education and civility. Anyway businessmen had two perennial ways of looking at other people who depended on them, the one who was closer to heart, with whom businessmen have personal relationship and thus conceived them as important people to whom they owe something, to whom they have some duty and so on; and the other one who was distant, accidentally related, seen mostly as people who were to be squeezed to the limit needing no care for the future relation. Naturally, the modes of bargain changed with such perceptions. At times internal checks were put to harness the ruthless motives of profiteering in the bargain and at times, it became a matter of tug-of-war, each pulling with might and tending to win at times, but in the final run, the winner must be the businessman. Hence, the perceptions in business changed from the view that the customer has no right to the view that he has every right when it comes to profit and good. With the issues of rights, obligations and duties, were introduced the conception of justice as fairness in give and take. The emergence of the ideas of good of the purchaser and their rights and the ideas of justice, honesty and integrity took us to ethical considerations in business. Therefore, for the businessmen the questions of moral desirability, right and good became important.

The most important aspect of the business practice is that those engaged in providing some goods and services at some price to others have been tragically branded as egoists or egoistic hedonists, who for their benefits and pleasures act Shylock because they are by virtue of being profiteers, necessarily immoral and anti-social. Hence, in a society none but businessmen should stay hands down, they are good only when they do no good for themselves. Hence, there are myths about businessmen and their morality. The myth about business as gross egotistic enterprise and thus immoral did not grow in one day. Dated back to Aristotle, business as an economical activity of household trading (*oikonomikos*) was not only an activity that does economic welfare of people in society, it is also closer to illegal trading practice for maximisation of profits or what he called *chrematisike*. Aristotle had no good words for these people because they were egoistic parasites in the society. Robert C. Solomon has observed in his essay "Business Ethics" (1991) that this vast background of business enterprise we find the history of socially conscious and morally charged people attacking these parasites—"Jesus chased the money-changers from the Temple and the Christian moralists from Paul to Thomas Aquinas and Martin Luther followed his example, roundly condemning most of what we today honour as 'the business world'".[1]

The inherent conception of ethicality in business practices was, therefore, the conception of brutality of rich men for profit at any cost, which needs to be checked by any means, that is, the scale of profit needs to be tilted to the consumers. The consumer unfriendly and brutal attitude of businessmen labelled as unethical needed some change in the later times, which we have seen just now, did change phenomenally. In the western part of the world, the ethical conception in business emerged rapidly through the writings of Adam Smith, which owed it partially to the medieval business guilds that constructed codes of ethics for businessmen. With this, the business and economic activities gained different importance in society and the status of the businessmen in public perception grew stronger. Businessmen as moral agents were thus seen differently not merely as persons of gross hedonic interests. However, this does not mean that suddenly rich people were conceived as very good social beings who donated huge amounts for the poor despite their urge to make great profits. Business ethics is not as simple a matter as this. The rise of business ethics in our times is mainly due to the discovery of issues in business that apart from many other issues cared for ethical analysis and the justification that theoretical and practical moral philosophy opens for relevant studies in the field of business. This is far away from courses in the older versions of codified ethics in business and the discussion of moral values and virtues in the context of business enterprises.

Contemporary interest in business ethics is not easy to point out in terms of mentioning any day or date. Yet, Norman E. Bowie in his account on "Business Ethics" (1986) claims that "One might date the birth of business ethics as November 1974—the date of the first conference on business ethics at the University of Kansas and cosponsored by the Philosophy Department (Richard De George) and the College of Business (Joseph Pichler)"[2]. This must be historical account of American Business Ethics truly speaking if we mean to say that in other parts of the world business ethics was discussed well before 1974 no one really contests that idea, not Bowie to the least because what he means to say is that the full fledged academic discussion involving ethicists, businessmen and others that is ethically relevant in the field of business was the said 1974 meeting at a global level. Though the history that we have already traced, tells us that ethical interests in business activities date long back, but they were stray, unorganised and more of intellectual discussions among a tiny group of people here and there or eminent in the writings of some economists. I have some reservations to call a body of knowledge business ethics if either extensive contribution of the field of ethics or extensive contribution of the field of ethics to business has not been clearly and systematically discussed by people interested in these things. Stray writings reflecting the value of human virtues and values in business or the value of Indian or Western value system in business, does not construct a profound body of business ethics. Business ethics, in this logical, systematic and profound sense was really a construction through the ages by many thinkers and writers in this area, which bears distinctive character, something unique to it. An interesting example in the construction of business ethics through its *nature analysis and justification*, which is a rare commodity in very early or medieval or later writings, until what Bowie rightly thinks, came to be so distinctive of business ethics with effect from global meets, seminars, symposia, congresses and a huge body of writings by a number of interested people. The formative years of business ethics expectedly did not have desirable elements unique to it, but that does not prevent us from conceiving an early history of business ethical writings outside America. What is asserted here is that beyond 1974, business ethics was nearly full grown, its desirable features emerging with prominence and the stray and scrappy features quickly withering in course of systematization of the field. With this, several misconceptions were withering away about which I have mentioned above, but that does not prevent us from discussing several virtues and values in business. Business ethics has become different beyond 1974. Truly therefore, though business ethics had germs of Aristotelian and Platonic reflections and to some extent the germs of the *śāstric* wisdom of India, it did not remain just what these genius said or thought. Bowie writes: "The field of business ethics was not created *ex nihilo*, Plato and Aristotle both discussed albeit briefly, matters of business ethics; Plato identified the proper function of business—a view very much in live with the twentieth century economist Milton Friedman. Aristotle provided an account of economic institutions and at least a partial account of economic justice"[3]. Bowie further explains that gradually in the late eighteenth and nineteenth century business ethical reflections started pouring in with much extension, some of which were "crude" and others "critical". The clash of the pro, anti and moderate opinions in business ethics gradually evolved a body of knowledge so profound and varied as we now know it to be, which however, does not mean that the final words have been written.

Bowie thinks that the rise of business ethics was on two directions, one is the broader or the *macro* way to the rise of business ethics as something that occurs within the broad field of economic ethics, for instance, the ethic of certain business practice dealt in the light of broader conception of the ethic of economic affairs; the other is the narrower or the *micro* way to the rise of business ethics, that is, narrowing the ethical discussion to the corporate practices or the ethic of the practices of the firms. As usual, ethicists parted way to disagree on the value of these approaches, they tended to either follow a macro-way or a micro-way exclusively because they either believed that economic ethics paves groundwork to any business ethical analysis or they believed that business ethics does not need such groundwork for the number of readers who are unaware of the economic intricacies, rather, zeroing on business firms and their activities, one can gradually assess what lies beyond it at the economic strata. However, the debate is on, for Bowie, it is 'a tempest in a teapot' because none wills to believe that business ethics should be rightly approached on both ways because that is hopefully the course of its rise. For me, the point is extremely important as a *meta-study* because analysis and critique of contesting justifications of business ethics is itself an important *task* of business ethics. It is interesting to note in this regard that the approaches towards business ethics through the micro and the macro-levels is not exactly the same for some writers. For instance, what is for Bowie the micro approach is *molar* for Solomon, and micro and macro bear different significance. Solomon thinks that the rise and growth of business ethics has been through three ways, the micro, the macro and the molar. The micro way to business ethical discussions is marked by the ethic of fair exchanges between two people, that is, at the basic level of business activity, ethically sensible points are raised, analysed and criticised. On the other hand, business ethics grew through macro approach as well, that is, the ethically relevant study of issues inherent in the huge world of commercial activities, the institutional activities so to say. Finally, business ethics grew through the molar approach, that is, the ethically relevant discussions pertaining to commercial units or the corporate so to say. What issues cohere in these approaches and thus construct the whole of business ethics is a matter to be taken up in the due course.

It is important to trace the rise and growth of business ethics by knowing what it was thought to be and what later on it turned out to be the case. Hence, knowing what business ethics is not helps us in understanding how it grew up gradually from misconceptions to a new conception. We had some hint that business ethics did not grew by virtue of the attacks on business as either an immoral practice or valueless practice or amoral practice because in our times no one is ready to buy the idea that at any point in human history trading, buying-selling, need fulfilment through give and take and making profits at the ends of the sellers and the buyers were immoral or valueless or amoral practices. Even the modern corporate houses are not completely undesirable because we wonder how else we can flourish at least physically if there were no houses to fulfil our legitimate needs! The rise of business ethics is thus by virtue of revaluating the desirable ways of corporate functioning, participation in the market for need fulfilment in desirable ways, providing desirable services and contributions that is expected of them. No one really feels any moral shame or a guilt in the matter of profit-making because "the new concern is just how profit should be thought of in the larger context of productivity and social responsibility and how corporations as complex communities can best serve both their own employees and the surrounding society"[4]. Hence, one way through which business ethics has evolved is breaking away from the notion or rather the 'myth' that business is all maximisation of profit by some hawkish people at the cost of maximum exploitation of masses, which is amoral and valueless. There can be no business ethics because business has no ethical face, is the old and misconceived idea. It has been an important task of business ethics, therefore, to break such negative myths, to make us understand that even if in the worst case, some business practices are valueless, immoral, grossly unethical, there is still a business ethics because business devoid of an ethical face has no logical relation with ethically relevant studies in business or what we call, "business ethics". Unethical business remains enough wide for business ethics because probing the pathway to hell a critique explores its ethical darkness to lead us to brightness. The grossly exploitative business, even if it be true in many cases, does not to the least prevent (or has prevented) the growth of "business ethics" because rather than preventing, it has invited us to see what is dark and thus move to what is brighter. In fact, "there is no ethics in business" may be a more challenging view if that means to show why there can be no ethically relevant study in business. We have seen that the big brother of business matters, economics so to say, was equally thought to be beyond the reach of ethical interceptions, which, nonetheless turned out to be wrong. The same may be true of business ethics, but we have to wait for that. For now, let us conclude that business ethics grew at the cost of breaking myths about business because business for long has been tormented by critiques as "profit making activity" wherein strangely "profit making" has been equated to a "very bad thing to do in society". What an ideal civil society does without a profit making business activity is simply mind blowing to understand or what is done there bereft of business is a bizarre idea. Coming out of such fool's paradise was one reason why business ethics grew with the truth that "profit" is always in the air because business goes with it as a natural ally, though "making a profit" is fortuitous, business involves "loss" as well, and it is interesting to know whether neutrality and loss of profit makes business glorious or society without business makes civil society glorious. Let us also debate whether remaining paupers is ethically good or whether remaining decently well without any business around is both ethically good and to be intellectually honest, practically possible. In one sense then business ethics has grown from the ashes of *cannibalistic conception* of business, that is, business is basically *jungli* activity where businessmen in corporate are after another's throat, ready to finish competitors for making maximum gains. Hence, the inherent idea is that in a *jungli* atmosphere, there can be no ethical discussion because in the jungles the beasts have a natural course; there is no ethically relevant talk there. Again, let us remember that that worst *jungli* modes of business life remains for us encouraging to make an ethical hunt because unlike the beastly tale, here we deal with people, who do not only cut throats, they also restrain, react, revolt, criticise and ethically scrutinise what is right, good, desirable and just. Most painful is to imagine a society where glory of civility and ethicality has banished business altogether. Is it imaginable? Hence, "it is the tendency to see business as an isolated and insulated endeavour, with values different from the values of the surrounding society that characterizes all of these myths and metaphors. Breaking down their sense of isolation is the first task of business ethics"[5].

With this background of the rise and growth of business ethics, we now move on to the unfolding of the "nature" and "justification" of business ethics. Our task of the nature analysis of business ethics has now become relatively simpler because in the earlier chapter we have already analysed the nature of "ethics", which forms an important aspect of business ethics. We have seen that unlike common morality or moral opinions and beliefs, ethics as a branch of philosophy is known for performing the normative, metaethical, practical and virtue-based tasks. We have seen that ethics approaches fields like economics, which is known as a science. We have also seen that economics approaches ethics for some relevant scrutiny. It is important now to find out the ways in which business matters approach ethics for yet another relevant discussion and how ethics approaches business matters for relevant discussion. What we have not seen thus far very clearly in terms of a definition or meaning analysis is that what "business" as a field of study amounts to, though in our foregoing discussion we had some idea about what business activity or business enterprise amounts to. It is not difficult to find out that a study of business is a body of systematic inquiries about the unique human enterprises called business, in which the individuals and the private and public sector companies are engaged in distinct economic activities among themselves, mainly dealing in human need satisfaction, that also involves production, pricing, marketing, market transactions, bargain, profit, loss, accounting and so on. This may be at basic level, that is, among few individuals or between two persons, as well as among individuals and corporate and companies. Hence, business is an intricate human enterprise at micro and macro levels in which human needs and wants are satisfied through production and distribution of goods and services that has a market value and in which profit and loss in terms of commodities and money is natural phenomena. However, this is not a definition of "business" that aims at satisfying us with all necessary components of business clearly spelt out. On the basis of this simple explanation of "business" we are drawn to imagine that business is primary economic activity, and business enterprises are primary economic enterprises or institutions that contribute towards the production and distribution of goods and services among the people of a particular society or of different societies who have some common aims like need satisfaction, whether that is satisfaction of monetary needs or basic needs of food, cloth and shelter. The urge for the such satisfaction brings together discrete individuals of a society or societies to engage in the use of whatever scarce resources are available to them to become a party to *production* to turn these resources into usable goods or services, and that cannot remain idle because other party to *consumption* of such goods and services *pay* the needful to use the desired usable goods and services. Hence, we have a nexus of basic economic activities in which producers produces desired things for the consumers and distributes them in the form of consumer products, employee salaries, return of the producers and the taxes that are imposed by the governments of states where the nexus is in function. A modern business institution is, therefore, not like a market place barter of goods among secluded anonymous individuals as a low-key activity. Modern business involves a number of things like tilling, mining, manufacturing, retailing, marketing, arranging transports for marketing, selling, insuring, banking, advertising, accounting and so on. In the modern times business is not restricted to government and semi-government companies and corporations either; we now have a wide non-government or private business houses or corporate houses. Covering both, we can say that modern business is marked with sizeable enterprises called the *corporations*, which are constituted by virtue of law and run under legal bindings of the land, and enjoys unique rights, duties and powers. Their sizes vary according to their investment and turnover of the products or the marketable goods and services and the subsequent profits. These corporations need not be always huge in terms of involving work force or human labour; many modern corporate are huge in terms of involving sophisticated machineries and modern gadgets. The paradigms of business called corporate in their new *avatar* is only a precocious youth, it is vastly different from the joint stock companies of the medieval era. An interesting feature of such modern corporations is that they are perceived by us as embodied individuals, that is, as "persons", who enjoy rights, obligations, powers, are bound by law, may be sued, might come into a coherent relation with persons of contracts as per suitable rules and by-laws. In the words of Velasquez: "Modern corporations are organisations that the law treats as immortal fictitious "persons" who have the right to sue and be sued, own and sell property, and enter into contracts, all in their own name"[6]. An important aspect of modern business is that the corporate business houses conceive of different roles, liabilities and benefits to the *stock-holders*, the *administrators* and the *work-force*. The division is conceived according to the division of labour that has become a part of modern enterprises. The stock-holders are mainly the asset and capital holders or chief investors but not necessarily the immediately involved persons in production and distribution, their liability is fixed to what they invest in terms of money and assets. The administrators are the officers administering the assets of a corporation who have for their function a number of managers and office bearers to do the allotted tasks. The work-force is the employees of a corporation, the persons providing labour directly to produce something and to distribute them as well. They are also involved in different types of labour, physical as well as mental. The business houses are also known for their hierarchic systems, that is, a ladder of rights, liabilities and powers which are intricately woven in a nexus to achieve an end though the difference in *status* can be seen easily. These corporations can be seen as law abiding; every individual irrespective of their status are seen to abide by certain rules and laws, they do not normally transgress their limits of functioning. However, if the responsible parties transgress laws of the corporate, they are deemed to be punishable.

The modern day business is also marked by crossing the boundaries of a particular society or a nation, most of the time these large to very large corporations are called *multinational companies* or simply, "multinationals". Hence, these corporations are active in production and distribution of goods and services in number of countries that host their activities. It is important to note that these multinational business houses have no hesitation to play in the fields made open to them by a host country. Hence, they freely hunt cheap but skilled labour, extract natural resources for manufacturing goods and distribute or market their products to their maximum advantage in open markets, thus making world a huge market not always obliged to sell things where they are produced and by whom they are produced. This is not to say that in modern business, the governments have no role to play or that they are powerless because many governments have found effective ways to check the unlimited freedom of the multinationals when it comes to ruthless extraction, exploitation of labour, displacement, pollution, ill quality control, crude profiteering and depriving the masses of their due benefits. The multinationals are in fact bound to the laws of the land and partial or total confiscation of their rights and profits cannot be ruled out. Another important feature of modern business is the extensive use of latest *technology* in business because with its help companies manufacture, process and distribute goods and services to a greater extent and more effectively. Modern business has succeeded in its rapid evolution mainly owing to the quantum leaps in technologies. The extensive use of heavy duty machines, motors, robots, computers, airways, rocket technology, biotechnology, genetic engineering, medical engineering nano technology and may others have contributed tremendously to the evolution of modern business. Keeping these things in mind, we can now analyse what "business ethics" amounts to.

In the ordinary parlance, business ethics is defined as a 'branch of ethics or rather applied ethics, which studies the moral adequacy of the business related decisions and actions of businessmen or corporate on the basis of the available ethical norms we have under normative ethics'. In this ordinary way of defining business ethics, we are obsessed by the idea that normative ethical applications for evaluating business related decisions and actions are what business ethics is. I will argue later on that business ethics is not a branch of practical ethics if that means application of some standard norms like teleology and deontology in evaluating business actions. Another simplistic definition is that 'business ethics as a branch of applied ethics strives to evaluate business actions on the basis of common human values and virtues'. Again, I will argue that business ethics as a type of application of ethics is not merely evaluation of business actions based on *our* value systems. However, before we find out the objects in such definitions of business ethics, it is important to make a cursory remark on the possibility of "defining" business ethics in order to clarify its meaning and to analyse its nature. We have seen before that nature analysis of concepts do not necessarily and sufficiently beg a logical definition or even definitions popular in the ordinary discussions of the subject. Often these definitions are either too narrow or too wide. For instance, the definitions given above are too narrow because they do not clarify important aspects or *tasks* of business ethics rather cursorily touches on the normative and the value related tasks leaving out other important tasks. First thing is that we can hardly doubt that business ethics being a field of study in which 'ethically relevant' discussions are held, it is within ethics. To jump and say that it is within applied ethics makes things difficult to understand because we have assumed that the readers know what applied ethics is and why business ethics is within applied ethics. In fact, we can show (as we have shown in case of nature analysis of economic ethics), that 'ethically relevant' discussions in the context of business decisions and activities of persons and corporate is wider, because the metaethically relevant discussions along with the normative, the practical and the virtue based discussions are included in the 'ethically relevant' discussions regarding business. During our analysis of the justifications of business ethics, we shall know more about it. For the time being, we need to understand that if we have followed truly the tasks of ethics (as stated in the earlier chapter), and therefore, the sense of "relevant ethical discussions", we are much better placed to know what are the tasks of business ethics because ethics as a branch of philosophy having important tasks, when approaches branches of study like "business", shows signs of not merely normative and virtue based discussions. Related to this is the truth that calling business ethics under applied ethics can be seriously confusing because one might have an idea that in business ethics all that is done is resolution of business related dilemmas based on the wisdom of normative ethics, which is in reality a theoretical enterprise than practical. This is owing to the basic confusions about application of ethics, which needs to be dispelled. (For details, see Vol. 1). In any case here we are poised to see what business ethics does or what are its tasks, if we really want to have a proper analysis of the "nature" of business ethics.

Nevertheless, for a better understanding of what business ethics is, it is always useful to dispel some of our common confusions, we come to know what the case in reality is. Let us continue with one of the most common misconception of business ethics. We have some idea of it by now, but let us analyse it further for clarity. First take this assertion by K. E. Goodpaster in his essay "Business Ethics" in *The Blackwell Encyclopaedic Dictionary of Business Ethics* (1997), which we expect to be authentic in so far as beginners of a subject is often introduced through Encyclopaedias: "Business persons confront ethical issues, whatever their position in the corporate structure and whatever the size and complexity of the organisation. Sometimes responsible judgement and action are clear, but not always. Consider the problems surrounding sexual harassment in the workplace.... What managers often need is an early way to think through the moral implications of policy decision—a perspective and a language for appraising the alternatives available from an ethical point of view. For many, this is the most operational definition of business ethics"[7]. It is important to note that though Goodpaster has been careful in mixing non-committal terms like "for many" and "operational", it is by far clear that he would not have much hesitation in accepting this "working" or "operational" definition either. However, an option was open to him to say that any definition be it workable, common, or popular, is not necessary for clarification of the meaning of "business ethics". Most important point is that the operational definition is not satisfactory at all. Hence, it cannot be useful for all or even many of us interested in business ethics. The instances, which Goodpaster cites as problems of business ethics, are of concern but what is of greater concern is that business ethics does not consist in dealing with such problems and their resolution based on one or more normative ethical theories. It is also interesting to read a passage from Velasquez's book. He writes: "Business ethics is a study of moral standards and how these apply to the systems and organisations through which modern societies produce and distribute goods and services, and to the people who work within these organisations. Business ethics, in other words, is a form of applied ethics. it includes not only the analysis of moral norms and moral values, but also attempts to apply the conclusions of this analysis to that assortment of institutions, technologies, transactions, activities and pursuits that we call *business*"[8]. Velasquez is clearer in accepting that what is 'applied ethics' in 'another word' is what application of 'moral standards' in business is. The analysis of moral norms and moral values and their application for resolution of practical issues in business holds key to business ethics. This is strange. Why should application of ethics be application of ethical norms and standards in business crises and then the same be termed 'business ethics'? Moreover, why should business ethics do such things only? Is it not important to analyse the nature, significance, tasks and justification of business ethics, which is an ethically relevant task in the context of business but in no sense application of ethical standards? In fact, what we are dealing now, that is the nature analysis and justification of business ethics transcends the normative discussion, and enters into a *metaethically relevant* discussion in business ethics. The analysis of the meaning of "business", "ethics" and "business ethics" is in no case exclusively normative discussion. Interesting is to note that the ethically relevant discussion of the justification of possibility of business ethics sans normativity is metaethical in nature. Hence, to think that business ethics is application of norms in business is over simplistic. It is most interesting to see that both Goodpaster and Velasquez know very well that ethics is not merely norm related study, it is something more, but somehow they are under an illusion that business ethics consists of some such issues, which makes case for ethically relevant inquiry only when norms are applied by us. It may be that people like Goodpaster, Velasquez and many others were more worried about justifying business ethical discussions within the broad field of practical ethical discussion. Some writers are also worried to justify that business ethics is under professional ethics. They forget that both practical and professional ethics are within the broad field of ethics, which is a fact more important to be clarified because first we are concerned about the relevance of ethical interventions in business, which is a different field altogether. The relevance of ethical interventions with regard to individual and corporate decisions and actions is very wide; it calls for many things like showing the metaethical, normative, practical, professional and the virtue ethical involvements, all within ethics. We have seen in the first chapter that our effort to show such wide-ranging involvement of tasks (and thus branches) of ethics in fields other than ethics like economics (and now business) is to bring out clearly what economic and business ethics are. Both Goodpaster and Velasquez have been careful enough to show that ethical involvement in business is clearly stated when we come to normative ethics and value-based ethics, which is worth commending and with which we shall deal later on, but what is missing here is what we are already involved with, the metaethical involvement in the field of business. This is needed to clarify at the outset that business ethics need not be defined in popular ways or in workable ways to unravels its nature because that leaves out important aspects of business ethics. Despite our basic disagreements about the normative and practical ethical involvement in business, we can still turn to Goodpaster and Velasquez to agree that the field of business and the studies related to business have numerous issues, which invites ethical involvement. Hence, it is important and interesting to show the ways in which business provides ample scope for ethics, particularly normative way to justify that business ethics is within ethics, and that it is a sensible study. However, getting involved into the clarification of ethical involvement in business and business involvement in ethics is to enter into the realm of *justification* of business ethics. This is to say that nature analysis almost inescapably drags us to the justification because knowing what business ethics is, amounts to the clarification of 'tasks' of ethics, and the tasks of ethics are better known when business opens to ethical study and when ethics opens to business studies, which are finally two best ways to "justify" why ethically relevant study of business or why business ethics makes sense. Hence, it is time now to leave the question of definitions in nature analysis and indulge into statement of *tasks* of business ethics, which I said, is inescapably related to *justification* of business ethics.

Nevertheless, we cannot overlook the value of ethical scepticism in this regard because there are arguments against any involvement of ethics in business or business in ethics because the said enterprises are pointless, they make no sense in so far as unrelated things cannot be related. One field called business has nothing to do with ethics and other field called ethics has nothing to do with business, because they are unrelated categories; hence, they are unrelated. Nature clarification of business ethics is possible when we answer this important but stiff question because if we can show that scepticism is pointless, we immediately come to know that nature of business ethics is such that in it two different relatable things are logically related. Let us come to business ethical scepticism. Some writers of business ethics and management ethics like L. T. Hosmer in *Ethics of Management* (1991) have argued that an important feature of ethics of business and management is that it assumes ethical interception in some such financial and economic matters as if not doing it will be less glorious or less humane. However, the truth is that in a free market even if the players are profit oriented and competitive, without any ethical interception they would be perfectly sociable through their decisions and acts, they would be thus most beneficial to the people and the society. It should be, therefore, one-point programme on the part of the competitive producers and managers of corporate that they ensure what is most desired and valued by the customers or consumers of a society and guarantee that in doing so, the company gains and not lose. In this atmosphere of all win-win position, there is hardly any scope for any party in business to unnecessarily impose their values and ethical norms so that some glory is added to what they do. When business activities are *per se* of great value, socially speaking, no ethics is needed because added query of business is only an assumed relevance, not truly so. In reply to such ethical scepticism in business it may be said that there are no universal perfectly competitive markets wherein players maximise profits in the atmosphere of close competition without any laxity in quality because in reality, without being worried about any competition, business houses may go clear earning profits at will with complete or partial laxity in quality of goods and services. This is best understood by us in the so-called 'third world' where third grade things are consumed at the will of big houses at good price amounting to good profit to the houses who appear to compete and profit but without a sense of quality. The important point is that Hosmer completely overlooks this truth and with it the greater truth that ethically speaking if profit is so dear without an uncivilised competition, quality of goods and services must not be irrelevant. If Hosmer argues that 'quality' always makes a sense to these houses that are nevertheless, bereft of concerns for ethical value in business, then he is invited to come to India and consume soft drinks of different companies for some time till he knows what quality *vis-à-vis* profit means here. Next, he is completely unaware of the idea that the justification of profiteering in the climate of perfect competition, in an open market with a view to quality are so dear value to businessmen and managers because some values are *objective*, recognised as ethically desirable so far socialization of business and management is so important. The grounds for justifying the business values do not come from the *businessmen* only rather from ethically charged people or interested people. Equally true is that any disregard for value of say profit or perfect competition or open market economy or quality control is not bound to the businessmen or economists; they are truly open for social people who are concerned about value questions, which is however, a matter of constant debate before some decision is reached. In any case, deriving any conclusion for or against profits and competition etc. are matters to be referred to the ethical experience and knowledge of concerned people, the knowledge of the "desirable, just, right and good". Hence, in-house values in business are not in-house values drawn from the field called business, they refer to objective values that crystallize in society when conscious people in and outside the house debates. This point is crucial to what I will later on say about the practical ethical involvement in business. From this, we can further remind Hosmer of his mistake that though there is no inherent unethicality in making profits by any sector in any business, but the point is its ethicality needs to be justified, and we do so, Hosmer needs to remember that businessmen do not do so at their subjective whim. It may well be that the ethic of profiteering transcends all arguments either based on reasons drawn from the field of business or economics; the same may be true of unethicality of profiteering. More often than not, the profiteering in business is good because these grounds remain open for further ethically oriented questions. It is due to this open-endedness of economic justifications of profiteering that the touted "social benefit" is challenged and replaced by "social injury"; in both cases nevertheless, we forget that the desirability of "profiteering" has transcended positivism of economics and business and entered the realm of the idea of "benefit", "altruism", "welfare" and even "egoism" or "egotism", which are all non-economic, ethical grounds. This is much like asking doctors why euthanasia should be or should not be done because falling in the trap of replying such questions, we transcend non-moral to the moral grounds. Hence, scepticism about ethical interference in business is a little too much because business often drags us to non-economic justifications of economic decisions and actions because such decisions and actions affect individuals and the society at large positively or negatively. Hence, to say that profiteering is bad because it gives rise to environmental, social and cultural pollution gives way to wider ethical grounds of badness of such pollution. Hosmer is also at pains to justify that need or desire satisfaction is one glorious goal of business irrespective of caste, class, and creed and so on. However, all needed or desired things in society do not reflect the social psyche or social value because there are stiff value-disagreements about the *desirability of desired things* in the market. It is due to this that in India we constantly debate whether many desired consumer goods are at all desirable. The point of "desirability" more often than not transcends positivistic grounds for desirability and embraces *ethical* grounds for desirability. For instance, the desired junk foods and its correlative increase in production, price, consumption and profit often transcend the positive grounds of desirability that such foods reflect social needs and values or that they are handy and easy for jet-age people; they even transcend the point of health benefits and are grounded on the conception of "pleasure satisfaction", which is in reality an ethical ground. However, we can argue about undesirability of the same on economic and medical grounds that takes us again to ethical grounds such as "well being" in the final run, which is truly ethical in nature. Hence, business matters are always open to ethical interference, not all of them, but most of them. It is important to notice that Hosmer has himself agreed to a great extent to value the *norms* in business that are beyond business, that is, they belong to ethics. When Hosmer says that it is the duty of the businessmen and the managers to have one-point programme to enhance profits for the company as well as to respect human needs, he is in fact, speaking about certain assumed *moral norms* for business, which may be put as simply as the norm of maximisation of benefits; the ethic of such norm is however, a matter of further scrutiny, which is again a fertile field in ethics. This is important because any assumed norm in business, which truly begs ethics, cannot be accepted without rational justification. This becomes clearer when we consider that in business there are a number of such so-called positivistically justified grounds, which are in reality, non-positivistic ethical grounds, often forgotten, mistaken and camouflaged. A good example of this is found in the writings of Michalos and Friedman[9]. They argue that business owes to the managers, who are the architects of decision making and moving the corporate in a desired direction, which is in the main benefit maximisation of the corporate, that is, maximisation of profits apart from other benefits, wherein the considerations of ethics does not make any sense. The pragmatics of business thus rules out any normative considerations. If this be the case, we can go on extending the argument to mean that managers can obtain suitable or deemed to be just means for the attainment of the said glorious business objective. More often than not, a logical manager, who happens to be a responsible agent in covenant, obtains every other business tricks to maximise profits even if in doing so the stakeholders or the shareholders are harmed or overlooked. For the sake of business, the agent is then good in doing some wrong or injustice. This "loyal agent's argument" thus clarifies how important it was to consider the ethical questions, which are nearly impossible to overlook. Even if we support the pragmatics of Michalos and Friedman, we need to remember that their clarion call for neglecting ethical consideration in business was a hoax because the call itself is guided by the assumed validity of an overreaching ethical norm, which is the "profit or benefit maximisation for good of the firm"; precisely, it is "economic egoism" on the part of the firm and the managers. In the garb of the above-mentioned pragmatic business ethics, therefore, we have an ethical thesis, which was overlooked by their whims. Further, if we look critically from the point of any sensible stakeholder, they may well contest the case fairly well, but surely, on ethical grounds that criticise the said economic egoism. Hence, the assumed validity of economic egoism at the cost of deliberate harm is contested on ethical grounds. This shows that business ethical scepticism is a wayward conception. The defect of such scepticism amounts to a number of ethically relevant queries in business, namely, the desirable duties of stockholders towards stakeholders in business, the stakeholder based benefits and the rightness of the case, the covenanted role of the managers in the firm *vis-à-vis* legality and morality in the society at large. It is this wider perception of what should be done by the managers despite the covenant, calls for ethical scrutiny of supererogatory duties of the managers and their status as whistle-blowers if that is deemed to be unavoidable. Michalos and Friedman forget the basic truth that an analysis of "duty" of the firm and the managers is not merely a drab positivistic analysis; it costs the legal and the moral features of duty as well. Here, it is important to notice the difference among the covenanted, the legal and the moral duties of the firm (including those of the managers). It is one thing to say that managers on contract have certain 'contractual duties', the performance of which is an imperative as per the rules, by-laws in the contract and the benefits one gets out of performance of duty, and it is another thing to say that it may not be necessarily a 'legal duty' on the part of the manager to respect the covenant and thus go to any extreme to cheat a person or another firm to maximize benefits because what is just according to the *company rules* may not be so according to the *company law or acts* as laid down in the law of the land. Further, what is good according to the rules of the company cannot be necessarily so according to the ethical perceptions of the community. In some cases law of the land that suits the greater benefit of a company or companies cannot be morally just and desirable in the public perception. This is often reflected in our part of the world almost regularly, particularly in the open markets like India. The tension among the covenant the legal and the moral further shows that it is nearly impossible to overlook the ethical inquiries regarding economic and business matters.

Dispelling some of the doubts of the business ethical sceptics we are now in a position to justify the case of business ethics or the case of ethical inquiries in business, which I have said before is possible in at least two ways, to find out the ways in which business opens avenues for ethical scrutiny and the ways in which ethics opens avenues for the scrutiny of business activities. Let us first consider carefully the ways in which business provides opportunities for ethics. It is said that there are at least three ways in which modern business provides ethical opportunities; the first being corporate operations and the other being individual functions in corporate and the status of the consumer/ shareholder on whom depends the success of the corporate. Knowing fairly well that a corporate is a body or organisation constituted by a number of individuals who serve in it, we can still speak about the desirability, good, right, just, duty and obligations of the corporate and only about the individuals who constitute it. It has been a fashionable debate among the ethicists for quite some time now that any ethical discussion about individuals who serve the corporate, leaves no point in transgressing the limit of ethical discussions, which is a limit owing to its dealing with sane, grown up individuals' intentional actions, and therefore, it is not sensible to speak of ethic of corporate as an organisation or rather the ethic of an impersonal entity. Hence, a moot issue in business ethics is whether corporate activities can be taken as good as human intentional activities separately to evaluate them as based on standards available to us. Related issues are whether corporations have any moral duties, obligations, rights and so on, and whether they can be qualified as morally right, just, good, wrong, unjust or evil. Those who believe that corporate as impersonal and anonymous entities having no moral duties and rights are thus neither good nor bad, only individual member in corporations are so. This confusion is popular among some ethicists and non-ethicists because many of them have argued that we cannot sensibly speak of ethicality of non-human beings and things because ethics is an exclusively human affair, it judges human activities. Hence, like corporate ethics there is no issue like animal rights ethics and so on. This becomes a fertile area of debate when we find that on the one hand the decisions and acts of a corporation are not necessarily the same as those of an individual or individuals and on the other hand the truth that without individuals' decisions and acts corporations become a lifeless entity. For some people the rules of the corporations and their common objectives lay the basis for calling them morally responsible and judging their decisions as moral, immoral and so on. For others, though the corporations run by following certain rules, they are themselves unlike humans and more like programmed machines performing unintended tasks, which are not amenable to moral evaluation. Ethicists point out defects in the *personification* or *anthromorphisation* of companies as wells as the *demoralisation* by virtue of anonymity of the companies. There are problems in treating the company exactly as persons because imposing penalties on a company, for say, pollution control rule violation because that is ethically unjust does not amount to say that individuals in the company are also unjust and the penalty should be distributed equitably. Further, to say that companies are inert and thus beyond the scope of ethicality would amount to say that at many instances when collectively members of a company participate in gross unethical act, for instance, punching intoxicants in an edible substance, the company as such being inert cannot be penalised though individuals are penalised. Professor R. M. Hare reminds us of a grave mistake we often commit in such matters, that is, to accept the truth of any one of the alternatives as absolute when all of them may be true in some sense. It is important to remember that though companies are like machines if we look them as body of offices, vehicles and so on, they also nevertheless, full of life, consisting of people thinking, intending, deciding, and acting and so on. Velasquez in his book takes an important insight from the John R. Searle's work *The Construction of Social Reality* (1995) where he argues that the enjoyment of a *moral status* need not necessarily and sufficiently go with individuals alone because the same status may be enjoyed by a social organisation, which Velasquez says, a company is by virtue of what Searle calls the primitive elements of *collective intentionality*, *assignment of function* and *constitutive rules*. In a company, individuals form a coherent group, a collective to intend to achieve certain ends through certain means. There are assignments of such functions in a company by individuals, which are not intrinsic to certain things, and there are basic rules through which the entire organisation is expected to run. Hence, apparently inert, mechanical and anonymous companies enjoy a moral status: "Because corporate acts originate in the choices and actions of human individuals, it is these individuals who must be seen as the primary bearers of moral duties and moral responsibility"[10]. If this be the case, corporations are deemed to be right, good, just, dutiful, immoral, and unethical and so on. A corporation thus has moral obligations and duties; they do have moral responsibilities. Further point may be whether or not we have definite grounds for the evaluation of corporation as morally good or bad, dutiful and obliged. However, this is a different issue because it may either take us to fixed set of norms of evaluation or flexible moral arguments that involve normative thinking. We cannot for the time being avoid the conclusion that corporations have their own ways to decide and act, have a unique culture, choice and beliefs that affect human society in many ways, which often call for moral evaluation. Nothing much changes when we consider the case of multinational corporations and their business strategies. A number of issues in multinational business open for ethical interception because these companies fix some such ends and means, that is, their decision makers and members participate in such means–end nexus which, by virtue of being intentional affects not only humans but non-human beings and things. Precisely, the choice of ends and means of the multinational corporations affect our environment or ecology to a great extent, which is further subjected to ethical evaluation either on the basis of norms available to us or on the basis of moral debates amounting to moral judgements. Many multinationals like ethical agents also face the ethicality question of supererogation, that is, whether they owe something to the nations in which they operate. It may not be spelt out in memorandum of understanding or legal document; nevertheless, people of a nation expect certain advantages when it comes to agreeing to allow the workers and the shareholders of a particular country where a multinational company works and the environmental safeguards are but natural for companies to consider seriously. It is also important to consider whether it is ethically just to get involved in other things like providing free education to some deserving people, and in India for instance, we may argue whether there is an ethic of caste based reservation guarantee on the part of the multinationals. Interesting is that the later option may not be of supererogatory status because in India in the near future, it may be an imperative duty on the part of the multinationals which is backed by legal imperatives. With this we come to conclude that the business houses or the companies, whether small or large, enjoy the status of a moral agent and are thus amenable to ethical scrutiny of their activities, which is nevertheless, undertaken by a group of people. In the words of Jack Mahoney: "The growth of powerful business corporation with their distinction between multi-ownership and professionalised management, and with their expanding influence over the lives of million of earth's inhabitants, whether as employees, suppliers, customers of commodities, has resulted in the spotlight of ethics being switched from considering the conduct of individuals in their business or working lives to being directed more at the corporations by which such individuals are employed and of which they are perceived to be the agents or representatives. Many of what have become the classic case studies of modern business ethics show graphically this switch of ethical attention from individuals to considering corporations themselves as the object of ethical evaluation and as morally accountable for their actions"[11]. It is exactly in this context that we are doubly reminded by the ethical tension between the "fiduciary responsibility" championed by Milton Friedman and the "socialist responsibility" of the multinationals as well as national business houses, the latter sometimes crossing the limits to be more like "supererogatory duties". For Friedman, supererogation is on the part of the company's hidden socialist agenda, which is averse to free market economy, the rise of the business houses, the ideal of the profit and the aspirations of businessmen in free societies. The capitalist ethic of fiduciary responsibility thus calls supererogatory duties *unethical* because *per se*, business houses are not expected to invest in social causes. Though public investment does not increase business, they may not be against business, because lack of it is nothing but cheating the stakeholders in business, which is however, completely neglected by Friedman. Friedman's argument thus points towards gross unethicality on the part of the managers of companies who act more like amateur social activists by extending company services for the public; their role is to maximize benefits of the stockholders though they have little or no interest in public welfare. Welfare at the cost of the company or at the cost of the stockholders is thus unethical because moral saints who act like that by virtue of stockholder's money, is unethical cheating. It is important to note that Peter Drucker in his work *Management* (1979) argues almost similarly to prove that managers of a company are "competent" to partake in works related to the interests of the company and incompetent in taking up social projects because they are not the best trained people to do these things notwithstanding the tension of maximisation of basic benefits to the shareholders. However, such arguments have been squarely attacked mainly on the basis of unrealistic sketch of both business in free markets and desirable role of managers in such business houses. There are few takers today to agree that modern business means profit maximisation at any cost, because it completely neglects the land, environment and welfare of the people where business activities are in full swing. Truly there are equally less people who believe that managers are competent in large scale social welfare, but one can easily see the unethicality involved in the grosser cheating and neglect of the masses of the country in which houses do business where at least some benefits, welfare, environmental protection, education, infrastructural developments are expected because in free markets benefits are derived from where the houses play, wherein the workers strive and people participate. Mahoney also argues that power tracking by the business houses are noticed as well because among other things, the growing pressure of profits have given the ills of bribery and corruption at the official and political levels in a society where the companies are active. The allied issues of discrimination in jobs and wages, substandard working and living conditions and in case of monopolistic business, vices of mass exploitation in pricing and safety of consumers are widespread. One cannot suffer from a Friedmanesque syndrome to say that everything is fair in profit-making business. Business opens a wide vista, therefore, for interesting ethical debates, which is a good way to justify why business ethics or ethical inquiries in business holds good.

It is the growing concern for the ethical concerns in business that some writers have vehemently opposed Friedman's conception of business free from ethical pressures and R. T. De George's idea that to speak about an ethically glorious social responsibility of business houses is "ambiguous". A.B. Carroll, for instance, in his papers "The Pyramid of corporate social responsibility towards the moral management of organisational Stockholders" (1991) argues that the modern business as we understand, considers the *economic*, *legal*, *ethical* and *philanthropic*. Friedman and many others did recognise the truth that economic, and legal responsibilities are unavoidable, they were far too ambiguous about the social responsibility and almost pooh-poohed the philanthropic responsibility, when the later has strong ethical basis for its desirability in modern business. The 'social' concerns in business, almost each of them pose ethical questions for us, that is, economic responsibility itself opens for us ethical concerns or ethical evaluation particularly when we are poised to evaluate it in the context of stockholders' and shareholders' good *vis-à-vis* stakeholders and larger social good. To keep in mind cr not to keep in mind, the society's 'economic expectations' of providing quality goods and services at competitive rate without much environmental hazards may be ethically more desirable, says many. If one has strong arguments against it, is welcome but that does not in anyway jeopardise the possibility of business ethical discussion like this one. Similar is the case when the ethic of 'legal responsibilities' is on cards because we can always have fertile debate about the ethical viability of following legal imperatives imposed by governments on business players so that there are no cheating, malice and malevolence against the workers, people and environment. It is always extremely challenging to face the music with our staunch capitalist businessmen who disregards on *ethical grounds* the good of such legal bindings imposed on those who can never flourish and thus complain of red-tapism, step motherly treatment and even forcible benevolence and taxation, all of them ethically evil. It is queer but possible to discuss the ethicality of the 'ethical responsibilities' in business because we can always argue about the touted ethical-value-expectations in society that business houses (and people therein) should be honest, benevolent, sympathetic, fair, dutiful, rightful and so on because *ethical relativism* enables us to argue whether these touted ethical values are at all desirable on ethical grounds available to us. Why 'honesty' is ethically good in business if that means "honesty" as perceived in a society that counts houses to be so good to distribute some earnings to the poor people where they do business? Can one be honest to the poor at the cost of being dishonest to the in-house members? Ethical relativism really does not allow us to be universalists in this regard because within our societies, the socialist might argue that, moral disagreements about value-perceptions are natural phenomena. If that be the case then why do we need not accept the possibility of relativism in the conceptions of honesty and other touted human virtues? Such controversies in any case make way to business ethical considerations.

When we turn more specifically to the ethic of ethical responsibility of a company we have for us interesting questions. First is the ethical basis for continuing with injurious substances and production processes in a public or private sector either by deceit or by agreement. Both cases are in plenty. Deceit is most of the time to be blamed for fatal accidents in which poor workers die, but cases of contractual risk-taking in business is not difficult to find either. Not too long back did we have in India private coal mining, knowing well what are the hazards in risky mining without preventive measures, and the result being too many deaths of miners. This is not uncommon deceit even in public sector mining when peer pressures for production compel miners for risky mining, resulting into loss of life. In contractual risky production/extraction for business houses, end results are not different. The problem is of moral responsibility because we ask who needs to take the blame for accidents and loss of life for mere profits. Who has to take the moral responsibility, the worker, who took risk either in ignorance or wilfully? Should the managers and the peers be not blamed and thus be morally responsible for such things? Do wages guarantee the moral ground for ordering for risk-taking? Are payments everything for workers? Should profits be not linked to care for wage earners' safety and security? These are issues for ethical scrutiny of moral responsibility in business. More interesting questions regarding this matter come up when we consider the cases of *ignorance and inability* on the part of the business houses to prevent any fatal or undesirable end. Here, ignorance, unlike the above case is not deliberate but genuine, not deceitful so to say. Similarly inability here is not negligence but genuine. More important is that the participants in risk-taking activities know that certain dangers are lurking around but either on unforeseen or unforeseeable grounds they cannot be completely blocked or prevented. In such cases, we are open to argue whether it is ethical to charge a manager or a stockholder on grounds of moral irresponsibility to have allowed risk-taking? One opinion is that genuinely ignorant and unable person or group of persons cannot be held morally responsible because in such cases they lack moral freedom and genuine moral intention to do any harm or deceit; hence, they are free from moral blame. Another argument is that peers and workers are all sane people and for their benefits, they cannot shake off moral responsibility in their intentional participation in risk-taking business; hence, mere ignorance and inability cannot be good excuses against moral blame. Those holding the first view like, Aristotle in *Nicomachean Ethics* and R. M. Hare in *Freedom and Reason* (1965) are often backed by those who argue that those involved in business, which involves some uncertainty as well, cannot be held morally responsible because the participants in business may be either sure about what he is doing but uncertain about consequences or may be free to avoid participation but it is difficult or unavoidable to do so or the person might minimise injury in participation, but it is not completely possible to avoid participation. Such cases may not fully but at least partially help risk-takers in business to skip moral blame. Our ethical concern of ethical responsibility helps us in going deeper into these issues. This is one way how we find business opens vistas for ethical inquiry[12]. It is important to note that peer pressures and individuals' profit hankering cannot prevent us to thoroughly analyse dangers in business activities. Alan Donagan in *The Theory of Morality* (1977) argues much like this. Similarly, Peter Singer in *Practical Ethics* (1979) argues that idea of a passive spectator to a wrong decision in business decision-making may not be obliged to warn a danger, is itself ethically wrong. Still, there are arguments and counter-arguments in this matter, which I have said is most interesting for us because they show us that business opens many ways for ethical interference. Now what interests us most is that the foregoing discussions have revealed that when we speak of moral responsibility, duty and obligation and the ethicality of such discussion in the context of business, we are reminded of three important aspects: the moral responsibilities of the stockholders (the peer group as I have said) and that of the managers and officers on the one hand, and the responsibilities of the workers, who are in fact, stakeholders within a company, as well as the responsibilities of the corporate or the company on the whole. We may thus say that the ethic of moral obligation in business is a wide discussion involving the peers, the corporate and the subordinate members of the corporate. We will consider the case of moral responsibility or ethical accountability in terms of the peer group a little farther before we move to the corporate and the subordinate accountability.

The field of business gives us many ethical dilemmas in the context of peer group discussion and actions, the group not merely consisting of the capitalist, who is the stockholder-in-chief rather, the shareholders, the managers and the individuals representing the policy making and implementing authorities in their official status. These people are those who decide how their employees or subordinate workforce should act. It has become important for the modern business houses (whether public or private), to fix responsibilities or accountability and thus become subject to moral praise and blame. In this atmosphere the companies construct their own *moral codes*, which they believe are the set of desirable modes of behaviour for in-house officials. Whether such moral codes are moral, is an interesting question. What the moral codes reveal is known through careful deconstruction and normative analysis. It becomes important to find out whether the set of codes or rules are at all moral by any normative ethical standard or are they sets of non-ethical codes pretending to be moral on the grounds of common-sense morality or arbitrarily fixed moral dogmas and opinions of some in-house bosses. In any case, if they are arbitrary opinions, the ethic of such moral accountability becomes an important matter for discussion. Mahoney remarks: "Of course, such documents on occasions be no more that window dressing or examples of bandwagon mentality; and if that is the only step which a company takes to identify the values for which it stands and the types of actions for which it claims it will not stand, then the credibility of its code is subject to question. For the production of a code of conduct is only a stage in a corporate ethics process which should also involve its regular monitoring and revision as well as other corporate structures"[13]. We need not forget that in modern business in public and private sector companies, "shareholders" play an important role because they are in one way stockholders in terms of investment, and must enjoy the legitimate access to all benefits due to them by virtue of business. The point is whether they should not be held accountable morally for decisions and actions taken in the company because they cannot be at the same time enjoyers of fruits but not carers of the trees to the least. *Shareholder activism* as we know today thus opens for us the inquiry of the ethical basis of for such activism, that is, the ethical inquiries regarding the control of the shareholders in management, policy making, finance, economic betterment, and worker's benefits and so on. The interest in corporate governance may not be liked by all; many others are critique of such activism on ethical grounds. The lines are drawn mainly regarding the unethicality of *lay-involvement* for bridging the gap between the owners and the shareholders; whereas others find that moral watchdog policy in business is always good for the larger interest of the company. In fact, much moral tension is also due to extension of the notion of *management* because it now tends to include shareholders apart from the experts in-house. It is believed that if the greater financial good of the firm is crucial in business, we need to assure that management must have a lot of playing ground of its own beyond the erstwhile capitalist red-eyes dictation in business. Nevertheless, the counter ethical correction is that in the name of bridging the gap, which is however, welcome idea in running a big company, we cannot allow the owners to go scot-free when it comes to fixing moral responsibilities, duties and praise and blame. If widening and heightening of management responsibilities is desirable, we cannot forget the truth that those who own the business have even great accountability in their business, they cannot play a blame game when evils come on them and lick the cream when victuals are at hand.

Let us now come to the question of ethical responsibility of the corporation as such, the collective institution, the firm so to say, which covers the peers, the managers and the shareholders in the main, but in this case we do not speak about individuals of the collective body separately though for an act of deceit or foolishness the collective may be thrashed or else may be morally praised. The main argument in favour of corporate responsibility is that corporation are representatives of collective thinking, decision-making and actions; hence, the collective body must be held responsible for ethical or unethical acts in business. This is to say that though the board of policy makers and decision makers are few, the responsibility of implementing the policies may be in the hands of few people, it is the corporation which is taken *as a whole* though many of its members were least involved in policy framing and decision making because on principle the institution as a whole is an embodiment of cooperating people, people are under similar contracted rules, working condition, work ethos and a unique corporate *form of life*. It is due to this that though a number of people had nothing to do with the risky practices in the Bhopal unit of the Union Carbide, it is the company in the final run which was held responsible for the unethical business practices as embodied in their risk-taking practices and appropriately charged for criminal acts as well for gas-leak and deaths. Hence, moral responsibility and the ethical questions relating to such responsibility takes on the issues like fixing accountability on companies, which however, percolates to its policy making boards and members therein. The problem is that though a company as a whole is accountable, only a decision-making board is immediately responsible for an unethical decision and action, in which case should each member of the board be morally blamed? W. L. La Croix (1976), and T. M. Garrett and others (1986) argue that each member who has intentionally decided to do something should be brought to be morally booked. Further, in such acts, the members make other means towards achieving what they have decided to do. Naturally moral agents were made tools for a successful misdeed, which peers must be doing knowingly may be for reasons of compulsion. These people cannot be left out of moral purview but the person or group of people who were mainly responsible in using others as evil ends, should be morally accused or morally accountable. Similarly, these people are in the main held morally responsible because by virtue of their decisions and actions, other stockholders of the company may be equally harmed. Writers like Christopher D. Stone (1975) and Peter N. French (1984) have argued that in case of a corporate moral malady, whosoever may be the culprit, a person or a group, the responsibility should ultimate go to the company because any group or individual in a company represents the company and in that sense it does not enjoy an independent status. Hence, only the corporate must be held morally responsible. The counter-arguments follow immediately, which is not so important for us to elaborate at this place. We are here to justify why business activities are amenable to a number of ethically relevant discussions under business ethics. In the broader context of moral responsibility, it also becomes an important point to argue whether an individual or group should be held morally responsible if what they did were most unintended, or done in ignorance or even were used as tools by virtue of a cunning peer. In fact, in corporation, the subordinates or the employees are often voiceless when it comes to obeying others because the hierarchy and associated peer pressures often compel subordinates to do what they would have otherwise avoided doing. It may well be that the subordinates either know it fully well what are the objectives of the people in hierarchy or they are completely ignorant of it, but the working conditions, rules and ethos are such that they have no option but to follow the orders. Business practices like these further open gates for ethical inquiry, particularly when the inquiry is about the ethical validity of moral responsibility of subordinates to follow orders unconditionally. One view is that "following orders" and "compulsions" are not good moral excuses at all when someone knowingly participates in an unethical venture in business. It may be that by virtue of malpractices one gains nothing, but his or her wish to be praised by the company or the executive by following orders cannot be seen as any less intentional to participate in the wrongful practices than going to the extent of being dismissed or discharged from duty as a protestor. Similarly is the case with compulsion, but others might argue that both the executive and the subordinates do not hold the same level of moral responsibility in such cases because the person who has been used by another person is the main motivator of an unethical act and holds greater moral responsibility to not only hatch an evil plan or to do a harm; hence, he or she should be accountable to use humans or to pressurise or bribe to fulfil evil designs. Hence, the proof of being used as a criminal shows the greater criminal role of another party. These are thus interesting business ethical questions needing answers. With this we come to justify business ethics as a sensible discussion in the context of the role of the stockholders/ shareholders in business, both at the individual and the collective levels.

The conception of 'stakeholder based thinking' has grown phenomenally in modern business and with it has grown the possibility of ethical evaluation of such thinking that brightens the chances of business ethics as a meaningful enterprise. The line of thinking goes like this: Shareholders or broadly speaking, the stockholders have the right to get what is legitimately due to them by virtue of investment and owing capital in business, but the claim-right presupposes others who have the duty or who are obliged to pay what is due, which is mostly the function of managers and administrators, including a board that looks after business functioning and distribution of claim-rights to stockholders. The point is, their duty does not end with this because many stakeholders have equal claim-rights, not merely in terms of gaining or having paid back what is monetarily due to them or what are due to them as cash and kinds, rather, in terms of services, satisfaction, quality, honesty, non-malice, non-harm and in some cases monetary and other physical benefits. Most of the time these people and the ecological community at large expect from the company managers to give them what is due to them as consumers, citizens, natural entities and employees. It is in case of the "employees" that managers are obliged to pay back in terms of cash and kinds, but unlike the stockholders, not in terms of what they have invested rather in terms of what they have done or how they have served physically and/or mentally and to what extent. To be precise, we can say that in business atmosphere the stakeholders are the public, the employees and the ecological community at large who owe for what they serve. Modern business thus came to realise a simple truth that if we speak of stock and related claims of the holders of the stock, it is sensible only when we speak of stake and related claims of the holders of such stake because business cannot run in an atmosphere of "no demand" or "no claimers" of products and services. Hence, the claimers of products and services who are in the main, the consumers or the public should be adequately paid back what is due to them keeping in view what are their aspirations and demands and what they pay for that. The addition of employees as stakeholders is due to the fact that they are immediately related to what things are produced by serving physically and mentally, and labour cannot go without paying back adequately what are due to them (cash and kinds but not the capital), mostly as parts of salary, perks and welfare measures. In some cases, adequate claim for some *ex-gratia* payment owing to good profit of the company, bonus payments as a recognition of extra work done becomes rightful stakes of the employee. The third factor, that is, the stake of the ecological community ensues from the eco-consciousness among responsible people, businessmen inclusive, to realise that the business activities go on in the vast ecological community, which is more often than not disturbed by such activities, particularly when we extract minerals, manufacture goods and distribute them. Many services need to disturb the ecological balance. Most of the time the serenity and balance in nature is disturbed by pollutants of manufacturing units and to build and run service providing sectors. The companies cannot disregard or overlook the stake of the ecological community to be undisturbed or not to be vastly disturbed just for meeting demands and making profits because it is people who need things and people who meet demands, they cannot be party to disturb the 'household', which is their happy abode. Hence, non-human beings and things can be stakeholders as well. In a sense the stake of ecological community covers the stake of the public at large because apart from business related demands and aspirations, their larger interest to live in an unharmed atmosphere is taken care of through such claims. Another important aspect in stakeholding is that neither the stakeholders should desire undesirable things to be produced and served at any price, nor should undesirably, desired things be produced by stockholders. This also percolates to undesirable *use of employees* for producing and serving both desirable and undesirable goods and the undesirable *use of natural* beings and things for producing and serving both desirable and undesirable things. This also covers the undesirability of *maximizing desired desires* on the part of the consumers and *coping with desired desires* at any cost by business houses. Often affluence is an evil if desired desires go unchecked because businessmen might exploit it for undue benefits which often boils down to the exploitation of the employees, public and the ecological community. But that does not mean that we need to be poor to be good because among paupers business does not run too far. The elements of what is desirable, good, just, rightful on ethical terms in business activities involving the public, employees and natural beings and things thus makes an interesting inquiry. We call it 'stakeholder-thinking' in business that opens for ethical inquiry. Ambler and Wilson think that probably such conception in business ethical writings emerged in 1960s by virtue of the wide use of "stockholding" in business studies. It was found that the conception of stake-holding is much wider as it enables us to see the vast responsibility of the business community including the managers towards employees, their dependants, and the public of all ages, castes and the environment in which we thrive.

However, ethical questions in stakeholder based thinking are not as simple as taking care of people, beings and things. Questions like "quality products and services" might take us deeper than we imagine in this matter. On what does the said "quality" depend? There must be certain criteria fixed by the company not by whims but in the light of the desirable standards of products and services fixed by the public bodies and the government agencies as backed up by arduous and careful researches on products etc. The first point for ethically relevant query is if researches to judge the "quality" of some products are themselves open to ethical scrutiny, especially the drugs and cosmetics, then can the quality be assured by virtue of a greater evil? Should the quality of a lipstick be determined by the tests on monkeys? (See volume 3). Moreover, most of the consumer items are tested for "quality" to find out the items' subsequent effects on human health, that is, how far are they safe for human use. Further, companies have to put on labels of items, for basic ingredients and the risk perceptions if any for human health, particularly those for the children. Such items may not be edible or drinkable or smoked, they are things like toys made of plastic or films made for watching or songs recorded for entertainment or flavours made for pleasant smell and so on. The quality of plastic used, hues added and the likely effects on chewing them must be taken care of while toys are marketed. Films should bear a U or A or U/A certificate for right choice and songs recorded on disks should contain details for making a proper choice. Ethical questions do not emerge at the level of why should risk factors be spelt out? Rather, at the level of to what extent are the products liable to spell out these risk factors and why? Is it not a moral responsibility on the part of the consumers to use things properly or guide those who are not able to do so when scanty or no information about contents and risks have been provided? Certainly plastic toys are not meant for constant chewing and for sure not all high quality plastic dolls are affordable by the public. Surely, when colours used in sweetmeats are clearly visible, was it not an ethical responsibility on the part of the consumers to be careful in their use because producers cannot always afford to market super-class products at cheap rates? This must be raising eyebrows of the consumers of the northern part, but in the southern part of the globe, a number of places just do not imagine getting consumable items at high prices which are excellent quality-wise, and people have to choose for desire satisfaction among inferior to very inferior things at low prices. Moreover, what can companies do when committed smokers, despite all warnings and high prices still smoke? Is it not ethically unjust on their part to be careful in consumption? The consumers' irresponsibility syndrome or idiot attitude raises many ethical questions, which are nevertheless, tough on the producers as well because they too are pressed for a balance between public good and quality at affordable price.

Ethical questions in consumer satisfaction are profuse when we consider the cases of *marketing* of products and *promoting* them through *advertisements*. There is nothing ethically evil in product marketing and advertising because products cannot lie idle, they have to be sold for they are normally in demand, and in competitive (not monopolistic) markets they have to find a place among buyers by elbowing out others. It is not always that cheaper goods sell better by virtue of aggressive marketing in terms of quantity and advertisement. What if, cheaper or inferior goods elbow out better ones by virtue of greater supply and advertisement? Nothing must be too bad ethically on the part of the seller because idiosyncratic buying is always bad. Yet, what if companies persuade the buyers through many cunning tactics of advertisement and marketing? What if companies create an atmosphere for the buyer to believe that a product is in heavy demand, the stocks are running out though in reality they are lying in plenty and not of good quality? What if, companies create an atmosphere of persuasion in which irrelevant information are highlighted for selling a product? What if in marketing a product a company chooses to be sarcastic, comical and derogatory to competitive products? What if, companies play on human emotions, feelings, sentiments, faiths, creeds and so on to sell products? The 'what if' poses for us 'what should be the case', that is, what is ethically just and right? The guilt and shame of nudity and indirect insult to women for selling products notwithstanding, ethical questions asks whether stakeholders universally be seduced by companies through barrage of persuasive tactics that goes against the dignity of humans as humans. Borrowing from Kant: When we live a world where humans are merely *means* to our ends, dangerous implication of such seduction are well seen all over the world—young men and women are seduced for their lovable dream-life, old are seduced for their proactive good-life and the sick are seduced to go over-the-counter to buy medicines without taking any notice to side-effects, which may be fatal. Strangely every other uneducated to educated Indians go on popping pain-killers and ayurvedic drugs having lead and mercury residues that may damage their kidneys, yet boastfully brands are sold in the market. However, companies too have no moral obligations if idiotic consumer behaviour does not pay heed to their risk-warnings and information. The pro and con arguments which are ethically focused in these matters make business ethics an interesting study that it is.

As we now turn to the employees, we find a number of searching ethical questions when their 'stake' is in question. But what are the stakes of the employees, the manual and the intellectual workers, and mangers? One view is that ethically speaking no businessman or organisation is in the market to do a lot of welfare for their employees at the cost of getting poorer in a stiff competitive free market. Hence, it is better in such market to be wise in perceiving the workforce as "commodity", which is hired at some cost, not too high of course but to be sure, *used* to the optimum for greater production/distribution and profits and when needed, they may be let off and replaced by sophisticated machines or men. The perception of employees as commodity for optimum use and benefits of the company asks for ethical scrutiny. The questions of human rights, obligations, duties in the capacity of employees come to the fore. We do not and should not avoid many ethical questions like these because civil states run by law and moral concerns always keeps the business houses on toes so that the erstwhile serfdom and exploitation of wage earners do not come back. Yet, there are counter ethical questions regarding the role employees should play in corporate, particularly when the same is the parent institution on whose good the good of the dependants depend. To what extent should the employees be loyal, dutiful and so on? If they are treated as mere commodities, is it not ethical on their part to treat companies as happy hunting grounds? If that be true, in many welfarist societies under the veil of a just fight for a worker's rights, politicians, union leaders and middlemen join the chorus to exploit companies by educating the workers to play hide and seek with their supervisors and play the politics for petty gains. What should be the right ways to protest against employees' exploitation, and to what extent should companies be politically coloured? These are some trifling questions. To what extent should the workers contribute to the nation's growth even in private sectors with claim-rights in their heads, becomes important ethical questions under stakeholder based corporate thinking. It is exactly in this context that in business ethics today we enthusiastically speak about work-culture, work-ethic, quality-of-the-work-life, and deference to corporate culture. We raise these issues in business because on the one hand we believe that whether we are in a socialist or a capitalist society, the companies owe much to the employees and for that reason, proper wages, work conditions, time limits and welfarist measures are ethically just steps to be taken. On the other hand, we believe that employees in contract come to do specific jobs having full knowledge of what they have agreed in the contract and thus liable legally and ethically to serve though certain limits are also well known to them by virtue of the contract. They should know how important it is to serve properly in cooperation but not completely hands down when they are exploited. In fact, both parties should know that in society people and common men have great expectations from those who run a company, earn profits, and from those who eke out a living in contractual work. Naturally social good or social welfare remains supreme in our mind whether we are stock or stakeholders. It is often argued that most of the stakeholders are bereft of such ethically good objective in mind particularly if they do not belong to a country. In many cases rampant profiteering causes a lot of injustice to the employees, and the practices of bribery and malevolence runs deeper in society causing economic colonialism and capitalist exploitation to the extreme. The proponents of open market and free trade thus argue that foreign companies and workers are anti-nationals in so far as a nation's good are concerned. The argument extends to the joint stock holdings because being a party to exploitation and deceit a nation's citizen joins the anti-national forces to exploit masses through business, doing no social good. The same may be true if purely *desi* company becomes a party to same mischief. In any case the exploiters are anti-socials no doubt. Many proponents of open market and free trade do not buy these unethicality arguments because they argue that despite the capitalists having profit motive, they contribute tremendously to the growth of a nation's economy in terms of production, jobs to millions, welfare of workers, and rise in foreign reserves and so on. Hence, nothing is anti-social in free markets; the stakeholders are very well placed compared to what they were at the time of Uncle Tom.

Stakeholder based thinking in business in the recent times has taken us to debate about the ethical basis of "whistle-blowing", which is related to the concept of *supererogatory duties* (if any) of the employees. It is like supererogation on the part of the employers as we saw in case of fiduciary duties and philanthropic duties. Many ethicists hold that whistle-blowing by an employee to bring to notice and protest against the hidden malpractices and malevolence of companies is something beyond what has been explained in covenant and for what the person is paid. However, ethical imbroglio about the matter is, why should such an act be so glorified, when from the company point of view, such acts may be ethically unjust because an employee should be first and foremost loyal to those who employs, plays and looks after their welfare. How can a person be so unjust to his or her masters without whom their own existence is at stake? Moreover, certain so-called in-house malpractices on the part of the employer are wrongly so-called because they are rather commonly accepted business *tactics* without which existence in a competitive market is impossible and without them the companies die with the employees. Why should then employees do something unwanted or supererogatory? It is interesting to note here that I personally know a case of *so-called* malpractice in a public sector company, which is however, commendable in the eyes of that company though most interestingly the sufferer of the malpractice is none but another public sector company. The case is interesting because generally whistle-blowing occurs mostly in private sector companies though the public sector is touted as noble for doing public good without heavy profit motive. Of late, we came across the case of Satya Prakash Dubey in public sector, and the one I am speaking about (which dates long back), is in a coal company that played hide and seek in quality control to supply low-quality coal at good prices to steel companies in the public sector. Should people like Dubey or the quality control personnel or others in private sectors blow whistle against their parent bodies? The question is a good example of how business has opened vistas for ethical queries. Many people argue that though much is said about stakeholder based ethical thinking in business; we are not sure about ranking the stakeholders in companies for their needed good and welfare. The question is really of finding out the *deserving* stakeholders, and among them, the identification of the most and the least deserving ones is important because when it comes to the ethic of extending benefits to the stakeholders, we cannot forget that they constitute a heterogeneous entity and as such, cannot claim for equal benefits. This takes us to a number of troubling issues in benefit distributions. The questions of legitimacy of extending greater benefits to skilled employees than the unskilled ones, or, to differentiate intellectual *vis-à-vis* physical labour for benefits, or to differentiate dedicated, honest labour *vis-à-vis* undedicated and dishonest employees raise stiff ethical problems. Hence, stakeholder based thinking may be ethically wise but many ethical issues that comes up are not simple to handle. Jack Mahoney conceives that stakeholder based thinking in business consists of "four concentric and expanding circles", the innermost representing problems regarding the company activities that affects employees positively and negatively. The next one representing problems regarding the company activities in relation to other companies and the last outermost circle represents problems about relation of the companies with the whole of the *environment* in which it functions, because we have seen that environment is a stakeholder.

Thus far we were involved in finding out vistas in business and in business studies that opens for ethical intervention to justify that business ethics makes a strong case. In the course of justification we found that interesting and fitting answers have been provided to the business ethical sceptics. What we have gathered are that business as a cooperative activity involving human society and using many beings and things demands basic thinking about the right, good, just, duty and responsibility on the part of those involved in such activities. It is also important to refrain from talking plain untruths to customers, and to be honest, and show respect to agreements and so on. Not only should businessmen be honest to others, they should be honest and responsible towards their own managers, workers and the environment. We have gathered that business as a pursuit to earn legitimate profit should thus be sensitive to ethical inquiries about the profit motive itself and the conception of the legitimacy and limits therein. The rationality of business bereft of profit or lack of the same *vis-à-vis* ethically conscious business practices even if profit is not put to stake are important questions. We have seen that business opens to ethics when questions of gains or benefits are considered at the ends of all parties involved in such practices. Should one party deceive, malign mistrust and bluff another party or parties when gains are most important for all parties? If there are gain-related deceptions, do others have ethical right to retort in equal measure? The moot point is that the problem: Does ethical behaviour on the part of businessmen and organisation pay? Is crucial in understanding whether business as a field of activity and study has something that asks for ethical query? I do not believe that empirical inquiries can be any closer to reply either in the positive or in the negative; what is for sure, business ethics remains open ended as we go on debating that when business opens for ethical interceptions, is it just to be in business but not think and act ethically or is it just to be in business and remain neutral to ethically thinking and acting. With this, we now move on to another set of justifications, which as we have seen before, tries to show ways in which performing different *tasks* of ethics makes sense in the context of business; for instance, whether metaethical inquiry makes sense in business related discussions, that is, whether metaethical-talk is involved in business-talk. Further inquiries are about the involvement of normative, practical and virtue-ethical-talks in business-talks.

It is fairly easy for us now to justify that metaethical-talk makes good sense in business-talk, that is, the metaethical task may not be isolated from a number of non-ethical discussions and labelled as "exclusively ethical". Some people do not get the point so easily that philosophical discussions of morality or what we call ethics, includes some such non-normative, that is, beyond normative discussions and for that matter "meta" discussions in ethics (metaethics), which has distinct role to play when it makes an entry into other discussions most sensibly because these "other discussions" by virtue of a "family resemblance" are "meta" discussions or discussion "beyond" their respective positivistic discussions as are the business discussions, biological discussions, technological discussions and so on. This is a unique feature of philosophy when we consider it as a discipline of language clarification or conceptual clarification or analysis of language. Philosophy by virtue of its unique task makes entry into many positivistic-talks or discussions like psychological, physical, biological discussions and so on. For instance, by virtue of "family resemblance" psychology apart from analysing positivistically *what happens in our mind* when we think, forget, remember and so on, strives to know what is the *meaning* of "mind", "thinking", "remembering" and so on, and in due course of explanations emerge many theses about these things, the clarity of which and the critiques of the same are aided by philosophical reflections about such matters, which gives us the field called, philosophical psychology and philosophy of mind. Almost in the same vein, when we discuss the language of ethical discussions, the analysis of meaning of ethical concepts and ethical language, it makes an easy entry into discussions related to business which has some relevance to the said linguistic discussion because here we are interested in not merely what controls business activities, discussions, profits and losses, it strives to know what amounts to "business", "profit", "loss" and so on, and in the course of explanations, emerge some theses, the clarity and critique of which are aided by philosophical reflections about the issues, which constitutes business ethics. As I have said at the beginning of the discussion, things are easier for us now to justify metaethical entry in business-talks, taking a cue from what has been said right now, readers are aware that we were involved in the process of language clarification for quite some time now in this chapter, which constitutes business ethics through metaethical interests in business related issues. It is important to remember that the said "meta" discussion amounts to meta-normative at the ethical plane and meta-positivistic at the plane of business studies. The urge of linguistic clarity at both planes enables an apparent mismatch possible to match. We were thus indulged in this chapter to know *what amounts to* or *what means* "business" and "ethics" and "business ethics", and what do we mean by "corporate morality"; "multinational corporate ethics", "business and corporate responsibilities", "moral praise and blame in business" and many other building blocks of the business discussions or what constitutes the "language of business". This is one way to justify metaethical entry into relevant talks in business and thereby enable us to see why "business ethics" makes a good case. Equally true is that in this chapter we were committed to justify why business ethics should be discussed with all philosophical élan, that is, why sceptics are not just to refute it as a sensible study beyond business studies. Thus far our effort to justify the ways in which business related discussions enable ethical reflections to creep in is to show *at the plane of business studies* there is something *non-positivistic* or meta or beyond business studies (positivistic), which demands *logical reflections* to *justify* why some business activities are *not* merely expected to be done but what *should be done*, that is, what ethical interests it *should show*. Interestingly business might need different sets of logic to justify why it should open for psychological discussions, sociological discussions as *meta-inquiries* which goes on not to justify that such business-talks are sensible or that business ethics holds good so far as "meta-inquiry" is a sufficient ground. What we are doing right now is queerly meta-study again because now we are at pains to show why an inquiry into the language of ethics percolates to fields other than ethics, that is, to business. We are also at pains now to justify the logic of ethical involvement in matters like business. Hence, we are involved in logical justification of "business ethics" in another way, and such "justification" is basic to metaethics. However, our involvement in language clarification is clear to understand by this time, to repeat them to show what exactly do we mean by metaethical interest in the language of business is wastage of time, it will be repetition of what has been said.

Many enthusiastic writers of the subject focus mainly on normative ethical involvement in business matters to justify business ethics because for many ethicists and non-ethicists business ethics is nothing but a body of *application of ethical norms* in business. It is time now to club two things together and discuss what normative ethical and practical ethical involvement in business means in the real sense and thus provide two strong bases for justifying business ethics. What is hidden in the present agenda is to show that the conception about business ethics as 'application of norms available in academic ethics' is unfounded, though normative and applicative ethical involvements in business are not unfounded. First let us start with the "unfounded" idea that business ethics is application of normative theories in business matters. Relatively speaking, perhaps the most unfounded idea is that common sense ethicality of the convictions of common men about principles or rules of thumb that help us in deciding and judging what is right and good in business behaviour like telling plain untruths to clients, dishonouring agreements and so on is what we should understood as application of ethical norms in business, which in turn justifies business ethics. However, things are not so simple in the realm of business because in business related thinking, deciding, choosing, judging and acting there are a number of *dilemmas* which moral agents face either owing to personal or inter-corporate decision-making and behaviour, or owing to corporate decision-making and behaviour. These inter and intra-corporate dilemmas that the agents face are not as simple as applying one's own moral ideas and ideals to the dilemmatic cases for resolution. In fact, subjective ethical conceptions about business matters do not amount to practical ethics, nor is normative ethics, establishment of subjectively determined norms. Ethics being a *critical reflection* on matters pertaining to the desirability of intentional decisions and actions depends more on universally acceptable logic than whims and predilections. In fact, it is also a critique of common sense moral thinking about business related evaluations. In due course of such critical reflection of what should be the case or what are universal bases of evaluation of intentional decisions and actions, we do have a number of normative theories or first principles or morality, most important being teleological and the deontological theories having many sub-types. What I call relatively less "unfounded" thesis is that normative ethics in business related dilemmas like bribery, dishonesty in payment and so on amounts to artificial application of these theories by expert ethicists in cases of value-crises. The conception that normative ethical involvement is nothing but involvement of teleological theories in business matters, amounts to justify that what is crucial in matters like business is, "interest-fulfilment or interest-satisfaction" of both the client and the corporate. Hence, any decision and action on their part will be judged for value (and not disvalue) if and only if the *consequences* of the decisions and actions have been put under rigorous empirical tests, and calculus to find out whether they meet the end, that is, *interest* (to be precise), as valuable or good *means*. The beneficial consequences are prescribed in business, which becomes standard means or cues to the teleos or the good—itself. Nevertheless, what is good—itself in business is a matter of dispute. It is argued that the "interest–fulfilment" of a businessman or a company is good—itself, which is based on the normative thesis called egoism, and by parity of reasoning we can call the thesis "egoistic business norm". It is not beyond dispute because the egoistic thesis faces many unhappy consequences when we come to *stakeholder* based thinking in business, which many say that it derives its logical strength from altruistic normative thinking or simply, ethical altruism that cares for good over evil of other individuals, companies and the social well being. Notwithstanding further disputes about whether interest fulfilment of one's own or of others begs the concept of pleasure, which gives us egotism and utilitarianism respectively, we urge that the teleos or purpose of interest fulfilment in any hue or colour is bereft of ethical value because it confuses ethical good-itself as non-ethical good because 'satisfaction of self and/or others' or 'pleasure of self and/or others' are all non-ethical ends in the true sense of the terms, they do not have ethical contents, and therefore, fail to be ethical theories. The contesting party now argues that in business, the universal norm of decision-making and acting should be ethical, which is performance of duty or undertaking obligations and responsibilities by virtue of their *intrinsic value*, that is, not for any higher idea of 'purpose' but for its own value or in the *respect* of the principle itself. The *deontologists* as we call them, argues that in business only that is ethically desirable which has intrinsic value *not value as means*. In this sense, respecting one's responsibility towards the company and the agents therein and respecting one's duty towards other companies and clients are good or desirable. The same may be extended further when we consider greater social good and even good of humanity at large, to say that in business we (individuals and companies) have welfaristic duties for their inherent value or for their own sake. In case of whistle-blowing they might argue that as moral agents, for greater social good and arguably for greater good of the company it is good to warn of malpractices within parent *organisation for the value of the act*. In any case as such the crucial point is to do something for the value of doing that thing. The debatable point is whether respect for the law of duty is itself not a teleos? Anyway we are not interested in going for elaboration of such disputes, but we are reminded of the truth that disputes of justifying one norm over another that is begged in value-crises in business is a testimony to critical ethical thinking, which is logical in nature, and if we did not forget our first lesson, it is a 'metaethical' venture. Of late, some ethicists held that involvement of normative ethics in business matters is not restricted to teleology and deontology; we have *contractarianism* and *libertarianism* as two more contrasting normative theories that find application in business. These theories hold that more than speaking about non-moral interest fulfilments and morally based performance of duties, we need to beg the norm of *protection of claim-rights* of the beneficiaries in our societies. But to the question, which rights needs protection? It is said that the right to *fair distribution of wealth and benefits* which social beings enjoy by virtue of living in a *contract*, needs to be protected, which is the *contractarian* normative thesis. It comes to justify that the stock and the stakeholder based moral thinking in business is grounded on the norm that justice as 'fairness in the distribution of wealth and benefits' (Cf. Aristotle in *Nicomachean Ethics* and John Rawls in *A Theory of Good*), should be regarded as supreme whereas *libertarianism* argues that rather than facing untoward consequences of doing great injustice to groups of people in society in the hoax of doing justice or rather equal and appropriate just distribution of wealth and benefits, it is just to protect the right to human *freedom and basic liberties*. When this norm is active in business, it amounts to justify why individuals in corporate as well as the corporate themselves enjoy basic rights and liberties to benefit from what they are able to do, and what they really do. Hence, for stock and stakeholders, it is just to derive full benefits out of their right to be free agents in business enterprises as a natural phenomenon to strive for profits. Again there are tensions within normative thinking because teleologists do not buy the argument that "enjoyment of rights" can be itself an end principle, they are truly, good as means to other purposes like pleasure/happiness/welfare and so on. Deontologists do not buy the arguments because "enjoyment of rights" as non-ethical good is out of ethical contention until 'respect for the responsibility of protecting rights' is in view. Whatever the case may be let us remember for our further discussion that normative ethics is a bundle of end principles, each contesting for monolithic status and we are (wrongly) contesting to apply one or more such principle or principles in the field of business to say that it is in this way that normative ethics finds place in business matters and thus business ethics holds good. We will take up this "unfounded" idea for a critique shortly but before that let us come to the spiritual/religious ethics in which the normative thinking is somewhat different. The moot issue is whether such normativism has anything positive to contribute to the field of business. We can pay attention to two such theories, the *nirvāṇic* and the *non-nirvāṇic*, the former is found in the spiritual/religious ethical systems in India that includes non-theistic, systems like Jainism, Buddhism and Sāṁkhya because despite differences in the recognition of divinity these systems accept that the supreme ethical ideal in human life should be the attainment of *nirvāṇa* (or alternately, *mokṣa, kaivalya* etc.), though in human life lived on earth, the social life so to say, there are other ethical ideals which are *means* to the realisation of this higher ideal. Though, the corporeal relativistic ethical ideals have their own value, they are only inferior to the supreme *nirvāṇic* ideal of life in so far as life is not wholly as we imagine to be, that ends here on earth with our corporeal non-existence. Our actions producing effects binds us to fruits and thus the urge to enjoy them and subsequently fall in the pitiable cycle of life and death, pains and pleasure are natural. Acting in a manner that a wise man having clear conception of ultimate end of life will do, that is, to come out of this vicious cycle or to attain *mokṣa*, constitutes ethicality. Norms at the social level prescribes us to do something as social beings so that our actions are judged to be right and good, which enables us to pursue the path to *nirvāṇa*, which is the overreaching norm, without which morality in life remains incomplete. Such a state is possible here, in this life, when wise liberated people strive for liberation of all humans by imparting unadulterated valid knowledge of the *summum bonum* of life and thus the knowledge of what we are as humans. The *non-nirvāṇic* spiritual/religious ethics preaches almost in the same vein that in the capacity of social beings we have different ethical goals in life, though attaining them remains of lesser value if we do not unfailingly pursue the *non-nirvāṇic* ideal to attain *Godhead* for instance, that is, to be one with the Supreme Divine Reality. In some cases, the non-theists speak of the realisation of *non-nirvāṇic* ideals like the Absolute Reality, Self-Realisation (Selfhood), Self-Fulfilment and so on. It is argued that until such highest ideals are achieved, morality remains elusive in our life in the real sense of the term. Whatever may be the difference among the different versions of the *nirvāṇic* and the *non-nirvāṇic* normative theses, when we come to business decisions and actions, they find good exposure. Many writers of business ethics and management ethics in India and abroad have discovered that business (let us leave management for the time being), is a field, which, when bereft of spiritual/religious ethical ideals or such normative conceptions, is bereft of value or that it becomes a *disvalue* (not valueless because that is soft term). Hence, enthusiastic business *gurus* speak of things like "spirinomics", "ethico-spiritual or ethico-religious business ideals" and so on. In fact, such extreme normative thinking goes to the extent of urging a life in business for both the individuals and the corporate that is permeated with the ideas expressed either in the *nirvāṇic* or in the *non-nirvāṇic* normative thinking. Hence, a number of so-called issues or tough problems of ethical values in business are superficial; they are reducible to the basic problem of ignorance of the valuable ideals of business life, whether we speak of ideals as means or ends. Whether we go for a *nirvāṇic* or a *non-nirvāṇic summum bonum* in life through our business activities (as means to the higher goal), we should never lose sight of what means in business leads us to the ultimate end of life. Such wisdom can only help us in resolving crises in business, this is the crux of the *application* of ethico-spiritual normative ideals in one aspect of life, and that is, life lived in the corporate—whether private or public. This is basic to an understanding of quality-of-life and quality-of-work-life. Without indulging into criticisms at length, it is often said that both the *nirvāṇic* and *non-nirvāṇic* ideals preach nothing but ethical *teleology* in other words, and they should be too happy to share glory and infamy that the said normative thesis has. In fact, it is a queer way to define "teleos" of life, most of which is blurred with a number of pointless presuppositions that are essentially *non-moral* and thus do not refer to basic critical ethical reasons about the standards of moral evaluation and moral ideals of life. Some people famously argue that there is nothing such as ethico-spiritual business ideals because ethicality and spirituality are different categories altogether which leaves no room for an amalgam that is unreasonable because from two metaphysical or spiritual premises why should we validly derive an ethical conclusion is not known to us. In fact, ethics has enough logical strength itself that enables it to derive ethical conclusions without vague non-ethical presuppositions. Why should all non-spiritual and non-religious people like ordinary men, tribes and non-believers are unethical is hard to understand. That non-believers are not good businessmen or constitute a good company, is equally arrogant illogic. Ethics, when it is spiritually soaked, harms its nature. Then do we say that the conception of "duty", which is ethical and not non-ethical in nature, what is propounded in the *Gitā* or by Bradley is true ethics? Let us not forget that in both we have clear cleavage of life lived as social beings (when we do things like business in our station of life or by virtue of our training and temperament or *svadharma*), and the life lived as humans (when we *should* pursue for the Realisation of Brahmahood or the Absolute), which is however, impossible without duties done in life (in business, for instance) having no inclination to profits, benefits, pleasures and so on. Hence, both *Gitā* and Bradley are *not* supporters of *monolithic deontology* that urges for a unique ethical ideal that is overreaching, they are *qualified–deontologists*, and truly, *teleologists* in the *qualified sense* as well. This is, however, a good example of how both teleology and deontology may be put together in a relativistic system. But what mars its ethical status is the constant urge for the ethico-spiritual supreme ideal of life which was perhaps not needed in the final run. It is very difficult nevertheless, to remain spiritually unadulterated deontologist in the true sense of the term; perhaps Kant had his own jittery reasons when he too spoke of God and Holy Will in his deontological scheme of things.

Before coming to the possibility of applying any of these normative theses in real life business problems, we are at hand the conception of "virtue ethics" or virtue based thinking in ethical matters, which, of late has been promoted to a normative status by some writers. Some thinkers are of the opinion that there is no use of speaking about norms in life and applying them in real life situation for value-based decision-making and acting unless we, the moral agents, first and foremost become virtuous or persons having based our thinking and doing on certain values. Virtues being values or properties of worth or properties epitomising the good, are expected to be *inculcated* and thus create virtuous characters referring to their nobility and ethicality by the business and the corporate. Without these things, it is useless harping on different noble teleos of life or on duty. First we need to be *dutiful*, to understand the value of duty and then perform our duty. How can a person bereft of the value of duty and dutifulness be a person who does duty because it is an overreaching norm of life? Similarly, how can we follow the utilitarian norm before inculcating altruistic virtues in us? Hence, for a person and a corporate in business, it is first and foremost as a standard perhaps to "inculcate virtues so needed before blindly applying deontology, teleology contractarianism and so on. Virtue ethical thinking thus assumes a normative status in both stake and stockholder based thinking in business in so far as it provides moral agents in corporate some such worthwhile properties or traits or habits that makes them persons who do not base decisions and actions on so-called norms rather on their character that is good by inculcating noble properties, traits and habits of character. Once we concentrate in our practical life (as in business), the importance of cultivation of needed virtues or traits and habits of character, we gradually go on building a desirable or good character, that is, we become a person of high or noble character. If that happens, we need not bother whether we respect duty or are altruistic because among other virtues we *are* dutiful and altruistic. We are also temperate, courageous, just and prudent and so on. For the stockholders, it is thus important to recognise the value of being virtuous in terms of cultivating the traits of honesty, justice, truthful, right, responsible, diligent, hard working, and ecologically conscious and so on. For the stakeholders, it is important to recognise the value of being virtuous in terms of cultivating traits of honest, truthful, right, responsible, non-aggressive, temperate, equations, non-gluttonous and so on. The list of virtues is too long to be mentioned here. To be more precise, thinkers propound the idea that for the benefit of the moral agents who are conscious and serious about virtue inculcation, should remember that there are *aretaic* and *deontic* virtues awaiting inculcation. The 'aretaic' virtues (come from the Greek term arête or 'virtue') are those traits of character or those needed properties of good life that relates us to the most *desirable ends of life* or the *desirable teleos* in life. Hence, these virtues become crucial in choosing our means and ends in practical life. The life in corporate and of the corporate being active life epitomising choice of desirable ends and means in business, should be based on these virtues. The virtues fix a habitual state of mind in decision-makers in business to fix their priorities and abstain from undesirable acts. The *cardinal virtues* (as conceived by Plato and Aristotle), namely, prudence, justice, courage and temperance are foremost in this category, and others are honesty, dedication, fidelity, compassion and many more. The corollaries are the vices, which should be carefully avoided. Further, we have the *deontic virtues* awaiting cultivation because having these virtues the moral agents (as in business), relates them to other moral agents by *respecting* the inherent value of certain things that needs to be done in life as universal maxims. For instance, to respect the freedom, and rights of moral agents and thus the duty or the responsibility of an agent to respect such things. In business, these deontic virtues are of great importance because having this enables managers, stockholders and others to change their ways of looking at and dealing with the stakeholders or a number of clients, beings and things. It keeps those in business to see that notwithstanding valuable choice of means and ends, they need to have the virtue to value the freedom, rights and welfare of other beings and things. It is this that enables companies to do a lot of good to human and non-human beings and things while they are involved in business. It is often argued that individuals and organisations in business should care for the cultivation of both these virtues because business does not end with *expressing* oneself in the just choice of means and end, nor does it end with effecting others with the just ways of dealing, it is both (bifocal); hence, organisations should take care for induction of some such people possessing both sets of virtues. Nevertheless, there are strong criticisms of virtue ethical indulgence in business. Some argue (Cf. W. K. Frankena in *Ethics*) that there is no non-normative or rather free from normativity virtue based thinking because the point that we should inculcate virtues before we follow theories is preceded by the charge that only normative theories can help us in knowing that such and such virtues are properly so-called and that we have them in us. How do we know and claim for instance, that we are really courageous and responsible until we have some norms or standards to tell us what amounts to be "really courageous" and "really responsible"? In fact, this problem was faced by the *adi-guru* of western virtue ethics, Aristotle when he said that courageous *qua* courageous is a matter known to the *phronimos* or the philosophically wise person, but who is a *phronimos*? The only reply is, he is the one who apart from other things, knows what it is to be courageous *qua* courageous. This *circularity* is threatening the virtue ethicists constantly because the moot issue is, how do I *know* (this is an epistemological question), that I am courageous? In fact, Aristotle and others should either fall back on *intuition* in this regard or they must refer to a normative thesis. For instance, one might argue that "I am 'courageous' to be sure (that is, to know without doubt), because either I chose the most appropriate end in business, that is, pleasure maximisation for all section of people whatever may come to prevent that or I chose to be respectful to uphold the rights of all humans whatever may come to prevent it". In any case, my being courageous (surely) depends on the truth that I *follow* either a teleological or a deontic standard in my life. However, as I have asked before, can virtue based thinking be a normative thesis, that is, the norm of evaluation is "to be virtuous"? Well, it may well be in imagination but the norm "to be virtuous" begs the question, "*How* to be virtuous?" and then we fall back on hackneyed enlisting of virtues that further begs an answer to, "*Why* are these virtues?" Thus, we look at the norms of ethics finally. In fact, normative and virtue based thinking are complementary to each other, there is no non-normative virtue based ethics. Another point is, how can there be *absolute value* or worth of a said virtue, like, "justice"? It may well be that to do justice in distribution of wealth and benefits, even for its respect so to say, we have to deliberate on some unjust measures that are sure to affect affluent people. Hence, unjust or non-proportionate distribution may be itself a *means* to the desirable justice. Hence, at times injustice becomes ethically permissible for greater justice on different *normative grounds*, for instance, for social well-being thus refuting the idea of absolute value of justice as a equitable distribution of wealth.

Whatever the case may be, many post-modern ethicists are of the opinion that they can contribute *de novo* in business ethical justification by showing how ethical conceptions of solidarity and conceptions inherent in feminist ethics are aids to such justification. The impact of such post-modern thinking in the field of business and management has been well explained Norman E. Bowie (1998) who bases most of his arguments against the anti-objectivist or rather *relativistic* arguments of Richard Rorty and Ed Freeman, both drawing impetus from the philosophy of *deconstruction* to justify that ethical theories are essentially relative to place and time, they emerge, change and fizzle out in the actual contexts of their meaningful use by humans in different places and times. Hence, there are no objectively arguable theses in ethics, no objectively valid norms that can be drawn in the real contexts of issues like business to find absolutely valid and universally acceptable solution. Hence, whatever ethicality remains as residues in business practices that enable us to derive some solidarity among our race are relative to *us*, they are completely *subjective preferences*, and they cannot be argued for. All this is much in tune with the pragmatics of Dewey and the effects of deconstructionist theses more popular in literature. It also reminds us the famous declaration of J. L. Mackie that "there are no objective values" (1978), and therefore, ethics is wholly subjective or relativistic, there is nothing we can say that amounts to emerge a "solidarity" in human societies around the globe that can tell us that we perceive these as moral and others as immoral. We are also reminded of the deconstructionist theses that though art is a play in and with the *medium*, what artists accomplish are *contingent* to the severe or moderate *constraints* imposed by the medium on the creator, and for that matter in the art of intending and doing good, serious constraints are imposed on the moral agent by the prevailing moral taboos, opinions, criticisms and so on, which shows why "solidarity" in ethical matters are far too impossible and why there are no objectively valid moral theses. Drawing blood from such deconstructionist presuppositions, some writers argue why business ethics cannot be a body of normatively valid theses drawn to business matters. In fact, business happens in an atmosphere of constraints as well, which are imposed by several socio-economic, political and ethical forces. Hence, there is nothing objectively valid in such enterprises to imagine that by virtue of such things some solidarity in the business community all over the world is imaginable. In fact, moral constraints imposed on business at different places and at different times enable us to argue that moral agents in business enterprise play under its influence thus emerging no objectively valid normative principle or ethical practices in business. There is thus no objectively valid and universally acceptable ethicality in business, ethics in business practices is thus relative to place and time, relative to us so to say, "contingent", to be precise. Norman Bowie has attacked elaborately on the conceptions of deconstructionism as implied in cases of ethics and business ethics to disclaim normative objectivity and solidarity. It disclaims the idea of 'solidarity' as a subjective construction. There are several interesting points in the deconstructionist thesis that pour new wine in old bottle. It is another way to show that if relativism holds good, it is not that there are no values or no values in business or that there is no business ethics, but that business ethics is 'non-normative' in status. It is nothing but the ways in which moral agents *use* their ethical opinions in actual contexts in a space and time within the complex texture of social, political and economic taboos and their critiques to come to a 'construed solidarity' about desirability, right, good, just, duty and so on, which must be essentially relative. Hence, the most interesting aspect is that though there is ethical reflections in business matters, it is not the same as normative reflections, and bereft of it we can still have ethical solidarity, which is merely a matter of convenience in so far as moral agents are concerned to put their minds in the matter to find out what is good in business. I think these reflections need serious consideration when we shall shortly come to the practical task of ethics and its impact in the field of business. Whatever may be the outcome of our analysis, whether Rorty or Ed Freeman or Bowie turns out to be more logical, it is interesting to notice that we are already in hand the impact that normativism and non-normativism in ethical discussion have on business related talks, which is our contention at this point. To be precise, Bowie argues that Rorty and others have missed the Deweyan point in pragmatic thinking that though 'medium' imposes some constraints on artists when involved in an art creation, it puts a limit to what the artist strives to attain and what he really attains by overcoming the limits pressed on him. Nevertheless, in literary creation, there are least constraints put by the medium on the creator because he is more or less free to put *his ideas* on the medium. Hence, it is not necessary and sufficient for us to buy Rorty's argument that the subjects in art-creations have more or less no liberty in imposing ideas on the medium. It may be possible, therefore, to claim further that though ethicality is seriously constrained by socio, economic and political factors, in the art of thinking and doing the rightful, moral agents are free to press on their critical thinking on moral matters and come closer to a moral "solidarity" through certain *objectively valid* moral conceptions, principles, norms and so on, which is far from what Rorty thinks to be mere subjective construction without an objective normative validity. Drawing this in the field of business Bowie achieves his goal to press the point that though ethical thinking put serious constraints in business, we can still find certain moral principles which have universal appeal in business matters that amounts to certain "solidarity" among the global citizens. Bowie explains it nicely in these words: "I apply some of the insights about art to business. Just as the clay imposes constraints on what the potter can produce, facts about the material world place constraints on the kinds of economic institutions one can have and even more importantly, morality places constraints on the behaviour of most economic actors in a free market economic system. If a free market economic system is to be viable, most participants in that system will need to adopt certain moral principles such as respecting voluntary exchange, honouring contract rights, and avoiding free riding. In other words, free market economic systems require that most participants adopt a fairly Kantian perspective"[14]. This is not to argue that free market economy will be a universal phenomena or that it will persist or that in the free market economies, whether in America or Japan (or its new incarnation in India), despite several ethical constraints that it faces, we are still as moral actors able to overcome constraints as artists do to the clay despite so many constraints in achieving what he wishes to create. Hence, we are able to crystallize certain morally justifiable set of rules and principles, which are based on overreaching objectively valid first principles of morality like Kantianism. Hence, normativism might still be as good in business ethical matters though it appears to have fizzled out in the face of subjectivism and relativism. Before coming to the appraisal of Bowie's position, it is important to remember what James Rachels has argued in his seminal paper on ethical subjectivism, particularly in the course of his refutation of J.L. Mackie's conception that 'there are no objective values'[15]. Rachels has argued that the world bereft of objective values in the world in which both barbaric Callatians who consumed corpse of fathers is as ethically good as the Greeks who burnt the corpse of fathers. Is it not objectively true that the ethical value of eating corpses is incomparable to the value of either burning or burying them? Will it not be ethically just irrespective of place and time, culture and taboos that we do not eat corpses because apart from health hazards, it goes deeper to the point of human well being? But what do we do when we run out of woods, when nothing is left for us? Should we not turn cannibals? Where is ethicality when we are mad in hunger? These are good emotional blackmails very popular among cultural relativists, which really do not force by any logic to justify ethicality of cannibalism because that is good for human welfare. Or, do we argue that human welfare depends both on eating our dead and live parents, children and at the same time on not doing so when we are well fed? Do we not prefer dying without food but save our parents and children because such sacrifices might do more human welfare than consuming our own people? Carry this a little farther; do we not agree to the objectively valid ethical truth despite cultural differences that racism, mass genocide of the Hitler-era, female foeticide, *sati*, child marriage and, telling plain truths like telling the correct time as per our wrist watch when asked for it? Take this to business, let us conceive of free markets, corporate culture and so on, is it not objectively valid to be respectable to our clients, not to cheat them in the bargain? Is it not objectively unjust in business to manipulate financial accounts to deprive shareholders of bonuses due to them? Both Rachels and Bowie and many among us would prefer to say that there are certain ethical truths which are objectively true; they withstand pressures of cultural relativism. Hence, there are moral agents who withstand pressures of society in business to do ethically what is good on objectively valid grounds. Hence, normativism is in the offering in business and not completely banished by the cultural arguments. The deconstructionist's appeal to non-normativism in business may be thus refuted and pure subjectivist solidarity (pseudo?) be given up. Nevertheless, we might ask Bowie why Kantianism is the normative thesis that has positive impacts on business matters like business in a free market and its allied value conceptions? Is it not true that the basic normative impact on free market business practices and values therein is that of utilitarianism and even contractarianism? Is it not possible to see the truth of cultural relativism at least partially that impacts of overreaching normative principles vary according to place and time? Is it impossible to imagine that within the Indian society at this point of time different normative conceptions may be active to influence the evaluation of free market business practices? Is it not possible that the touted value of 'untruth' in business be not justified on contractarianism or utilitarianism than Kantian deontology or even taking them together? Rachels in his wonderful essay has recognised the truth that understanding the defects in cultural relativism does not amount to say that 'there are no relative values'. This is another whimsical orthodoxy of objectivists. Relativism teaches us that we should not completely trash the values of any society on the false vanity of our civility. In this sense, the values in American capitalism cannot be taken to be godly to trash some values in Indian mixed economy and business therein. We cannot buy the argument that Americans are more ethical and civil than Indians because American capitalism has given them more moral authority and civility by virtue of *egotism* as a moral thesis which Indians lack because their mixed economic ideal has given them less moral authority and civility by virtue of foolish *altruism*. Hence, Americans should not trash the Indian ideal to curb rampant profit-making by the corporate by rolling down its public sectors; or, alternately Indians have no moral authority to trash profiteering in business by saying that it is based on a rogue philosophy of ego-satisfaction. Hence, Bowie makes some reservations about an apparent absolutism in his thesis to say that: "A different economic order at a different point in history would have a different underlying morally.... If market considerations are to be overridden in the interests of other values, then other moral principles may trump the morality of the marketplace as well. There certainly are times when it is morally wrong to enforce a contract. However, to limit the morality of the marketplace is not to adopt Rorty's extreme relativism"[16]. Given this respect to relativism, we can say that Bowie will not be less happy to curb his deontic leanings because that cannot be the only objective moral truth in changing places and times, respect for other theories may be equally good. Nevertheless, his love for the capitalist economic system enables him to conclude that ultimately there will be agreed or consensual ethical practices in the world in the realm of business in so far as international phenomenon of free market economy sustains the phenomenal spread. Hence, for Bowie, what must be objectively true is the force of capitalism that will bring human solidarity through business practices as based on normative principles like Kantianism. Well, we can go on debating about Bowie's contentions but his tension to recognise the truth of relativism on the one hand and the recognition of the truth of Kantianism that strengthens a capitalist based business practice is clear. Our *respect* for humanity *per se* may not allow such strengthening of capitalist based business enterprises in India because we are still afraid of becoming global-boss in business affairs by virtue of capital. We are really suspicious of what is happening in the South East Asia. Yet, I must agree that the position of Rorty and Bowie have given us important points while we engage in unfolding the role of ethics in business and thus justify business ethics. This is clearer when we consider some of these points when we discuss practical ethical involvement in business.

Almost with the beat of heart people in business and ethics should say that business ethics should be active and not passive; however, what it is to be "active" is not agreed upon by us uniformly. For the analytic philosophers the activeness of ethics is not determined by dragging theoretical reflection in ethics to fields alien to it for the sake of resolution of some practical problems therein because there is perhaps nothing in store in academic ethics that can solve practical problems in our society, whether these problems arise in the fields of medicine or accounting or business or whatever. To argue that the so-called 'practical problems' are in reality "value-laden", that is, they are laden with unique questions about ethical desirability or about why should such and such decisions be taken and actions be done, are also unfounded because we cannot plant value questions in stark practical issues at our wish to take them up as our noble task because problems need not be created and solved in this manner. Hence, an active ethics is nothing but unique activities with the clarification of language of ethics, and arguably to discuss about norms, better said, normative language analysis is more appropriate task of ethics. These arguments advanced by the analytic philosophers thus takes metaethical activities in ethics as proper ones because only such activities are better suited to the philosophers, the moral philosophers so to say should not have synthetic interests or wrongly understood practical interest. The restriction of ethical "activities" to linguistic analytic activities has been well faced by a number of ethicists since long (see volume 1 for details). It is proper to say at this point that the virtue of metaethical and normative activities in the field other than ethics, like business have shown us why ethics need not be restricted to mere analysis of language of ethics. It has also shown us that the metaethical tasks of conceptual clarity and justification are well knit in a whole where normative, and virtue and value related discussions appreciate each other for a wholesome ethical activity. This is also true of applied or practical activities within the whole called ethics, which has close relation with metaethical and other activities (see volume 1 for details). It is sufficient to tell here that the present effort to explain the nature of applied ethics and its relation with other tasks of ethics as well as the justification of application of ethics in business is all *metaethical* in nature. Similarly to inquire about normative involvement in application of ethics in the field of business shows how close practical activity is to normative activity. To discuss how close practical activity to virtue inculcation is when it comes to business is another way in which we come to know what it means to be ethically active.

Now the most debatable issue for us is, whether applied ethical activity in business is the same as applying norms of ethics, which is in one sense applying theoretical ethical knowledge in the field of business. If it is the case, we have to find out how we can do such things and in doing so what exactly do we achieve. Or, alternatively we may discover that practical ethical involvement in business is *non-normative involvement* but practicality does not lose its significance in being so. Similarly, we can either find that practical ethical involvement in business involves inculcation of a number of virtues or to find that the same is not the case though practicality is least affected in being so. It is important to mention at the outset of the discussion that business amounts to the application of one or more standard normative theories like utilitarianism and/or deontology so that the business related issues or problems under consideration are resolved with ease and success. This can be seen in a number of works in business ethics, which finds a reflection here at the beginning of this chapter when we found that business ethics as a branch of practical ethics is nothing but application of normative ethics in business matters. We have also seen while discussing post-modern conception of business ethics that most post-modernists are either of the opinion that application of ethics in business is a *subjective* affair where normativism makes no impact in so far as applying them is concerned or of the opinion that application of ethics in business is a *collective* affair where Kantian norm in particular is of great help when it comes to applying it in business. Hence, the story of application of ethics in fields other than ethics, for instance, in business, is a story of hard fought battle between normative application and non-normative application, sometimes called a battle between *engineering* with ethics and non-engineering with ethics (for details, see volume 1). The real tension is not to trash normative ethics or normative thinking in ethics rather, non-normativism in this regard is the possibility of non-engineering with normative theories in business though normativism remains sensible within ethics. What we call normativism in this regard is the possibility of engineering with normative theories in business, though normativism, independent of application of standard theories in business makes perfect sense. Hence, we have to discuss whether normative ethical engineering amounts to business ethics at least in a major way or there are application of ethics that amounts to business ethics without it. The tension is well portrayed by Jack Mahoney in this manner: "It would be oversimplifying to consider business ethics as just routinely applying general ethical or moral values or rules to different business activities such as voting on a particular company policy.... Frequently, general ethics can be led to develop its thinking by considering various business activities and recognising that experience of real-life situations can lead us to refine and develop our understanding and appreciation of moral values or principles"[17]. Further, he asserts, "It follows...that business ethics is not the unvarying imposition of ethical standards on the gamut of business situations. It is more of dialogue between the science of ethics and the conduct of business"[18]. There are important points in what Mahoney says much in abeyance of both postmodernists Rorty, Ed Freeman and Bowie. Mahoney's position differs from Rorty and others because his refusal of normative engineering do not logically imply acceptance of subjectivism in which decisions in value-charged business matters amounts to what moral agents find most *convenient* at a particular place and time, given the contesting moral opinions and their critiques. Mahoney differs from Bowie in so far as for Mahoney's, involvement with Kantianism or other principles of morality that claims a sacrosanct status is to get entangled in the web of normative engineering, which if far too artificial and improbable at the ground levels of reality. Another view that needs more careful scrutiny after we have analysed

Mahoney's position a little farther is that of George Enderle, who happens to take major cues from Amartya Sen's conception of "goal-rights-systems" (*On Ethics and Economics*, 1990). This is needed because the position appears to be a half-way house, trying best to put together the puzzle blocks of normative engineering and non-normative (also non-subjective) decision-making. What is most important in the position of Mahoney and some of his supporters including me is that at the ground level in interdisciplinary attempts like business ethical resolutions, the entire talk of application of ethics in business makes sense in the exclusive contexts of value-charged business issues, which irrespective of any ethical training and ethical wish, philosophers and non-philosophers alike are able to *know* by virtue of their participation in this world teeming with multifarious intentional decisions and acts why such and such issues do not leave scope for neglect in so far as they affect us in pro and con manners to answer whether certain things (decisions and acts) *should* be done though they are done on regular basis. On regular basis kickbacks are needed for a big contract in business whether in the public or in the private sectors; people are almost naturally involved in such things but philosophers, businessmen, administrators, managers, laymen, labourers and many others in a civil society might feel an implicit ethical heat that evokes their pro and con views or criticisms to find out whether 'what is done, should be done'. The concerns for ethical good, right, just and so on are not subjective constructions—business ethical problems are not constructed by us, they are there for our consideration, lest we are caring about such things in life. Another point implicit in it is that business ethical considerations, when they are at the ground level of resolution of value-laden issues, neither begs expert ethicists nor expert economists or business magnets or managers alone. To add to it, the entire issue of resolution may not be possible without the involvement of many *non-experts* in ethics and business. This takes us gradually to an understanding of people's participation in interdisciplinary efforts like pressing ethics to the service of business related value-resolutions. What is undesirable in ethical engineering in such matters is intellectual bossism or experts' chauvinism. Why should wise people in governing bodies and management in a business house assume that the issue of widespread computerisation and robotisation in their house raises practical problems having no moral questions of desirability? And why should wise men think that even if they feel some moral heat by virtue of nagging charges of unethicality in terms of lay-offs and other repressive measures towards the workforce that does harm to a number of families, the wise intellectuals, the experts so to say, are best suited to resolve them all by themselves and the sermons be accepted by those who directly suffer from misdeeds? Why should ordinary labourers, supervisors, office *babus*, union leaders be not party to the *moral debates* that resolves ethical crises in a democratic and peaceful way? Why should only economists come up with theoretical models, one after another to press their assumed solutions to ground level as if social issues are subjects for their lab. tests? Why should economists not participate in people's discourses about stiff value-charged matters before their intellectual interplay with the theories they have learnt and the things that happen are put face to face to revise their ways of thinking? Can theory and practice be put in categories unrelated to each other and a division of labour that demands intellectual technocrats, the economists and the management people to move in the way of theory to practice, but not in the way of practice to theory and then a *return to theory and practice*? These are important questions in the methodology of ethical application in business matters which poses serious threat to engineering of the experts with theories in ethics or even with economics, business principles and management principles and practices where the public has been partially or completely neglected. If economists, business theorists and management *gurus* imagine that practical ethics in business is much like what they do in their subjects, that is, armed with theoretical wisdom try to be practically wise, they are completely mistaken. If they imagine that their painstakingly framed models of *being ethical* in business and other economic enterprises *on paper* are terrific theoretically valuable projects where monopoly of norms or a *kitchery* of them are placed in all sorts of jargons and figures and/or diagrams like a complex mesh of electrical circuit, they are completely mistaken.

Application of ethics makes great sense in an "action oriented business ethics" (Cf. Enderle), no doubt but that does not mean that "action orientedness" is application of norms of ethics in value-laden cases by ethics or economics experts because apart from the fact that it is based on misconceptions that one more theories can mend moral malfunctions in business as engineers do with their tool in tool-box, its absurdity lies in the fact that either subjective whims or an absolute principle can solve *all* problems provided experts are at work. It is interesting to see *how* welfarism or libertarianism or Kantianism or Rawlsianism or goal-rights-system are picked by experts in business ethics just as a fixed wrench can fit a fixed bolt to tightened up things when they are loose. I am sorry to comment that persons having little knowledge of the ground reality of *doing things with ethics* will surely do engineering, they will make models out of theoretic knowledge and try to fit in proper situations, which never tightens the loose ends. Doing something with ethics in business is to be "theory non-coopted" (see volume 1), that is, to move away from ethical chauvinism of ethics experts or of economists with some theories. The needed objective is to resolve value-crises in business with most of the concerned parties, that is, parties feeling the ethical heat in business matters and thus tending to be pro or con in moral matters, based on the "moral experience" and "moral knowledge" (see volume 1), they have by virtue of being members of this vast ecological community who act, influence, gets influenced, react, retort, submit, disagree and come to consensus. This takes the 'non-theory coopted ethicists' and business scientists to de-class their arrogant *gurudom* and come to the public and their ethical concerns to respect them and then fearlessly *debate* on business related value-crises, for which they construct a *questionnaire* which brings out best moral critiques. "Intersubjective corroboration" (see volume 1) in business, is not a construct of theoretical knowledge, it is an outcome of the moral urge to pass the moral authority to those who have them, which is a concrete experience that comes with involvement. The questions for the moral debates are still not chauvinists' construction that is, not made at the whims of an ethicist. It is also a learning process which comes with reading news and views about moral matters, talking to the people who have moral concerns and one's own rationality to put the questions systematically, simply and straightforwardly. Hence, the questions that are used in moral debates by either ethicists or others who are best to come forward in such interdisciplinary matters, that is, best in terms of moral interests and public debates, are *non-structuralist*. It appears that then anyone other than the ethicist can do this job, that is, frame questions, arrange moral debates and moderate them to reach consensus. If this is not the case then there is some role of intellectualism and bossism so to say on the part of the ethicists and/or business-theorists/economists. Well, nothing can stop a businessman, economist, and management experts like ethicists to be respectable to public critiques of value-laden issues in business. Nothing prevents them to read ethics, business ethics and things like that to gather information and then frame ethically relevant questions for moral debates. Nothing prevents them to arrange debates and moderate them. However, these 'non-philosopher experts' fail to do certain things without a proper training in ethics including metaethics, normative and virtue ethics. First is, they and many other ethically concerned people (as said above), fail to construct "relevant ethical questions" for debates *not* because these questions do not have normative orientation rather they might lack in the *penetrating power* that relevant questions often have or should have to push the analytic abilities of participants in ethical matters, that is, they fail to squeeze out the needed ethical critiques that agents often want to produce but abstain when they are not pushed hard. Second, the non-philosophers (a sweeping term that covers common men interested in ethical matters) fail to do what is extremely important in ethical wisdom to analyse the moral reasons displayed in debates, that is, they often do not have the needed ethical wisdom to *analyse* the *moral reasons* displayed in debates by different parties and thus come to know which normative theses and rules if any were *active* though implicit in their criticism of the issue. This is what I call "post-corroboration analysis" (See Volume 1), which is an important role of person trained in ethics. Hence, training in metaethics and normative ethics may be extremely important for any interested party other than the ethicists or the non-philosophers who want to apply ethics in the way I have spoken above, that is, non-theory co-opted tending to moral consensus through ethical debates. There are three charges: One is that ultimately intellectualism of academic ethicists is at hand. Next, at least *gurudom's* vanity is restored in "post-corroboration analysis". Finally, ethicists' interest in normativism cannot be overshadowed. The charges are baseless because they are based on a great misconception that a model of ethical application stated above should not have any academic ethical involvement and role for trained ethicists' if it is truly non-chauvinist. It is also based on the misconception that having no cooption with normative theories in application is to say that no analysis that reveals any involvement of such theories in real life debates is needed. The problem is, why should we confuse practical ethics in business as an activity that completely sidesteps academic ethical knowledge when it is evident that what has been urged in this model is that ethicists and non-ethicists or all interested people in resolving business ethical matters should keep away from artificial application of ethical norms in such practical affairs? There is no clarion call to abandon academic ethics partially or wholly, that is, whether in framing questions, guiding debates, and analysing contents of consensus reached in debates.

Rather, non-philosophers interested in applying ethics should train themselves in the whole course of ethics but they need not be interested in applying theories they know. It is due to this that pages of economic theories read by economists should give way to practical involvement with the public in economic matters to reach a consensus or to learn from them, and it is too bad to apply what great theories have taught them and be satisfied that their task is complete. Ethics applied in business by any interested party may be thus non-chauvinist though not non-ethical. Further, application of ethics does not end with debates because the point is the fruits of the debate may be further put to scrutiny. First, we have to see which decision-making rules found in consensus should be adopted by businessmen, managers and so on when they are further placed in ethical crises. Second, we have to find out which moral reasons emerged in debates as based on moral were not artificially applied, non-coopted and even untrained people display the powers of normative theses in debates to overcome dilemmas and to reach a consensus. Hence, 'post-corroboration analysis' that begs normative ethical training is a way to see the *dynamics* of moral theories at ground levels of reality because they are not handmaid of experts' wisdom, neither do they drop *ex-nihilo*, they are active but implicit in our ethical knowledge, which is not necessarily *academic* mostly owing to the ethical experience we have on earth. In fact, wise ethicists have formulated these principles and theories to construct a body of academic ethics, which is normative ethics, but that does not imply that only they know it or apply it. Nothing prevents our uneducated workers in coalfields, for instance, to understand that their good do not end with wages, that their welfare is broader concept and it is *desirable*, and for this they do not have to attend economics classes. In any case, application of ethics is a vital activity that enters the field of business which Enderle says should be "action-oriented". Thus business ethics is justified through involvement of application of ethics without a normative cooption. Enderle says that "business ethics should be *fundamentally oriented towards decision-making and acting in business*... the proposed conception essentially differs from two other approaches: the "deductive-descendant" approach that first deals with general moral norms and values and then tries to "apply" them to various situations, and the system theoretic approach... (that) excludes the actor at all three levels (micro, meso and macro), and hence, eliminates also the question of moral responsibility"[19]. He continues: "I want to argue for a '*problem-oriented approach*' because compared to a comprehensive theory... it offers a better chance of finding a way out of the enormous plurality and heterogeneity of approaches, dogmas, theses and results in the field of business ethics and contributing to the solution of urgent problems"[20]. Interestingly, Enderle says: "today's crises of moral orientation be taken seriously and that the 'fact of pluralism'... be faced squarely. For this seems to be a *conditio sine qua non* to find stable orientations for collective actions supported by a large *consensus*"[21]. Rightly, Enderle clarifies that such 'moral consensus' should take into account the social, cultural, religious, economic and political conditions and there should be constant scrutiny about such consensus so that no obsession and orthodoxy about desirability of decisions and actions prevail in societies. But Enderle could not resist his normative interests despite his apathy to the said "deductive descendant and systematic theoretic" approaches because for him it is very important to have a "goal-right system", a 'moral system' in the imagined action-oriented business ethics wherein consequentialism and deontology are not overlooked or are not seen as anti-theoretical rather, they are 'combined' (also by Amartya Sen). And what is the aim of such combination after all? It is one thing to find out through moral debates and consensus that in the public criticisms, goals and rights need to be such and such and that they are most of the time 'combined', and to urge that in the capacity of ethicists and other interested allies "whenever collective action is at stake requires normative ethics"[22]. This (conclusive remark) is in accordance with what Enderle says in the introductory passage that an "action-oriented" conception of business ethics that provides a framework within which the discussion of substantive issues can be conducted fruitfully.... I take up the *normative ethical* (my italics) approach of a 'goal-rights-system' proposed by Amartya Sen"[23]. Yes, we agree that to talk about goals and rights are extremely important in business ethics, we agree that at all levels of activity in business talk of goals and rights are important, we also agree that recognition of these truths might reveal that normative ethical pluralism in a pluralist society holds good, but it is difficult to agree that in a business ethics which is action-oriented, talks are *about* goals and rights as if that becomes the normative basis for our activities, related to ethical resolution and decision-making as necessary and sufficient. In "intersubjective corroboration" when moral talks or debates are held as a vital activity, we focus on moral consensus about moral impasse in business, in the course of which many crucial aspects of moral desirability, good, right, just, duty, obligation, responsibilities, praise and blame are hotly contested keeping a value-laden issue at the centre which gradually gives us decision-making rules after agreement is found among disagreements but that is not pressing into service a substantive or normative "goal-rights-systems" in the dialogue.

There was a need for some details of application of ethics in business to justify business ethics as a sensible enterprise because in due course of the discussion of ethics we have come across the method of application of ethics with the help of which some crucial economic, business and management related ethical issues are resolved. This book, a major part of it is also "action-oriented" because after necessary theoretical groundwork, it moves to what should be done in business ethics, that is, dialogues for business ethical resolutions and analysis of the dialogues for *discovering* the implicit normative theories in action. We have now come to know that an action-oriented business ethics should be respectful to people's ethics, the ethics of classism with normative engineering fails in this respect, though legitimate roles of ethicists and experts in economics, business and management are not snatched away from them. We shall turn such activism shortly after we have discussed in the next chapter the nature and justification of management ethics or ethics in management.

NOTES

1. Solomon, Robert C. "Business Ethics" in Singer, Peter (ed.), *A Companion to Ethics*, O.U.P., Oxford, 1991, p. 355.
2. Bowie, Norman E. "Business Ethics" in DeMarco, J. P. and Fox, R.M., (eds.), *New Directions in Ethics*, Routledge and Kegan Paul, NY, 1986, p. 158.
3. *Ibid*, p. 158.
4. Solomon, Robert. C, Op. Cit., p. 356.
5. *Ibid*, p. 359.
6. Velasquez, M. G., *Business Ethics: Concepts and Cases*, Prentice-Hall of India Pvt. Ltd., New Delhi, 2002, p. 15.
7. Goodpaster, K. E., "Business Ethics" in *The Blackwell Encyclopaedic Dictionary of Business Ethics*, Vol. XI, Werhane, P. H. & Freeman, R. E. (Eds.), Blackwell, 1997, p. 51.
8. Velasquez, M. G., Op. Cit., p. 15.
9. For details, see Michalos, A.C. *A Pragmatic Approach to Business Ethics*, Sage Publications, California, 1995, pp 44-53 and Friedman, M., "The Social

Responsibility of Business Is to Increase Its Profits", *New York Times Magazine*, Vol. 13, 1970.

10. Velasquez, M. G., Op. Cit., p. 18.
11. Mahoney, Jack, "Business Ethics" in *International Encyclopaedia of Business and Management*, Warner, Malcolm (ed.), Thomson Learning, London, 2002, p. 475.
12. An introductory account of ethic of moral responsibility in business is found in M. G. Velasquez's *Business Ethics: Concepts and Cases*, Op. Cit., pp. 45-51 and in details in a collection of essays in the matter by J. M. Fischer and M. Ravizza in *Perspectives on Moral Responsibility*, Cornell University Press, NY, 1993.
13. Mahoney, Jack, Op. Cit., p. 475.
14. Bowie, N. E., "Postmodernism, Business Ethics and Solidarity", in Morcher, E. O., Neumaier O. and Simons P. (eds.), *Applied Ethics In A Troubled World*, Kluwer, London, 1998, p. 180.
15. For details, see James Rachels' paper "The Challenge of Cultural Relativism" in *Ethics: History, Theory and Contemporary Issues*, Cahn S. M. and Markie, P. (eds.), O. U. P., NY, 1999, pp 548-557.
16. Bowie, N. E., Op. Cit., p. 189.
17. Mahoney, Jack, "Business Ethics" in Warner, Malcolm (eds.), *International Encyclopaedia of Business Management*, Vol. 6, Op. Cit., p. 474.
18. *Ibid*, p. 474.
19. Enderle, G., "Business Ethics As a Goal-Right-System" in Malcom Warner (ed.), *International Encyclopaedia of Business Management*, Vol. 6, Op. Cit, p. 156.
20. *Ibid*, p. 156.
21. *Ibid*, p. 156.
22. *Ibid*, p. 163.
23. *Ibid*, p. 151.

3

The Nature and Justification of Management Ethics

A careful study of some of the textbooks and references on business ethics reveals that ethical issues pertaining to management finds a place in the context of business ethical discussions. It appears that talk of business goes along with the talk of management and ethical talks of both goes together as if one involves the other. However, there is no reason to believe that talks about business are the same as talks about management, and for those matter ethical talks about business is not the same as the ethical talks in management. Hence, both are not synonymous, they need separate treatment for clearer understanding. Nevertheless, among many ethically relevant studies in business, we do study about the management of business and related ethical concerns. It is due to this that though management ethics forms a part of business ethics, they are not one and the same because in business ethics, many non-management issues are taken up for ethical inquiry. For instance, under business ethics we may talk about the *desirable goals* of business among which may be the "effective management of human resource" but under management ethics, we may talk about the *desirable goals* of management among which may be the "desirability of managing humans treated as *resources*". There are number of ethical issues regarding ends and means in business and management which shows why both are related but different. Yet, it will not be out of the way to call ethical discussions in management under ethical discussions in business despite their differences. In this chapter, therefore, we move on to consider in some details the clarification of the nature of management ethics, which obviously clarifies the differences between management and business ethics, and we attempt at clarifying why (or for what reasons), management ethics is a sensible study. As usual we shall obtain the same method obtained thus far. First, we will analyse tasks of "management" and "ethics" to find out what amounts to the nature of "management ethics", further, we shall find out the ways in which the tasks of management invites ethical inquiries as well as the ways in which or tasks of ethics covers the field of management. Another important discussion, which we will consider during the nature clarification of "management" is the ways in which management is *included* in the broad spectra of "administration" but at the same time different from it in some respects. This gives us a glimpse of value aspects of administration overlapping the value aspects of management. To start with, let us analyse "management" in "management ethics".

Management comes from the root *maneggio* meaning thereby "the hand", which amounts to convey the idea that management is in essence a *human activity*, that is, an act having a skilled human hand to direct or control, train or use, or treat available resources, both beings and things, so that through such effective leadership an organisation or institution achieves desirable goals. Management is thus an art or a skilled act to channel available resources in business to fulfil its desired as well as desirable objectives. We can say that there are many goals of *organisations* which are attainable through the *process* of management, for which human and non-human *resources* are needed for effective use and control and in doing so some *value* is continuously added to the existing state of affairs. Management is, therefore, effectiveness in attaining the organisational objectives, which is well marked in instances like *effective* use of resources that avoids spilling and damages, *innovative* improvements in process of production and outputs and *responsible* acts towards the good of the stock and the stakeholders. Management is thus a process epitomised in organisational effectiveness, innovation and responsibility. If the two important aspects of management are the material and the technical aspects, the third aspect reminds of ethical or the value aspect of management. It is truly a feature of the process of management that it adds value to the world. A.D. Chandler in *The Visible Hand: The Management Revolution in American Business* (1977) and P. H. Werhane in *Adam Smith and his legacy for modern capitalism* (1991) remarks that management (as *maneggio*) is an effective process, a process which reveals a "visible hand" that manipulates what has been left to the managers by the "invisible hands" or the stockholders. What the invisible hand leaves for use, is used extremely efficiently by the "visible hands" active in the private, public and other sectors globally. The visible hand thus plans, controls, guides, leads and so on to add value to what has been left to them. The impact of management results into qualitative improvement in organisations' activities to achieve their goals, the net gain is huge advantages in a competitive business over those who spill opportunities and thus suffer loss. This may be true not only of a business house; it may be true of our families, states, nations, educational institutions, hospitals and so on. However, focussing more on public and private sector organisations one can say that management can be effective and ineffective, depending on the merits of using available resources without minimum spill over. An ineffective management when it is overt causes many damages to a private or public sector company in terms of shares, profits, confidences, goodwill, costs, products, services, cooperation and so on, which therefore, need from the top intervention by the "invisible hands" to put mismanagement in line. In the government or the public sector the 'invisible hand' is the "government", who comes to the rescue. An ineffective management when it is covert, results into a number of backlashes in terms of retaliatory and subversive acts of the producers or the workers contributing in production units. The same may be true of the service units. Managerial ineffectiveness thus results into some such retaliatory acts on the part of the humans responsible in production and services that the ultimate sufferer is the company. It is here that ethical work culture may be more important, which turns the uncompetitive companies back to the rails of competition and profits. More often than not in the face off stiff competitions companies resort to subversive techniques that boomerang on them, this demand better management of the workforce than their abuse.

Keeping the basics of management in mind one might now ask, who is an ideal manager? Or, what is ideal management? It will be too simplistic to say that ideal management is the one that enables organisations to attain its ends and add value to the world. It will be equally vague to say that ideal management is the one that cares for the stake and the stockholders. In fact, the notion of an 'ideal management' is realisable when we review the prevalent goals or the tasks set for management experts. Not necessarily by virtue of a theory of management believing that the "ideal" is the only one available to us. Whereas the truth may be that the "ideal" may be a confluence of ideals expressed in a theory. There are at least four such management theories that gives us these ideals or tasks set for ideal management. First, we have the *rational goal theory* advocated by Fredrick Taylor in his work *The Principle of Scientific Management* (1911); the *internal process theory* established by Max Weber in his work, *Theory of Social and Economic Organisation* (1921); *the human relations theory* of Elton Mayo in *The Human Problems of an Industrial Civilization* (1933) and *the open system theory* supported by Paul Lawrence and Jay Lorsch in their work *Organisations and Environment* (1967)[1]. According to the 'rational goal theory' the tasks of management experts should be that of *producer and director* to set goals, take initiatives, increase production and optimize output. These are the tasks of managers in a company when as managers they are agents taking organisational goals valuable from outside, that is, as those external to the organisation. The involvement of such professionals in an organisation is as those *controlling* agents who more or less act as governors having less involvement with the workforces as motivators, empathisers, mentors and so on. Almost similar "externality" of the managers could be noticed in the 'open systems theory' propagating the tasks of managers to *innovate and broker*, though with a basic difference that they do not act merely as controlling agents rather as relatively *flexible* agents not governing others from outside rather getting involved in the cultivation of organisational learning capabilities, developing the skills of incessant creativity instigating competitive abilities and to learn to adopt to political cross-currents to negotiate external resource acquisition. We can thus say that both rational goal theory and open system theory takes management as a process in which experts are expected to assume the role responsibilities as external agents to organisations notwithstanding their variable roles as either controllers or flexible adapters, who at times learn how to cope up with the queer role of a middle-man between the workforce and the stockholders to face stiff political exchanges within companies and to gauge the numerous external developments and changes to make necessary changes in the company's ways of actions, production, distribution and so on. On the other hand we have two theories, one is the 'internal process theory' much similar to the rational goal theory in being conceiving managers as *controlling* agents, but with a basic difference of being more *involved in* more *internal* to the company's affairs, including the workforce and the stockholders. Management as such is taken as a process which has the task to coordinate and *monitor* information, documentation, processing and to consolidate the functioning of the company and its structural order. The empathiser role of the manager in the basic good of the company and its structural consolidation is well marked in this ideal of management. Much like this we have the theory of human relations with a difference that it is less in advocating the spirit of 'control' in management and thus 'flexible' in attitude, which is well marked in the role responsibilities or tasks of managers as *facilitators and mentors*, involved *internally* to the affairs of the company, not acting as agents external to it. These managers thus assume the role of creating openness, encourage wider participation in the good of the company to build the morale of the team of workers and to commit oneself to have consensus in and outside the company about debatable issues and to resolve conflicts. It is interesting to note that all the four theories stress on important tasks of mangers in company management but hardly any one theory constitutes the ideal manager by considering only *two* unique role responsibilities. J.F. Quinn and others have stressed on the fact that to define the task of management and thus the "nature" of management in terms of any one theory, or in terms of two arbitrarily selected role responsibilities is to make management *linear*. If we choose two theories and thus any four responsibilities arbitrarily, it becomes *complex*. Whereas if we choose to be *synergetic* to balance the entire eight basic role responsibilities expressed in four theories of management, not only does management become "ideal", it assumes a "desirable" status. This point has been well taken by P. M. Senge (1990). Petrick and Quinn (1997) thus brings out the truth that any one theory either loses sight of the fact that management cannot be wholly power assuming but not empathetic or the fact that it cannot be wholly empathetic without having some assumption of power and control. The reason is that for the good of the company, the public and the employees, a synergy among employees' freedom or flexibility, their value to remain under control and checks, and the perfect harmony among stock and the stakeholders is needed. The authors write: "To sustain the synergetic balance of outstanding management, all four theories need to be understood and mastered. Taken alone, no one theory or set of role competencies has the range of perspectives, the increase of choice, and the potential effectiveness provided by considering them all as part of a larger integrated framework"[2]. It is not difficult to follow the minor tone of what this integral conception of management holds. It holds that without comprehensive managerial tasks being performed, we do not have an ethically desirable management. Petrick and Quinn argue that when we integrate all the four sets of managerial tasks into a whole we integrate the conceptions of management that conceives of people (employees) as "inherently valued" on the one hand and as valuable to "goal attainment", that is externally valued. It also combines the conceptions of managers as experts having external and internal focus, and those caring for environmental changes and stability and continuity. These things amount to the construction of the *behavioural complexity* of managers and enhance their performance, which is a "cognitive complexity" combined with ability to perform "cognitively complex strategy" by virtue of multiple role responsibilities in an integrated and complementary way. Hence, "extremely low and high behavioural complexity on the part of a manager can lead to undesirable managerial role performance"[3]. We can, therefore, conceive of three levels of management (and thus managers) the *underdeveloped amoral*, the *masterly moral* and the *overdeveloped amoral* management. Both the under and the over developed amorality is not immorality, rather, some sort of valueless attitude, value neutrality one can say, which are the "negative" aspects of behavioural complexity in managers. The underdeveloped amoral manager represents those who do not perform any role responsibility in a balanced way and thus fail to make any impact in the company. The overdeveloped amoral manager represents those who either become aggressive directors and producers to harm cohesion among individuals. They become overindulgent with the role of the co-ordinator and monitor and thus become derogatory to progress. They also become extremely dependent on the role of facilitator and mentor amounting to sluggish in authority. Finally, they may be over-reliant on the role of broker and innovator to waste their energy. Hence, these managers do what is undesirable to push positives to the extreme negative limits. Far different from the amoral managers, the moral managers are at the balance level of performing their role responsibilities, which we have discussed above. Hence, management as a process is expectedly a body of balanced role performance, the normalcy of their complex behaviour is ethically desirable as well. Nevertheless, Petrick and Quinn reminds us of the fact that "management conduct within the acceptable variation range of good management practices remains a cross-cultural standard"[4]. This is much in line with ethical relativism that considers the desirable complex behavioural patterns of managers contingent on "transnational global cultures" ruling out any absolutism with regard to what is valuable for managers to do in their respective companies that play in an atmosphere of peculiar cultural value-systems. Hence, despite universality of the integral theory of management spelling out balance among the said sets of tasks it *should* take up, nevertheless, the relative merits of one or some of the tasks (mentioned in the theories) might be predominant in certain cultures, we just should not avoid it either. However, bowing to cultural values in management practices and for their sanctity to sacrifice the universal value of integrated management approach may not be ethically justifiable but this is a debatable issue. The universal value of 'moral ought' in management may be equally overreaching when it comes to the overpowering of sacrosanct values which might turn out to be disvalues in reality. Yet, not all cultural influences on management may be so easily snubbed or should be snubbed. Managers thus stand in the territory of turbulence, a moral turbulence that is presented by universal values from within and those cultural values gifted as taboos from outside. Hence, as managers in modern management the underlined task comes out to be steadfastness in the face of *moral complexities* notwithstanding the behavioural ones. This is a cue to the ethical concerns in management, to which we shall turn in a short while.

We tend to believe that with an exposition of sets of managerial tasks, we have explored the "nature" of management but is it not true as we are still apprehensive about whether management is a mere part of *administration*, which is in fact more oriented to value questions than management which is more oriented to factual questions and only derivatively being a subset of administration borrow value-related insights. Or, is it true that talks about management is well considered by administration and thus redundant? Do we feel the need of any factual talk about management and for that matter any ethical talk about the same when such talks are well cared within administration? If we reply in the negative, the whole of management related discussions will come to be futile, but most of us do not reply in the negative for obvious reasons we have to make distinctions among management, business and administration and the fact—value related opinion we have just seen. Christopher Hodgkinson in his work *Administrative Philosophy: Values and Motivations in Administrative Life* (1996) remarks, "Administration is inescapable. We live our lives in organisations… (Man is) an organisational animal… we are utterly administration dependent. This dependency means that the class of specialists known variously as managers, administrators, leaders, executives, officials and functionaries has a profound significance for the quality of human life. The expertise of this class is administration"[5]. From the presuppositions that humans live life in organisations, which is always administered by specialists called as managers and so on, he derives the truth; therefore, management of organisation having different goals is but administration. Hence, "management, itself a subset of administration, is pre-eminently disposed towards facts. Its superset administration is pre-eminently concerned with values"[6]. There is nothing logical awkwardness in this informal argument because from what has been said earlier, it is not difficult to say that what we call "management" is truly within the great whole called "administration", that is, the former is a part (subset) of the whole (superset), but the point is, does it amount to say that the subset is redundant? And that management is a value-free enterprise, whereas its superset alone takes up questions of value? Hodgkinson is careful about a likely confusion about the redundancy of "management" because it is only a synonym of "administration". He clarifies that "Although semantic usage varies, and important conceptual difference exists between the terms administration and management"[7]. However, he continues with the awkward categorisation of facts and management on the one hand and values and administration on the other hand, to which we shall turn shortly. Nevertheless, for the purpose of nature clarification let us first continue with the superset-subset thesis and the idea that subsets still have distinguishable tasks and thus extremely important by virtue of its own merit. The basic idea underlying the superset-subset relation between administration and management is that though management is a process related to realisation of organisational control, not all forms of administration are called "management" though all forms of management are called "administration" without any doubt. Hence, management of public and private sector companies, whether they run any sort of business or enterprise that is concerned with production and distribution of goods and services and with which goes the conceptions of investment, profit and loss, depend on unique process of administering these companies or corporate by experts trained in such things, but when we speak of various other forms of administration, they are not necessarily dealing with business enterprises and related concepts mentioned above. For instance, when we speak of family as a micro-organisation or the nation state as a macro-organisation and imagine their effective guidance, we do speak of unique processes of administration having goals different from the business organisations. To run a family efficiently or administering a family is not like running a hospital or a factory, because their ways and goals are different. Hence, we use the word "managing" with regard to running family, which is not the same as use of the word "managing" with regard to running a company. The first use of the word is in the context of *administering* a family, that is, to guide, channel, control and flourish in certain ways not by trained experts like able manager, whereas the second use of the word is in the context of *management* of a corporate needing trained experts like able managers performing sets of duties which we have discussed to guide, channel, control and flourish in certain ways. Hence, common usage of words "administration" and "management" are often overlapping, they appear to be the synonymous causing the sense of redundancy of one or the other, but a careful analysis of contextual use of the words clarifies that they are *not* synonymous rather, "it is not always that we manage while we administer but we administer when we manage". The crux of the superset lies in the broader perception of *guidance* of organisation of various types, not only business organisations, needing organisers who are able but not necessarily formally trained having motives of monetary or material gains in their minds. In fact, in administration, management of corporate bodies is neither necessary nor sufficient, but in case of management in particular we do speak of guidance of organisations of different types, needing unique goal oriented trained professionals who care for the benefits of stock and stakeholders in material terms necessarily and sufficiently. It is interesting to answer whether families and nation states need "managers" in the second sense and thus not non-material benefit oriented, non-professional guides. If we argue that modern families need trained parents, perhaps trained in home science and thus managers in the second sense, and the nations need trained lawmakers much like Plato's trained Guardians, do we not accept the truth that our distinction between "administration" (as superset) and "management" (as subset) breaks down? Not really because home science is not necessary and sufficient for our families to run efficiently, because homes do not presuppose or beg a science to run, though the science might give us important cues to run homes more methodically, in which individuals' well being is underlined carefully. The nation states, the most civil ones so to say till date, does not choose lawmakers on the merit of their managerial skills they have learnt in institutions as did Plato's Guardians necessarily and sufficiently because nations do not beg skill to run nations in a certain way, though political science does give us important cues to run states more methodically in which citizen's well being is underlined carefully. Precisely, homes and nations need administrators who are not necessarily and sufficiently trained managers having definite corporate organisational skills, goals and means to achieve the goals in mind. Hence, it is not always that administration amounts to management of an enterprise, though management of an enterprise is a form of administering an enterprise that is, guiding, channelling, controlling and flourishing an enterprise. This is for me the superset-subset relation conveyed by people like Hodgkinson that truly tells us that "management" for its nature clarification should remain careful about compelling vagueness in the usage of the terms "management" and "administration". It is important to remember that the former is a form of the latter but not *vice versa*. Much like this was mentioned at the outset that though management is a process within an enterprise called business, the latter enterprise is not necessarily and sufficiently a management enterprise, it is something more. Hence, a qualification like "business management" is often needed to differentiate "non-business managements" like managing a family or a nation, which we have just seen, is "management" in the "broader perspective" of the term, conveying the idea of non-business "administration" to us. Nevertheless, rightly Hodgkinson says, "Administration is inescapable".

If there is no doubt that administration is an essential aspect of human life and that management is only an important form of administration, where "management" refers to "business management" in particular, that is, managing a broad range of business enterprises involved in production and distribution of goods and services, then we should look into some important features of administration which includes business administration. It is only then that we are better placed to see what makes business administration or business management distinct from the more general or broader form of "administration" that cover subsets of "non-business administration" as well. After drawing the distinction we can find out why concerns about values or better said, ethical values is important for any form of administration, and therefore, for business management/ administration.

Administration is an essential aspect of our life or is 'inescapable' because we are born, brought up and become self-reliant and successful in organisations like family, state and nation; and these organisations are administered in different ways by different people because organised forms of life, different from unorganised lives are marked by their characteristic ways of administration. Organisation cannot remain a body or an existence without being kept together like a close knit unit to act to achieve ends without administrators. Administrators are thus authorities holding rights, duties and obligations to unify and activate forms of life in our societies which have unique aspirations or ends to achieve. It can be large or small public or private sector business units, having distinct entrepreneurial form of life or large or small families, states and nations having distinct dynamic forms of life, each needing guides or authorities bound by their role responsibilities which are either codified or non-codified, having rights and duties to see that a 'coherent whole' functions well and achieves what is desired and what is desirable. Hence, human life as organisational is administered and thus administration is 'inescapable'. We are thus members of complex mesh of organisations, who thrive in a network of organisations ably controlled by administrators/ managers. Every individual encounters organisational administration of complex features because individuals become members of a number of organisations. As member of family an individual is ably guided by unique administration, not of a formal type but most informally, yet, ably. As member of a state and a nation, the individuals are guided by different formal administrations, which are found in schools, colleges and in the different stations of civil life wherein a body of administrators are always vigilant in ensuring what are our legitimate aspirations and rights, duties and obligations. Further, as a member of workplaces, large or small companies or enterprises, individuals are guided by formal administrations of a different type, where ensuring the business goals of parent organisation are primary because for that covenanted members are paid to meet their ends. Hence, we are increasingly under administration, even in death to be sure because the family, society and social institutions have to ensure effective management of the corpse for appropriate payments or legitimate dues to the bereaved ones. Even issuing a medical certificate for natural death or the registration of the same becomes aspects of institutional administration. Private or public hospitals are also responsible in such management. Hence, before birth, after birth, and in death, administration is inescapable though it is not necessary and sufficient that business administration is also an integral part of our life because an individual can escape all sorts of enterprises and managerial administration by remaining a perfect idle or a classic sage for metaphysical reasons. Yet, a solo enterprise of a tiny scale or a well camouflaged religious enterprise of a sage cannot be free from the management intricacies because no business enterprise should be unmanaged or unorganised if it needs to be a business of some sustenance and growth. Even organised begging or crime can be efficiently or inefficiently managed by some people, but in civil societies we do not learn the science of administration or managerial administration of begging and crime, though it may not be altogether queer to learn the finer points of management of a religious enterprise involving workforce and money as well as the management of unemployed self rehabilitating enterprises. It may well be that studying the finer points of administration of a begging or criminal enterprise gives us some cues to the way *undesirable* business practices are run so that we can correct our ways of management of business or we can detect the undesirable ways of business and management to catch hold of them. Hence, it is not always that any form of administration including business administration is desirable, though we accept that they should be "desirable", that is, should have rightful goals to be achieved and proper means to be obtained. It is, therefore, an important and incessant inquiry to crack the desirable and the undesirable techniques of administration and business management. Having organisational forms of life and definite goals are not enough, care for a good form of life and desirable goals are always important. Administration (including business administration) cannot be value-free; therefore, it cannot be unethical to be sure. We can also say that cooperative venture in society almost naturally demands administration of some kind which should not be ethically either neutral or unethical.

Before turning to the value aspect of administration of any form we have to find out the reasons for distinguishing business management as a unique form of administration and thus making sure that business presupposes some administration at least. Taking some cues from the worthwhile writings on the subject by Andrew Dunsire and C. J. Gardner, Christopher Hodgkinson argues that though he (and Derek Allson), do not fully agree to a classification of characteristics of administration *vis-à-vis* management, it may be of preliminary help to note that administration in general is taken as an art which deals in *policy making*, cares for *values* needing some definite *strategy*, *philosophy*, *upper rankings* and *qualitative and reflective approaches* through which, it is *concerned with humans*, a feeling most needed at the *top levels* of management involving a lot of *deliberation*. Whereas management (or what we qualify as business management) is a *specialised science of execution* depending on *factuality*, *tactics*, *action*, *lower rankings* and *quantitative and active approaches* through *material* management at the *mid-level*, and for which, *details* are most important. Granting the truth that there are many incompleteness and ambiguities in such distinction-making, which is far from being clear, Hodgkinson stresses that "in general, however, it can be said that by administration we mean those aspects dealing with more value-laden issues and the human component of organisational life, and by management we mean those aspects that are more routine, programmatic, and amenable to quantitative methods"[8]. The definition needs some clarification. What we understand from the dichotomy of tasks of administration and management is that administration is a generalised form of guiding, controlling and flourishing our forms of life in society, which in turn includes many sub-forms or particular forms of guiding, controlling and flourishing, the best example of which is business administration or what I prefer to call business management. We have also come across the truth that in social administration or in political administration, we do need management and thus the managers, which I preferred to call 'non-business management', the sub-group within the robust superset or super-group. Keeping this basic distinction in mind we can further proceed to see that while the complete activities of administration are carried on at some levels, the management processes that goes within it turns out to be in the main a *means* to the realisation of an administrative *end* in an organisation. Hence, it is not out of the way to speak of administration as *end-focused* whereas management is *means-focused*. In a business house or organisation we do conceive of administration and its end or ends which take on different *methods* than those taken up in non-business organisations. Hence, methodologies of administration differ from business houses to non-business organisations. Nevertheless, in business (as in non-business activities) to fulfil the ends, the administrators need trained people to use the methods at the real levels of moving from models to application and achievements, which are done by managers in management. Management in general administration or in business administration is thus ancillary or auxiliary to effectively choose means to achieve administrative goals or ends. In the human resource development ministry, for instance, the chief administrator, is by virtue of people's representation in democracy the elected minister who ensures the objectives of the office to be realised. For this general administrational objective to be realised, management of various aspects of functioning of the ministry is needed, which is taken up by the management force of the office or the managers in the ministry. The executives and others of the ministry are thus the managers who choose effective ways to realise the desired objectives. The same is the picture in the business houses, private or public, which have different sectors to be administered for goal realisation by obtaining useful methods, which are applied as means by management forces. In this way, even in business administration, management becomes a different *aspect of* administration that ensures the ends to be realised obtaining suitable means. Therefore, the basic difference in administration and management is not that the former means a process that underlines business and non-business goal realisation, whereas the latter means a process that underlines business goal realisation. The difference lies in the truth that administration and management despite going together in business and non-business organisations, the former uses the latter as *means* to its goal, that is, management as an ancillary to administration is nothing but a "means" of fulfilling administrative objectives. However, we must remember that management itself obtains certain means or methods which are useful for its own goal realisation. Thus we have to differentiate management as *means of administration* and *means of management* for administering. It is equally true that general administration has its own methods or models, which are also called "means" in yet another sense. For administration, there are different ways or methods which are different means for its goal realisation. An aspect of one such means or model of administration may be giving all assuming liberties and powers to the managers involved in the management so that the staff members remain more or less "distinct", which is *administration-at-a-distance*, but within this model, the management people might have other sets of means and models, for instance, *managing-by-incentives* though remaining at a distance, whereas others might prefer *managing-by-rod* and remaining at a distance. The whole picture may be different when administration is with the help of a model of *care or feminine empathy*, whereas its means, that is, management takes on models such as the manager as *liaison-taskmaster* among staff or the manager as *integrated-member among staff*. Whatever the case may be it is important to notice that management is an auxiliary science to carry on the art of administration to achieve definite goals and both administration and its auxiliary science have different approaches or models or means to achieve their respective goals. In this sense going to the roots of society, the modern nuclear family of a typical patriarchal trend, there is a conceivable administration that aims at well-being of its members, but to do so its means is perfect management of the unit. In a patriarchal family, household management is taken up by parents by virtue of a division of labour, the financial management going to the wage earner father and the non-financial management going to the householder mother. Hence, at the microcosm, administration uses management, and management uses methods, but both strives to attain definite goals. In the democratic Indian society, the CEO is the Prime Minister heading administration and in the states the CEO is the Chief Minister, who uses management forces to manage the number of tasks to achieve certain goals, the administrative officers or the bureaucrats do a lot of management work here. Hence, the PM and CM as well as the bureaucrats are all parts and parcel of the general administration, they are in one sense managers who manage different things needed for a good administration and thus the well-being of the state and/or the nation state. We should thus say that management as sub-process in the process of administration is hardly separable as two watertight compartments; they are rather inseparable from each other, one involving the other with a difference that it is not necessary and sufficient for all managers to be business managers and thus all administrators to be business administrators. It is also not necessary and sufficient to imagine that as administration subsumes management, all involved in administration must be involved in managerial tasks. The truth is that though staff members of any rank in an organisation some time at least are in administering something, they are least in the management job for a while, because the latter, we have seen, is more of a *technical* task performance as means to administering something needing expertise and know-how of doing things in certain ways better suited than other ways. It may be said that *management is a technocratic job*, a scientific one but suited for some skilled people in the greater body of administering job. In this sense, going back to our roots, in a family even children are found administering when perhaps a renovation work is going on in a household, they are nevertheless, not managers of the household. The petty staffs in government office or a college is found administering when some shifting work is going on, for instance, but they do not become managers of the office. The clerk is administering in a cabinet secretariat office at times, but does not take up management tasks of the secretariat. The peon in a corporate house is found administering some time but not a part of management. This makes clearer why *not* all cases of administration are management, though all cases of management are cases of administration, and therefore, subsumed in administration. An administrator is a manager but not always, but managers are administrators. It is important to note that in most non-business administration amateur administrators are well occupied. Strangely our public colleges and universities have amateur CEOs as Vice Chancellors who have little or no knowledge of management of educational institutions because it is believed that the public educational institutions are non-profit organisations, depending for their funds on grants and subsidies. Of late, with self-financed studies, fund generation and profit making, the universities are gradually feeling the heat of inducting professional managers. Here again, not all involved in running universities may be mangers, only few need to be so, others may be seen contributing variously as administrators. Hence, management, unlike administration is a specialised enterprise, it is organisation focused, that is, specialised as per the needs and aspiration of different organisations. It is due to this that educational management is a different expertise than technological management or hospital or hospitality management. Yet, these organisations need universal or generalised form of governance, that is, administration. Administration in this sense is dealing with general governance and fixing strategies for which expert managers are used for effectively carrying out the strategies fixed for attaining desired goals. Most of the time when management is left to non-experts or non-technical persons, a number of malfunction and unethicality creeps in. This is characteristic of many organisations in India, even those which are profit-making.

When we turn to the types of administration, such as business administration and educational administration, an interesting question is whether it is proper to qualify the more generic notion of administration with specific enterprises like ‘business’ and ‘educational’ and so on? Is it not true that such qualification truly refers to types of management? Hence, when we speak of “business administration", we are really speaking of "business management", and for that matter a study of business management should be distinguished from a study of general administration. The methods and principles of administration is thus differently studied whereas business management studies aspects of general administration and specific features of specialised administration or specialised means of administration, called "business management". In this sense, "business management" must keep in mind features of administration and try to find out the ways or means of special application of administrative theories in business practices. In a sense, administration gives us policies to achieve ends, which policies are based on certain philosophy of action, planning and politics or the impetus to translate philosophy into action, whereas its *means*, that is, management is to *implement the policies* based on mobilisation, managing and monitoring. Whatever the case may be, administration *per se* requires a clear goal and a *leadership* to attain that goal. Very often "leadership" is taken as synonymous to "administration" because to administer or to deliver or to govern a body amounts to lead the same with efficacy. Truly, it is extremely difficult to imagine an organisation bereft of leadership and management. Hence, we do not speak only of administration and management, rather of leadership as well. This focuses the importance of philosophy of action on the one hand, and translation of such philosophy into action on the other hand, juxtaposing the missing link, the flag-bearer of an organisational goal, a philosophy and its ground reality application, which is the task of leadership. Leadership is thus an essential element in both administration and management with a difference that in administration the leadership is taken more as a desirable trait of a person who has goals set to be realised, whereas in management it is not only a desirable trait, a valuable requirement, rather, a real life personality who takes on occupational challenges almost as a matter of factual necessity expected to be naturally present among the managers without any exception or option. In this sense, management turns out to be real life affair at the ground levels of translating administrative philosophies and policies into action. Management is thus an involvement with facts given the system of administrative values. This is not to say that management is value-free rather, it is permeated with values through the generic administration of which it is a sub-set, but it is more of dynamicity, and actions as based on the given values. It is through the process of management that the collective interest of the organisation is fulfilled. Administrative value system does recognise "collective interest fulfilment" as extremely important but to *talk* about values is not to have them at hand; to have them at hand, we need actions at the level of management as based on values. Without translation of ideas into practice, policies and decisions into actions and great utopias into reality, "the administrator is diminished to managerial factotum and a value antisepsis is achieved which in theory defines reality but in truth constitutes a sort of hypocrisy"[9]. If administration and management does not want to be Hippocratic, the gulfs between values and reality, and ideals and actuality need to be bridged. More often than not great administrative ideals back up our managers to act but the great hypocrite does the other way round, he or she acts as per own values to idealise it as a system and thinks that everything is all right in the world. The valuelessness and the unethicality are common phenomena in today's administration and management owing to the nagging myopia that the harsh real world awaiting administration, control, guidance, and management and so on has one value, "do as you wish for the realisation of the organisational goal". The liberty of the moral agent in decision-making does not guarantee ruthless subjectivity in imposing values or even sticking to an obsessive role of goal achiever. It is extremely important to find out what things are worthwhile in administration and management. Let us turn to the conception or worthwhileness in the more generic administration, management will follow suit as its sub-set.

The first issue in value considerations in administrations is whether "organisations" waiting administration, at all pose problems of values, such as moral values? The scepticism emerges from the idea that values, particularly moral values makes any sense in the context of humans and not non-human beings and things which have no system of evaluating the worth of their intended voluntary actions and the worth of their ideas, thoughts, opinions and so on. Hence, a system of values makes sense only in the context of human thoughts, ideas, opinions, beliefs, knowledge, acts and so on, and for which some evaluative function is needed at the intersubjective level. We have considered this issue in the context of finding out the importance of value-related talks in business and corporate activities. We came to the conclusion that though corporate (and also organisations) are our conceptions, constructed out of the group involvement of individuals with regard to production, distribution, profits and so on in intricate business activities, they are as such *not* mute or inert because organisations are essentially bodies constituted by some humans who come together for fulfilling their wants and aspirations and thus take intentional decisions and act accordingly, which in turn affect them and others in the society amounting to moral evaluations based on available criteria. Hence, even if organisations appear to be mute physical existential, they are nonetheless, represented through a gamut of unique activities which cannot be left out without proper moral evaluation for right, just, good, and so on. Hence, it is always sensible to talk about ethical values in particular and other non-ethical values in general with regard to the organisational decisions and acts. We have seen that organisations are inseparably bound with administering and thus administration, the said dynamics cannot be left without evaluation, and for that matter talks about ethical and other values are natural with regard to administration. If that be true, the means of administration, that is, management as unique dynamics is within the focus of values and evaluation, both ethical and otherwise. As such, if organisational dynamics are bereft of the focus on values, especially ethical values, we must say that it is value-free or even valueless, in which case (though it is difficult to understand), organisations as organisations lose their intrinsic character because as organisations, the bodies are essentially oriented towards *value-charged dynamics* or dynamics continually considering the "desirable" aspects of "doing" as most important. In that case, administration, and management as administration, lose their basic characteristic bereft of value-orientation because they fail to remain constantly focused towards what "should" be "done". Therefore, talks about values including ethical values are built-in the nature of organisations and inseparably to aspects of administering and managing the organisations. With this we must say that the sceptical challenge to conceive of organisations as bodies without consciousness and will, and thus value-free, is itself an unethical or valueless conception about the most basic aspect of social life because looking at organisations in such a manner amounts to some kind of aggressive neurosis among the individuals who are its members, who will never aspire collectively to achieve "desirable ends" in life overcoming many challenges to evolve as law abiding and ethical states. Some degree of freedom left to treat organisations as 'moral primitives' would amount to the rise of self assuming leaders or chauvinists, who for petty gains and power would champion power-tracking than moral-tracking resulting into dire states of immorality. Hodgkinson refer to Victor A. Thomas who holds that the value-free conception of an organisation amounts to "bureausis", a kind of neurotic vision that tends to exploit "mute organisations" for ego gains, that is, to loot, conquer, sabotage and so on. It is a pity to say that the nation that is India has been looted, conquered and sabotaged by minor forces more so as the outsiders since 1947 owing to such neurosis. Many Indians go on vandalizing social organisations mercilessly till date; one good example is to tatter into pieces the Nehruvian era public sector industries by the "bureautics". Our birth right to remain valueless has made the mixed economy the farce as it now stands amidst the back-thumping orchestra of privatisation and globalisation, and free trade. Well, that does not mean that these are neurotic visions, what is true is that they have only grown on the ashes of public sectors, which were left over of our effigies burnt to the last straw. Hence, we have to give up the neurotic vision about the organisations disoriented toward values, ethical in the main, so that we do not lose sight of the truth that organisations are for our well-being. William G. Scott and David K. Hart, says Hodgkinson, have maintained that organisations stands of the good of the collective and the individuals and the good of the organisations is possible if its members have a vision for the good of the organisation. Hence, if organisations have built-in ethical aim for human well-being, humans should reciprocate ethically. If this be the case then people or groups of people responsible by virtue of their temperament and training to guide, control and run the organisational dynamics for the desirable goal, then the administrators and the managers must have all respect for the ethical values like maximisation of administrative efficiency or be rational to administer. They should be loyal to the organisation or are stewards of organisations and should be expedient to concentrate on short term objectives for higher realisations, that is, they must be pragmatic. A careful consideration tells us that on the whole the administrators must be ethically oriented or must be value-oriented or must be value-charged. How can managers (as administrators), in management be callous to these basic ethical aspects?

Nevertheless, once we are engaged in ethically relevant discussion, that is, administrative ethics, we should not forget that skimping ethical criticisms are not good for ethics. Hence, it may not be essential for us to accept without qualification that the conception of ethical administration of Scott and Hart is acceptable *in toto*, rather we might argue that this is though a new vision in administrational value-orientedness, it is "paternalistic" than matriarchic because despite the universal values of the ends of organisations and individuals, we cannot universally agree that being rational, efficacious and pragmatic in the sense in which Scott and Hart has taken them to be, is ethically acceptable. We may thus start an interesting debate whether such American ethicality can be universal in organisations as such? Why should administrative 'rationality' be the same as (or only as), optimisation of efficacy of the leaders, when that is nothing but expected from our managers? Why should materialistic achievements be placed at its peak? Is organisational and human good exclusively scientific and materialistic? Further, we may ask, why expedient and efficient administrators be myopic in recognising the short-term goals by putting long-term ideals in abeyance? If human good be supreme, can it be guaranteed when we are so practical to some good for the humans 'now' and leave out the future generations? Moreover, it is not always that stewards should be primarily obedient and committed to the good of the organisation. This may be only largely true of society as an organisation or the national organisation, wherein the administrators take great interest in the good of the collective because in that way, good of the individual members are taken care of. However, steward model always opens the question whether organisational well-being does sufficiently take care of individual good that is, involved in an empathetic way to the most downtrodden individual's well-being. The same may be the case when we consider the stewards acting for the good of the company on financial terms and thus either leave out employees' well-being or the well-being of the customers; or to place customers' good as supreme to tax the employees. On what does holistic good of a company depend remains an interesting ethical question. The ethical debate might thus reduce to consider whether organisational well-being can be ethically superior if there are some degrees of imbalances in individual well-being. It also takes us to consider whether definition of organisational well-being should be peer-determined? If peer-determination be the case, there may be everlasting conflict among the peer-leaders in administration and their value-systems taken as sacrosanct and those whose good is at stake. Should it be corroborative, the ethically desirable objectives and ways are *discovered* collectively and that too in an objective fashion? If that be the case, how organisational values are discovered is interesting to notice. This may be the major consideration in the chapters to follow.

It may well be that organisations are always at the cross-roads of determining the desirable ends and means. It is most likely that those in administration and management feel some heat in the face of such tension, but that is an unavoidable ethical crisis. The crux of the crisis is who should have the ethical authority in determining the value-system in organisation? Should it be enjoyed by administrators, those exclusively trained so that their choice of desirable ends and means are accepted for our good? Or, do we refrain from giving absolute power to administrators for their ego-satisfaction because absolute power corrupts absolutely? Hodgkinson reminds that "For the organisation to survive, to satisfy its metavalues, sanctions must operate to ensure at least a partial hegemony of discipline over indulgence. Typically, these are of two kinds. First, there are collective sanctions, reinforced by society, of conventional norms, conventional morality, and the "axioms" of political value, the constraints of consensus, law, rules, regulations…. The second sanction to discipline occurs when there is self-commitment, the individual attachment to or investment in an organisational collective value by way of ideology, religion or philosophical reflection"[10]. This reminds us of the external and the internal sanctions mentioned by Bentham and Mill to explain why transmutation of egoistic hedonism to altruistic hedonism is possible. However, here ethicality do not depend on completely bashing administrators' value-system because despite their legitimate satisfaction by choice of ethical goals and means, they have the moral authority to see that the collective morality does not overrun ethical values of administrators just for accommodation? This may be important for us in a later discussion. In fact, we must remember the fact that administrators as administrators are faced with many ethical challenges and their resolution in a complex atmosphere of overriding cultural values which need stiff ethical evaluation from within, a party to which should be administrators as social being whose overriding academic/technical values awaits internal and cultural checks.

Overall administration makes a good case of ethical interception and thus administrative ethics makes a good case for study. Justification of administrative ethics is never complete when such a brief study and sweeping remarks are made, but our task is to move to management as a form of administration and find out why ethical interceptions are needed there, and why management ethics is justified. However, winding up the present discussion we can say that "administrative ethics" as a branch of practical ethics discusses ethically relevant issues in the field of administration in general that includes the desirable end or means of administration, the desirable types and structures of administrations, the desirable models or methods of administration and so on. A careful study reveals that at the point of administration there are many value-laden issues needing resolution. We discuss under administrative ethics how these issues ought to be resolved. Similarly, when we approach ethics, we find that performance of some of its tasks, like the normative, the practical and the virtue related pervades the field of administration and thus makes ethics sensible in these non-ethical discourses. In any case, administrative ethics turns out to be an encouraging field of application of ethical knowledge to explore and resolve value-laden issues in administration. We have seen that though general administration is basic to management, the specific field of management is a means to fulfil the administrative enterprises in a technical or scientific manner by some qualified or skilled managers in the field of business and elsewhere. We have argued that management as administrative enterprise is filled with value-related issues or it is value-oriented. As a branch of applied ethics, it is our task to find out what it means to deal with "management ethics".

To call "management ethics" as concerned with ethically relevant topics in management is vague, it needs clarification. However, our discussion about the nature of "management" has made things easier because thus far we have seen what is the enterprise called "management", how it is related to administration as well as different from it and why ethical questions are nearly unavoidable when management appears as its subset. Avoiding any repetition about the nature and tasks of ethics, we have to say that "ethically relevant" topics or issues in management are many and not one, but before we enter into the details we can say that broadly speaking, management ethics is ethical interception in the non-ethical matters of management of the different organisational functions. Such ethical interceptions are at the meta-level, where such interception is about the justification of the ethical interception in non-ethical matters like management. Much like this was discussed before when sceptics challenged why should there be any ethical interference in the matters of business, corporate, administration and so on. At the *normative* level ethical interception is about the *bases of evaluation* of managerial decisions, policies, actions, means and ends as ethically desirable, good, right, just and so on. At the *virtue ethical* level of interception, we find out *which virtues are needed* primarily and essentially for any managerial enterprise to be evaluated as good, right and so on. At the *practical* level of interception, we discuss how ethically charged issues in management, that is, issues about right and just of management practices be *resolved.* These four in the main clarifies what amounts to the 'ethically relevant' study of management. However, this may be supplemented ably with a clarification of those managerial intricacies that opens vistas for ethical inquiries, that is, why should such intricacies be not taken as merely technical but ethical as well. Readers already have the glimpse of the two broad ways in which we can "justify" management ethics as sensible within ethics. Hence, to discuss the nature of management, ethics will take us to its tasks or its concerns and getting involved into that means we are in the realm of the two-pronged justification. Nevertheless, a little different from jumping straightway into the above justification we should first see why is ethically relevant study of management so needed or valued by some of us. What if we do not care for ethical study of management matter? If management is left alone, does it progress without ethicality? Is it not a kind of trespassing into a field which does not need ethics in any case? One strong argument in favour of ethical interception in management matters is that bereft of it management is conceivable, but a *progressive* management and progressive managers are inconceivable. A dynamic management that is progressive does not remain within the shackles of old hegemonies and traditions to show signs of inhuman attitudes because that is not desirable of management. Hence, to consider the value of management towards a desirable human progress is measured through the moral progress we have made. The ideal of moral progress is so cherished because its corollary that is, regress, means back to our animal basics that loses the progress we have made through the ages by dominating our animal instincts, and gross wants, desires, motives and intentions, by way of criticising and evaluating them and so on. The number of progress that we have made by virtue of the things mentioned above traces mainly to the biological and the psychological evolution. We have been further able to make quantum progresses in understanding the nature, its governing laws and manipulating nature for different purposes, which is the basic to the sciences, though the scientific progresses in turn owes to the more basic biological and psychological powers we have grained through the ages. However, the scientific and technological progresses have so eluded our minds and rationality that we forget that we have been always critical about the progresses that do harm than good. We know that certain things would be injurious to human progress, yet we proceeded with them and were criticised for unethicality. We know that certain things are injurious to us, we go on encouraging such so-called scientific progresses because ethicality in the scientific domain is stipulated by its own positivistic definitions. In the name of "human good", "well-being", "human progress", the great ethical ideal that they are, we continue with the so-called scientific and technological progresses we have made. Nevertheless, we strive to be ethically focused and make strong statements to show why the said ethical ideals are antagonised by scientific ideals. Of late, we came to realise that human progress cannot be attributed to the scientific progresses, much in discontent to Karl Popper because human progress is evaluated in complex terms, it is not so simplistic. Other aspects of phenomenal human progress are that we invented languages, literatures, arts, crafts and so on. We were also progressive in terms of rationality to see the value of contract and co-operative life. In such terms, we know the value of barter, market, corporate, business, profits, and financial prowess and so on. We came to know that human progress was unthinkable if people had no zeal to produce and distribute goods and services. No doubt our linguistic, artistic and commercial progresses owe to the progresses made in the sciences, particularly the positive sciences; nevertheless, the linguistic, artistic and commercial progresses *per se* cannot be diluted, they can be said to be aided progresses or *subordinated progresses*. This must be done of educational progress as well. The cultural and civil progresses cannot be said as completely unaided by the scientific progresses. Yet, we need to remember that the aided progresses themselves contributed or supplemented the sciences greatly for its quantum progress. All things said and done, can we not say that scientific and other non-scientific progresses owe much to our *moral progress*. Refraining from the role of the moral progress in scientific progress and many other non-scientific progresses, let us concentrate on the commercial progress through which we shall move on to the progresses made in management, taking commercial management as paradigm.

In an absorbing essay Stan Godlovich states that though there are stiff arguments against the conception of commercial progress fully realised if and only if through moral progress, we can still refute them to show that business or commercial progress is *subordinate* to moral progress. He mentions the famous argument of Kant in *The Fundamental Principles of the Metaphysics of Morals* (1785) that commerce and morality are at odds when, for instance, we take the case of "honesty", which is an evaluative conception used in ethical parlance to evaluate things like commercial or business activities, which for Kant is "savvy honesty" as distinct from pure "moral honesty". Kant argues that "honesty is the best policy" amounts to an ethical or evaluative statement if and only if "honesty" in business is taken as a "moral" policy in business, that is, a policy which is not valuable for its consequences or *teleos* or purposes, rather, as good itself or for its *intrinsic value*. In this sense, the above statement is an ethical imperative that speaks of the practice of "honesty" for its intrinsic worth as one's *duty* and not to *use it as means* for ulterior ends, which is the case when "commercial" or "savvy honesty" is in question, that is, stated as hypothetical statement reading: "honesty is a *useful* business policy". When "honesty" becomes "policy" or "tactics" for getting ulterior ends, commerce and ethics are at the loggerheads. Hence, what we call, "commercial or business honesty" is in fact, morally neutral or even unethical honesty. Nevertheless, Kant's arguments nicely portrays why commercial activities have lost the moral ground, which it have gained. If Kant meant to say that commerce in itself is bereft of moral vision, he must have mistaken the truth because he must have remembered that there is every possibility of moral orientation in commerce or a moral progress that supports commerce or that morally subordinated commercial progress, lest there is least truth in deontology. Why should it not be read as argument of Kant which shows why commercial progress in its "savviness" is not a full progress until it orients interested people in such enterprise to value the necessary enterprises as intrinsic and thus be treated as duties? In this sense, the much abused "profit making" in business may be a deontologically glossed ideal because the inherent value of profits and not losses, drags entrepreneurs to profiteering in an ethically oriented manner. There must be no reason to abuse profiteering in commerce, therefore, either in terms of abusing gains or in terms of necessary nuisance because with it we abuse business itself as an activity that has given humans the needed progress we have discussed before. What is a good or ethical business without profits is not understandable. Hence, business can be ethical and thus progress when we take cues from Kant to say that business ideals, strategies and methods needs to be deontologically good or we take cue from Mill to say that they need to be utilitarian good and so on. There is thus scope for us to throw some light on how business can progress aided by ethical orientation, and without it, we are as I have said, back to our basics like "honesty is good in business in so far as it gives me optimum corporeal pleasure". This is much better hyped in the older feudal economy when in the matters of distribution of wealth the widening of poor-rich gap was preferred. However, the act of distribution becoming more and more humane is a testimony to the ethical questions of "just" distribution where gaps are not widened or maintained but closed as far as possible through proper methods. The study of such methods becoming a pet issue for awarding Nobel prizes is nevertheless, not glorified by Mr. Nobel and his successors; the ethical urgency of "just distribution", which is inherently an "ethical just distribution" came to the focus, when advocated very strongly by a Greek called Aristotle. The moral anomalies in distribution thus shows why moral progress is so required on our part in matters of commerce. Nevertheless, this does not amount to say that morally oriented or a morally progressive business practice makes us well-off. This may not be the case in reality. More often than not being "well-off" is a terrific vague conception because it begs paradigms of flourishing economically, most of the time meaning monetarily well-off through huge monetary and other physical gains. However, without being well-off in such terms we can still conceive of our non-material well-being in cultures. Hence, it is difficult to maintain that relatively less monetarily or physically well-off do not attain their well-being. The morally progressive commerce may not be a poor commerce or non-profiteering commerce, but equally true is that it may not be optimally physically gratificatory commerce because optimum physical gratification indulges us to moral corruptions or undesirable practices which are harmful to society at large. It is, therefore, important to be under moral cheeks to evolve as morally charged persons and take on business as an enterprise which is on the one hand physically progressive and on the other hand indicative of multifarious progresses made by humans. However, it is debatable whether evolution of a morally progressed person who involves in business practices is so because one is an avowed deontologist or a teleologist. Are standard ethical norms isolated to be morally progressive? Do we imagine that an avowed Kantian or Utilitarian has morally progressed and for that matter should either apply such progress related theses in business practices for having a progressive business? Can there be a morally progressive business practice without normative predilections? We shall find out an answer to this in the following chapters. For the time being it is important to note that business practices without moral orientation is not progressive in the "full" sense because in that way humans as humans do not progress to their full potential by doing some such things which were not expected of them though they had every opportunity to do the desirable. Business practices, when they are only *raw*, that is, materially aggressive progress, when they are *cumulative* or merely purposive and when they are *ameliorative* or mere improvement on earlier states, are not fully progressed, says Godlovitch. Moral progress, which is far different from these and that becomes a strong aspect of the moral man in civil states is thus needed over and above the man being a businessman. Godlovitch writes: "Can one seriously contemplate as preferable a world governed *superordinately* by commercial or technological imperatives? Unlike these domains, morality credibly illuminates what we do generally and always in our collective interests.... Of all domains to which we attribute progress, morality allows us not only to measure improvement retrospectively, but uniquely provides intelligibly clear, global, weakly teleological ends in the form of determinate and absolute constraints"[11]. Thus we have the argument that ethics in business is extremely important. Now the point is, why should the same be the case with management? Why should we argue that management of business should be subordinate to ethical practices? First argument is derived from what was said earlier in this chapter, that is, management is an inseparable aspect of effective business practice because without it there is no good business practice in the practical sense. If business is itself a subordinate to morality, its contributing means cannot be immoral.

Based on the conception of ethicality as basic to the scientific, technological and commercial enterprises and the idea that the "positive tone" of management, which is management based on ethicality is truly "master management", we now proceed to see what exactly management ethics is and why is it so valuable. Let us proceed with this explanation a little farther. It is argued that management ethics or what we have been calling 'ethically relevant study of management practices' should be at the outset distinguished from moral management and even amoral and non-moral management for its nature clarification. Morality as distinguished from ethicality consider the uncritical or unphilosophical moves, habits and customs because the social practices cannot wilfully negate or abscond the moral taboos, obsessions and prejudices, which have been as a matter of habit accepted by us without any critical inquiry. Among the social practices, the practice of management as a tool of administration, particularly in the field of business is not completely free from the obsessive moral pressure that have also uncritically become a way of managerial life or even corporate life. In the course of such traditional moral practices in management several evil or immoral taboos have crept in which is as distinctive and shameless as it was in the ages of serfdom and feudalism. Hence, the term "moral" or "morality" cannot by itself save the face of management if the same amounts to acceptance of traditional or customary laws or codes of morality as have been given to us through the ages. Traditionally in the name of moral management, we have followed an unwritten but popular code of morality in the business houses in India that the best way to manage the utterly reluctant and politicised workforce is to give favours to the notorious leaders among them to do a cliché with the group and in the long run blackmail the leader to the optimum to not only pull the venom out of the leader and the group, but when needed throw him out as a needless trash. And the cycle goes with fresh notorious faces coming up. The policy of divide and rule, and the unwritten moral wisdom to do so *for the good of the company* as a covenanted manager has been seen by many of us in the coalfields, tea gardens and in almost all small and large production units. The morality of "for the good of the company", a paid manager can thus divide and rule and can play a game of dirty politics, can be immoral, commend a disvalue and not a value. Why is this case? The reason is that the ethical critiques of such so-called morality or customary moral behaviour are most needed when inherent unethicality calls for urgent rectification. Hence, it is not always that ethicality is morality or the *vice versa*. It is due to this that rather than using loosely the term "morality", it should be qualified with the term "*philosophical* morality" to remind us that armed with a philosophical inquiry, our customary morality can be tested for validity, otherwise should not be accepted. Hence, a philosophical critique of the moral practices or the practices that are thought to be not only *natural* to the science but *customarily moral* as well, is what constitutes ethics of management or ethical management. D.M. Green (1994) and C. C. Walton (1988) in their works thus justify that though 'moral managers' pose as 'ethical managers' through many resembling behavioural patterns, the former is the customary manager, taking what is going on for the good of the corporate as good itself, whereas the latter always inquires whether what is going on good for the corporate and if it be so, on what grounds or on what norms and if it is not so, on what grounds or on what norms? An ethical management is thus systematic normative inquiry into the corporate governance, its desirable aspects, right, just, good, duty, obligations put to the most thorough criticisms before acceptance and subsequent practices. Management ethics is thus applied branch of ethics that ensures the several managerial practices are thoroughly scrutinised on the bases of available ethical grounds before indulging into any practice, and shaping decision-making rules that *should* work in the future management. One important question is whether 'ethical inquiry based on ethical grounds' is taken necessarily as an inquiry based on normative ethical theories? This will be answered later on when we argue that ethical inquiry is not merely normative/theoretical inquiry, it is something more. Further clarifying the nature of management ethics we can say that ethical inquiries have a disposition to permeate into different fields because many relevant issues in non-ethical fields await such an inquiry, which is also true of management because here we shall see shortly that many value-laden issues await ethical resolution. Taking cues from the earlier chapter and the paper by Godlovich we can say that management ethics is ethical inquiry into *macro* or *global* economic orders and corporate practices, *molar* or *organisational* issues that ranges from within an institution to between institutions and micro or individual behaviours and practices that are either for or against business enterprises. With this, it may be said that management ethics is ethically based inquiry into all levels of managerial practice.

To embark upon the value of management ethics something has been broadly underlined in the early part of this chapter. Still it is worth noting according to Petrick and Quinn that management ethics enhances individual business judgements and performance through "stimulation of the moral imagination, identification and ordering moral evaluation. Tolerating moral disagreements and ambiguity, integrating managerial competence and moral competence and eliciting a sense of moral responsibility"[12]. The authors also make a strong point that improvement of managerial performance in all the corporate sectors is possible by virtue of management ethics because such ethical orientation enables managers to know the disvalues of unethical conducts in corporate, non-awareness of value related issues in managerial role-responsibilities, non-integrity in corporate, corruption in organisation and undesirable organisational order. Correlative to those are the values of management ethics, that is, it enables managers to be ethically charged in workplace conduct, respond to value-laden managerial roles, integrate in and with the organisation, avoids corruption and strives for desirable organisational order.

We are now well placed to see why management ethics is a justified study within ethics, thus making a strong point to those who argue that management has least involvement with ethics or *vice versa*. First we shall find out the cases in management that involves ethics almost necessarily, though this is a gigantic task, nevertheless, I will touch on key issues. We have seen that management of business organisations (refraining from non-business management henceforth), is an act of a leader. A manager needs to be a leader in a corporate, without which apart from other things discreet individuals having their own motives, goals and aspirations, their egoistic desires may not "team up", which is most needed for an organisational function. Hence, leadership trait and teamwork are important aspects of management. It is most expected of a corporate leader to be a good *educator* and a good *speaker* because the manager-leader has to unambiguously express what the company wants him to do and thus how he wants to fulfil his goals with the help of his comrades-in-work. It is also important for him to convey the message and thus educate comrades the ways in which things ought to be done so that goal-fulfilment without any inhumanity is possible. Hence, governance of the employees demand that managers as leaders should not be value-neutrally goal-oriented or what Kant says, is a "savvy" person who is a mere middle-man in the extraction of profits for company by exploiting comrades-in-work or the employees. The idea of the "ought" opens the door for an ethical inquiry into the "employee based" thinking in management. Does employee based thinking in leadership help? 'To help' does not mean to say that some physical benefits needs to be siphoned from the shareholders to the employees because it is equally ethically important to ask whether foolhardy extraction of benefits out of the core body to those who are not willing to contribute to the corporate, is ethical? Does leadership not demand legitimate basis to combine expression of shareholder benefits and the education of how that can be achieved and why the same should be done with a human face? The crisis in ethical management is thus a crisis of ethically based leadership in which employer's and employee's good together save the leader who is standing at the crossroads of choice of norms to meet the crisis. It is at this point that the fiduciary duties, and the supererogatory acts of the company and the leader open up for ethical scrutiny.

As said above, a leader-manager in the modern day management need not be chauvinistic not only because it is unethical but also unpragmatic. The approach of "bossing from the top" or "the carrot and the rod" does not work ethically and practically because a manager needs to be wise to realise peer-needs and the needs of the comrades-in-work. In this tension, a manager has to team-up with many others in a corporate who have different role-responsibilities though together they strive for the corporate good (and also human good at large). The problem of managing the workforce or the employees, which is also known as *human resource management* (HRM) (to the distaste of many because humans are taken as "resources" like other natural resources though the humans have a vanity that they are the peers in existence), anyway demands that at the end of management force and at the end of human resource there are ample scope for ethical inquiry into the legitimacy of ethical basis for *teaming* and *re-teaming*. The most widely talked about ethic of teaming draws strength from the conception that management through division of labour or classifying managers in watertight job-allotments does not have the ethicality of cooperation and thus the more ethical, holistic management based on the idea of management of the 'knowledge era' is missed out. Charles M. Savage explains: "Instead of fitting people to jobs, people will team with others to seize emerging business opportunities. Instead of closely controlling people, we will set cultural norms and values and trust people. And instead of assuming blind self-interest, we find interest in other selves sets a whole new dynamic of creativity in motion. This last point is key to opening up the Knowledge Era."[13] The ethical brooding into the affair of leaders in management seeking cooperation and empathetic involvement with other managers and employees reminds of the deontic argument that as managers, one has imperative duty to *respect* the covenant one has entered into by being a member of the corporate and thus to respect the corporate integrity, as well as the teleological argument that as manager one has the duty towards teaming up or empathetic involvement in corporate well being because that amounts ultimately to the manager's own advantages or benefits; or, alternately, there is a spurt in social welfare. In any case entering into the deontic ethical theory unilaterally is fraught with problems because other theories are at liberty to challenge them. In management ethics it is always important and interesting to find out the logical strengths in normative thinking about these issues. The above statement of Savage cannot be thus a scared prophecy in management ethics because ethical inquiries do not stick to sacredness of truths. Hence, it will be always asked, why should taking "interest in other selves" in management be ethically justifiable if comparative calculus of the interest of the firm and the paid leader is not fulfilled? Why should covenanted officers not take prime interest in the health of the firm and themselves by having some degree of "sympathy" but not overindulgent in "empathy"? Why should teaming be all imposing and good if too many cooks in reality spoilt the soup? Is it not true that losing control over employees by not acting from a distance is unethical because that kills the parent organisation surely but slowly, which has been a feature of the history of public organisations in India? The flip side of the coin is equally interesting when the success of knowledge revolution enables us to see the truth that through effective corroboration of managerial knowledge as well as employees value perceptions, corporate emerge as integrated units, and integration pays because it is based on the ethic of holistic well-being in cooperation. Ethic of teaming is thus based on the conception that leaders are good when they act in a coherent whole. Members in an organised whole thus have opportunity to reflect on what lies 'beyond self', which is pathway to the more ethical *teleos* of *self-realisation.* It may well be that with some *spiritual inputs*, the teaming-up thesis might make a heavenly ride to *realisation of the Self,* which is more encouraged by a number of prodigal *gurus* of business who, much like Cephalus in Plato's *The Republic* at some age at least counts the merit of being honest to pay the debts to the society by being nobler; and nobler is to be spiritual, which is to be ethical (!). The beauty of ethics is that it may be too acidic to a *teleos* in management that dwells in the realm of the ethical on the merit of being 'spiritual'. The merit of being non-spiritual (not anti-spiritual) but corroborative, integrative and so on should not be downplayed. Why on earth should management take a piggy ride to the seventh heaven on the back of spirituality is difficult for many others to gulp. Anyway, it still remains interesting in management when it opens gates for ethical entry into its teaming-up strategy.

Speaking of strategic management reminds us of *public relations*, that is, the managerial prerogative to be master *communicator* because the same has apart from other bases to be called worthy, based on the ethical conception of "justice is unity". However, we should not be nurturing the wrong idea that to be able "speaker" managers have to be physically present, because apart from making a physical pressure and speaking to other managers and employees, managers communicate in many ways today. Today communicative management is also not restricted to a company or some companies at a locale, it is trans-locale and trans-national. With the acceptance and growth of free-trade, multinational companies have gained great value, wherein managers need not always govern or manage within a space; they transcend defined boundaries and even defined time through several means of communication. With the complexity of communication emerge complex ethical crises for the managers, particularly when the person has to communicate needed ideas and orders across different groups of people who are expected to perform allotted tasks. A manager has to communicate across people living in different cultures, value systems, and moral trends, social, political and economic conditions notwithstanding certain basic national values, mores, social and cultural values under which the manager himself exists. Most peculiar fact is that the manager has merged with a definite organisational ethics, work ethics and atmosphere of work-life, which cannot and should not be given up because any member of an organisation, whether he or she is a trans-national employee or manager, cannot jump the basic ethos of the organisation and the basic aims of the organisation. Hence, respecting these, the managers are found standing at the ethical crossroad to *integrate* a workforce that is essentially discrete in many ways and the stakeholders or the clients who are divergent in many ways as well. Why is it extremely valuable to integrate on the part of the manager who has to find methods for cultural transmutation? Why should managers be a party to find out a basal corporate culture and impose it as a necessity on the clients and the employees by means of strategic transmutation of individual's basic culture to the alien one? What is the ethical basis for discovering a unique corporate value system combining work ethos and work culture etc. and expect from people of various cultures to integrate into an alien systems? This must be very painful and unethical to many among us. The opening up of Indian economy has imported many cultural and corporate ethoses, whose managers are at pains to sell them hard for alienation. Why is this alienation ethically desirable? Some Indians argue that with several corporate ethoses and basal corporate culture of 'gains at any cost' has come many diseases, in particular a diseased perception of values, ethical and non-ethical. Interestingly, when certain so-called basal corporate values are objected by members of a particular culture and even a particular corporate body, why should managers still act flag-bearers of the integrated values? This must be far too complex worldwide, if the company has global connections. Yet, one might argue that a company within and outside a community takes on huge responsibility to do some social good. A company does take up the challenge to uplift the economic status of its own people (including the manager) and all shareholders, employees and stockholders across the globe. In doing so, though not perceivable at once, a lot of good to the economically backward and the socially deprived people are done. Is this not a driving ethical objective so that managers are induced to act a PRO-in-chief to integrate people across the cultures? The organisational social responsibility of the managers must be basic cultural transmutation and integration. Nevertheless, in management ethics we will hotly contest on the ethical basis of whether the simplistic vision of a universal corporate ethos should at all call for cultural scapegoats to sacrifice.

Closely related to the management role of relating to the public across the globe and manage based on values and not power, are the ethical issues that emerge in cross-national alliances and international technology and man-power transfer, which in turn may be evaluated in the broader perspectives of globalisation, privatisation and liberalisation of economies with the growing glitz of a "global village". Collaboration has been the key to the success of man through the ages. How can commerce or business be far behind? Business is a collaborative effort and so is management because both refer to close interaction, relation and integration among stakeholders, stockholders, shareholders, employees and so on. In the modern times, the business collaboration has transcended boundaries of nation states, it has truly become trans-national or cross-national, and so has become management of cross-national organisations. However, it is not that there is a sudden growth in such alliances, it has been gradual through the ages, changing its features with changing stress on resources, growing needs and aspirations, and the phenomenal changes in markets and communication systems with subsequent dependence of them. The business alliances can be of short or long term among many or a few companies involving a few nations. The global interdependence thus calls for the global alliances for managers, each of them crossing boundaries of nations, cultures, value perspectives for the search of an "integration" because that is touted to be ethical on the grounds of deontology and teleology. It is a truism that as human societies have flourished through the ages owing to cooperation, it is "just" to be in unity and not to remain in diversity. For this there is a need that ethically oriented management should educate managers and others such as the employees and even the public that without giving up some of our compartmentalised values, mores and norms, we cannot be citizens of the global village in which activities such as business flourish. Naturally, therefore, we ought to have a universal vision of welfare through economic exchanges, for which managers have to strive hard. Modern management thus takes great ethical interest in evaluating why strategic management should be transmutative, where managers come out of their comfort zones of value-isolation to mingle in a milieu of administrative ethos that serves the organisations best for their goal achievement, mainly 'profiteering with a human face'. Nevertheless, cross-national alliances face stiff ethical questions from the management perspectives. The point is, there is hardly a friendship among weak and strong or among the unequal and for that matter in allied management we have to see the nature of alliance. Taking the case of weak-strong alliance among mangers of two corporate, we have to ask first for the defining limits of "weak" *vis-à-vis* "strong". More often than not "weakness" lays either in resources or in their use and distribution or both. Though India has been a land of strong resources (including humans), America is the land of strength. If they try to collaborate through their managers, who gains? Is it ethically desirable of the stronger party who needs the abundant quality resources (because they are relatively weaker in that regard) and thus impose their corporate values, ethos, work culture and other values on the weaker party who needs the necessary funds and expertise to use their resources and gain by that? Should the stronger party gain by virtue of value impositions on 'a culture' in the name of a 'global culture'? Should they impose managerial methods suited to them on other managers and employees of the weaker party who have a different philosophy of work-life and value-systems? It is not that transnational alliances do not change their nature, often opening up of economies inviting such alliances ends up in rapid growth and economic flourish, which is the case of China and India at the present. At times such economies grow in near Frankenstein proportions to outwit the stronger party in many respects, does it amount to a shift in cultural and ethical values from the 'now stronger' to the weaker? Or does value-systems that overpower and are overpowered, conflict and then calm down gradually to a universal system of values which is so good? What does that calming down amount to? Is it a typical capitalist value-system and their correlative work-ethos and work-culture, which should be universalized? If yes, on what ethical grounds should it be allowed? Let us not forget that with the constant efforts of mono-polarization of capitalist ethical values in business and management based on them, the world does not really become mono-polar with regard to a quantum shift in values. Still in India, a case of *kitchery* economy transmuting to capitalist economy *via* globalisation, free trade and privatisation, many believe that on certain ethical grounds the business world cannot be governed on the said universal value-system, and, therefore, the managers cannot be spokesmen and transmitters of a global capitalist value-system borrowed from the West. Many among us in the business schools argue that if capitalist goals and work-ethos in business and its management is added with 'spiritual inputs', it becomes nobler and acceptable because spiritual values are universal in nature and they thoroughly paint capitalist philosophy in white. Taking resort to spirituality, theism in the main, has been a long tradition to glorify things like global alliances in business. Of late, Vedānta and the conception of "the world is our brethren" have acquired a brand status in this regard. The spirituality of the non-theistic Jaina and Buddha not left aside. The point is their ethics does not rule out management alliances if that does social good and leads further to a *higher good*, the liberation from the many pains of existence. Well, the inherent managerial strategies cannot have any glorification like this, says others because on the one hand, it may be argued that non-spiritual and non-capitalist welfarism is a higher value-system and on the other hand the point that management as an earthy affair should better aim at non-exploitative, pro-people or pro-human attitude in governance of organisations than taking a *nirvānic* attitude. In the recent times, the spiritual entry into strategic management and transnational alliances have done a disservice by making it vague or blurred, thinks many, which is against management and thus unethical.

Many things are common when we come to the ethic of international technology transfer and aspects of management of companies going for such transfer. This is again a result of globalisation when government and private business organisations engage themselves in the transfer of technologies, including information technologies to build networks for effective and wide communication and productive and distributive efficacies. Both amounts to the growth of business around the world. It is easily understood that such a gigantic project needs extremely capable managers. Hence, management becomes an important aspect or feature in the cross-national technology transfer. Those who have lived through the 1960s to the 1980s in India knows it very well what it means for a nation (weaker) to be thrown into the weird net of international technology transfer, which was truly a 'one way traffic', the flow was to the weaker from the stronger parties. Strangely the masked socialist countries were not left behind to exploit the economy to the brink for hefty gains. Any way, the scene changes with globalism; very late though, the proponents of international technology transfer argued that managers of companies across the world should try collectively to ensure that the greater universal aspirations of business houses and thus the nations and masses be fulfilled by getting access to the most wide, effective and cheap means of production, distribution and communication. The managers should be quick and wise to capitalise on the merger of erstwhile narrow governmental control with the ideals of globalism, that is, corporatisation of nations, because this does overall material good for the people of all nations and thus brings isolated people into the economic mainstream. The 'multinational companies' should thus become real contributors to human well-being for which managers stand as most important parties. Management of the MNCs is thus a great ethically charged task because in that way the companies come out of the shackles of hedonic enterprises and for that matter, from narrow perception of human good, particularly the good of the downtrodden nations and their people. This is a popular pro-corporatisation argument by R.T. De George in some of his papers and books. It has been argued by such thinkers that the managerial efforts to strive for paradigm shifts in value-systems in any kind of international corporation in business cannot be accused of unethicality on the ground that capitalist values like those in America are imposed universally. However, the truth is that universalisation of values in management of international cooperation as in technology transfers is based on the ethical conception of human welfare, for which the recognition of some guiding rules such as maximisation of good of people of host nations, respect to human rights, fairness in payment and taxation, respect for work-ethos and cultures of host nations and cooperation with national government are most important. Nevertheless, as stated before, the ethical arguments against it are based on the notion that for the good of a downtrodden nation which happens to be a new home for the MNCs, it is extremely difficult to corroborate the obligations of the MNCs and the host countries for different reasons. Norman Bowie in some of his writings claims that the ethical inquiry into international technology transfer depends mainly in answering stiff questions about conflict in obligations. Management ethics should thus look for answers to questions like, 'who shares the moral responsibility or obligation towards the stakeholders? Should it be the host country, the government so to say, who has nevertheless, lost some bite in allowing globalism to play? Or, should it be the MNCs transferring technologies and thus party to the maximisation of profit, which has to take the moral responsibility for welfare of stakeholders? De George thinks that if MNCs fail to take sole responsibility because such responsibility cannot be shared or shifted from the chief player to the host, the MNCs should quit. Bowie starts an inquiry whether this may be the case because the stakeholders enjoy the right to fulfil their interests to which the managers are bound as a necessity and to which the government which had the basic responsibility to do some economic good are also bound but which they fail to do alone. Hence, welfare being a shared responsibility, the MNC managers and the companies should not quit business just because only they were bound to necessitating duty to maximize stake-holder's good. To this may be added that stakeholders of the MNCs do not refer to host nation's stakeholders and the employees, rather, the company shares a broader responsibility to do good to a number of stakeholders, shareholders and stockholders in the entire fold. Hence, the basic principle of human well-being enables us to say that in any case stakeholders' well-being is supreme; thus in international technology transfer, managers are bound to ensure stakeholders' legitimate rights and needs. Not only this, ethical wisdom calls for a close scrutiny of different factual circumstances that influences the role responsibilities of managers in the MNCs at home and in the host country. The same is the case when we consider the different moral principles that influence the role responsibilities. There is always a tension because conflict regarding justification of moral principles and their supremacy vary in the cultures. Yet, one might discover the overriding value of universal principle of "stakeholders' good" in MNC management. Bowie and many others thus calls for management ethics to find out the value of a universal moral thesis that is an answer to relativism with regard to individual and cultural values that disturbs managers acting as agents of home organisations in a host organisation. Though George and Bowie bases their ethical inquiries on teleological ethic that provides answers to the role responsibilities of the MNC managers, T.J. Donaldson and M. Velasquez in their works pays more attention to the questions of rights and freedom in the broader perspective of management of the international technology transfer. This takes a clear deontological turn in the writings of W. C. Frederick (1995) when the roles of managers are outlined in upholding the human rights and fundamental freedoms for their intrinsic value. However, it has always been a good ethical challenge by the thinkers that the role responsibilities and duties of the managers of the MNCs as listed above cannot be ethically (teleologically or deontologically) glorified because it becomes extremely unpragmatic and undesirable of company managers when seen from the organisational side, that is, from the side of its well-being or the chief good of its shareholders and stockholders to engage into a number of fiduciary acts despite clashes in interests, values and stiff host resistances in forms of political pressures, red-tapism and extra-gains. It may well be that the blurred strategic management owes much to the Cephalus-type (Cf. *The Republic*) of conception about the duties and responsibilities of a rich towards not so well off or poor, who in the main does not belong to my culture. It may be equally true that poor may not be valueless beggars; they may not take pride from external gratis when his own people have failed. Well, can that be an ethical passport to *swadeshi* exploitation by the poor man's own people?

The vistas of management ethics as it unfolds gradually shows the different ways in which management as a highly technical process awaits ethical interpretation because such process continuously gives us issues that cannot be treated merely as practical issues rather having ethical worth, that is, inquiring why such and such methods, decisions and actions in management are ethically good, right, just, obligatory, duty and so on. We are thus continuously presented with instances of justification of the study from the side of management. In due course of the discussion we have seen that a number of management problems may be conveniently clubbed for their family resemblance under what we call 'value-laden managerial problems' in the environment of globalisation, free trade and privatisation, and many other value-laden managerial problems are about the perception of the status and treatment of stake and stockholders of corporate. However, there are problems regarding the role of managers in a corporate as leaders and team-makers. Anyway, we are in dire need of ethical interceptions in the atmosphere of globalism and its spill-over or its subsidiary issues. In this respect the role of corporate managers in the MNCs and the national companies towards the treatment of employees become extremely important because employees are integral members of a corporate, sometimes they become shareholders as well. In any case they are one of the stakeholders whose rights and needs cannot be overlooked. Yet, for the interest of the shareholders and the stakeholders there are needs of the corporate to be revamped, modernised, restructured, and renovated and so on. Not only this, in this age of globalism, companies are often shut down or are sold or disinvested, which also gives rise to a lot of problems for the employees and the managers. In the light of such fluidity in corporate existence, not only the employees but the managers live in a fluid state. This is not only true of the private sector, but of the public sector, whose health must have gone wrong awaiting some treatment. Hence, in management we have some value-laden problems that are truly in the overlapping zones of globalisation, free trade and privatisation, and the status and treatment of stake and stockholders, particularly the employees as the stockholder. Certainly the covenanted managers are also paid employees of a company who nevertheless, have to justify that they are needed or are valuable in the governance of or administration of other employees in the face of overreaching shareholder value in companies. Hence, taking corporate downsizing, restructuring and re-engineering as business imperatives to enhance shareholder value notwithstanding stakeholder and managerial values, we find many ways in which management opens up for ethics, and thus management ethics is justified. It may be said that the trends in contemporary business takes downsizing, restructuring and re-engineering as natural processes for mainly the good of the shareholder or the stockholders, and is also touted as good of the company at large because its existence and well-being assures the well-being of its dependants, the employees and the managers. Let us not confuse that such things are found in large production houses or manufacturing companies rather in many petty businesses, non-manufacturing houses like educational houses and health care business.

Downsizing is thus a process or rather a strategy of the business houses to close units, scale down activities in business, closure for some time resulting into lay-offs because it was running loss or was not satisfied at the stockholder satisfaction level or a simple need to diversify, modernise and even quantify business with a thoroughgoing overhaul. The main objective must be to incur and enhance profits and not loss. Nevertheless, except for a prolonged closure and complete shut-down, downsizing cannot be seen as a necessary evil if it is followed by restructuring with the left over employees or even with some excellent substitutions, altered methods of functioning, altered objectives and even more effective administration by the managers. In any case, one cannot deny that the evil of curtailing the workforce, replacing manpower with machines and either cutting on costs on employees' salary and welfare measures or, investing more on modernisation and up gradation always leave room for ethical justification. Hence, downsizing and concurrent restructuring of companies affecting the stakeholders and their dependents always have enough reasons to ask why such things are ethically just. Restructuring as an alternate to downsizing might appear in many forms; forced retirements with updated due-clearance, transfers and conditions created for voluntary retirement are some of the ways, each awaiting ethical scrutiny. Re-engineering is a form of reorganisation of a company by first of all wiping out all old workforces and starting the organisation *de novo*. This is also backed up by new business goals, methods and management techniques. Most important feature of all these ways affecting stakeholders, particularly the employees is that managers face the best music uniformly because it is their prerogative as administrators to ensure stockholder's good by managing the turbulence owing to retrenchment, lay-offs and so on. Hence, the ethical crises in such steps taken in business are mainly crises for the managers, which managerial ethics considers seriously. The crux of the crises is 'man qua man is needed to do some harm to some men for great benefit to other men'. Why this is ethically right, just and good? In the tone of Plato, we might ask: "Does it amount to justice as right conduct? And according to Aristotle, is it justice as fairness? Further, in the vein of Rawls, we might ask: Does social justice consists in relative injustice at some levels? The point is that ethical issues in the management of downsized, restructured and re-engineered companies addresses to the questions of rights and justice. Popular ethical analysis is that downsizing etc. is justifiable because it is for the greater good of the stockholders who are responsible in running a business. It is thus good for the business at large, and if it does not exist, there is no point in speaking about the good of some employees. In popular parlance, downsizing is ethical because incapable and redundant workforce corrodes the corporate fund and the work culture, which is in the long run detrimental to the company as such and thus to a number of stake and stockholder. It is also detrimental to the social good to which the company contributes in its own way. In the popular parlance downsizing is unethical on the ground that it is anti-employees and pro-capitalists, it is one repressive way to exploit those who are the pillars of corporate success. Yet, pro-view is that employees in corporate should know well that for flourishing business several steps like downsizing are needed, and for that matter by virtue of entering into a contract they must face the necessary evils. Though there are several ethical tussles in downsizing etc. they are not to be so simply and popularly approached. Management ethics in particular approaches ethical inquiries into the management role in downsizing with a deeper vision. Management of such things thus opens vistas for the deeper inquiry into the ethic of downsizing by asking what managers contribute to *social justice* when he is a party to employ downsizing (which is a macro-inquiry). It asks what do managers contribute to *organisational justice* (which is a meso-level inquiry) and what managers contribute with regard to justice to the individuals or the employees (which is a micro-inquiry). The manager might ask deeper questions like, who is he, that is, who is a manager *qua* manager? What`are the values of the company that employs him? And what are his values in the context of a good governance and good society? Managers are thus at work to ethically find out why *qua* humans they should sack humans and why *qua* managers they should be related to the organisations *externally*, that is, as individuals *used* for the good of the stockholders? In the milieu of these difficult ethical questions there are a number of sub-issues of importance. For instance, the managers have to find out what amounts to a just society, which is for a MNC manager more troublesome when the conception of a just global society has to be imagined. This call for several social, economic and political theories of justice. But of great concern is the way distribution of primary goods, burden, benefits and opportunities are to be evaluated as good. In this context the manager has to further evaluate the impact of downsizing on a particular society and distributive justice therein. Does social justice diminish with downsizing and disintegration occurs, which is unethical because social disintegration is the loss of social well-being? Evaluation of such ethical questions cannot be completely context independent or independent of the finer considerations within a particular society.

Nevertheless, many among us might argue that certain things are themselves derogatory to human integration universally; independent of social relativism and thus it is for the respect of certain universal ideal that managers should refrain from being a party to human exploitation and also social disharmony. At the level of meso-inquiry for instance, it becomes imperative on the manager to inquire whether universal principle of respect for humanity does not prevent him or her from depriving the employees their right to live honestly and undisturbed? Do organisational peer pressures for economic flourishing outwit the rights of employees as humans to live an honest life? The acute question for managers in this regards is whether to treat humanity as means to an organisational end? This needs serious ethical review. How do we realise the value of finding "cutting down" methods having a human face, where managers are not sympathetic, they are not chauvinists as well, rather they are empathisers, who find the methods of fairness upholding basic rights of employees to "cut down" costs of company, to whom they owe much but not forgetting what they owe to human society. The contesting models of patriarchy and matriarchy are thus important to evaluate in such ethical matters. However, there are problems when management related to organisational downsizing opens for ethical evaluation because managers are often at the cross-roads to find out the way to ethical evaluation. What does it actually mean? Is it opening up for the induction of one or some principles of ethics, which we have just seen, finding inroads in such matters? Or, does it mean that managers have to apply their ethical knowledge of right, good and just to evaluate such matters? Or, do they have to apply ethical knowledge along with many others, most important being the employees? Management ethical literature is testimony to a debate about application of normative ethics in these matters. Many thinkers now do not prefer theoretical ethics as most important to find out what is right and just for managers to do in these regards. We shall turn to this issue at a proper place. For the time being we shall leave a hint that manager's crises in downsizing is really not his problem, it covers a number of people, the stake and stockholders, the society and the humanity at large; hence, the resolution of the crises cannot be a peer effort.

At times ethical inquiries send wrong signals because one gets an idea that ethical business and management must be pro-people or pro-stakeholders and not against them, but are not stockholders/shareholders humans, and demand some pro-attitude? Is everything ethical when in management we become darling of employees but shareholders, the investors doing business are seen as villains? Are managers good when like a Bollywood icon he or she teaches capitalist a lesson or two, sacrifices self and becomes a hero of the employee? Does shareholder value and managerial value necessarily conflict and the former is necessarily defeated to be ethical? Management opens this door for ethical inquiry as well. These questions become all the more important when in public and private sectors we aggressively debate the ethic of the supremacy of shareholders because in the atmosphere of globalism, the health of the company nourishes the employees, managers and other stakeholders. Shareholders need to be valued for the integration within the firm, for which managers are directly responsible. Only able corporate governance can keep up the shareholder value despite many populist pressures to keep it below the stakeholder value. The crucial point is whether managers should take and ethical stance to balance the two pressures or should they be more ethically speculative to keep up the shareholder value first and foremost? If they do so, there must be ethical justifications and if they do the other way round, they must justify their shift in loyalty. The manager, says Peter Koslowski, must be a "speculator" than a production master—he or she must not be a manipulator to the least who plays a double game without any professional commitment and thus ethicality. How should managers be ethically oriented to "limit" the shareholders and the stakeholders? How can managers be oriented in merging their and shareholders' values and interests? The ethical basis of "limit" might be traced to the holistic good of the firm or the complete welfare of the society or the intrinsic value of their professional duty. It is a matter of great interest, therefore, in managerial ethics to inquire how managers' perception of ethic of profit and benefit are effective in putting a limit to the ideal of maximisation of both things for the shareholders and the ideal of maximisation of the same for the stakeholders.

The discussion thus far reveals that management is a process that invites a number of ethical questions to be answered, which shows what ethically relevant talk in management amounts to and why is it justified. Before turning to the ways in which ethics approaches management, we should know that many interesting ethical talks are about the misconceived role of managers, which must be true of almost all professionals. First, managers are often engaged in *non-managerial roles*, that is, what they do in organisations in the capacity of their positions but such efforts are for one's own good overlooking the good of the firm. All kinds of extra benefits, earnings, bribes, embezzlements come under this category, which awaits moral reasons to be called unethical. Related to such acts of managers are their *distorted roles*, that is, roles that are professionally fine-tuned for some benefits to few stakeholders, almost none to stockholders and almost everything to the manager himself. The distortion of professional ideology is a matter for ethical evaluation. Further, some managers are involved in *overexertion*, which is again a matter of ethical evaluation because such acts of managers do some good to a few stakeholders by unlawfully ditshing a number of other advantages to the firm or the stockholders at the cost of great harm to many other stakeholders. Most important ethically questionable act like this is the intentional act to damage the *environment* to give some short term advantages to the firm. Most of the time such managerial role distortions are not unethical because they are *un*professional or are *anti*-profession, but because they are responsible for complete or partial disintegration of the organisation, the firm and the society at large. Hence, social and organisational integrity stands as an important ethical basis for evaluating managerial role performances. We have seen before that the model of *positive* management neither amounts to a *moral* management nor *over*-management because both loses sight of moral management that is a perfect integrative management in which a professional manager does not abide by a particular role or some roles as advocated in the four theories of management stressing on partial truths but not combining them in an integrated whole. The question is which normative ethical theory justifies this integrative management?

Let us now enter into the realm of justification of management ethics through the clarification of ethics making in-roads in management affairs, for instance, how we find normative ethical involvement in management related matters. However, we will start with inquiry into non-normative ethical involvements. Metaethics or what is known as first order ethics studies the nature of moral concepts and discourses and the truth and meaning of moral language. It is also a study of justification of the different normative theses needed for moral evaluation. It is interesting to note that the main aim of this chapter is metaethical analysis of the nature of "management ethics" and the justification of the same as a sensible discussion within ethics. It is a poor idea, therefore, to nurture that metaethics makes sense only within ethics proper or morality proper and not when we consider non-moral studies such as management studies. There has been a long tension about what is ethics proper. If we take it for granted that ethics properly so-called is the study of 'moral language', we cannot leave out the nature analysis of language that makes unique appearance in the field of management related discourses with an added qualification of being value-laden or pertaining to ethical value. The question is if *per se* management is a non-moral field of study, that is, positivistic or scientific, how can it have a body of unique appearance of value-laden language? The answer is that though management as such is a positivistic study, it does not imply that it possesses exclusive positivistic language or the language of matters of fact and not of value or ethical value. Nothing prevents sciences to have unique value-laden language because scientific language reveals after a careful analysis the features of a language in which the evaluation of certain human decisions and actions have been evaluated for their ethical good, right, just and so on. In a sense such language falls under ethical language. It is not that the whole of scientific languages, such as language of management is value-laden, but such language does have truly features of value-language or simply, the language of ethical value. There is a difference, therefore, to speak of "Globalism is by definition such and such" and to speak of "Globalism amounts to exploitation of workers class and thus bad". The former is a purely scientific or management language, whereas the latter is not so, it is a language of evaluation or ethical evaluation. Hence, unique appearance of value-language *in the context of* management science is a subject of study of metaethics and not management. And as metaethics is within ethics, the study of language of value in management contexts is within ethics and not management. It is due to this that management as a science does not take much interest in unfolding the nature, truth and meaning of its either value-laden or purely scientific language because that is not the task of management, but we do expect such things from philosophy or a branch of it, called ethics. The moot issue therefore, is not why ethics should analyse the value-laden management language rather, why should ethics take any interest in non-ethical studies. We have answered this, that is, closely related to the metaethical justification of management ethics at least in part, and now we are trying to look it from another side, that is from the side of language that appears in management. It is important to note that without justification (metaethical) of management ethics on the basis of management making way to ethical interceptions and on the basis of ethics crossing to management for a linguistic analysis, there is no truth and meaning of the conception of "management ethics", which is injurious to us who thinks management ethics is so important to be discussed within applied ethics. Hence, the metaethical task of justification of branch of ethics, that is, applied ethics as consisting of management ethics, is of great value. We cannot suddenly spread water over the huge body of managemental ethical literature as sheer nonsense by not addressing to the metaethical task of "justification". Turning now to the "other side", that is, the side from which ethics takes on the unique language of management which speaks of value of management related intentions, decisions and actions, responsibilities, duties, rights and so on, it is most important to know what does it *mean* when we find concepts such as "managerial role responsibilities", "managerial duties", "employees rights", "managerial justice" etc.? One answer is to define these concepts found in management language in their own scientific terms, but it is certainly not proper and possible to analyse the meaning of "responsibility", "duty" and so on as based management science because these concepts are analysed for their meaning in the field of ethics (within metaethics), to be precise. One who does not know what is "duty" or "good" cannot understand what is "managerial duty" and "managerial good". Hence, it is the task of ethics (and not management) to analyse nature and meaning of basic "value" concepts or "evaluative" terms which are used to qualify managerial intention, decision, actions etc. based on some ethical grounds, that is, the logical strength of such evaluation is derived from ethic and not management. Joel Feinberg in *Essays on the Theory of Responsibility* (1970) clarifies why it is so important as *first order task* of the ethicist (and not managers) to analyse the nature and meaning of basic assumptions of management, among which is the assumption that humans (managers inclusive) have some *moral autonomy*, that is, they are capable of intending, deciding and acting without any aid of authorities, peer pressures and external commands, otherwise as moral agents, it will be difficult for us to determine who is *responsible* of an act and its consequences, and to evaluate whether when it is good or bad, it bounds the agent or someone external to him or her. In management, therefore, it is important that ethics or metaethics approaches its language containing value-elements to analyse its nature and meaning. An analytic knowledge like this enables managers to realise what exactly is moral responsibility and autonomy and what it amounts to in the context of management. Managers may be further helped to understand why managers having moral autonomy and responsibilities are subject to moral evaluation of their autonomous and responsible intentions and actions. Hence, the vast body of management discourses which stands on the blocks of language have distinctive body of language that does not state what the case is, but what *should* be the case when something is the case. Such evaluative language needs clarification from metaethical inputs, which may vary greatly. The evaluative language may be considered as meaningful on the grounds of subjectivism that is, the language *describes* the speaker's state of mind or feelings or emotion. Or, it may be taken as emotive language that either *causes* emotions in the speaker and the hearers or *expresses* emotions of the speaker to the hearer. Or it may be considered as *prescriptive* language that suggests what speaker thinks to be just to do for the hearer as well. The evaluative language in the context of management may be also considered as language expressive of cultural values which are *relative* or as expressive of universal values which are *absolute*. It is extremely interesting to know from our managers that when they use value-laden language in management parlance, what do they mean and on what basis they are true. Any care about such things falls back to metaethical analysis. This is the way we can justify why ethics as taking on metaethical task make in-roads in management and what we mean when we speak of "management ethics" in at least one sense.

Ethics is also a study of 'description' of certain necessary psychological components needed for ethical discussions, for instance, the description of what is motive, intention, feelings, emotions, will, wish, desire, and so on. These are built in and with ethical discourses, particularly, when ethics is taken as a "human centred" study of not what happens in their minds when they intend or feel or desire, because that is proper to the field of psychology and not ethics, rather, the distinctive features of human intention, feelings, will etc. that have some effect on the decisions, actions, conduct and character of moral agents. When use of notions such as these are marked in management literature, we have to be careful about analysing their meaning and how they stand in the context of evaluation of human conduct and character. It is important to ask our managers what does having a good character mean? When we evaluate that for such and such reasons, a manager is said to have a good character but not conduct, what does it really amount to? What exactly do we judge in the name of character? This takes us to what is the description of character as distinct from conduct. These are some descriptive issues in ethics that take cues from psychology. However, what we call *descriptive ethics* as an *empirical* aspect of ethics is far more varied. It takes on the empirical methods much like the social anthropologists and sociologists to collect data, observe facts and phenomena having clear importance in the ethical contexts, explain human behaviour and find out the factors around us that have direct bearing on moral events; for example, to observe the fact of changing ethical values among students in the schools and colleges with regard to sexuality education or corporeal punishment. Similarly, it becomes important to find out the changes in the perception of employees in the public sector industries about their participation in shareholding. Or, the changes in the managerial strategies as based on the value perceptions of managers with regard to environmental refugees. It is extremely important to collect such information for value-based decision-making, planning, fixing goals, strategies in management, and resolve the moral crises with regard to such things.

Management ethics is thus justified when ethics as empirical ethics has enough reasons to enter into the field of management. The same is true or may be best instantiated through the involvement of *normative ethics* in management. In fact, for many managers, it is norms that make ethical study, which is however, a wrong idea. Normative study is only colloquially, historically and emotionally the prime or the first order task of ethics. Let us find out how normative ethics is engaged in the management affairs. We should keep in mind the truth that normative ethics is not merely a body of standard evaluative theses like teleology and deontology; we speak of many standards of evaluation such as social and political though for the purpose of evaluating the *moral worth* of intended human actions, for instance, actions coming under the realm of management. The reason is that it is pointless to speak (ambiguously) about "moral basis" of evaluating moral worth, when "moral" of "moral basis" is unclear without resorting to some *non-moral explanation* of what is "moral". This appears to be at the outset a contradiction in terms because explanation of what is "moral" basis cannot be based on "non-moral" terms. Nevertheless, many ethical thinkers are of the opinion that if we rule out the possibilities of explaining moral bases on non-moral terms, we shall unknowingly rule out *ethical teleology* or teleological basis of moral evaluation, and with that we have to accept a peculiar thesis that *ethical deontology* is the only justified moral or ethical basis of moral evaluation because in it, the explanation of "moral" basis is based on an exclusive moral or ethical notion, namely, "duty" (*deon*). In this sense, we have to say that egoism, altruism, hedonism, self-realisation, god-realisation, *nirvāna* as standards of moral life, as bases of moral evaluation and ideals of moral life are wrongly conceived normative theories, they are, non-moral theories and thus needs careful avoidance. In this sense, then, social and political explanations of "norms" of ethics need to be ruled out. For instance, we have to rule out that the norm of conformity to democratic rules as laid in constitution cannot be ethical basis for evaluating *some* of our intended actions. Or, we have to rule out the possibility of acting according to the norm of social welfare and social justice. Even, we have to rule out the possibility of acting according to the norm of economic justice at the grassroots. The main argument in rejecting the traditional teleological and the so-called non-teleological bases of moral evaluation is that their acceptance leads to 'naturalistic fallacy' because it amounts to equate the moral with the non-moral or the natural which can never be the case logically speaking. Yet, it is extremely important to understand that the said illogical equation holds good when one intends to *logically define* the "moral" with the help of the "non-moral" terms intending them to be equivalent, that is, one can be replaced logically by the other term. However, in due course of *clarifying* the meaning or analysing the meaning of the "moral" we do need the help of many "non-moral" notions because they are helpful means or aids to explanation or clarification. Hence, without intending to define by logical equivalence, there is every possibility to say that moral norms can be clarified for their meaning on non-moral bases, including the available traditional teleological bases because their meaning cannot remain concealed in ambiguity. It is nearly impossible to tell what "moral norms" are without taking recourse to teleological or social, political, spiritual, economic and other such non-moral bases. Hence, moral norms as found in normative ethics can be social, economic, political and other ideals which stand as overreaching standards of ethical good, right, just and so on. It is perfectly well, therefore, to speak of hedonism on the one hand and economic welfare on the other hand along with deontology touted as the exclusive moral thesis to evaluate our intended decisions and actions, which is one of the concerns of academic ethics. Academic ethics thus provides us with normative theses for the *actual social acts* for the evaluation of decisions and actions of various types, the political, medical, environmental, and commercial or business decisions. Many ethicists are of the opinion that it is unnecessary to differentiate the traditional *teleos* and the recently advocated ones because a careful study of the social, economical and political norms are in reality, different examples of "teleos" in moral life or ideals of morality that stands as bases of evaluation. Some of us are serious to say that the whole of Indian normative ethics is "teleological" in the true sense though it is jammed with several social, economic, political norms as ethical standards in the "social life" and spiritual/religious norms as ethical standards in the "transcendental life" of the individuals or moral agents. The idea is that moral agents as 'social beings' have a life different from agents as 'Beings they truly are' or as 'Transcendent Beings', and for that matter, what they intend as social beings should be evaluated on different teleological standards sensible at the *social plane* which include obeying authorities and social, political, economic bases as found in different teleological thesis. Moreover, at the *transcendental plane* individuals either have hedonic ideal because they are wholly material Beings (Cf. Cārvāka) or have non-hedonic transcendental ideals as wholly transcendental Beings (Cf. the six orthodox systems and the two heterodox systems in Indian philosophy), which may be simplified as "*nirvāna*". In any case, the *corporeal* and the *spiritual* ends or *teleos* of life shows that having an *ethically justifiable teleos* or purpose in life is what underlies ethicality. It is in this sense that on the one hand ethically justifiable ideal may be economic welfare through business or social and political fairness, and on the other hand ethically justifiable ideal may be spiritual liberation. I have taken the case of Indian ethical thinking in particular to show how to accommodate norms within a system of normative ethics even if they are *non-morally explained* in terms of "*teleos*", whether the traditional or the broader one. Indian ethics serves another purpose in this regard. It shows us how to accommodate the ideal of "duty" even understood in Kantian terms as acting in the respect of the Law as "social beings" because that is ultimately the stepping stone to Self realisation as the supreme *teleos* in life. Thus the *purpose* in transcendental life is never ruled out in a peculiar normative system best identifiable as *ethical pluralism*. Parallels in Christian ethics and Hegelian ethics are not difficult to find out, though the moot point is about the "ethically justifiable" *teleos* in life, when we live a social life amongst the complexes of business and management. The point is to discuss why not all *teleos* are "ethically justifiable"; for instance, why not corporeal pleasure maximisation is ethically just in business. Or, why being a *trustee* in corporate management is justifiable ethically though being professional who maximizes profits is *not* justifiable? This may be further intensified as why a *professional duty* may *not* be maximisation of corporeal profits of corporate only or of one's own self? Contesting justifications may lead to the final consideration of the highest *teleos* of human life or the 'chief teleos'. The evaluation of work-life of managers may be thus based on a debate about whether a normative thesis of evaluation *vis-à-vis* other theses be overreacthing? The debate is perennial and intense. Many among us argue that though nothing prevents ethical pluralism in normative thinking, everything included in the name of teleological norm *cannot* be ethically justified because religious and spiritual *teleos* in life may be nevertheless, rejected for belonging to a category which has *nothing to do* with ethical category. Hence, to avoid a category confusion in normative thinking teleological theory should abstain from advocating transcendental *teleos* that cannot be a part of a coherent system of theories. If this be the argument, the advocates of spiritual teleology hits back saying, in that case all social, political and economic *teleos* as well as egoism, altruism and hedonic *teleos* needs rejection for category confusion, which is to complete the circle by conforming to the deontic norm. Hence, deontology argues forcefully that when we talk ethically about the basis of ethical evaluation of managerial decisions and actions for instance, we should only apply the ideals inherent in deontology and not teleology because it corrupts ethical thinking by means of non-ethical thinking and thus confuses categories, which is a blatant mistake. There is thus nothing in ethical normativism that enables us to prefer non-monolithic or non-absolutist normativism whether in management or elsewhere. Equally true is that normativism should be deontic normativism. Tragically, this tends to jolt Indian ethical thinking and many teleological ethics that advocates pluralism. Monolithic deontology jolts many monolithic teleological theories like pure hedonism and altruism as well, but we have to be careful about the monolithic assumptions of ethical deontology and its likely value in evaluation of managerial decisions and acts. I am reminded of criticism of deontology that says, it would be a fantastic world in which everyone else does something for the sake of duty and nothing else. For instance, someone visiting a sick person is merely doing a duty and nothing else, the person has no human feelings, attachments, and purpose than coming to the sick because visiting a sick is intrinsically good. Now, how many sick can we visit for the sake of its value? The point is which sick do we visit? May be our near and dear ones, not even best doctor visit all sick people and go on visiting some at least *merely* for visiting them. If the doctor does another duty, that is, collective health care but *merely* for its value and nothing else, the person has no feelings, attachments and purposes higher than that. Is the world good? It may not be a liveable world says many when every other manager of companies govern or administer, contribute for good *merely* because that is their duty. The managers are not interested at all in doing duties and other things as well, for instance, they are not interested in any fiduciary or supererogatory act or even welfare of the family of the employees or flourishing of managerial capacities and so on. Others ask how duty for its intrinsic value can be *known* by common people? Are allotted duties, the covenanted ones, duties as such? Do we not find extension of defined duties of professionals? Are changes in duties not possible? Is it not true that performing duty for its value is itself a purpose of a professional? Anyway, normative ethics with its huge repository of questions and replies approaches fields like business and management to inquire whether monolithic or pluralistic norms are justifiable in corporate governance and which among them is justifiable on what grounds. Management ethics is thus justifiable by a normative nexus.

Nevertheless, normative ethics is itself a weird realm within ethics, which has influenced the writers of business ethics, management ethics and many other branches of practical and professional ethics so much so that either they take ethical involvement in the fields other than ethics as wholesome normative ethical application or they take the ethical involvement as a particular game of jigsaw puzzle to fit one theory to an managerial/business and other such issues to find resolutions. Wholesome normative ethical involvement amounts to show how *all* available ethical norms somehow or other gets involved in business and/or managerial issues or how an available ethical norm may be pushed for the same purpose. I must say this is most unfounded and tragic in normativism, whether we extend this beyond traditional teleology and deontology or not. The point takes us to the important aspect of *using* the available body of normative ethics because in essence, academic ethics does not pretend to be purely academic, that is, all good to read but not good to apply. However, the matter of use of available normative theories in management takes us beyond normativism to practical ethics or applied ethics. We will not jump immediately to show how practical ethics enters management to justify management ethics because I have a task to show how some management theorists manipulate pluralistic normative systems for their application. Let us consider the explanation of Petrick and Quinn. First, the authors classify the body of ethical normativism into four parts, the traditional teleological theories such as egoism, utilitarianism and eudemonism; the deontological theories such as the theory of negative and positive rights; the theory of social contract and the theory of social justice; the virtue ethical theories such as the theory of virtuous individual character, virtuous work character and virtuous professional character, and the system development ethical theories such as the theory of personal improvement, organisational theory and extra-organisational theory. After a brief explanation of these types of theories (which I do not want to elaborate), the author turns to play the famous jigsaw game. They discover that teleological norms fit with the rational goal theory in management where managers are producers and directors in the main, which is however, an incomplete thesis in management. Hence, teleology is apt in the fields of evaluating managerial roles as producer/director and is useful in the resolutions of ethical crises that approach them in the said roles. Other things remaining the same, deontological theories fit to internal process theory where managerial roles are of monitor and coordinator and useful therein. More elevated are the virtue ethical theories which fit human relations theory where managers are mentors and facilitators. Finally, the system development theories fitting into open system theory where managers are innovators and brokers. The authors have stressed that amoral and immoral management is to take up one or some role responsibilities and thus one or some theories for managerial acts. Hence, moral management integrates all theories of management and thus the said roles, and for that reason integrates all the four normative theories in management practices. This would mean on the one hand that the integrated norms leads the business administrators to desirable directions or goals to enable them to have an ideal ethical life of integrated ideals, and on the other hand the integrated norms provides the business administrators and others the bases for evaluating managerial decisions and actions. Further, this amounts to an integral application of normative theories in practical planes of managerial roles in corporate not forgetting the unique role of a theory in case of a particular value-crises or in case of appropriate performance of each role resolving problems therein. But for sure, like all jigsaw games, we must know that this block of norms fits that block of roles, and this must be an absolutist paradigm because normative fixity in practical cases are far from being relative. Yet, pluralism is well covered because not one theory but normative theories permeate management as such in the capacity of a guide, a beacon light and an evaluator. This must be a fantastic thesis lest we find some gaps in it. First is ethical teleology does not cover religious/spiritual theories. Second, deontology does not have proper reference to Kant, Ross and Prichard, though finds place for many others. Most interesting aspect is that each of the teleological and deontological theories are projected as having unique roles in management, like, having unique role in cases of productivity and profit management for pleasure maximisation (utilitarianism) and human resource management by the book (social contract theory) and so on. Third, in a huff virtue ethics has been given the status of a "theory" (normative) without any consideration of its *anti-theoretic* stance. Why should we not debate about the issue that virtue ethics as has been advanced as a post-Aristotelian revolution by Ms Anscombe and many others is seen as anti-theoretic, that is, not as a normative revolution but as a non-normative stance in which stress is on inculcation of worthy traits of character or virtue, whether he or she is a professional manager or an employee or a stockholder? It is important as managers to have basic virtues of cooperation to coordinate or enterprising to direct, or, guidance to facilitate and inquisitive to innovate. Virtue ethics stresses on the basic virtues which the managers having the eight fundamental role-responsibilities under four management theories should possess, and not that virtue ethics itself is a normative thesis that advocates like other theories to evaluate actions on the basis of finding out whether *all* worthy traits are found in managers when they take up all their duties either at a time or some time at least. Nevertheless, to find out whether some managers possess a virtue in reality is to discover whether she takes a role responsibility desirable of her most effectively. Can one learn about virtues in virtue ethics academically and then inculcate them as managers to do certain things? Do managers learn to inculcate virtues by simply learning about managerial role-responsibilities and then performing them ably? What does it mean to be virtuous without being inclined to an academic theory or norm? Some virtue ethicists say that virtue ethics is not in essence anti-theory because it begs theories. The reason is that any worth or virtue of a manager is clear to us or that we discover them in managers when we call a theory into service. How do we know that this manager is *cooperative* (a virtue)? The answer is when she performs her role as *coordinator* under the desirable management practice advocated by the internal process theory. But that is not the end, we ask, how do we *know* that the manager having powers to coordinate, is in fact, virtuous or worthy of being like that? Why at all is coordination a virtue and not a vice? The reason may be that it is a virtue because in doing so, the ideal or objective of holistic management is fulfilled, which in turn amounts to the flourishing of the self of the manager, which is to beg *eudemonism*. It may be said that it begs deontology and so on. Hence, virtue ethics need not be anti-theoretic, it begs normative theories. Nevertheless, how do we *know* that self-fulfilment is the ideal of managers as co-operators when the manager does not beg to inculcate the virtue of being a self-fulfilled person? The point is that virtue ethics has moved much beyond a hackneyed linear thesis, either tending to be a pure theory or anti-theory. We forget that both may be equally important, that is, *to be* virtuous and *to have* a theory to know when a person is virtuous. How can we thus have a blind eye to the truth that the three sub-types of virtue theories that our authors advocate for management neither proves that a particular virtue-inculcation is good for a particular managerial role, nor does it justify that normative thesis read above have no role in virtue ethical discussions. It would be a good exercise for a manager to know why the virtue of courage and wisdom may be needed as an individual trait to possess the work character of being cooperative and to have the professional character of being collegial. There are in reality no isolated compartments of virtues for managers. It may well be that individual, work and professional virtues support each other in a coherent whole

Most strangely the *system development* ethical theories though they have nothing wrong in them as normative thesis because being non-moral standards for managers, they do not stand rejection, but I wonder why should there be a need of such a normative thesis beyond teleological theory! Whether a manager strives for personal improvement or organisational improvement or extra-organisational improvement or all of them, does it not amount to the same as having a *teleos* of "development of ethical self or ethical persona" or simply, "self-realisation" (containing a small "s")? What is most interesting about the work of our authors is that they have neglected the applied task of ethics and shown that what it amounts to is application of normative ethics in management. However, we have seen that they have unambiguously stated that management ethics is a branch of applied ethics but does that clarify the sense in which it is a branch of applied ethics? It is a common practice among writers to take it for granted that applying ethics in management means applying anyone or more or all (as in case of Petrick and Quinn) standard normative theories and more such theories to the field of management for two reasons, which we have seen. Coming particularly to the reason of managerial decision-making and subsequent acts, the authors have no doubt that what we apply are normative theories either singling or in combination or wholly, first two applications are mistaken, the last, the integral application is proper. This is commendable because the authors have come very close to realise that chauvinism with anyone theory is to forget that the chauvinist manager is not ethical, she is either amoral or immoral. Hence, "a narrow moral point of view in ethical decision-making that provides a one-dimensional, single quadrant resolution to all management problems... expose the lack of skill in handling moral complexity required of managerial integrity"[14]. Further, "management judgement integrity requires the balanced use of all four ethics theories in the analysis and resolution of moral issues"[15]. What interests me most in the last passage is that using *all four ethical theories* amounts to *analysis and resolution of moral issues* in management. Let us first ask, 'by whom the same needs to be done?' The answer is stated above: 'by the managers'. Hence, application of all four ethical theories *by managers* in managerial crises is application of ethics is management. Truly, the commendable anti-monism in ethical application 'by managers' is replaced by a bashable integralism in ethical application 'by managers' because that is ethical application wrongly understood. The first point is application of ethics in management is not an exclusive managerial affair, not chauvinising of any theory in the second sense because application of ethics, as I understand is not application of any normative theory possible and probable by a professional or a group of professionals or even ethicists or a group of ethicists and managers (See volume 1 for details). Application of ethical norms, one or all, does not make any sense because this application is not a game of jigsaw puzzle played by ethical experts who know which block fits where because unlike a standard jigsaw puzzle, moral puzzles are far too complex, where experts are refuted by others or there are disagreements for complex patterns of fitting blocks, which is a matter of *consensus* or *corroboration* in ethical analysis and resolution. Here, *our* ethical knowledge of what is good, right and just are applied in association in debates tending to corroboration, which might reflect features of standard theory but that is *non-coopted* by any party in the dialogue in artificial manner. Ethical knowledge reflects theories when they are applied in real life by not only managers but many others who have equal moral authority to analyse and resolve ethical issues in management. Why should managers alone have the moral authority to resolve ethical crises in management through theories? A proper answer to this leads us to integral approach in ethical application, and not by answering which theories should managers apply in management. I will develop this approach in the next chapter. For the time being it is important to notice that the weird but interesting field of normative ethics, virtue ethics and applied ethics ushers new hopes for us to have an effective and meaningful management ethics. When ethics opens doors for management and when management awaits ethics to enter with its functions, we have "management ethics" for sure. We thus find out what management ethics is or what is 'ethically relevant study of management'. Nevertheless, we have to answer the effective way in which ethics is really applied in management ethics. This book is not purely a theoretical enterprise and for that matter we hope to find an answer to application of ethics in management in the next chapter.

NOTES

1. For a synoptic account of these theories, which has been cryptically represented in a schematic model, readers may consult the work *Becoming a Master Manager* by R. E. Quinn, S. R. Faerman, M. P. Thompson and M. R. McGrath (John Wiley & Sons, NY, 1996). The authors bring out the concept of ideal management through a synergy of managerial tasks desirable of master managers which has been depicted in four types of writings about the matter.
2. Petrick, J. A. and Quinn, J. F., *Management Ethics: Integrity at Work*, Response Book, New Delhi, 1997, p. 8.
3. *Ibid*, p. 9.
4. *Ibid.*
5. Hodgkinson, Cristopher, *Administrative Philosophy: Values and Motivations in Administrative Life*, Pergamon, Oxford, 1996, p. 3.
6. *Ibid*, p. 105.
7. *Ibid*, p. 27.

8. *Ibid.*
9. *Ibid*, p. 33.
10. *Ibid*, p. 170.
11. Godlovitch, Stan, "Varieties of Process: Commercial, Moral and Otherwise" in *Business Ethics in Theory and Practice: Contributions from Asia and New Zealand*; Werhane, P. and Singer, A. E. (eds.), Kluwer, London, 1999, p. 219.
12. Petrick, J. A., and Quinn, J. F., Op. Cit, p. 44.
13. Savage, Charles, M., "The Ethics of Teaming: The Key to the Knowledge Economy" in Chakraborty, S. K. and Chatterjee, S. R. (eds.), *Applied Ethics in Management: Towards New Perspectives*, Springer, NY, 1999, p. 218.
14. Petrick, J. A. and Quinn, J. F., Op. Cit., p. 63.
15. *Ibid*, p. 53.

4

Some Economic, Business and Management Related Ethical Dilemmas and Intersubjective Corroboration

We have seen thus far that the ethical involvement in economic, business and management affairs makes a strong case. Hence, to speak of economic, business and management ethics is perfectly sensible, which is, however, not the same as economic, business and management morality if that amounts to the study of traditional moral opinions, beliefs, trends, dogmas, codes and so on because ethical study is apart from other things, a thorough critique of moral dogmas prevailing in a society or in sub-organisations therein to find out whether such prevailing morals are at all justifiable on *ethical grounds*, that is, on unique ethical reasons. We have seen that the 'ethical grounds' for a thorough critique of traditional morality need not be those found in normative ethical literature traditionally, that is, utilitarianism, Kantianism etc. because many more non-traditional reasons for evaluation of dogmas are available to us by virtue of especially framed non-ethical reasons, that is, reasons beyond traditional ethics, which extends to ethical matters and are thus proper bases for ethical evaluation. We have seen that normative ethics as we should now look at it is not the hackneyed body of traditional theses of moral evaluation. Evaluation of what is ethically justifiable in intended human acts which makes proper cases of ethical evaluation, is thus not to press into service one or more traditional normative thesis, though we habitually press at least one or some norms in evaluation. However, we have contended that it is a gross traditional conception that ethics is all good to read but not good in practice because we cannot make a sensible case of practical application of ethics on the ground that what is applied in ethics is ambiguous or even unfounded. The common conception about this matter is that application of ethics is application of anyone or more norm or norms of ethics which we know thus far by ethics-experts or other parties equally apt in ethical expertise to find one thesis to restore ethical crises or to fit one thesis to evaluate a value-laden problem. Those who are critiques of such ethical application hold that norms of ethics cannot be applied so artificially by experts, and for that reason there is no ethical application, norms are at best of 'pure academic value'. We have argued that truly, norms are not to be applied by experts in an 'engineering' fashion because on the ground realities of value-crises and their resolution, there are little or no scope for theoretical pondering and choosing theories by experts. It may be said that to the experts such things come naturally or automatically, but we have argued that even if mechanically ethical engineers find norms to fit in situations of crises, only they do not or should not have moral authority to do such things because ethical problems involve many parties—the people of different occupations and professions and those directly affected who have the moral authority for ethical evaluation and resolution as well. Moreover, the evaluation and resolutions based on normative theories by expert ethicists may be easily (or are easily), refuted, disagreed and replaced by equally competent non-expert moral authorities, who are without theoretical or normative cooption able to debate about evaluative issues by virtue of their moral experience and moral knowledge gained as members of a vast 'household' or 'ecological community'. Moral norms, which are traditional or new or undiscovered are not invented by ethicists or experts, they are generalisations of some experts in academic field though non-experts having no idea of such field are well placed to give such moral reasons as expressed in normative generalisations because the germs of theories are embedded in the 'household', they are not pure intuitive findings or *a priori* findings—norms do not drop from the blue in fertile minds of experts, they are not subjective either. However, if they are believed to be both, we have grounds to refute them as predilections, having no value in generalisation of norms. What *should* be done or what is ethically desirable, right, and good and just is thus neither mysterious findings nor predilections of mind, they are rather outcomes of *social criticisms* which we find in the community life of the 'household'. The experts' generalisations are unique academic abilities of some trained minds to put moral things in a coherent shape or who builds a system of norms and shows how they are logically justified. Nevertheless, constant debate about or ethical critique of a particular normative generalisation by an expert to banish its monistic supremacy in ethical matters is a testimony to the fact that like all empirically based norms which are logically grounded, relativism and pluralism holds good, and there are distinct gaps in the logic underlying the monistic norms. This does not mean that for one issue all available norms are as good as a particular norm because a number of norms may be *logically weak* to justify a norm as having enough evaluative dispositions, whereas others are *logically stronger*. Ethics is critique of norms as well, which is therefore, reflected even in the common man's disagreement about evaluation and resolution of value-laden issues based on a particular norm or some norms. The difference may be that common man's normative inclinations and justifications are clear only through ethical debates or dialogues in society about value-laden practical issues, and not the same as what system builders have done or are doing through their trained enterprises of explaining, contrasting, comparing, criticising and appreciating norms in a logical manner, that is, by following standard rules of formal logic or informal logic or heuristics. Hence, we come to conclude that value-laden practical problems or simply, ethical problems should be approached by concerned members of society (if not by all), in a normative non-coopted manner so that through lively debates, disagreements find grounds for agreement on value crises to evaluate and resolve them. Such theory non-coopted ethical dialogues may be thus an affair in which expert ethicists and non-experts participate to find ways out of impasse. We all have moral freedom to face moral crises. This may be true when we come to fields beyond ethics (or philosophy), such as business and management because the value-laden practical problems in economics, business and management follow the same rule of evaluation and resolution through theory non-coopted participation of the concerned parties, including the expert ethicist, expert economists, businessmen, managers, administrators (who are however, non-expert ethicists), and many affected people, who are non-experts as well. Coming to the 'affected' people, we may say that though expert ethicists and expert managers, for instance, are affected in some ways when there are lay-offs in companies, the workers and their families as well as those in the government, judiciary, executive and others as common men, are affected in other ways. Ethicists might eke out a pittance for the "directly or intensely affected" workers because what has been done *should* not be done calling moral evaluation and to find a way out of the crisis; the managers are affected because what has been done needs reality level evaluation for practical or useful value and for some 'soul-searching' (may be). The managers are only "indirectly or moderately affected", whereas common men and others may be similarly placed, though they might be intense "soul-searching" people who wants to evaluate what managers and stockholders have done. Anyway, they all become parties to evaluation and resolution of the complex crisis, the one that is practical and moral. Such "practical ethical crisis" or "value-laden practical problem" brings people of society having moral authority for ethical resolution in one fold. If we forget this, we end up in ethical engineering of experts or what is "ethical chauvinism" notwithstanding normative obsessions in artificial atmosphere, which is itself ethically understandable as it is based on an anti-people or better said, pro-expertise but anti-corroborative and thus *anti-social methodology* of ethical resolution. Hence, we should abstain from moral engineering and moral chauvinism as ethicists, managers, stockholders and commoners. We should thus find a *method* to come together as *pro-social* beings who are theory non-coopted even if some of them know theories, which is however, not the same as the Rawlsian 'under the veil of ignorance' rather, 'under the influence of *logical forces* in ethical debates, readiness to give up any cooption on ethical matters if the forces come to *consensus*', which is not a consensus among anti-socially oriented members of arbitrarily selected morality of a fixed order, thinking its sacredness over everything else. This pro-social and anti-engineering but non-chauvinist method of ethical evaluation and resolution is, what I call, *intersubjective corroboration*, which is applied to resolve value crises of different kinds. (See Volumes 1, 2, 3 and 4 for details). Now, in this chapter, I take this method of ethical application as dynamic ethics, to see how it works in evaluating and resolving value-crises in economics, business and management without theory non-cooption. Intersubjective corroboration thus enters into a range of value-laden practical problems in field other than ethics to resolve them.

Intersubjective corroboration assumes value-laden practical problems permeating in economic matters, business enterprises and management on *empirical grounds* because we do have direct experiences of some such problems at the ground level of reality which do not merely call for what has to be done or needs to be done rather, why and how, what needs to be done, *should* be done, that is, on what ethical grounds do people (of all types of 'affected' categories), come to corroborate through moral reasons that they display during arduous moral dialogues to establish that such and such things are desirable and thus to be taken as courses of decisions and actions. Economics, business and management as expertise-oriented fields thus paves way for social beings having respect for *our* moral experiences and knowledge and *our* moral authority to come together to thrash out ethical disagreements in the evaluation of the right, good and just to come to conclude what should be done. Moral dialogues or debates are thus the crux of intersubjective corroboration, but this is not all, we have something more in store. We have discussed before that the first step in intersubjective corroboration is to "discover" value-laden problems. This is needed because value-laden or ethical problems cannot and should not be subjective constructions, that is, outcome of intellectual or emotional parleys of experts who are so-called 'conscious-about-ethicality'. A practical problem does not become value-laden when experts in ethics and management or in other fields by virtue of their great academics come to put value to practical matters. Some practical issues are value-laden is a matter of discovery of a sane person in society who luckily has not become a moral islanders, that is, one who still acts and interacts among vast number of people, beings and things, and thus come to *experience* the pro and con impacts on these beings and things, and about the retro-effects of the actions of beings and things on the one who has either influenced others favourably or unfavourably by his or her own decisions and actions. Hence, common moral experience enables *us* to discover the number of ground level practical affairs, that is, those intended actions of moral agents here in the world, which are marked by their characteristic disposition to churn our moral being or the moral experiences and knowledge which we have for a thorough critique. If we follow this explanation, not a single practical problem *is* value-laden in itself making a different category. Let us accept the truth that lay-offs in companies are not value-laden in itself because lay-offs are stark facts or phenomena in companies which can be explained on given factual *descriptive elements* or features. Lay-offs do not *become* value-laden by any external input such as subjective input, much like magnet that induces its properties in iron when they come in contact. Humans, some of them at least, when comes in contact with stark fact of lay-offs in companies do not realise or know that this is value-laden by virtue of their intellect or whim or wish. If this were the case, almost any fact could be turned into value by whimsical subjective inputs. As such Hitler would be able to turn a Jewish escape from gas-chamber to be value-laden, in fact, for him having an evil value, and a capitalist will be able to turn a lay-off as an evil because worker's demanding for better living was against a better life for themselves. Nothing in lay-offs thus calls for its *being* value-laden or its *becoming* value-laden. A lay-off in a company is value-laden if and only if a number of sane head ordinary people or even extraordinary ones, by virtue of their being members of a community come to realise that from within, they have an urge to find out that the said practical problem before them (lay-off) should not be left aside without an ethical *criticism*, that is, without resolving whether what is the case, *should* be the case or is desirably the case not on paradigms of social moral dogmas or corporate dogmas, but moving beyond them to the grounds which counters such dogmas in *association*. A practical problem which is value-laden or ethical is "discovered" by *us* by virtue of *our* moral experience and knowledge in this world of beings and things when we come to realise that critique of certain intended decisions and actions are needed in society for their desirability, ought, right, just, duty, obligation, responsibility and so on, on grounds different from what is or what happens or was happening. Such discovery does not belong to a class or a clan of experts, is the conclusion. Hence, no class or clan have unique rights or moral authority to resolve them either. If that be the case, trained businessmen, managers and ethicist do not enjoy moral authority to resolve the moral crises in lay-offs in companies, it should be extended to the *people* for dialogue, for the concerned parties at least, the most important being, the workers, their associates, administrators, judicial experts, law-makers, social activists and importantly, the ethicists. The final addendum to the list might raise eyebrows because one may be apprehensive about my whims as trained ethicist to save my clan and thus champion ethical clanism in the resolution of ethically charged practical issues. The reason for not excluding ethicists from the list are two; first, ethicists as members of the civil societies having moral experience and knowledge apart from academic ethical knowledge which gives them the needed attributes for a "discovery" of moral issues and the resolution of the same, not by applying their theoretical knowledge all by themselves but in association with other concerned parties, and second, it is by virtue of their depth-study of theoretical and practical ethics, not only are they best suited for finding out the reasons for supporting the *ethical pro-people method of applying ethics*, they know *how* should they proceed to take adequate leadership with others to conduct ethical debates, try to corroborate ideas to give us decision-making rules, and finally, to *analyse* the ethical debates to reveal which theory or theories of ethical evaluation were dynamic in ethical corroboration. Hence, there is no point in banishing ethicists or the expert managers who are or are not trained in ethics from the said ethical discovery and the dialogues or what we call, intersubjective corroboration discourses.

From this it is clear that an interested party in dynamics of ethics in management, business and so on should not only discover one or more value-laden practical problem or problems awaiting resolution, they should come up (at least some of them), to lead from the front to arrange moral dialogues, as extensive and intensive they can be. Two things are important here; one is to keep in mind the specific features and demands of a society in which value-laden practical problems are found, and the first hand idea of the practical problem. Hence, someone interested in resolving the value problem regarding lay-offs, should first know the technical aspects of lay-offs which is obtained through technical literature. Further, lay-offs have different facts, impacts and perceptions in different societies and in changing times, which makes a case for caring the specific conditions, features and demands of societies. In this sense, the value crises in India owing to lay-offs may be viewed with all care than dealing it as a general issue globally. It may well be that the features of value-crises owing to lay-offs in companies in India is distinguishable from its Japanese counterparts or, that in India, the crises we face at the present time of opening up of economy is distinguishable from what was at a remote past or a few years back. The debaters should thus be careful about the nature of the crises we 'now' face. These two points are all the more important when we consider ethicists taking a lead in ethical corroboration in arranging and moderating moral dialogues. However, it is not an imperative that non-ethicists cannot lead in such matters, but I must say that if post-corroboration analysis of moral debates is an integral aspect of ethical application to discover which theories of ethics were dynamic or applied by *us* non-mechanically, there is no wayout to have knowledge of academic ethics, particularly normative ethics. Hence, not everyone among us make a good party to lead in application of ethics if that amounts to intersubjective corroboration. Leaders in arranging a debate and moderating them need not have depth knowledge of academic ethics, but analysis of dialogues as theoretical enterprise needs such knowledge. Again it is not necessary that only ethicists are the party to do such things, anyone, for instance, businessmen, managers, and economists may do the same lest they have good knowledge of academic ethics. Hence, intersubjective corroboration understood *wholly*, does leave enough room for a post-debate theoretical enterprise suited best for ethicists or those trained in academic ethics. Like an interdisciplinary approach, application of ethics in management, for instance, begs on the one hand first hand *technical knowledge* of practical problem in consideration and on the other hand *theoretical ethical knowledge*. Leading in application of ethics thus rules out those who lack in both, though those who have both attributes make good leaders, may be they are ethicists or non-ethicists, not a clan at least. Hence, though academic knowledge of ethics and technical knowledge of the problem in consideration are not expected of parties concerned with value-laden issues and their resolution by thrashing differences in debates, both these things are needed of those who comes forward with the responsibility to start the course somewhere. Leaders are always needed in a dialogue but in this case, the leader does not belong to a class or a clan, nor do they mental gymnastics aided with normative theories. Intersubjective corroboration is through free-flowing debates, ably controlled to avoid deviations by the leader, the leader is not a moral engineer, she is much like an able moderator in any debate. Nevertheless, the leader of debates should do two things: First, to prepare a *questionnaire* fine-tuned to explicate the ethical reasons of debaters so that *points of corroboration* could be jotted and a *closure* reached to suggest a number of decision-making rules for concerned parties when they face a value-laden issue in future. Resolution of value-crises thus involves moderated debates reaching a closure. Again this is not classism because the said leaders are neither ethicists nor business managers to name a few; they are the one who are marked for their quality to conduct wholesome application of ethics that includes post-debates theoretical analysis as well. Hence, framing questions that brings out the ethical reasons of the debaters nicely and to control and reach a consensus during debates are tasks not to be shared by anyone among us. Again, this is not chauvinism because neither ethicists nor managers do such things exclusively; anyone who is trained in ethics can do so. Hence, intersubjective corroboration do not have any fixity in discovering a value-crisis and in resolving them through debates, it does demand from leaders of the application of ethics, knowledge of technical issues, ethical theories and analysis of ethical debates. It is also important to note that without any scope for structuralism, the model demands "ethically oriented questionnaires" to be framed by the leaders of debates because it is they who have shared the responsibility to make explicit the implicit ethical criticisms advocated by the participants. Yet, one must know that knowing ethics and management is not sufficient to frame proper questions for a dialogue because the discoverers of value-crises being common people, talking to them before they are invited for a debate and learning about their moral opinions from different sources always make good material for the preparation of ethically oriented questions for debates. Hence, leaders of debates should have all moral wisdom to not only know which cases make up for a debate, they should have enough respect for common people's moral opinions before they can gauge that along with academic information, which factors or elements should be integral parts of an "ethics oriented questionnaire". Selecting parties for dialogue need the same respect for people or respect for the most concerned ones, which is again vital for a lively dialogue in which intellectualism is not supreme or in which technicality and chauvinism has been kept aside.

Keeping these things in mind, we can now proceed to find out the value-crises in economy, business and management in India needing urgent care for resolution. There is no doubt that such issues are many, looking at the importance and urgency I have sorted out three in this chapter for discussion and one to be discussed in the next chapter. To be clear, my selection is not arbitrary, it is guided by recent literature, people's reactions and concerns, government's concern, concerns of technical persons or experts and of course, my own wisdom as a member of the Indian society. According to this selection, the most important and urgent value-crises for resolution in India is "globalisation of Indian economy and its ethical pitfalls", which will be taken up in the next chapter in a different way. In this chapter, my choice is to consider the ethical crises owing to "computerisation and modernisation of industries", "marketing and advertisement" and "taxation". It is interesting to note that these value-crises cuts through the fields of economics, business and management, which is always pragmatically valuable to discuss. The difference between considering these issues here and the other border issue in the next chapter is that here I will expound the aspects of intersubjective corroboration partially, that is, I will leave for readers to go for dialogues for which questionnaires will be provided to them, which is again matter for making the necessary changes if needed. However, first hand idea of the technical aspects of the practical problems and the moral currents therein will be provided here. In the next chapter, a full course of intersubjective corroboration will be provided, which expectedly becomes a matter for hot exchanges among our economists, businessmen, managers and others for validity, changes and acceptance. It is a great benefit if people revise my efforts with more sensible inputs. Let us proceed with the value-crises in computerisation and modernisation of industries in the Indian perspective.

First we have to know what is computerisation of various organisations like educational institutions, banks, insurance sector, government and non-government offices, railways and so on and why is it so needed in India. Further, we have to find out why computerisation is fraught with many 'practical problems', and why is it ethical or value-laden as well. This should be followed by key ethical controversies raging computerisation, the pro and con views likely to emerge and a questionnaire that might help us in debating about this matter for ethical resolution. Nevertheless, we must note that the modernisation of industries is a separate but linked value-laden problem, which is best treated in the perspective of pitfalls of globalisation. Here, we have to see what modernisation amounts to, particularly in the global environment of technological advances, population growth and subsequent increase in needs and demands. It is important to find out why modernisation is needed, what it poses in the Indian society and in what sense is it value-laden. Our questionnaire for debate should include ethical questions about this issue as well because one aspect of modernisation of industries owing to technological advances is the rise and growth of computers and the computer-culture (if we like that term). Looking at the linked issues of technological advances, modernisation of industries and computerisation of various organisations, I think it is best to start with the state of technological advances in India and its impacts that include value-related impacts.

Humans have virtuously (or viciously !) developed brain, its intricate functions, the powers to think, imagine, manipulate, create, change, modify and so on. Humans are particularly apt at playing with Beings with the nature and structure of what is available to them in the 'nature'. In due course, they create and modify so many things out of natural beings and things, but that is best done when they have certain physical or material aids or means or gadgets. For instance, we need types of levers even in our daily practices, which are the basic tools for manipulation, modification, creation and so on for meeting our needs and aspirations. We also found complex tools or means to meet our needs and aspirations, and a gamut of such means that makes our works easier and quicker thus enabling to meet the needs of a number of people at a rapid rate. The art of using the means effectively and appropriately by humans in and with nature evolved what we call "technology", or what may be called, the science of or scientific/systematic method of doing things and manipulations of natural beings and things. Generally, the scientific way or method of manipulating the natural bounties for human use, aided with adequate tools is the technical ability of humans or the technological advancements of humans, mostly needed in commercial practices. Technological advancement of humans is also testimony to the scientific advancement because advances in positive sciences in particular, have led us to the path of discovering newer and bolder techniques or ways to manipulate entities available to us in nature. This is of course owing to the diverse and wide knowledge advancement. However, we must not forget that the advances in techniques of manipulations or simply, technologies have given spurt to newer and bolder scientific advancements. Hence, advancements in knowledge, and scientific and technological advancements are correlative to each other. We can say that the human race has come of age to reach the modern times having a much more different life than what was before due to the three basic advancements. Technological advances thus contribute to the evolution and growth of human civilisation. It is the technology of a bottle cork opener that we do not use cumbersome methods to open corks. The same advancement gave us comfort in changing a leak tyre of cycle or car. Also it has given us rockets to fly and fight. It is technology that has given us way to blast rocks and earth for paving paths and extracting minerals. The same has however, given us the way to devastate humanity and environment. Anyway, technological advances have not waited for their negative uses, but they have been put into check whenever humanity felt the need. With the rise of modern and ultramodern technologies have risen industries and with it, has grown individual civilisation and culture through out the globe. Again, it was not without a point. Its rise was owing to the growing needs and aspirations of nearly geometrically progressing humans, at least at the different parts of the world. However, industrialisation was heavy to very heavy at different epochs not only due to population growth and to meet physical needs, it has grown for a specific need fulfilment, the growth of *power*, financial, commercial and military. The growth of commerce was certainly related to the growth of industries, and industrial growth reciprocated in commercial activities. With the accumulation of money in some hands, industries grew and the industrial spurt gave money in some hands. The accumulation of capital showed light to industrialisation, whereas the latter strengthened the capitalists who showed it the light. The need to protect capital and different resources and to acquire more power, the power-seekers needed industries of war, which in turn grew to great propositions to give humanity its worst power-seekers. Strangely, it was also believed that not for power accumulation but for the destruction of human miseries and poverty, to give support to the last persons of societies, industrialisation was needed. Did industrial growth reciprocate to empathise with them and empower them? If it did, there is different commendation than if it failed doing so or if did not do it at all. These questions may be equally searching for the mentors of industrialisation and scientific and technological advancements. Somewhere do we feel lays the question: was everything all right with our knowledge advancement? Leaving these unpleasant questions now, we are at hand the rise of yet another thing, state-of-the-art industries or simply, modern industries. Again one can see that the history of sciences and technologies is testimony to the evolution from rudimentary, to the medieval and then to the modern industries (we can conveniently cover ultra-modern ones in this fold without much ambiguity). Sciences and technologies have thus grown, marked by changes in their nature, structure, methods and dynamics. Some growths have been steady and gradual, others rapid and yet others by quantum leap and bounds. To my mind, agricultural technologies have grown gradually at a steady rate though this has been the prime economic occupation almost all over the world for quite some time and continue to be so in India. Whereas production technologies in manufacturing industries have been rapid, the same is the case in India. However, war industries have grown by quantum leaps in many areas of the world, and looks to continue at that pace though we had two devastating wars. Correlative to what we find in these cases, industrialisation has many states, the moderate and the rapid to the very rapid, the latter being a sign of what we call, modern industrialisation. Modernisation of industries is expected to do the best trick; it should push the output graph phenomenally whether that is in agricultural, manufacturing service and war industries through low to intensive replacements of older ways of production. This is well noticed in the *restructuring* and *re-entering* of industries. Modernisation is thus coping with situations, global and local, that is, to cope up with demands of people, their well-being and the profiteering of the corporate, the last being most dominant motive in the modern industrialisation whether that is undertaken at the private or the public organisations. One of the main reasons of rapid rate of modernisation, is that we have to cope up with the spirit and objectives of "globalisation". It may be said that modernisation of industries is a key to the globalisation of economy. Naturally, if globalisation is ruled by the ideology of the capitalists, most expectedly, except the agricultural industries, the others mentioned above, particularly the manufacturing and the war industries should grow tremendously, though service-based industries cannot lag behind. The worst sufferers have to be the small and the medium scale industries. Modernised industries are however, not always large to very large industries in terms of workforce or payments or output, there may be industries with few workers, few payments and not too much outputs, but mostly demanding a lot of investment and adequate profits. A modern industry may thus have robots and computers to replace workers, cut payments, welfare measures and produce what is needed, not too much though because there may be no market at all for such commodities, but things must sell at good prices incurring profits, at least at the expected level. With globalism in view, business houses in collaboration with the Indian houses might either prefer a huge capital invested modern industry with cheap labour and even few workers if workers can be replaced by modern machines even if investment on such replacements may be high enough. It is always taken as a wisdom for companies doing business at a distance to pay less, manage human resources at ease, invest less on welfaristic and fiduciary measures, but earn heavily. It is believed that these things can be helped best by good managers, curtailing unnecessary emotions and foolish humaneness. Corporate moving to and fro through the imaginary global boundaries at ease in business is thus helped by modernisation of the industries that they have. It is a matter of common sense that with the age old technologies and industrial units, corporate get old very soon; they are simply out of the global race for economic growth. This may be the case why many of our *desi* private and public companies are not coping up with many modernised companies, but (alas!) that need enough capital for investment. Yet, capital do not drop from trees, they are earned by virtue of moving in and with the global changes in commerce, and therefore, needs modernisation of productive units. One among many means of modernisation of corporate is through the computer technology. Let us come to it now, which may be called, the phenomenon of "computerisation" of organisations involved in commerce or business, whether it is a production, manufacturing, service-based, war-based, agriculture based, educational and many more types of business.

Computerisation in this context thus amounts to a specific method or technology with computer machines that is placed, replaced and enhanced for giving a modern boost to the company's objectives of production, distribution and profits. Here, we are not dealing with non-commercial computerisation in our household purposes having other than commercial objectives and gains. Modernisation through computerisation of companies has especial commercial significance in this context. We need to evaluate the ethical value of such a phenomenon, and not the ethic of having computers for our children at home and see what undesirable or desirable repercussions of the same are there. Clearly, we leave out many ethical issues due to computerisation in the broader social perspective. Our discussion thus far has also revealed that the ethical and social issues concerning widespread computerisation in business and homes is deeply related to the social and ethical issues related to modernisation in the face of globalisation of economy, and both in turn are related the social and ethical issues arising out of the scientific and technological advances. Hence, in this chapter referring to ethical issues in computerisation expectedly refers to modernisation, technological advances as well.

Technological advances and modernisation of industries as we have seen above in some cursory remarks, have deep impacts on global economies but it has defaced the geographical, environmental and social contours of nations. India is no exception, though there has been a huge hoopla all the way through their phoenix rise in the post-independence era because the touted great value of these things face some challenge when human well-being and social well-being is considered to a great extent. It has always been a *mantra* for the technologists and the modernists including the computer-technologists to base their success on a supreme *ethical* ideal. The problem of ethicality starts here, particularly when the glorious ideal is "human good", which is most expectedly at the broader level good for all sections of the society. Did technology and modernisation contribute to the broad-based "human good"? Did computerisation as an ally to modernisation do human good in the broader sense of the term? Some people say, if they did not do so, they are unethical because human good cannot be the same as doing good for a class of people and nor for many others. Many others say that even if they did good for a large number of people not sticking to the good of a class, it is further important to see whether the ecology has been harmed and whether the social, political and cultural environment of the population has been corrupted. Hence, it is important to ask, whether greater good of the humans has been done in the context of little or no corruption or huge corruption in the environment in which people exist. The broad lines of ethical belligerence are thus drawn. In India, we have been living under the prophetic vision of great technocrats backed by the industrialists, planners, economists and law-makers who said that the future of India is extremely bright with the rise of modern technology. We have witnessed the way in which technology helped an industrial revolution in India, and no sooner did the erstwhile alien computers enter the field, no one really doubted that the prophecy must be true. Yet, we have seen that not exactly did the great men do a Nostradamus, because there were yawning gaps. The gaps in the modernisation of industries through computerisation are clear, too. Where were the gaps? Critics said that they appear when "welfare" is understood wholly and not partly or scrappily. It may well be that modernisation did some good but took away many things from us. Computers did give us powers to calculate, restore information, pass on information, help in education, banking, railway booking, defence research, scientific missions and of late helped in what some people say India's best bet in outsourcing and knowledge revolution. Still the sceptics think that the unethical aspect is that all these hyped goods are still in the hands of some people, the masses really neither need them nor know them or both. The poor and the toiling masses engaged in agriculture, mostly as semi-bonded or bonded labourers or the migrating class doing physical work, are in large numbers, they have almost nothing for them to think positively about the said advances. In fact, all hyped goods are those for the well-off people who have the power to purchase technological and computerisation benefits. Hence, these advances are for those who have the economic power to get access to them.

Hence, computerisation as means to modernisation is not only pro-class, that is, pro-well-off class; it is also a means to the exploitation of the worst-off class because money-power added with technological power has always been the sources to the corruption of the corrupted class.

Even the so-called powerful class is also bungled for the so-called good. What is the said good of the class? Most of the proponents of modernisation and computerisation argue that the said good is their "happiness in life"; and what is the happiness quotient of the class? Able economist of our times does not hesitate to say that the consumer having the needed power to *buy* happiness, in fact, buys "pleasures" for them. Hence, the class is satisfied with the bungled out gratificatory sense pleasure that modern industries, computers have given them. The consumers having no such power to buy the above imaginary "happiness" must not be "happy" in any case, but they might have other ideas. They might say that though we lag behind in the power to buy gratificatory pleasures for us, we are "happy" in other ways. For instance, we are happy that the computers have not corrupted our youth or have made them physically impotent or have not entered our tiny, poor, village schools for extra fee, and so on. Well, none is satisfied with the debate of ethicality in monologues because each contestant argues with a wall in front him or her. However, our readers are already having a taste of the inner questions of ethical desirability, good and so on for a debate and not a monologue in front of a wall.

As we do not live in Europe or America, it is expected of us to consider some of these questions seriously in the light of the Indian social, economic and political conditions. Is it too odd to imagine that evaluating the technological advances, modernisation and computerisation in India should be in the light of the basic rural predominance till this date? Is it inappropriate to keep in mind that a large chunk of our population is extremely poor? Is it too odd to keep in mind our reactions to a growing social order and value-system that comes from the lands of consumerism and capitalism? What is good if the brouhaha of our speedy economic growth of 8 per cent *per annum*, the so-called glorious GDP and the showing of incredible India is bungled cloaking the truth that people eat mango seeds and a number of hungry people commit suicide or simply die of hunger? We just cannot be so unethical to walk in the shoes of a pseudo-capitalism that forgets own brethren who do not know what computer is, and for what it is to them. The punch line of criticism is not soft and cannot be left without answering them. My point is to come out of the comfort zones to a hot zone of debate. If we do not give our answers in the public, no ethicality is left for us.

There is no doubt that a majority of the questions raised above primarily asks whether technological advances and modernisation have any value. Going through an English Work Book of my son I found a chapter on the meaningful or sensible uses of technology, particularly if it is hyped as "modern". The point was to make children realise that though we live in an age of modern technology like supercomputers and many others, not all of them are sensibly used by the general public for their good. It is in this regard that "nonsense machines" are discussed for having no social value, and thus it is unethical to have a propaganda mechanism based on palpable untruths to bluff the consumers. Most interesting fact is that consumers having less wisdom but more money power are worst sufferers because they are easily carried off to buy nonsense gadgets. One way to bluff and sell these gadgets is to add to the advertisement of the product: "Fully Computerised" or "Digital Device". You might thus have a computerised washing machine that sounds an alarm when the job is over or an electric coil meant for heating/baking that rings an alarm but the point is, what it does to the money powered consumer? If it is a near hoax, modern computerised machines cannot be of any good and thus their production and marketing is unethical. Will it not be better in India if computers enable our farmers of remotest villages to know the wind patterns, cloud formation, changes in rain, its persistence and intensity? We can further intensify such questions to ask whether sophisticated, computer guided ultramodern machines that does wonderful diagnosis and operations in speciality hospitals are at all ethically desirable than having more and more general hospitals in villages for the most un-empowered people where basic amenities have dwindled? Can the ordinary masses in India buy such health care speciality even if the machines are too good to serve people? The point is, when we speak of goodness of computers for the health care of the people, we carefully abandon the thought of "poor or ordinary un-empowered people". It must be a tragedy, if the AIIMS, which sounds to be pro-people health care organisation, does the same consumerism-trick of the capitalist though its apparatus, the fully computer guided ones are of the people and for the people. Any consumer goods in India or elsewhere should be excellent in quality; they must be produced by obtaining latest technological advantages, the computers must be used when they are necessary, but the point of ethicality boils down to the pragmatics of use of the consumer items and the status of the consumers who are supposed to use them. We cannot and should not forget that any machine that helps in the production of a carcinogenic substance for instance, cannot be pro-people. Equally true is that having computers for billing in an ultra-modern shop in a glittering mall, does not justify computerisation in business. Yes, the billing system helps the shop owner in keeping accounts perfectly managed. It helps the consumer to keep his accounts straight and if needed to sue the shop owner for any bungling, but the point is whether computerisation may not be more generally useful for those who do not need it most for a 'cosmetic feeling-well', but for more realistic, 'being-well'.

Most of the questions that we have faced till now hovers in the field of benefits that modern computer technology might have or do not have when people of a particular nation is put to the centre, and when "people" do not represent a typical consumer class well-off in monetary terms. Shifting the focus now to another people-centred ethical debate is to inquire the impact of computerisation on the *working-class* of a nation. There is no doubt that this 'consumer benefit oriented' and 'working-class benefit' oriented questions are of global concern, but in particular states the problems might be different given the socio-economic and political shifts through the ages. This is no wonder because any concerned Indian has felt the heat that has been generated in different organisations after computerisation started with a bang, particularly, after Rajiv Gandhi became the Prime Minister of India. Before that many public and private sector organisations had to rely heavily on human work force, their manual and intellectual labour, so to say. Though, India has no dearth of human power to work, the organisations thought that not emotions but prudence controls business, and one prudent aspect is making payments and perks to workers who were nevertheless, not as fast, precise and accurate as machines. Well, how can a biological machine be as fast and as accurate as a material machine? It cannot be the case in practice, but to imagine that it should be the case because that is a 'desirable desire' of business houses, is basic to the ethical inquiry. Why at all should sane humans in the name of business be so inhuman to imagine that humans as workers needs to be as good as machines? The man-machine or the human-machine interface is the crux of the ethical problem. Through the ages all over the world, the interface of humans and modern machines have created value-laden practical furore, because machines undermine human power and dignity. Machines also undermine human right to eke out an honest living by sheer hard work in any civil society. The threat of machines replacing workforce is thus brought under ethical scrutiny because not always our desired desires are desirable. It may not be granted without any challenge that sophisticated machines will suddenly snatch jobs from millions and thus leave them to ignominy. We have seen interesting things in India once computers were widely introduced in the railways. Immediately some of us were extremely appreciative of the system of reservation where *babus* do not make hay or the agents do not play truant. Yet, the trade unions were up in protest. So was the case in the nationalised banks, power sector, coal sector, insurance sector and so on. There was heavy crunch in the jobs, the unions always demanding that they should not be made the scapegoats, though huge cases of voluntary and forced retirements made the atmosphere heavy. The other side of the coin is that gradually workers coped with the situation and they became faster, accurate causing much benefit to the customers. It is learnt that with the rise of stiff competition in the banking sector in India, not only did banks go for more sophisticated computerised services, they spread network of banks in far-off areas involving less human work force but creating fresh jobs once more. Similarly, a loss of workforce was ably covered by fresh needs of the same in the newly evolved information sectors. Hence, one cannot deny that computerisation and modernisation always did some poor trick with the workforce. The ethical questions we have now thus hover around the desirable good that computerisation does even at the cost of retrenchment and even the most drastic re-engineering of firms in the name of modernisation through the introduction of sophisticated machines. The moot issue is whether it will be at all ethical to follow the steps of nations having enough money to invest in modernisation though they have little workforce? Will it be ethical for those nations to bypass their paltry workforce to either induct cheaply paid skilled workers from other countries or to outsource the job? Is it ethical to cope up with the shortage of workers with mechanisation and induction of cheap labour? We cannot skip these questions now. Our time is a testimony to the growing unrest in European and American states regarding foreign hiring and outsourcing. Even if the workers of a nation are to be paid higher salaries, how can they be deprived of employment in the competition of cheap labour? Is it not true that with computerisation an unethical attitude in the corporate has grown to measure the value of workers purely on economic terms? Did it not give an unethical impetus to the exploitation of the workers at both ends, that is, at the end of hiring and outsourcing and at the end of deprivation of nation's workforce from their right to earn and live justly? Have computers in modern industries become the exploiters of the masses? If it does contribute to exploitation, a means to the hawkish capitalist, it is party to unethicality.

The readers should never lose view of the fact that none of the assertions and the arguments produced above is mine. I have tried to act as pro-con characters in an imaginary debate to show what value-laden issues amounts to and why is the issues value-laden needing emergent resolution. To carry it a little farther, let us enter into another realm of debate. A common sense analysis of the disasters owing to intended abuse of computers reveals that though the machine itself is not evil, its users may be so. In fact, computers were not invented to play trick on humanity but it started playing tricks only when some users had anti-human and anti-social goals. Nevertheless, the technology must face the blame game if it cannot plug the holes after so many years of its invention, modification and use. If computers were invented out of the genuine needs of complex computations made easy, and subsequently people went on for various uses, most notably in storing and passing information as well as storing and using data of different kinds for different purposes, then in itself the technology has nothing to be blamed but the users and researchers in this field do have some responsibilities towards the general public to prevent its abuse, that involves abuse in the manipulation with data, information and calculus. This broad view of 'responsibility' comes in the purview of "moral responsibility" because it does not simply speak of what needs to be done by some people but why something ought to be done. The question of oughtness takes us to the available moral reasons and moral arguments which freely draw from the different normative stands. However, it is not necessary that we need basic knowledge of either academic logic or academic ethics to display our reasons for the oughtness of human responsibility in computer practices. It does not take us to be computer literate to argue that deft manipulations of computer data by air or railway booking agent is grossly 'irresponsible' act because an agent in a responsible position ought to do such things with common people because that is acting against his or her social duties, and that violation of social duties amounts to a gross anti-social attitude that disturbs social cohesion and harmony. It does not need ethics training or even logic training to argue that passing on sensitive information in a simple diskette from the defence or intelligence department by responsible officers to those engaged in subversive activities is grossly unethical because that ought not to be done on the ethical ground of social good or national good. It does not take ethics teaching on our part to argue ethically that violation of duties in stations of life does not make us a self-realised person and for that reason, for a banker, it is irresponsible to pass credit card passwords/numbers to a party to mischief. However, what is beyond doubt is the importance of ethical scrutiny of the issue of human responsibility in the use of computer technology. Some people argue that companies like telephones and automobiles are amenable to both good and bad use, but the point of reference of goodness and badness is extremely relative and vague. It is very difficult to say that we have agreed on some such references as absolute that enables us to judge what is use and abuse of computers. It may well be that though the technology being so complex and so wide in use, it has capacity for opposites. Computers in this sense may be like humans, who have the capacity for opposites. Computer technology as such may be thus having the capacity to do a number of notorious things in society and a number of useful things. The question is, we have not made a chart of references for notoriety and usefulness. How can we say that stealing information stored in computers which is as easy as storing and keeping them safe, be notorious or bad, if for instance, I belong to intelligence group and is frantically after a gang to have basic information to bust them? It is just like tapping a phone-call by the intelligence to bust a criminal. How can it be bad or evil? Hence, computers, like humans, are capable of doing things; *we call them 'good' and 'bad'* on the basis of norms that suit us. Computers are 'good' as it suits intelligence officer to bust a crime; it is 'bad' as it suits criminals to pirate data. We have standards for evaluations that suits us, neither computers nor its users can be called ethically good or bad. We can say that computers and its users *do* certain things in association, what they do are free from any value; values are inducted or put by us arbitrarily as it suits us. Hence, it will be in a bad taste to say that human users of computer technology have moral responsibility to do such and such good things (ought), and not to do such and such bad things (immoral).

In fact, following this argument, there are no moral standards or norms that can be in any case called into evaluation of *our* responsibility in using computers and *our* ethicality in computerisation. This argument may be retorted by arguing further that though humans and computers have capacity for opposites and there is hardly any absolute standard of good and bad evaluation of computer use, we cannot deny that there are many objective standards for the evaluation of moral goodness and badness applying which we often come to conclude that at the global perspective and at the broader level of humanity, certain uses of computers are bad and not good, which needs to be plugged as soon as possible. It is due to this that globally computer scientists are trying to plug the loopholes in hacking, piracy and privacy. More research is thus not how intelligence can bust a secret stored in computer hardware rather how none can easily steal information or data stored by us. The moral ground might vary from the intrinsic goodness of honesty and privacy than dishonesty and breach in privacy. It may be argued that technocrats as per their work ethos and goals in life should assume the *duty* of preventing information stealing by any agency for any purpose than allowing them to some extent. Hence, responsibility and duty of computer scientists or of those who have opted for broad based computerisation is to abide by objective goods, like honesty, privacy and efficiency. It is in this context that we further realise the value of pro-people good of computerisation because computerisation for cosmetic good or specific good for some people may be tested seriously for moral validity till the technology survives. It may be thus a perennial objective for proponents of broad based computerisation to strive longer for extending benefits to the last person than for a limited defence, intelligence and banking purposes. It is believed that the queer trend of technological evolution, including computerisation is one of specific need fulfilment to spread out for more needs and then enter the alluring trap of cosmetic and class based use to neglect and exploit the population at large. The one-directed evolution of computer technology thus calls for spreading its tree so that it becomes pro-people. Therefore, we need to realise that computerisation in a global economy is not a mere need, a commercial or a material need of the businessmen. It is not a handmaiden of the savvy managers of companies who feels good when armed with technology to do what he or she is covenanted to do; computerisation is not value-neutral in any case even when businessmen and managers need them seriously. Moral agents, as the users of computers are, should take the responsibility to face the consequences of intended use of the computers if that is in particular not pro-people. Our businessmen and managers in the age of computerisation cannot remain value-neutral in the use of the technology because their intended use and their intended spread of the phenomenon is always under the moral scanner to evaluate whether what they do is amoral or anti-moral or immoral or moral, there is no scope for it being non-moral. It is due to this that in computerisation, the organisations making hay should never lose sight of the truism that computer technology with the software that are at our disposal, they are *intermediate* to us (users) and the consequences that follows from its use. Hence, we cannot shed off our moral responsibility as users of the intermediary to be cautious about intended courses of actions and the consequences that follows. It is not the intermediary which is responsible for good or bad consequences; it is we who should take the responsibility. Hence, it may be noted that in case of disastrous accidents owing to computer aided jobs of the technocrats, doctors and scientists, they cannot simply raise their index fingers to the intermediary and wipe off their moral responsibility. In case of an organisation, for instance, a business organisation, a managerial or technocratic mishandling which may not be intended, may be still under the ethical scanner to compel users to share responsibility and not bark about the mechanical malfunction. Even, the entire organisation and in some cases a nation has to take the moral responsibility if some irresponsible damage has been done to beings and things even by unintended accidents in computer use. It is exactly due to this that we do not put moral blame on the AK 47 rifles that kills thousands but on its users who are irresponsible and anti-humanity.

Another interesting aspect of computerisation is that its marvel lies in being not a machine but a *metamachine*, that is, a technological marvel that controls many other machines. Again, computers are seen as second-level machines beyond (meta) the first-level or major machines. In this sense, if basic machines are intermediaries available to us, computers are *super-intermediaries*[1]. It is thus not awkward to assume that in case of any disastrous consequences in the use of intermediary machines, the blame comes on the companies as if like humans they are taken as the most responsible agents that could not control rather trigger problems in the intermediary machines. It is due to this anthropomorphic view of computers that the focus of moral responsibility is (wrongly) shifted to non-human agents saving the human managers mostly responsible for computer control. It is natural these days to thus shift blame on computerised systems of first-level machines to save a human face. Should we, morally speaking, shift human responsibility to metamachines in this way? There is no doubt that once a computerised system is left to work normally as per its programme (which is however, a human affair), humans cannot or should not interfere in the functioning because interference might result into a complete shut-down or malfunction. Hence, the natural course of computerisation being a demand for non-interference, the pointer cannot shift to a person or some persons. Hence, the argument is either we are happy with ancient machines or we are happy with modern metamachines, though both might play truant. If humanity goes in the way of mechanisation and modernisation, it has to bear the outcomes of human follies. Well, everything must be good in this way of thinking then the idea that human follies need correction and serious moral inquiry because it is only then do we not fall in repetitive follies. Let us take it for granted that if bearing sympathetically with human follies until I am myself the scapegoat, is the way of moral life, then follies are glorified, they become so natural to us that we pardon people in the name of machines and continue to be party to killing fields.

Inherent in the above discussions and the range of questions regarding computerisation is the idea that despite relativism and scepticism about use and abuse, there is some objectivity to which the global citizens more or less agree, whether they are members of a company or outside the companies as common people having different occupations and professions. One distinguished abuse of a computerised system more or less accepted universally, is the individual and/or organisational intended anti-human and anti-social use of the system, which can be simply called "criminalisation" of the computerised system. If the whole of computerised system under an underground terrorist group be anti-human, it will be called "criminal" abuse of the system. If an individual does this, it is as worse a criminal abuse of computers as organisational criminal abuse. It hardly matters whether computerised systems available to a business house is used wrongly or whether someone in the house goes all by herself to use it wrongly. As I have said before that in this discussion of ethics of computerisation we are less interested in computer crimes conducted by individuals in non-business or non-commercial cases, we shall focus more on commercial crimes, particularly, by the organisations or by a manager or an employee in an organisation. Most noted business crimes of organised nature involving computers are those of consumer and contractual frauds. This might cover breach in consumer privacy, sales related malpractices and bluffs in data analysis thus affecting individuals or organisations or both. An interesting ethical debate regarding the matter of breach of privacy involves the civil libertarians and those against such views[2]. Supporters of necessity of breaching consumer privacy argues that the ethic behind such wrongly conceived subversive act is that for the greater good of the business organisation it is an imperative to have access to private information and data. Infact, a business organisation is primarily bound to some of its basic obligations; one of them may be providing good services to customers though for that some information from the customer's private files is needed. One instance is to survey market or to compare the state, status and relative benefits customers enjoy in an organisation in comparison to another parallel organisation. The civil libertarians argue that though services to customers are supreme ethical goal in business notwithstanding incurring loss as equally avoidable practice for business houses, it is ethical to value the liberty of the customers as free moral agents enjoying civil rights to safeguard against any intended abuse of their personal information. Business good cannot surpass individuals good by means of safeguard against their right to privacy. Hence, if an organisation uses personal data of consumer for higher gains or benefits not directly influencing the customer, libertarians ask for any data transfer which was uncalled for and unlawful. The supporters of breaching privacy argue that under the cover of a legal permission, sensitive information may be transferred to a proper authority. Taking a cue from breach of trust and privacy by the telephone departments (public or private) to pass sensitive information to the police, for instance, enables supporters a breaching mechanism to argue that when the greater good of society or nation is at stake, a business house being a responsible agent is bound to law to pass information which was otherwise unlawful. To this the critique say that law may be as overreaching as a sacrosanct system of absolute values that it confuses a consensus of legislative system which is by far a consensus of convenience disregarding the ethical system which is neither arbitrary nor a convenient consensual system. Hence, what is lawful under a definite banner for an organisation may be unethical under the normative banner. A social system that cares for blocking subversiveness should nevertheless, refrain from breaching privacy of customers of any organisation and look for other means for blocking the evil thing.

The problem of privacy in business is complex. More often than not it is the employees of a company who are at great risk in passing private information to the supervisor or the manager with whom the person is in personal contact or to whom the employee is bound by work-nature and responsibility. The risk is mainly due to computerised network to store and pass information. It is always a risky affair for an employee or a manager to exchange information through e-mail or voice-mail. It may well be that in-house politics of power, position and money always threaten to leak information about employees and managers to sabotage their work and career. The same may be true when two employees or managers exchange information either about management or workers, thus breaching their privacy and resulting into many unforeseen and unpleasant consequences. Those who support breaching privacy of non-managerial employees and managers in companies harp on the maximisation of the well-being of the company that ultimately does some good to the employees and managers because these people may be engaged in undesirable or unlawful or unpragmatic practices detrimental to the company. Companies even argue that with the gradually vanishing demarcations of home and work-place/office in modern business, it is often needed to keep a tag on the responsible people so that they refrain from irresponsible actions. Hence, the ethic of breaching privacy boils down to the benefit maximisation theory that has no hesitation in isolating benefits for a particular group, most of the time the stockholders and the shareholders. It is exactly at this point that anti-breaching arguments try to hit because for them humans at work places (home is also a work place), enjoy certain rights apart from having duties and responsibilities, which gives them the intrinsic value as professionals, as persons respectable for having a noble objective and freedom to achieve them to the best of his or her knowledge and ability. Computerisation is a means to the professional objective, which should be thus used with great acumen and freedom by the responsible people. Hence, the intrinsic value of a professional form of life calls for privacy at work-places, which computerisation should assure and not breach. Further, much like what Plato said, mistrust among people with intended harm makes bad people worse and good people bad. Hence, we should as humans are wise to refrain from mistrust and harm. For Gandhians, the two are evil as forms of violence in mind. Hence, the argument goes that computerisation should not in any way be used to breach privacy because it is based on the unethicality of mistrust and harm, which breaks corporate unity and thus against its well-being. If well-being of the company is so dear to us, the contributing employees and stockholders/shareholders should be protected from violence and disintegration which is possible when computer information is not breached for a private access to people's life. It is largely agreed by these thinkers that in cases of breaching privacy, it is not the law of the land or the company laws or codes that is of much help. It is best to take recourse to ethical thinking, debating and coming to a consensus about such matters. For employees, managers and stockholders it is imperative on them to respect human autonomy and not disrespect it, and for that the private individuals must be cared by not breaching their privacy. It is always a healthy ethical debate to find out whether without a clear conception of a theory of rights we will be able to discover an ethical system of respect for professional autonomy and privacy because "scholars are not in complete agreement as to whether a right to privacy is a hypernorm, though most would agree that some form of personal autonomy must be protected"[3]. Everything said and done, the antagonists are still in a position to say that the threat perceptions in business cannot be foolishly overlooked, and therefore, in the glorification of right to privacy and individual autonomy, private access to responsible people's life is not ruled out as unethical. Such nagging arguments are often calmed down by the protagonists by taking recourse to the conceptions of integration in work-life and accountability of responsible people. Ultimately, if professionals are not accountable to do what is not only expected of them to do, but to do what is also ethically valuable, and if professionals lack in integrity or consistency of values, then there is no resolution to the problem of privacy. To the question 'why ethically speaking professional integrity and accountability is so desirable?' It is said that without these things in mind a professional as such loses identity, that is, loses self-identity. Hence, the value of the professional self is best realised in the work-life integrity and accountability. A number of notable computer abuses in public and private sector companies (which involves employees, stockholders and managers), like computer related consumer frauds, computer related negligence and computer instigated victimisations, all refers to the individuals in companies to ask serious ethical questions about their intention, moral character, moral goals, ethical choice of means and their integrity and accountability. The searching questions are deeply related to the ethic of quality-of-life and quality-of-work-life. One important aspect of a life of quality is that people should be educated to live in association and harmony at home, in the neighbourhood, in the society and in the work-place. The last one being extremely important as a large part of our life is spent in the work-places, which must be qualitatively good as well. Apart from many things, it is important that the work-life should be ethically oriented, that is, we should never lose sight of the basic ethical inquiries about what things should be done. This is possible when employees, managers and others, even if they do not have any idea of academic ethics freely talk about what things are right, good and just as professionals and what should be done when they assume responsibilities and duties in society not forgetting the conception of the legitimate rights they should enjoy.

Intersubjective corroborative dialogues regarding the issues of modernisation, computerisation and the state of employees in India was arranged by me selecting the following people for the ethical dialogues:

1. Dr. J. Ashraf, Professor of Management, XISS, Ranchi.
2. Mr. V. K. Sharma, Head of System Analysis, SAIL, Ranchi.
3. Mr. U. Krishnamurthy, Regional Manager, Central Bank of India, Ranchi.
4. Mr. Manoj Kr. Tiwari, Director, Samadhaan Group of Companies, Ranchi.
5. Dr. Ramesh Sharan, Professor of Economics, Ranchi University, Ranchi.
6. Mr. Samir Kr. Dass, Jt. Secretary, BSSR Union, Ranchi.
7. Mr. Ranjit Roy, Human Rights Activist, Ranchi.
8. Mr. H. K. Roy, Ex-Labour Welfare Officer, CCL, Ranchi.
9. Mr. Sanjay Mishra, Bhartiya Kisan Sangh, Ranchi.
10. Sri P. K. Panigrahi, Asstt. Labour Commissioner (Central), Ranchi.
11. Mr. K. J. Anthony, "Johar", (NGO), Ranchi.

The dialogues were based on the following questions which was finalised by me after an arduous theoretical work consisting of collecting information about the problem in consideration from different papers, newspaper items and formal talks with economists and the participants to whom I met for arranging dialogues and thus had to go through a discussion about what I was intending to do and how the participants look at the problems. In fact, when an ethics corroborator visits some people to initiate them for a dialogue, he or she has to clarify the project and in due course comes to know what roughly each participant feels. This is very helpful in framing questions provided the ethicist or the person interested in dialogues do not profess or show his or her intellectual genius, rather listen carefully to what non-ethicists or non-coopted people say about the issue with which they are most interested. A good observer and listener often discovers what people think about morality and what they think is good or bad with the most prevalent and dominant perceptions about a value-laden issue (For details, see Volume 1). It is desirable that the corroborators should not put difficult questions in technical language. It is also good to put precise questions which bring value-perceptions of a participant clearly and the list of questions must not be too lengthy. Throughout the dialogue the corroborator should try to record each and every opinion and criticism, and be fair giving enough opportunity to each participant to express their views, but care should be taken to moderate the discourse along the ethical path rather than turning it to a non-ethical discussion. Care should be taken to find out the points of resolution which appears through corroboration of views despite stiff moral disagreements.

Let me now provide the questionnaire for the convenience of readers though it is not fixed. Necessary corrections should be made if someone feels that some more questions should be added or some questions should be deleted or modified. It is also important to note that one course of discussion as a starter anywhere in India is good for all practical purposes, but it needs spreading, that is, a number of such dialogues should be arranged by corroborators across the nation for which a wide network is needed. Great integration is also needed on the part of the ethicists to find out the broad based ethical agreement, resolution and subsequent formulation of decision-making rules, which need not remain as handiwork of theoreticians but must be pressed on a civil and sane-headed legislative for effective implementation. Professional life is not an edifice of theories; it is a life of theory put to practice.

QUESTIONNAIRE

1. What according to you should be the end or goal of technology and modernising technological units? In view of this, what should be the role and value of computerisation?
2. What is the value of humans *vis-à-vis* machines such as computers in commercial activities? In views of this, what should be the role of employees, including managers in commercial units?
3. Do you think that computerised and modernised companies can, and thus should contribute to a humane course of economic development and growth?
4. Do you think that there should be further care taken for the environment in which we live and act? In view of this, evaluate modernisation as a friend or foe of environment.
5. Do you think that in the Indian companies, the stockholders and the managers are linked to the machines and employed workers as exploiters and the exploited? If yes, justify why it should be the case, and if no, why should it not be the case.
6. Do you think that stakeholders enjoy some rights as does stockholders, managers and other employees dealing in the complex network of a computerised system in companies and beyond? Should there be right to privacy to each of these groups of people? Please justify your answer.
7. In view of the replies to the questions, please suggest some decision-making ethical rules for our professionals of India dealing in and with the computerised and the modernised units.

Now it is my task to explain why I have selected the parties mentioned above for the dialogues. A careful look at the list of the participants leaves some clues for the most interested parties in ethical corroboration to select, trained economists, management theorists, managers, and employees, trade unionists including the radical ones, administrators, computer scientists, engineers, human rights activists and NGOs in the fields of human welfare. It is also important to include in this list the politicians or law-makers, bank officers and labour welfare officers. However, as it was in my case, if politicians having different affiliations are not available, we may not include anyone of them. It is better to takc the debate further at the level of politics including some legal experts for more effective implementation of people's suggestions for ethical decision-making. We can now find out why one such debate is not enough and why a debate held in Ranchi is not enough. Nevertheless, all interested parties in ethical corroboration should note that rather than going nowhere, a movement has to be started—people's movement should begin to pick up momentum gradually. This is well noticed in the UK, USA, Australia and Canada. I have said that for instigating our readers, who might take interest in people's ethics which is comfortable with a social scientific vocation and empirical ethics (See Volume 1), should not be much interested in what followed next in a dialogue than finding for themselves what follows when they act corroborators. Hence, at least in this chapter, I will refrain from details of dialogues and the post-corroborations analysis of dialogues revealing normative involvement. I thus leave the two tasks now for our readers to move on to consider another case that is extremely important in the Indian context, which is the value-laden case of Marketing and Advertisement.

It is extremely important to consider ethical issues in marketing and advertisement seriously particularly in view of the opening up of Indian economy, freeing trade restrictions, encouraging the multinational companies and the new look of the government to disinvest in the public sectors. Why marketing and advertisement also poses value-crises, for people in management, for the employees and the commonmen is also interesting to note. As usual, the resolution of crises makes great sense following the method we have obtained here, though here we are committed not to learn much in details about real life resolution. Let us try to analyse what marketing and advertisement means to business and its management, and what value-laden issues emerge therein. However, at the outset it should be clarified that as usual here we are not interested in non-commercial advertisements or those done in the public interest without any involvement of transaction of money as fee or charge or profits at the cost of the public payments. What I mean here is that 'non-commercial' conveys a restricted sense of hiring services for marketing and advertisement by the common people, for benevolent purposes or for public good directly. In this case thus, the common public is not a direct paying body for the services meant for their good. Some stray cases at the lower intensity of investment might come under this category, when, for instance, we give individual effort by distributing hand-bills, notices and leaflets to advertise and market certain products or to give some information to some people without any expectation of monetary return of whatever low costs may be involved in it. Hence, the marketing and advertisement of family planning products by some welfare groups is one instance of marketing and advertisement of non-commercial nature, understood in its specific sense here; whereas, a football club's intention to market the skills of its players in a free for all exhibition match and to advertise the match without the help of any agency is another example of 'non-commercial' marketing and advertisement. There may be other examples but we must agree that at least a sense of "benefit" or "advantage" or "gain" may not be ruled out in every case of advertisement and marketing. Even a glorious example of an eye hospital marketing its skill of cornea transplant free of cost through ads all by themselves, that is, not hiring an agency for marketing and ads is essentially "benefit" oriented, otherwise why all these are done, is not known to us. This is so because "benefits" need not be necessarily "monetary benefits" or "commercial" in nature. We have to be careful here that our discussion of ethic of marketing and advertisement keeps in focus the purely "commercial" marketing and ads, that is, those in which public or private agencies, groups or individuals are engaged in hiring services by making direct payments to parties giving services, may be through a contract to thus serve their own interests including monetary interests. The commercial nature of marketing and ads may be high or low key in terms of intent, extent, investment and gains (monetary and non-monetary), thus taken up by individuals, groups of individuals agencies and the governments. It may well be that some business organisations might have their own marketing and advertising wings or they might take private services. Hence, marketing and advertisements as parts of commercial activities in public and private organisations may be either wholly hired or self-promoted. In all cases of such marketing and ads, there is an involvement of monetary as well as non-monetary advantages or benefits. Among non-monetary benefits may be gains in the catch of consumers' interests and sympathies, or even a feeling of satisfaction on the part of a company that markets products or services through ads. Also the benefits might be as good as satisfaction of professional self, the satisfaction out of displaying skills and aesthetic sense. Or, as bizarre advantages as persuading the public for a bad product at good costs, thus giving a satisfaction out of the negative impact that a skill can produce. Often in marketing, advertisements are taken as modes of propaganda and persuasion at any cost, anyhow, but there must be a drawing line between propaganda, persuasion and advertisement for marketing products and services. It may well be that *not* all cases of ads market things through mere propaganda or even persuasion because propagandas are not necessarily subjective models of advertising things for marketing them, they are used for many other non-commercial purposes, for instance, some political propagandas may be non-commercial in nature because that may be used to hit a vote-bank or to deviate people from voting a party or a way to create public panic or sympathy for ulterior purposes. Similarly, *not* all cases of persuasions are ways to advertise for marketing things, there are some non-commercial purposes of persuasive tactics, for example, to evoke moral sentiments in our hearers by uttering that democracy is a 'fool's paradise' just to make them react or go against the system or to pooh-pooh the system. Here, we are speaking of marketing and advertisement as modes of commercial and business objective fulfilment to have "gains" or "advantages" in the main, monetary advantages, being most crucial. It has also to be noted that though marketing and advertisements are different aids or means to enhance commercial and business activities, they are *not* key economic activities like the primary, secondary and tertiary activities, which are nevertheless, linked to organised human activities, at times done under the corporate settings. Hence, marketing and advertisements are *intermediaries*, to commerce and business but not organised human activities that are tantamount to the activities like the production and distribution of goods and services. Similarly, marketing and advertisement are related to trading practices under the commercial activities as intermediaries to enhance trade, but unlike trading, is not tantamount to the actual give and take of goods or produces among traders and consumers. In this way though marketing and advertisements are intermediaries in business, private or public, profiteering or non-profiteering, to enhance its enterprises, it is not tantamount to production and distribution of goods, and services to earn profits or to extend welfare to the buying and selling communities. Marketing and advertisements are thus human enterprises in organisational settings or at the individual levels that stands as intermediate means or aids to enhance business, commercial and trading activities. As all three economic activities are deeply related to economic activities, marketing and advertisement are linked to economic objective-fulfilment as *means*. Marketing and advertisements of goods and services thus have unique objectives of their own, but such unique objectives turn out to be 'means to higher economic, business and commercial goal fulfilments'. The management of marketing and advertisement is thus means to the higher level management of business, economy and commerce. Hence, they are conducted for the sake of higher levels of goal fulfilment of different organisations, private, public, profiteering and non-profiteering. In any case, marketing and advertisements are not ends-in-themselves; they are rather aids-to-advantages, commercial and non-commercial (which needs to be understood in the sense discussed above). It is also important to note that though marketing and advertising are related aids in commerce and business, as such advertising can be bereft of the necessity of marketing products or services or brands or ideas or skills because it is not always that we advertise for marketing these things, we may do so to *prevent* consumers from buying marketed products or to educate them about their rights and duties. Ads showing the value of 'right to information' or 'to have two children' or 'to give pulse polio drops to newborns' do not market the said right or family planning or polio drops. Nevertheless, when we market things, or concept, we do it with commercial and business motives, either profit oriented or welfaristic or both, that is, with basic 'advantage' orientation, but with a difference with 'advantage oriented' advertisement activity that in the latter, "non-monetary gain oriented information" are needless even if they are beneficial or advantageous. Hence, marketing things for welfare of people may be a common case in government efforts, such as marketing free condoms and iron pills, which needs advertisement as a safe strategy and not as a poor strategy, but it does not market welfaristic commodities as "non-monetary pure thoughts or ideas or concepts"; almost everything that are marketed have "monetary" links, directly or remotely. The welfaristic marketing of condoms involves money because in that way the welfarist state earns the cost of condom production and distribution to a great extent (if not fully) when the ads draws buyers to dole out the cost of the item and thus circulate the fund for public good. However, the ad for the use of safe condoms in unsafe sex to prevent AIDS does not earn money or does not intend to do so for condom production and distribution. It may be *educative*, which may be instigator to some people buying condoms, nevertheless, but that is not the same as direct involvement in 'selling a brand or commodity for collection of funds'. Hence, marketing almost necessarily needs ads though ads do no not necessarily need marketing for earnings. However, we cannot overlook the fact that an advertising agency itself needs marketing, when for instance, a new agency is floated. Hence, it is possible that while marketing, an ad agency might itself need advertisement. This is one way in which we come to realise that more often than not advertisement and marketing goes hand in hand in business, economic, commercial and trading practices as enhancers and thus needs management of the specialised enhancing methods. Hence, all basic money matters in our societies that involve advertising and marketing are related to the science of management. It is thus important to know about the management of both advertising and marketing. This makes clear why economics, business and management are related disciplines which also involve as diverse management as those of materials to humans and advertising and marketing things. Keeping this interrelation in mind and the basic information that we have acquired, it is now important to see what exactly are value-laden issues in marketing and advertisement in the contexts of economy, business, commerce and trade. It is also important to see what issues make good case in the Indian context.

In the stiff competitive scenario in an opening up economy like India, the private and public companies are first of all obliged to establish their goodwill and efficacy through marketing of quality products and services so that they do good to their respective companies, that is, to not only serve and flourish but to do what consumers expect them to do. Further, in such competitive market it is also important for the managers to ensure that what the companies must do and should do, are thus done as necessity. Moreover, the market and the companies expect from the consumers that they must do certain things and that they should do certain things to ensure good for themselves. The reciprocate obligations are thus not merely what are expected as a rational course for survival and flourishing, they are also what are expected as *moral* course for social good and moral evolution in society. Ethics is thus a field that reminds us of the value inherent in the discussion of a company's safe and efficient marketing strategy of its products and services. The most important value-laden issue in marketing management in India or any competitive economy is whether the business houses and commercial units have really done what they should do to the consumers. It is but natural that we expect from a company to supply us quality garments at a competitive price, but equally true is that it should not bungle quality at the cost of price or bungle price at the cost of quality. Taxing consumers for either quality or price is thus a kind of dishonesty in performing basic duties and fulfilling obligations, which is unethical. A related value-laden issue is whether in the face of multiple-competition a company should obtain so aggressive strategies to market things that a course of outwitting competitors ends up in either a cut-throat situation among company servants (the managers in particular) or a cut-throat situation when the outwitting company bosses the consumers for its all win condition by either compelling consumers to pay dearly or to adjust with the poor quality of things though they are at competitive price. Another related value-crises in places like India is whether the competing companies should abide by providing quality products at good prices to sections of people who can afford and thereby earn as much as they can from those sections of population, or, the companies should abide by providing affordable goods and services to the not so well-off population at large though some quality adjustments are needed or to leave out sections of well-off people who are nevertheless, fewer in number. Still more, crises is also about double standards in price-structure with a concurrent double layered quality control of the things marketed. Should poor people be happy with substandard things at low prices and affluent people are happy with standard things at high prices? Are double standards in business and commerce ethically good when that might corrode human unity from within owing to the gulf created among them? Questions are whether 'outwitting' competitors in marketing should be the goal of marketing? Is outwitting in marketing the quality of an ethical person though the person may be a winner? Is outwitting and aggression an ethical form of corporate life? Should stockholders and managers connive to bluff people in terms of money or quality and as a mistake committed twice, they should equally be belligerent against other forces in the market in the name of marketing? The crux of the flurry of ethical questions is whether there is a legitimate, ethically permissible goal of marketing in business and commerce? If there is one, should it be maximising gains and profits through selling products and services to consumers and nothing more? If we follow the Friedmannian *avatāras* and the capitalist *gurus*, companies are at best fools and not ethical if they do not care for their own good, which is maximisation of gains, monetary and otherwise. They are not primarily social service or welfare sectors in society who have come here to do a lot of good for the people by doing a lot of harm to their own resources, powers and funds. That public well-being is only secondary in marketing is a truism; the managers should thus be as aggressive as to maximise gains for their company by pushing products. This does not mean necessarily that the marketing managers are rogues, who are at another's throat at any cost because aggression in marketing is a specific technique, though it is argued that marketing needs a lot of planning, thinking, strategies and hard work than unethical black-tricks to root out competitors and bluff consumers. The problem is whether an ethical company has nothing to do for the commoners while they market their product with all zeal, might and intelligence? Should they not strive for the well-being of the consumers by virtue of whom they survive? This is the ethical question of *responsibility* of companies in marketing their goods.

The above questions focus the ethic of marketing from two sides, from the side of *marketer* (let us concentrate on managers) and from the side of the consumer. There are two views when we take the side of the marketer, one is that it is ethical for the marketer to strive for the maximisation of company's gains by increasing sales of products of the company because this is truly the sensible goal of any company and the other is that it is ethical for marketer to *create a market and a consumer* than the drab goal of gain-maximisation, which may be comfortably criticised for its snobbery and hawkishness. The critics say that the second is not truly an ethical objective rather a so-called ethical means to the basic so-called ethical objective of gain-maximisation. Hence, the basic ethic of marketing is gain-maximisation. For others, when we look at marketing as influencing the most valuable target group, the consumers, "marketing is a social enterprise". It occurs in society, with society's permission and support, and purportedly, in part for society's benefit. Presumably, it is therefore, to some extent subject to the moral regulations and expectations society and potential customers attach to it"[4]. P. F. Camenisch argues that when we look at the nature of marketing in our society, it is in fact involving a large chunk of any society and not only a small population of well-off people and businessmen. Hence, undeniably, as a social process, marketing needs to be ethical in the light of 'social good' or 'social gain maximisation'. This becomes doubly true when any marketer is also looked upon as consumers of various goods and services. When they look from their side, will it not be ethical for them that marketer be so good to look at the consumer's greater good? Yet, one cannot completely trash the idea that for the social good, companies cannot to the least maximise gains through marketing. Hence, the third ethical view (cf. Camenisch and R. T. De George) is that the business houses, the marketers as their chief party to marketing comes closer to the consumers by informing them about the products they purchase so that they come to know for what quantity and quality are they spending a competitive price. An ethical consumer has the responsibility to let companies know what they need and let them stand on their toes by pressing hard questions of quality control and price mechanism. Thus "assuming that marketing and marketers want to be part of morally defensible transactions, one might then say that viewed societally, the goal of marketing should be to increase the likelihood and frequency of free and informed transactions in the market place. Or, to put it negatively, marketing ought not to decrease the likelihood of such free and informed market transactions"[5]. We thus come to know the importance of ethical debate regarding the socially expected role of the marketers and the consumers. As we have seen before, this is all the more important in India, where the multinationals are finding out many ways to market their product most aggressively, all this is going on in a nation full of half-fed and unfed people (who are consumers without much power). Linking in this debate are two more ethically relevant questions: One is that of *ethic of marketing research* and the other is that of the ethic of *multinational marketing*. We shall come to those issues in a short while. For now, we shall provide our readers with some more interesting value-laden marketing issues. One is that even if in the age of consumerism, consumers need freedom in the matter of purchase of products and enjoy the right to information about product quality, quantity and price, this may not in reality bring consumers any closer to marketers. Rather, wider rift among them may be noticed when on the one hand bluff-game conjoined with blame-game mixes to make a queer market where nothing is truly ethical. The marketer now tries to find every other way to misinform in the name to inform and the consumer finds any legal and semi-legal pressure tactics to be applied to get proper information. Alas! the agency extremely powerful in providing information is the company and not the public, the ball is in their court which does not really empower the consumer though they have freedom and rights. It is exactly here that the role or advertisement comes in marketing and fresh set of ethical questions emerge. In fact, in India, for instance, one can easily notice a barrage of products marketed with bizarre techniques to catch consumers with either misinformation or low-key information. To emphasise quality, the marketers are finding new ways; one is to provide hard information, that is, some such technically obscure information that hardly matters for the public for their interest and understanding. It is of no use for a number of poor Indians to know that the nicely packed flour is marketed with an assurance that all *chapatis* will be as fluffy as humpty-dumpty and that it has vitamins added for the consumers. Most of us even do not know what A, B, C, and D to n-number of vitamins in flour or in other things will do to us. Jokingly, consumers ask: Is there no wheat in flour? This must be as good a question as whether there is water in water if there are only oxygen and hydrogen, but the consumer can't help. Apart from being free and right enjoying, why we must not be educated about 'hard information'? So may we argue that ethically speaking, seeking information is ethically undesirable as it does greater harm in creating mistrust and disbelief and in inciting black-tricks among trickster-marketer? Was it not true that all of us were ethically so good people when we had low-key information and trusted and relied on the companies for their marketed products? Nevertheless, the modern consumerism might retort back saying that older Indians lived in age of monopoly business, where they gulped what were given to them as gold by the companies, and their collective morality looked glorious because they were too few. Yes, the companies and the consumers were too few than what we now are, and truly free economy has nearly abolished monopoly, which was found to be good because they grossly devastated our faith on them owing to the ignorance of our freedom and rights of consumers. Moreover, they purchased or pushed to non-entity the public bodies responsible for quality-checks and price checks. To take two cases will be interesting here. Through the years hydrogenated oil was sold to us for cooking without any knowledge that the oil is not at all good for our arteries' health, and of late, that is, nearly in the age of consumer liberation in India did we discover that the million of vegetarians were even consuming undesirable substances, which created quite a furore. Truly, in this age did we realise that our favourite soft drinks contained brominated vegetable oils, which is bad for our digestive system. What is ethical about consumer pressures to be informed is that it allows the marketers to be more serious about advertising products and for quality control. It also keeps the government bodies to intervene aggressively in quality control, which is literally true when in both the cases, the governments had to intervene seriously pushing the companies on track. All these value-laden issues in marketing are closely related to the ethical role the marketers need to play as professionals in a civil society. If marketing managers are humans, are social beings, they do not merely have a profession and thus earn as much as they can as do their companies, true professionals have eye on the ethical questions of marketing and the ally that is, advertising. Their strategic aggressiveness cannot cross the limits of humaneness to beastliness. They cannot use humans, animals, and the sexuality of humans to exploit the consumers in the market for their good. Marketing thus does not depend for its success on cost/ benefit analysis; it depends on many social and ethical factors. Let us see what our readers feel about these questions when they go through a debate. The key question in marketing is thus: What is ethical in social marketing programmes?

We have seen that in India and in many Asian countries, economy is preferred to become secular in the sense of non-apathy to the introduction of any company of foreign origin to join hands with the permissible ratios of share in business and thus spread their own benefit network as well as to contribute to the benefit of the host people and the host nation. The idea of benefit has thus gained different meaning altogether in this cross-cultural and cross racial participation because people now believe that in business, trade and commerce it is too odd to encourage the rule of the home-grown products by in-house companies, whether private or public or both, though this must be annoying the *swadeshi* proponents who still live after independence. Hence, easy access to foreign markets by the multinationals becomes a key factor in the globalised world order in which globalisation of economy is a natural phenomenon. The problem is how *should* the multinational companies behave in alien markets though they have a local partner there, particularly in cases of *kitchery* economic system in India, where public control is not completely snatched off, and the multinationals are not free to do anything they wish to do for gains by breaching the 'laws of the land' regarding business, trade and commerce. It is a different proposition to sell the produces marketed by the foreign companies in collaboration with the *desi* companies because apart from the problems in pricing, selecting margins of profits, there are greater problems about quality assurance and effectiveness of the products in a land where people speak and understand different languages, have different customs, faiths, obsessions, prejudices, and dogmas in buying and selling and making profits. In India, for instance, it is always a difficult proposition to sell a consumer brand having foreign featurés to a number of people who are illiterate, poor and obstinate about home-grown things. Marketing of multinational products also poses several ethical questions, the most important being the marketing of undesirable things in connivance of a partner or a host. Undesirable things ranges from consumer items to manufacturing goods, and hi-tech machines and even expertise which are of sub-standard, defective, malfunctioned, spurious and even risky. The crucial ethical question is why should the foreign companies be allowed to market undesirable things and for that a national traitor should be a party? More troubling question is why should the controlling authorities and the governments be allowed to be a party to the connivance? Why should the government allow exploiting the masses when it has failed to do any good? Much hue and cry is thus about soft drinks, eatables, food grains, seeds, pesticides, pharmaceuticals, armaments, machineries and even expertise. It is often argued that no government and local companies ever want to betray their own people for business and other benefits. There are always stringent measures for quality of products and methods of marketing. In view of such safeguards it is always extremely important to allow multinationals to market their products in the best possible ways because economic gains matter in our country that enriches local partner, our people and the government. On the whole, therefore, multinational marketing is ethical as it is people friendly.

A lot of heat is generated when multinationals fix methods of marketing that includes strategies for sales and advertising, and the free use of corruption and bribery. It has to be noted that corruption and bribery do not increase with illiteracy, poverty and dire wants, as is with most of the Indians in some positions to either permit or control the marketing of multinational products. It may well be that educated, well-off and unsatisfied Indians in key positions may be soft points in bribing and corruption. Hence, it is a wrong picture to paint about the multinational marketing that they bribe and corrupt the *babus* and the low income people; in fact, they are more successful in icing the creamy layer involved in allowing multinationals to market their desired products. Is it not ethical to have rights groups conjoined with the judiciary as people's body to check such infiltration of corruption at the top because that is 'people friendly' in the true sense? Many stiff ethical problems arise when we come to the strategies for sales and marketing. An open eye in India could easily witness some such sales-strategies and advertising technologies that are not merely alluring or bluffing or violent, they are in bad taste. It may be argued that the multinationals do not have any right to market products by playing on the sentiments of the host country's people, their culture, faiths and ways of life. The free use of female sex, the body as a campaigner, the trade of flesh in another word, to attract customers come under ethical scrutiny. The counter view is that it is always in a bad taste to believe that our old and hackneyed ways of life, thinking and values have remained as it were in the past. It is thus in a bad taste not to allow technologies of sales and advertisements which are most effective and emphatic in attracting the people, who are also moving in paths of modernism and modernity.

An important value-crisis in multinational marketing in developing countries is *deceptions* in marketing *banned* products to the host countries. This is evident in the marketing of consumer goods, pesticides and pharmaceuticals in the main. A multinational company is always better placed to even deceive its partner to make deceptive changes in formula, compositions, labelling and branding to sell the banned substances. We often hear that such and such drug has been banned long back in the USA but working fine in India, but it may be too late before we discover the damage. Many health and environment hazards in India are owing to the free use of these banned substances. Yet, it may be controlled by an ethical argument that the multinationals are not legally and morally bound to accept norms of home countries in sales and marketing. They are not bound to follow the way government wants to see their products because the callous government is helpless, it has already failed to satisfy its people, and for that matter has lost moral authority in business control. It is the larger shareholder who has migrated all the way from the West or elsewhere to do business, help people and earn profits to decide what should be marketed. Nevertheless, there are international regulatory authority bodies, the international community pressures and the clarion call for human right to prevent itself from harm and deception that counter the above argument. R. T. De George argues that maximising good than harm to the host country as well as preventions against being deceived should remain the ethical guide in international marketing.

Let us come to marketing research and ethical issues arising out of such research. It is believed that ethical issues in the field of marketing and marketing management might arise when non-monetary cases are involved; for instance, when analysis of *information* gathered from well defined markets are used by the marketing managers for fixing sales and marketing strategies for the broader gains of the company, including monetary gains. Hence, marketing research is an aid or means to effective marketing of products, that is, it is a precondition of successful marketing management. Marketing research as based on 'information' is about consumers, competitors and the nature, feature and patterns of the market as such. It has to be remembered that collection of information about customers, for instance, does not amount to what customers like or wishes or prefers, rather, a range of inquiries evaluating his or her value-system. This does not mean that inquiries need to be made for ethical values, though one cannot rule them out particularly when consumers raise serious ethical questions about the marketers, the company's marketing strategies and the aid to such strategy such as researching about consumers. An interesting example comes to my mind immediately. A group of young people who introduce them as management trainees specialising in marketing management frequent the university departments these days believing that this is one good unprotected place where teachers and students are by far amicable to researchers. Soon they have a barrage of inquiries on products, mostly about popular books (because when it comes to other items, teachers frisk them aside immediately), which covers the value of books pushed to us. The practice must be arduous and we are very kind to these students, but frankly, they are 'disturbing' in our work-places during work-hours, more so when we are busy at home. Why *should* consumers be tortured for gathering information? What then should be done? What should be ethically admissible ways to research about consumers preferences? Most interesting is, why should the consumers be pushed to comparative evaluations about a competing brand already in the market? This brings to the fore, the ethic of researcher-consumer relation; the etiquettes, norms and approaches amenable to the customers and to the researcher; the responsibilities, obligations, rights and duties of the researcher and the customers and to value the perception of the researcher about the customer. In fact, the questions arising out of customer-researcher relationship and the value perception of the researcher about the customer are related but different. First, there are value-laden issues in marketing research when researcher has a predetermined value system as imposed or taught by the academicians or by the company big bosses while they impart in-house training to the managers/researchers. It may well be that the researcher perceives the customers as valuable as guinea-pigs and the whole market as pig-nursery, wherein each customer toys with a set pattern of questions in an expected manner that is well-known by the researcher through his academic lessons and comes out with a set of answers which can be no better or no diverse in a binary system. This 'guinea-pig syndrome' in management research that comes out of the fertile minds does not leave any proper evaluation patterns for the repliers or the evaluators. Bereft of subjective liberties, the fixed set of questions that gives fixed set of answers, always faces the ethical question that researchers often face when they frame questions for 'desire-to-get-the-desired-results' from an orthodox 0-1 programmed human guinea-pig. More often than not the answers reveal nothing at all to the researcher, not the values of the customer at least. For instance, when the researcher asks me what I think about the value of this picture dictionary in comparison to the one without pictures so that I reply 'yes' to the former and thus 'no' to the other, or *vice versa*, I may be completely bluffing the person who have gone out of wits to ask me whether both types are valued by me at the same time for different reasons. Or, more bizarre, I have gone out of wits to prefer dictionary having three language synonyms having phonetics of the three language synonyms and also having examples of usages of the synonyms. Why should the researcher be not so ethical to treat her as a guinea-pig first to put herself into a bizarre area of fuzzy questions covering indeterminacy of subjectivism in a growing and changing indeterminate society and market? If all this appears to be too relativistic, improbable and freak, why the researcher be ethical to ask consumer questions which are "false" because they are really "answered" and the researcher knows 'what if' this answer comes to us. In fact, unethicality in the dogmatic perception of the value system of a replier while collecting information leads to hackneyed researches. Hence, the dictionary publisher influenced by research sometimes adds pictures or deletes them. Or, change features slightly to make a good excuse to justify price-hike. This is key to understand the ethical question that arises out of client-marketer/researcher relationships. Should the researcher be so unethical to relate herself to the customers externally without any internal empathetic feeling? Is a 'closeness' expected of the researcher with the subjective freedom that the customers have? Is it ethical for the researcher to just fill his note-book with information because he is doing an allotted job and to analyse and use data as he has been taught? It may be said that in management, research is not to take care of subjectivism and individual freedom. It is need-based and thus must be methodical and patterned.

It may be argued that collecting information for marketing research does not amount to fill up a stereotype questionnaire, most of the time the researcher *observes* the consumer behaviour, needs, preferences and reactions in the market. It may be done also by means of *explaining* the product attributes and merits at the first instance, and then give *discursive* liberty to the customers about their preferences and evaluations. It may be also done by conducting research on the basis of *available information.* These ways are certainly better than filling up 'yes'/'no' type of forms, which we call, sources of primary and secondary research. Some ethical questions arise in both cases though. Observations as a source of primary research depends on electronic gadgets like close circuit TVs and cameras, which are definitely not open to the person or persons who are being observed. The way customers behave in markets can be nicely watched in this way with the risk of breaching privacy of the public and to some extent going to an uncivilised way to observe what should not be otherwise observed. The same can be done now with tiny cameras and sound recorders fitted to the researcher without having any idea of them, whereas the researcher simply studies the market and customer behaviour without anybody noticing it. This is again at the risk of breaching privacy and committing indecency. One can even go to the extent of breaching the most private areas if they so wish. The point of unethicality, as we have seen before, is the use of modern gadgets, that is, collecting *information through deceit.* Uninformed data collection is thus ethically distasteful because that goes against the people's right to know what others are doing with their liberty and freedom. We have every right to have own private life peaceful, not necessarily to be divulged publicly. We enjoy the right to use things without divulging them to others. Such privacy in using products should be respected for our 'right to privacy' in civil societies. Moreover, the companies do not enjoy any right to breach our privacy rights. Naturally, their right to get information for the good of the company does not imply consumer's right to give them all information candidly at their will. Though we enjoy right to express opinions and reactions to the companies about their marketed products that do not imply that we have to or we are obliged or we have duty to express our opinions and reactions as consumers. The proponents of marketing research say that they have the right to collect *consented* information at least as competent persons because they know best how to *analyse* and *use* them for the good of not only the company but for the maximisation of consumer's good and market good. For the greater pleasure of citizens, the marketers by virtue of their knowledge, expertise and skill are best placed even ethically to collect information. To this may be added that though researcher have all respect for customers' privacy and right to conceal their behaviour patterns, the same may be derogatory to themselves, the market and the company because that may amount to non-disclosure of truth, badness, inefficiency and ineffectiveness about products, persons and services. Hence, consumer non-cooperation may be due to shyness or lack of education or threat or fear or disgust, but these things only go against their own good and the good of the company. The marketer is in reality always at pains to compete with the best for quality assurance at a competitive price. Hence, it is a public/consumer obligation that they inform, express, react and even protest when they are cheated or when they are not served well. Such cases of non-cooperation and concealment are derogatory to the consumers and thus to the society at large, which often the companies enjoy by means of limited use of non-consented and uninformed research. Some noble researches on the tribes of India some years back was possible by means of concealment, but that was for the greater good. There is thus no ethical badness in the use of gadgets in a concealed fashion to research for the consumers' welfare either. Nevertheless, hard-nuts react to this saying that though non-consented research on animals and humans are for the good of the humanity at large, consumer oriented marketing research does no good to the humanity at large, it does some good to those humans who have specific needs and have the needed power of purchase. Most of the consumer goods marketed by companies are not comparable to the non-consented research on tribes for greater knowledge for the scholars or comparable to the concealed research of traffic behaviour of citizens in metropolis or comparable to the non-divulged study of public behaviour in departmental shops for security reasons. Closely related to this debate is the use of consumer informed data for marketing research through consent with an assurance for *anonymity*, which is however, disclosed for greater marketing benefits. It will be always beneficial for the marketer to show that a famous person is smoking their brand of cigar or taking their brand of coffee though the use of the pictures and voice were completely 'non-consented' in yet another sense because the person was assured of "anonymity". Similarly, the marketer/researcher might prefer remaining 'anonymous' and send fictitious address and letter-heads so that the consumer becomes more free at criticising or evaluating the firm, which is again said to be unethical. The first type of request for anonymity may be ethical in so far as the consumer does not want to be a party to public appeal about a product and thus become partisan though he might agree about the use-value of a product. Whereas unethicality charge is based on the consumer behaviour to not to be a party to common good, and thus the company is so good to be a party to common good by divulging the same. The second case of 'anonymity' of the company is said to be ethical because that allows the otherwise cunning but concealing consumer to flush out truth for the good of the company and the public. It may be called unethical because untruth and deceit cannot be a means to a greater good. Another debated ethical issue in primary research is when the researcher uses the respondents' replies (to questions) for *ulterior* purposes, that is, not for the expected purpose of marketing the proper products of choice rather to drag the respondent to buy certain things. It is extremely difficult to imagine what could be the ethically defensible thesis, but no doubt unethicality lies in the act of bluffs in the name of an academic activity.

When we come to the use of already collected information for marketing research, we find that value-laden issues arise when the researcher takes all benefits out of the information without having no regard to acknowledge the source of information because the researcher for some reasons do not want to divulge the source to the customers. This is often done to bluff the customer that the data from research has been collected currently with some pain justifying a higher price of the product. The ethic of such bluff may be that more often than not customers are very obstinate about both price rise and quality. If both have to be ensured, the secondary data-use with proper acknowledgement is needed. Whereas the unethicality lies in the undue advantages from the collected data for gains, which is at two poisnts— First, when falsely a previously collected data has been used and second, when the client is dragged to believe in a falsity as truth. Hence, 'falsity' becomes a key value-issue in marketing research. We will not indulge into this topic in more details now because we will take up this issue while discussing the case of advertisement. For now, we have two more value-laden issues in marketing research, the one relates to customer's and researcher's etiquettes and behavioural patterns and the other relates to rights and duties of the customers and the researchers. In the age of consumerism only consumers cannot be kings because the producers and the marketers are equally important. There is no doubt that though things sell when there are people to purchase them that do not imply that the consumers have either nothing to do with etiquettes or rights and duties or both. It is believed to be unethical on the part of a civil citizen to wade off all social responsibilities as customers to let other people aware of what they are using good or bad in comparison to other things. This basic right to inform about value of items and the duty towards consumers bind the consumers in modern markets. Similarly, the marketers/researchers are bound to the responsibility to enjoy the right to supply good things in the market for consumption and the duty to respect consumer right to have good things at competitive price. It is also unethical that the researcher should not be treated as fellow brethren who are also involved in a socially responsible act, whereas the same etiquette is expected of the researcher. The researcher should know how to approach clients for their views, how to take advantages amicably, how to behave when they talk to people in the market and how to be sympathetic, patient and emphatic when it comes to product value analysis. The clients are expected not to be harsh, untrue to the researcher and be behaviourally arrogant or meek or non-cooperative when it comes to greater human good.

We hope by this time our readers are ready with their views, they want to jump in debates to resolve crises in marketing and marketing research. However, we will refrain from such things until something has been said about the value-crises in advertisement, which is a close ally of marketing. The strongest proponents of advertisement holds that as a means of marketing products and thus as a means of attaining the goals of business, trade and commerce, advertisement is not merely one way to compel or influence people to buy what they would otherwise not buy, rather it is an effective and necessary way to *communicate* with consumers about the features and merits of products marketed with suggestions why something should be purchased not other things. It is thus a people friendly, beneficial service so as to empower them to be good purchasers and investors to become well-off. This is key to the understanding of the ethical goodness of advertisement. Whereas the adversaries of advertisement hold that it is adverse to people's general interest, it harms them than doing any good because it plays on the natural human cravings, wants and desires to thus exploit their feelings and emotions with all available gimmickry, untruth and deceptions so that through ill persuasive tactics, bad things at good prices could be sold to the public. Most interesting is that the advertiser is in all win-win position because they reach the target group with success and for doing that they need not pay for anything, the consumer ultimately pays for the advertisement because the value is added to the product. Hence, unethicality lies in multiple exploitation of the public, at the ends of cost, quality and need. Moreover, "to inform" is an extremely broad but ambiguous term. It is not necessary that all information is in the form of advertisements and that advertisements are necessarily informative because much information about a group or an individual is not to advertise products or ideas or concepts. Many of them are to educate us, though some ads are informative and educative. The information we get in our educational institution or railway inquiry or police files are not advertisements. Similarly not all ads are informative in the sense in which government ads to educate about the value of immunisation are. To get information that a talcum powder is as cool as the Himalayas in the summer does not educate us to the least, and what information does it really carry? Does it inform us that it has good quantity of borax or any coolant which is good for our skin in such and such ways? What information does cooking oil convey to us when it is hyped that it contains vitamins A & E, which is so good for even the heart patients that they can go on consuming deep fries in that medium? In fact, to call advertisements "informative" may be a half-truth because most of the time they lack in *proper* or *desirable* information and are full of improper and undesirable information. Hence, it is not the case that ads are informative in the true sense of the term because in the true sense ads are means to convey messages about product components, durability, safety, risk factors, uses and the most advantageous aspects that make it competitive best. More than that there should be clear indication about its carry-home price. Most of the time the audio and the audio-visual medias fail to do justice in this sense and thus unethical in practice. The best sources are print-media, particularly the consumer friendly leaflets and journals. It is clear that it is not sufficient to have information of any kind through advertisements; they should be loaded with proper and desirable information with all clarity, precision and necessary details. The unethicality thus lies in the pro-advertiser, pro-company profit attitude at the cost of buyers' loss. Hence, undesirable advertisements are to give 'biased information' not 'true and objective information' so that buyers are bluffed to buy things what companies push to them—it is thus an unethical pressure tactics. It is often said that the uniqueness of commercial advertisements lies in the 'mass communication' about features and advantages of products, which must be then different from many communications and information which do not have mass appeal. Hence, advertisements reaching to masses cannot be always as broad and as detailed as personal appeals. It cannot be satisfactory to an individual or groups of individuals because it has to spread easily to the general mass of different age groups, intellectual and monetary abilities, castes, creeds and temperaments. Advertisements, unlike the educative and so-called truly educative advertisements cannot be and should not be individual or group specific, and therefore, to expect it to be 'truly informative' on stipulated terms is itself an unethical attitude on the part of some consumers. One can easily understand that a toothpaste producer has a different desirability condition for advertising its product to the masses of enormous proportion and divergence in India than a cancer drug producer to a specific group, mainly the physicians, and government agencies to propagate the use of a specific brand of contraceptive pills to both physicians and its specific users. Looking at these problems in advertisement, it will be too unwise and harsh on our part to label commercial advertisements as not 'truly informative' and 'educative'. In fact, ads for mass appeal has its own models and ethics, it should be based mainly on the idea of a clear and catchy appeal to the prospective users of the product. Intellectualism and academic depths in commercial advertisements might mar its purpose and value, which does no good but a lot of harm to the common men, which is unethical. Hence, it is ethical for commercial ads to be simple, catchy, sleek, smart, funny, attractive and extremely appealing to the masses. This must be all the more important in countries like India where not only that many people are uneducated and semi-educated, they know little about what to use at what price and that they are broadly speaking, very emotional people. However, others think that such perception about the masses is extremely unethical. We should remember that the gross attitudes of companies, their deceit, untruths and attempts to fool the people thinking that they are uneducated and emotional people are itself unethical. The truth may be that education has perhaps little to do with the way we look at people, life and ethicality. The highly trained and skilled marketing managers or advertising managers are surely educated, they are believed to be civil, cultured and ethical, why should they think that the poor people, the illiterates and the untrained ones are fools or are so emotional that we can do anything to toy with their emotions? Is it then ethically just to exploit the masses through misinformation or poor information or no information at all? Is it just to be simple, attractive and even funny but not to be clear in the necessary technical details in advertisements? The most important thing is that we have to keep faith on the disposition of people to change with time because education is spreading, though it is slow; however, the way of life teaches ordinary people many things—many values, to be precise. The common sense of people, their empirical powers and ability to analyse good and bad should be banked on by the companies. This faith on the people, the faith on their values is key to advertising methods. The respect for people calls for the agencies to treat them as ends and not means to company's success. We thus have a good course of ethical debate at hand when advertisement relates to humans, their value as such and the value of information in commerce. It is exactly in this respect that evaluation of *use* of humans in ads is possible, the crucial ethical question being whether our body should be seen as a commodity. It is in this context of perception of humans that the problems of untruth *versus* stark truths, the creation of artificial consumer. wants and cravings and the breach of right to privacy comes to the fore. However, before coming to attend these ethical issues in advertisement we will go through some other ethical issues which arise out of the *impact* of advertisements on society at large.

An important ethical issue is whether advertisements need to be aesthetically good though keeping in view the *desirable* aspects of aesthetics. It is often argued that in the name of aesthetic worth or good, anything cannot be done because many things are ethically bad or distasteful though appeals our aesthetic sense (See Volume 1). Advertisements should be without any doubt aesthetically worthy. It should be linguistically rich as well if the advertisement is in print form or in audio-visual form because a good language not only conveys ideas with great impact; it becomes a part to 'beauty' of ads. Nevertheless, it is argued that a beautiful advertisement, that is, which looks and sounds *pleasant,* is not necessarily ethically good because not all pleasant looking and sounding things are desirable or should exist or ought to be there. Hence, the ethic of advertisement calls for serious checks on the impact of advertisements by virtue of its aesthetic appeals on human mind. One instance of aesthetically appealing advertisements may be thus conjoined with ethical rightness and become doubly appealing to the masses, whereas another instance of aesthetically appealing advertisement may be disjoined from ethical rightness and become doubly rejected. Again in this context, such as 'nudity' and 'eroticism' comes as a value-laden case in advertisement strategy to sell things like condoms, for instance, particularly if the females are exposed to a farthest limit. The most erotic and nude advertisements of condoms are no doubt pleasing to eyes, the background music, the light and shade, the features and facial expressions everything is immaculate to make them aesthetically great. But is it aesthetic greatness? Should it not be more appealing to the prospective users in another way? Can condom advertisement be not aesthetically pleasant but ethically charged not to be erotic and expose females for nudity? Is it not true that others cannot close eyes when they see such ads and thus become all the more inquisitive to vulgarity than value of condoms? Does nudity convey the true value of condoms? Still more, is it not true that in India, females still hold an esteemed social position, which should not be thus exposed vulgarly *in the name of* social value of use of condoms? The counter arguments start here. The point is that evaluation of aesthetic and ethical goodness is culture dependent. What is aesthetically good (or beautiful) and ethically good in that respect may not be accepted as a universal standard (See Volume 1). It may well be true even within India because a section of adults or others in different parts of India might think it strange to scrap erotic and nude poses in condom ads because they are not only pleasant to eyes and ears and appealing too, they are able to convey the idea of value of condoms in free and consensual sex among adults perfectly well. On the one hand they tell us that biological rationally should not be lost even at the height of eroticism, and on the other hand tells us that such things should be clearly among grown up people, who need to use such things as per their age and maturity. What is ethical is thus the clarity of message of what should be done, and as situation demands, it cannot be aesthetically good and emphatic in its appeal when we see people clad in veils stand apart and appeal for use of condoms. Hence, ethic of advertisement calls for judicious use of aesthetic appeal and for that ethical relativism gives us strength to use humans as when needed most ably and intelligently in ads. In fact, we ought to differentiate between vulgar or pornographic eroticism and nudity, which, without a social good, cannot be ethical.

The vulgar plays with people as sensual psychopaths, whereas the ethical ad does not do so. It is not that all ads should be valued on how it appears, but what it really means.

There are economists who argue that advertisements are unethical at the social level of their 'impact' if that is economically speaking, wasting the consumed resources to create an advertisement. In fact, generally speaking the advertisements do waste huge resources by consuming them in production, the cost of which is high in the form of "selling costs" though without any value because it adds no value to the product for the consumers, it rather taxes the consumers both by means of costly persuasive tactics and by means of money that the consumers have to eke out. Hence, advertisements are unethical as economic wastage. However, economists do not generally adhere to such view because many among them argue that advertisements are ethical in so far as they create a broad-based demand for the products in the market and thus rise in the production and sale of the products through which an economy is expanded. Greater production and sales amounts to the gradual decrease in the cost of items. All these turn out to be consumer friendly and ethical. This is, however, countered further saying that the unethicality in this approach is that it fails to recognise the value of high quality maintenance and good will in the market of products with low investments in ads thus refraining from unnecessary price hike. Effective marketing of high quality products can be without minimal expenditure on advertising. Hence, advertising is still wastage of resources, an unnecessary divergence of funds that corrodes quality assurance as such against the good of the public and thus unethical. To this stiff debate, which appears to be more or less "inconclusive" as says M. G. Vélasquez (2002); we might add another debate, again "inconclusive", is whether monopolists are able to create a deep impact through advertisements because in that way they sustain their headway lead in market bulldozing low key competition. The reason is that these firms are able to invest more on ads than the less well-off firms or poor firms. In this way the unethicality charge is that the monopolist firm is always at the helm of affairs though at the vulgar display of power on advertising investment which makes good companies scapegoats. An unethical feature is to grab the losing firms with their assets and resources to flourish more. This may be almost true even in case of oligopoly. The unethicality is not only in the anti-consumer attitude but in the vulgar pressure creation on small firms to make them non-entities. The ethicality of propaganda is much like 'all is just in love and war'. The corporate competition is not a place for camaraderie. Here we are not to help poor firm at our cost. Nothing should be unethical in being rich and powerful in business. Moreover, the idea is not to sell poor things through advertisements rather monopolists sustain pressures of competition due to quality products and goodwill, which is not merely due to arrogant advertising. Hence, monopolistic ways to advertise and create deep impacts are just. We can go on with many arguments and counter-arguments but let us leave something for our debaters. For now, let us move to the value-laden issue of advertisements as persuasive tactics to pressurise consumer wants and changes in the value perception of consumers about products.

Desires, aspirations and cravings are all in our mind, they are "psychological" in origin so to say. The problem is whether desires etc. or what we may call "psychic wants" can be created, and whether such things should be created in artificial or external manipulative ways. It is believed that though "physical or material wants" have their psychic origin because "wanting" something physical is not itself physical, it is psychic in origin. Hence, some wants may be directed to material things whereas others to non-material things such as realisation of the Self or God. In any case, the corporeal level normal humans have many physical wants and some non-physical wants. The moot issue is whether advertisements as an *external factor* is able to create some specific or *intended* desire, which was otherwise not there in subject's mind, and if it is possible, should we do that? To be brief about non-physical desires, such as becoming great or beautiful or elegant or intelligent, advertisements, particularly the commercial advertisements are hardly of help, but other things such as counselling, propaganda and persuasion are useful to some extent, but all counselling and persuasions are not advertisements, as we find in the case of teachers as career counsellors. Nevertheless, to make a point emphatic and clear the teacher might draw our attention to an advertisement related to what he is suggesting, but that is entirely different from "advertising". Similarly, not all commercial (or other) ads are persuasive or propagandist. Matrimonials are often neither persuasive nor propagandist. Hence, non-physical wants are often not influenced or changed by advertisements though physical wants do change as freaks by virtue of external or even internal influences. The point is whether physical or psychic wants can and should be influenced, that is, created (or incited) and changed (or modified) by external means such as advertisements of commercial nature which may or may not have propagandist, persuasive and counselling properties. Before entering into the details, let me clarify that not all make division between wants in the way I have done. For many, "physical" and "psychic" have different meaning, the first signifying more or less what I mean to say but in the latter case, are included wants that are "psychological in origin or mind-centred"[6]. For me, all wants are "in the mind"; hence, they are "psychologically based", but what others mean to say is that these wants are *aroused or caused or incited* in mind through sources outside mind and thus "psychic". If we take in this sense, there is hardly any difference in what I say and what others say, but the difference may be that I do not fully adhere to the view that all physically originated desire like food, shelter etc. cannot be influenced, changed and modified through commercial advertisements which are external to us. A few years back, Indian citizens, mostly in business and service, who could not afford buying a flat for them taking high interest bank loans are taking loan with much courage at good interest rates not only because they get tax exemptions or they can ease out the pressure of higher-purchase due to long-term repayment schemes, but due to an *urge created in them* by the banks in the public and private sectors, by the housing development boards and even by the government through attractive advertisements. A close look at these advertisements reveals that they hit the soft areas of the not-so-well-off but people having aspirations to instigate to buy a shelter for themselves than pay for rents. Without going into its ethic, we can say that such things have helped the housing sector develop phenomenally, the real estate business going high with concurrent rise in the consumption of cement, steel and other materials and thus help these industries. There are also works for a number of labourers, the migrating unskilled and skilled poor people. All these things count heavily on the ethical evaluation of a higher purchase, but the moot issue is that advertisements do play with basic human aspirations and needs to channel them in a needed direction. This is true in case of food. One can witness many poor and low income group or even well-off people in and around villages who erstwhile preferred rice, wheat, pulses and vegetables in the main, would now happily take some chowmein and fast food. How is this possible? Mainly due to the television sets reaching far-off areas with glittering advertisements telling us why fast foods are as palatable as or better than the dull *dal-bhat*. The rise in sale of chocolates, cold drinks, jeans pants, body sprays, cars are all attributed to fine tuned advertisements that takes on a physical or material good to instigate our aspiring/needing/desiring minds to create them as real demands. Suddenly the penniless Indian has started thinking that if he or she gets some money, he or she will fulfil some of his or her cherished desires that has been created in them from external sources. Truly, the inner cravings are stronger because they have their anchor in our fickle mind, which is like the flickering flame ever desiring things like becoming great, rich, honourable, dignified and so on. Advertisements target this soft spot nicely because they have unique techniques to flare up the flame in us stronger and stronger. These fanning techniques are many, the crucial being to ensure consumers desire and thus buy things which are produced by the companies. Hence, the company producing high quality and costly garments advertises in a way such that the consumer of ordinary to higher status is instigated by the inner idea of becoming as beautiful, smart, elegant and honourable as the individuals shown in the advertisements. Thus a consumer need is created which they try to get by any means if possibie. I think that the growing needs for specific good, cloth and shelter is not only due to the physical factors and so on rather, they combine with the inner incitements of becoming fashionable and so on to create wants which were not to be. The question is whether advertisements can be called ethically good in inciting wants which were not there or which were undesirable in cases of poor or very ordinary citizens in India or abroad? The first opinion is that the consumers have the right to choose freely in the market, they enjoy the right to choose the goods of quality at competitive price and for this, as moral agents having freedom, they should not be influenced in any way by external agencies (advertisements) that ultimately puts them in bondage, shows disrespect to their autonomy and makes them fools by thinking that people are basically emotional. Hence, advertisements as want-creator in autonomous and respectful moral agents are ethically undesirable. Ads are all the more unethical in so far as they become party to instigate ordinary people's suppressed desires to such extent that they are dragged to false prejudices, pride, hegemonies and obsession in mind to crave undesirably for things which they either do not have or should not have or cannot afford to have in any case. It is due to the creation of wants through deception among economically un-empowered and less empowered people that advertisements are unethical. Countering these arguments, others say that it is not advertisements that have to be blamed for want-creation because such things are created in us owing to the natural process of discoveries, manufacturing and marketing of "new products" by the companies. It is, therefore, natural that all sections of population want certain things which are "new" to them for use and consumption. Nevertheless, the point is whether any discovery and production of new things can go into oblivion without an un-strategic marketing that avoids advertising its products at the right time, to the right extent and in the target areas. How can people know that this is new for them to buy with ads? Hence, advertisements are parties to want-creation of new things. If this be the case, the pro-group might argue that if nothing new is created and marketed (through ads), and nò one buys these things, our society will be a dull place to live, it will be state of *laissez faire*, which is unethical as it does a lot of harmful things to people and society. Retorting, the con-group might say that no one seriously thinks that there should be no new things created and marketed and be thus purchased particularly if the things are costly and many people are poor, what is argued is that advertising agencies should be so humane as to know how to downcast and how to promote which things that are new because not all new things are needed for all and thus people should not be allured, and not all new things are useless for all because some need them and are able to spend for them. Moreover, some new things are needed though they are costly for the poor, but some way has to be discovered to reach these things to them at low cost, which is why advertisements are needed. Hence, it may be unethical to tease poor Indians by displaying ads of fast-foods and soft-drinks to a great extent than not downplaying them. This is all the more important if these things are also injurious to health. Though it may be ethical to promote vigorously the use of iodised salt among poor masses and others, and the government should assure its purchase even with subsidy arrangements. It may well be that a new ethical debate about the role of government to curb, control, downcast or upgrade ads by private players in the market is at hand. The government role to enter into ads for public education about new things produced and steps to market them makes other case for ethical scrutiny. Most importantly, new products should reach the public in their advocated "new" form, undistorted and un-manipulated. It is here that the ethicality of government intervention in private house ads becomes a good case for study. It is here that the revelation of untruth in ads and bribery comes to the fore. It is often said that private houses make salt but not iodised salt to manipulate price tags at least three-fold, and that many hyped good things have nothing good in them. Even two warring companies fight each other with *amoral* motives to reveal untruths about products which were otherwise hyped for public good. A good case in India is the fight over whether Wheel detergent bar had lemon in it. Hence, closely associated to the problem of advertisements for public good, is the problem of untruth or deception. The question is 'what is ethical in any case of advertisement of untruths? Or, are untruths in ads unethical in any case?

M. G. Velasquez has brought out clearly the important terms in advertisements as important mode of communication to the consumers by means of which their beliefs can be changed or modified with regard to marketed products. These three terms are the "authors", "medium" and "audience". The first being the party to ensue an advertisement, the second, its means through which the first party conveys something about the products and the last one being the receiver or the target of advertisement, the consumers. When we deal with the ethical validity of falsity or deceptions in advertisements we need to inquire into the role of all three factors. Undeniably, the author is the starting point in advertisement because it is the author who has to convey something about the products to be marketed or is marketed to the consumers (audience). If deception starts anywhere, it must be at this end because the author is the one who has the intention to convince/suggest the audience to accept certain information as truth, which is, however, palpable untruth. It is the author who knows that what he intends to convey is false and that the author adopts means effective to convey the untruths as truths to thus change belief system of audience. It is said that all intended actions that are palpable untruths, are also undesirable, and thus unethical. In this party should be included not only the advertising manager but the copywriter and the endorser, and in a broad sense the entire agency involved in deceiving the consumers who are wronged because their beliefs have been wrongly manipulated or at least attempted to be manipulated for wrong reasons, that is, for the greed of sales and profit and because the integrity of the agency has crumbled which reminded their epitome in markets. It is also said that the author intentionally chooses some such means or medium for bluffing the public, again for wrong reasons that they are held to be unethical. In such cases, a party to convey the message cannot shake off all moral responsibilities and blame if they know that they are helping in spreading untruths and deceptive ideas among people, which is of great harm to them. Thus, the print, audio and the audio-visual mass media are all party to the mischief of the author and thus unethical in practice. It is also interesting to note that though the audiences or prospective consumers do not appear to be in the esoteric coterie of bluffers, they become so when audience does a mischief intentionally to misinterpret the message conveyed to them, which was otherwise not a bluff. This may be due to an ulterior motive to make a fool of some people or to harm an agency. Hence, charges of deception and unethicality may be levelled in all three aspects of commercial or other advertisements. However, it is argued that the author's intended act is not unethical because that aimed at the sales and profit to their employers or to the company even if the message conveyed has been misunderstood or distorted by the audience or any other contesting party. It may be stressed that for managers or employees involved in advertisement the good of their company is supreme because it is the company which looks after their well-being. Hence, nothing is unethical in advertisements that conceal truth. Moreover, concealment of truth is often wrongly interpreted as untruth and deception. If a financing company does not fully tell us about the risk factors involved in investments in that company by highlighting those attractive to consumers, it is for the good of the company and in some cases for the public because lengthy revelations in ads are impractical and impossible, and semi-educated or less educated investors never benefit by divulging risk-factors to them creating unnecessary hoax. On the other hand it is argued that though ad agencies are not compelled to tell us negative factors in ads, their loyalty to the people, the consumers and the society outweighs in reality their loyalty to the company as their hosts. Being a trustee to the people outwits being a trustee to the employer. Hence, a good to the company should never be over-hyped and surpass the good of the population. In another way, company's greed cannot take off moral shine from an ad professional if they are truly nationals and not anti-nationals. Moreover, divulging some truths may be unpragmatic but they should be divulged fully beyond the advertisements when consumers need further clarification. Concealing truth to some extent may be thus a practical necessity due to paucity of space and time allotted for an advertisement but like all warning captions such ads should accompany "risk factor captions". Further, it is argued that though deliberate distortion of ads for malevolent reasons is ethically undesirable by any party, it cannot be a just ground to conceal truths, and even if certain things were misrepresented, it may well be due to deliberate vagueness or ambiguity for the fear of divulging truth. Hence, misrepresentations cannot be wholly dumped on consumers' head. Consumers have ethical right to know full truth and to tell them to others. If the latter is a reality, one should be doubly careful about clarity in advertisements. Coming to another aspect, it is often argued that though mass media is mainly responsible in conveying ads to the public, and that they cannot enjoy the right to convey anything without proper scrutiny, they should always find out whether what has been deemed to be practically fit for conveying is ethically fit as well. Many things being deemed to be practically good may not be ethically good. Hence, the mass media in public or private control are parties to be held for moral blame if they join hands with ad agencies to convey their message in the way they want without any ethical inquiry. On the other hand it is argued that there are no absolute standards for both the companies and the mass media or any agency to convey messages to the public which are ethically good. We cannot say that for such and such reasons we *must always* ban advertisements projecting female sex in nudity or semi-nudity in promoting an item because that is needed for a target group. A bra or a panty has no option to be advertised taking advantages of female body. Still, it is argued that despite relativism in standards of ethicality, certain things are objectively valid. It is always ethically distasteful to advertise female body in a semi-pornographic fashion for any promotion when intelligent thinking can make it otherwise. Thinking of the public as gross idiots living on the ancient psychic state of development is basically unethical. Similarly, it is argued that though the public has some moral responsibility while understanding and representing advertised things, they cannot be chiefly responsible because it is the agency and the company who owes chief responsibility to advertise items in all clarity. However, it is also said that in competitive markets, several undercurrents do not rule out public outrages as hoaxes, which are politically motivated. Moreover, a company cannot be held morally responsible for misrepresentation if the public is uneducated or headstrong or have low aesthetic sense. It is not company's fault if one confuses that in an advertisement eroticism is advertised rather than use of condom for safe sex.

The debate about intended untruths in advertisements by agencies gets fresh twist when we come to the point of conveying a truth necessarily and always. In a seminal essay, Robert Solomon writes: "Lying may always be wrong, but some lies are much more wrong than others. Truth may always be desirable, but the 'whole truth and nothing but truth' is just as likely to be a nightmare"[7]. This may be a good starter to the debate taking nearly a mid-position when it comes to lying in advertising for commercial reasons. It may be certainly ethically wrong to lie in an advertisement that a balm can *cure* arthritis, when it may just relieve temporarily from pain with a risk of great side-effect, which is concealed. Most of the time in India, advertisements conceal risks of steroids and pyregesics in ads published in broadly circulated mass-medias. This is a palpable unethicality as it does great damage to human life by encouraging another unethical habit of using medicines over-the-counter. Some advertisements projecting a mechanical device to bust fat to make us slimmer by some inches within a week goes to the extent of comparing a brisk morning walk with the machines for slimming, which may be a great lie. Yet, this is not comparable to the unethicality of advertising drugs with risks for human life. Similarly, it is just to be truthful in advertising products. To say that smoking can be relieving and stress busting but with huge health risks is welcome for it does some good to the non-smokers or prospective smokers, thus preventing a lot more committed smokers to increase in number. Nevertheless, to advertise the plain and whole truth that consuming eggs and red meat might cause deposition of harmful cholesterol and cause arterial damages, is never undisputed good because in that way sportspersons, people of manual labour and growing people are harmed in many ways. This is particularly severe if ads do not tell us that consumption of eggs and red meat should be backed up by adequate burnt up calories by exercising or physical work. Hence, the cases taken together shows why *telling truth and to hide some of it is ethically desirable*. Still, one might be suspicious about the "deceptive concealment" of whole truth and equate it with "palpable untruth" or "plain falsity". One might argue that though advertising a lie is not generally good, advertising a lesser lie is not as bad as plain lie and that advertising a plain truth is not as good as half-truth at times. On the basis of adequate logic we cannot derive that, therefore, *sometimes* it is ethically good to *lie*, meaning thereby to tell a half-truth or mixed truth. How can "plain lie" be a "half-truth" or "mixed truth" or "concealed truth"? A lie or plain untruth is not synonymous to either half-truth or concealed truth. Hence, the natural course is you prefer lesser untruth or you prefer greater truth, you cannot at the same time prefer truth with mixed varieties of it, that is, half or concealed. Half-truths are "truths not fully disclosed" which come out to be "concealing some truths", whereas it may well be "concealing some untruths". Similarly, "concealed truths" may be "truths not fully disclosed" and it may well be "some untruths not disclosed". In any case, not telling a "plain truth" or "nothing but truth" or what may be not telling a "greater truth" amounts to "everything else but truth", and for that matter it is *not* a "plain lie" either because a "plain lie" or what is a "greater lie" is "everything else but truth, that is, untruth with no truth". Hence, the moot issue in the ethical evaluation of a lie or untruth in advertisement can never be based on a lesser truth or lesser untruth or mixed-truth. The advertisements should be either ethically desirable if they are complete truth or they are ethically undesirable if they are complete lies as well as half-truths or mixed truths or concealed truths or untruths. The debate between the justification of lie in advertisement may be then all the more difficult when "lie" or "untruth" is understood in this way, which is different from what Solomon holds to be the case. Some commercial justifications such as advertisements telling a plain truth that the marketed drug is no better than its competitors is foolish; hence, can this be a good case to tell a "lie" or untruth by concealing the plain truth? It seems not because telling a plain truth *about* the said drug is at the first instance, not the same as being "foolish" to tell that its competitor is as good or better, rather the plain truth *about* the drug amounts to the *characteristic features* or *components* of the drug with elaborate risk factors and advantages explained clearly. We just do not expect any company to be so truthful to *compare* its products as equal to or as equally good or bad as others. Then is it not true that the *whole* of truth has not been advertised? Did it not amount to a lie or untruth in the said ad? No, perhaps, because again if the "whole of truth" has not been said, it is just a mixed-truth or incomplete truth but not a plain lie by definition. Further, if one has to really be so good to tell "all or whole truth" about the drug by telling what is basic in its quality than others, there is perhaps no plain truth on earth because in that case, any prospective drug of say malaria which has been thus far not discovered and yet potently extremely good or a "paradigm of good" has not been compared and thus a lie. We need to remember that even without committing us to brand comparisons; we can be plainly speaking in ads. It is in this way that evaluation of ethical goodness of advertisements becomes extremely difficult to ethically justify that advertisements should be wholly truthful in the sense that it has taken notice of all comparable truths. In fact, to know that whole truth has been said about a drug is extremely improbable because when scientific discoveries are marketed as products or brands, like drugs for malaria, the truth is only partially known to us in case of any available drug research. Thus only *probable truths* may be expressed not *complete* truths or untruths in ads though "nothing but truth" remains an ethical paradigm. To this one might add that probable truths are tantamount to complete abolition in later researches as untruths. Hence, when we "imagine something as plain truth" or even "plain lies" in ads they might turn out to be "probable truths and untruths". So advertisements in commercial respects in *many* cases can never be fool-proof for truth and nothing but truth. Still, one can intend to be truthful and not deceptive so that paradigm truth is achievable.

Finally, we come to the ethical issue of privacy in advertisements, which we have seen before is closely related to the issue of privacy in marketing. Here the key to the debate is breaching the right to privacy of both human subjects involved in advertising a product and the consumers who are subjected to go through a barrage of information using humans. The issue of "body as a commodity" is raised in this context. The use of humans is almost an imperative in commercial advertisements, the use of female sex in advertisement appears to be wide and more needed than the males. Not stopping here, we have involved many beings and things in ads. We used animals extensively and important landmarks, such as rocks, rivers as well as a number of objects or materials things for advertisement. Almost all these uses have raised some furore over the years not because they are merely impractical or distasteful to our senses rather, they were undesirable on ethical grounds. The extensive use of human body as a commodity for commercial benefits is attacked vigorously on ethical grounds, particularly if female body is used for material gains. The use of animals in advertisements has been equally forcefully attacked by animal rights activists, particularly if endangered species are displayed or if animals are shown to be taxed physically for an ad show. The ecologists who speak ardently about the use of rights of natural entities are equally vocal in objecting to acts such as defacing rocks or destructing flora and fauna for advertisements on ethical grounds. We find that the bone of contention in such arguments is whether on ethical bases we can at all justify using human body, which is otherwise *private* to an individual or we can justify breaching the private life (in a unique sense), of any animal small or big which is otherwise undisturbed by non-animal interventions, or can we justify disturbing the privacy (in a unique sense), of natural things, which is otherwise undisturbed by non-natural interventions. Hence, what can be the ethical basis of breaching the right to privacy of beings and things in nature? I have argued elsewhere (See Volumes 1, 2 & 3) that it is perfectly sensible to speak about the "rights" of non-human animals and material things in nature though they do not cry for such "rights". The reason for a *human* cry for rights of non-human beings and things is that holistic well-being of the ecological community is an ethical conception that conceives of upholding the natural rights beings and things enjoy including human beings. Further, our cry for "rights" of other beings and things may be conjoined with *our* cry for "right to privacy" of *all* beings and things, that is, to uphold the right to "avoid notice, use and disturbances" or to "be in a state of originality in seclusion". Every individual in primitive to modern societies enjoy the right to live a life of *seclusion* when that is deemed necessary, that is, when *retreating* from public notice, use and disturbances are needed, which is to have a 'right to privacy'. This may be extended to mean a right to "*secrecy* of possessions, assets, words, thoughts and acts". Every animal small or big enjoy the right to have a life or seclusion, retreat and secrecy when that is most needed to them. Almost everything should be thus left to seclude its possession, assets, and dispositions to some extent at least, when that is deemed to be necessary. In this sense then, humans, animals and things in nature despite enjoying such rights, *when deemed to be necessary*, opens some chance to breach the same rights because an absolute conception of these rights would amount to absolute 'no use or no interference' of such beings and things, which cannot and should not be the case. The point is that a limited use and interference of privacy when deemed to be necessary must have *ethical grounds* as well. It may be said that humans need to be used and interfered for the good of himself or herself and for the greater good of the society. The private life of animals should be interfered with and denuded when that is most needed for their good and for the greater good of the natural environment in which they exist. The natural things must be brought out from seclusion use for and interfered when that is most needed for their good and for the greater good of humans and non-humans that thrive on natural things. It is argued that though ethically speaking, upholding the basic human and non-human right to seclusion should be respected and thus beings and things should be left undisturbed and unused, this is not an absolute requisite for existence as such, the privacy may be thus "breached" on ethical grounds. It is interesting to notice that if we put two ideas together, it comes out to be an ethical support to the *limited or qualified right to privacy* of humans, non-human animals and natural entities. Hence, there is a natural right of lions to prey on deer but humans do not enjoy the right to prey on lions and deer, though they have every right to breach the privacy of lions if they are found hurt or sick wherever that is possible because they are to be saved and cared to their and nature's well-being. We have similar right to allow some deer to be in a sanctuary to feed the lions and thus breach the privacy of deer, and the right to protect them and put them under closed barbed circuits if their numbers fall sharply. Similar rights are enjoyed by rocks that we do not paint them for advertisements though we breach their privacy to stand erect as they were since long because a road-link is most needed to connect far off places for the good of the poor natives. Keeping these arguments in mind, we can face interesting moral questions about breaching privacy of humans and other beings and things for *humans only*. Now the question is more focused: Is it ethical to breach privacy of humans and non-humans for commercial gains which are only human gains? One answer may be that to disturb the private life of humans and others is perfectly well on ethical reasons of economic well-being of humans because we have seen that privacy has no fixed or absolute intrinsic value, it has a relative value thus giving opportunity to breach it when deemed necessary. Business, trade and commerce are most essential for the subsistence of humans and human society, and without them there is perhaps no one to cry for rights of non-humans. Hence, some humans have every right to interfere into the private life of humans and non-humans for human good. The opposing view is that though nothing is illogical and unethical in the conception of a limit to certain rights of humans and others like the right to privacy. Extremely important 'claim right' to maintain organisational privacy is now seriously challenged in the face of "right to information". In India, the companies and the government offices might feel the heat of a limit to enjoy privacy in work areas in the near future. Hence, it is the overreaching human good in commercial activities that rules out absolute non-interference in private lives of humans in particular, but the crucial point is "whose good is it anyway?" In the garb of "human good" what is really nurtured? Does business, trade and commerce do any human good in the true sense of the term, which is, nevertheless, hyped so much? It is argued that it is not "human good" rather "human greed" that is supreme in commercial breach of privacy of humans and others. The greed is so much so that it really transgresses all "limits" because the conception of these "limits" are defined by us for our convenience and it is we who manipulate it as desired (or as per our need and greed). Hence, using male and female body as commodities or resources in advertisements is to put an imagined "limit" to right to their privacy under the ethical grounds. Evil of human good, when it is only a limited commercial good and at best material good could be thus seen by us. In fact, it is the unethicality to maximise material greed that limits are put by a section of people on others, right to privacy and to use them freely as commodities for material gains. Humans and others are de-humanised and de-faced for their original being for commercial gains of the companies and the advertisers are thus showing deep disrespect for their nature, existence, rights and esteem. It is thus unethical. It may be said that advertisements make no sense without using anything. Hence, abstaining from any use of anything is to abolish advertisements as such because words cannot suffice all needs of ads. They are particularly useless in print media and audio-visual media because we have to refrain from all human figures and pictures or movements in any case. The same may be true of animals and other things with some liberty that their figures and pictures (not movements and manipulations) are used and thus *not* testimony to their use as commodities. In case of male or female humans not *all* pictures and figures may be allowed in this strict sense, and not all movements and acts may be accepted. In any case, as written or spoken words do not fulfil all needs to information, which is key in advertisements, they have to be abolished, which is unethical because it stops an artful means to inform the public of good things. To this may be added that when humans (male or female) are used in ads in several actions, pictures and emotions, they are *seen* or *valued* as commodities for which some price has been paid and as such they have no status, dignity, rights, privacy and so on. If this be the case, persons contributing through intellectual and physical labour at some price are all commodities, the inert things are thus bereft of rights and dignity. When same grown-up individuals apt at the art of displaying their beauty and skills in audio-visual media come as paid people, they have an occupation laden with some fixed set of tasks to perform. If they do that for their living honestly and in that way others are benefited, they are not seen as commodities but they are people having dignified occupations and of esteem. It is also clear that these people are not *forced* into occupation, they are not in serfdom. They are free individuals who have chosen to use their skills for conveying certain ideas and information for public and corporate good, and doing so they do a lot of good to themselves. Hence, they are ethically just in what they do and what advertisers do with them. This also makes clear that human contributions in ads are not merely for corporate good, it is unethical to distort truth to say that ads are means to good of greedy people or they are good only to a few exploiters of human and non-humans. Truth is that acting in *consent* in ads is not exploitative, it is covenanted and the good which is commercial in nature does not amount only to the corporate good. Why should we detach people's good from commercial good? Why should we not see the inherent ethical value of informing the public in an aesthetic way the value of some commodities for use? Everything appears to be so good with these arguments, but the critics say that the points of commoditisation, exploitation and greed in breach of right to privacy is not understood or rather misunderstood or completely distorted by the protagonists. What is conveyed in the above charges is that unethicality on the part of the advertisers is that though not all acts in consent stand for either legal or moral checks, acts such as participating in ads have certain *internal and external checks or sanctions*, under which they should be done. Commoditisation of human body and intellect occurs when people do not use themselves but when they are either *lured* to do what they should not do under the said sanctions or checks or when they are *pressured* to do what they should not do. When we use our body and mind for legitimate uses under covenant but within the said sanctions for personal, corporate and social goods, they are *ethical* and not unethical commoditisation. It is in this sense that females are commodities if they are hired to maximize gains or pressured for gains and thus *expose* their otherwise private or *secluded points of body* for the *so-called* advertisement goods. It is right to privacy which is thus breached unethically in advertisements. It is in this sense that they are used as only exploited thing for material greed satisfaction of others, and thus unethical as an anti-human attitude. Advertisements that are humane or ethical should not thus in the name of human good, exploit people with disrespect. A right to privacy of humans and non-humans is thus ethical even in the "limited" sense when advertisers use sanctions from within and outside to treat humanity and ecological community with respect and thus deem it necessary that need and greed does not do harm to holistic welfare. We need to thus remember that champion of women liberty or human liberty cannot and should not breach their own privacy for they "own their body" because sanctions are there to curb our "own" things to be shown with disgusting liberty to the public who have right to not to see obscenity and semi-pornographic items in the name of advertisements. Yet, the public is not a herd of sheep that has foolish moral dogmas; it is their collective agreement of aesthetic good which is also ethically good that initiates the needed sanctions to check the libertarians.

I have said that in this chapter I will not detail the moral debates arranged by me and analyse them for normative ethical discoveries. I wanted to clarify what value-laden issues are, why do we call them so, what sort of disagreements do they raise and how to proceed in an intersubjective corroboration for ethical resolution. Let me give you a questionnaire for ethical debate about advertisement and then move to the next chapter where awaits a full length course in intersubjective corroboration.

QUESTIONNAIRE

1. What according to you should be the just aims or objectives in advertisements in general and commercial advertisements in particular?
2. What should be rightful relation among the companies, advertisers and consumers in a market?
3. Do you think that commercial advertisements should be educative apart from being informative? Do you think that commercial advertisements are means to profit maximisation of advertisers and companies, which should overrule ethical and educative prerogatives?
4. Do you see any relation between "promise keeping" and advertisements? Should advertisers be held responsible for keeping promises such as upholding privacy and truth in advertisements?

5. What should be the rightful place for humans, animals and natural entities in advertisements?
6. Should advertisements use social taboos, faiths, customs and erotic visuals in advertisements?
7. Suggest some ethically acceptable methods of advertisements and some laws to counter undesirable advertisements in India.

The intersubjective corroboration debate arranged by me regarding ethic of advertisement was held in 1999 with the contribution from the following people:

1. Dr. Sivrama Krishnan, Professor of Commerce, St. Xavier's College, Ranchi,
2. Mr. Kishalaya, "Drishti Ad Agency", Ranchi,
3. Mr. Anil Kumar Singh, "Darling Ad Agency", Ranchi,
4. Mr. Ashok Kumar Sinha, Director, Sinha Institute, Ranchi,
5. Mr. S. K. Chatterjee, Sole Agent of Veedol, Ranchi,
6. A number of students and teachers of Philosophy, Economics and Commerce of Ranchi University.

NOTES

1. Ladd, John, "Computers and Moral Responsibility: A Framework for an Ethical Analysis" in *Computerization and Controversy: Value Conflicts and Social Changes*, Dunlop, Charles & Kling, Rob (eds.), Academic Press, NY, 1991, p. 671.
2. See Rob Kling's "When Organisations are perpetrators: Assumptions about computer Abuse and Computer Crime" in Dunlop, Charles and Kling, Rob (eds.), *Computerization and Controversy: Value Conflicts and Social Changes*, Op. Cit., pp. 682-686.
3. Hartman, L. P., *Perspectives in Business Ethics*, Tata McGraw Hill Publishing Co. Ltd., New Delhi, 2003, p. 669.
4. Camenisch, P. F., "Marketing Ethics: Some Dimensions of the Challenge" in Hartman, L. P., (eds.), *Perspectives in Business Ethics*, Op. Cit., p. 495.
5. *Ibid*, p. 496.
6. For details, read J. K. Galbraith's *The Affluent Society*, Houghton Miffin Co., Boston, 1958 and M. G. Velasquez's *Business Ethics: Concepts and Cases*, Prentice Hall of India, New Delhi, 2002.
7. Solomon, Robert, "Is It Ever Right to Lie? (On truth In Advertising) in Hartman, L. P. (eds.), *Perspectives in Business Ethics*, Op. Cit., p. 516.

5

Resolving Ethical Crises in Globalisation, Liberalisation, Privatisation and Free Trade in the Indian Context through Intersubjective Corroboration

Thus far we have seen that ethical study of right, good, just, duty and obligation makes sense in the fields alien to moral philosophy; this is particularly true when we consider the fields of economics, business and management (also administration). Hence, a large part of the book is concerned with justification of economic, business, management and administrative ethics as sensible and valuable. We have seen in almost all justifications that there are in fact two ways in which the ethical intervention in economics, business etc. holds to be good. From the side of economics, for instance, we found a number of issues properly called, 'economic issues' opens up for inviting ethically relevant study or ethical scrutiny of the said issues. This shows that what is otherwise known as stark 'positivistic problems' are not that constricted because the problems are open to a non-positivistic critique of the same, in this case, ethical critique. From the side of ethics, for instance, we found a number of important functions that belongs to that field is capable of entering the realms of non-ethics, like economics, and perform its functions fairly well. In this sense, metaethical function of ethics is not restricted to the traditional normative-language-critique rather, enters the realm of economics for relevant linguistic and logical critiques. Not only this, the normative, virtue-ethical and practical functions of ethics makes great sense when ethics enter different non-ethical environments. Hence, we are at hand strong bases to 'justify' that economic, business and management ethics are within ethics, and there is no point in relegating them to pointless studies or pseudo-ethical studies.

We have also seen that the traditional notion of economics, business and management ethics misguide us to believe that these fields takes up the burdensome task of resolving ethical dilemmas in economics, business and management by applying one or more ethical norm or norms available to us by virtue of the long history of normative discourses. This is all the more unacceptable if application of norms for resolution of value-crises is left to the expert ethicists and not to a number of interested people who have moral authority to participate in real life crises along with trained ethicists. Similarly, we have seen that it will be too odd to imagine that ethicists are mere onlookers in applying ethics rather, they have great responsibilities to *initiate*, *moderate*, *corroborate* and *analyse* moral debates. We have seen that for this ethicists should proceed with a *de-classed* attitude towards ethical resolution thus paving the way for a number of people who take interest in ethical matters, to act together for a moral consensus about moral dilemmas so that some concrete public direction comes to the decision makers in society which becomes difficult to neglect without falling prey to unethicality. We have seen that application of ethics in this sense leaves enough opportunity to those people who might belong to a different field like economics or business but have enough wisdom to initiate, moderate, corroborate and analyse moral debates to participate in what we call 'applied ethics'. This makes clear that though resolution of ethical crises by applying our common ethical experience and knowledge in ethical debates does not demand us to be trained in wholesome ethics or to be an expert ethicist, wholesome application of ethics involving things like selection of value-laden practical problems, selecting most important people for moral dialogue, constructing a questionnaire for ethical debate, moderating the debate, coming to corroboration of views, finding out decision-making rules and finally, the analysis of ethical dialogue to find out the normative ethical dynamics. However, we have seen that in all the above mentioned steps of application, people's involvement is needed, expert ethical knowledge or the theoretical ethical knowledge of the ethicists is not enough in perfect isolation, barring the case of theoretical inquiry of normativity in ethical dialogues, which is 'post-corroboration analysis'. Hence, if and only if ethical application in its complete sense includes 'post-corroboration analysis' for a normative study in particular, only then do we need in-depth knowledge of theoretical ethics, which the ethicists have. Yet, we have seen that even this is not unique to ethicists because others, namely, economists, managers and so on can have theoretical ethical training for doing something which otherwise ethicists will do, but in no case, the lay-persons, who are indubitably parties to the other steps in application of ethics. The comfortable inclusion of non-ethicists in application of ethics thus saves it from being chauvinistic or structuralist, which is unethical for its anti-people attitude. The safeguards to include expert ethicists in ethical analysis are *not* chauvinistic because without such theoretical or academic interest, practical ethics will still make great sense if the major part of ethical resolution has been taken care of. Nevertheless, to say that application of ethics should include this analytic task, is not returning to a hidden chauvinism because it still do not belong to a class or a clan of 'ethicists' more popularly known as "professional philosophers". To think that still, academic or theoretical ethical training is an imperative in this case, that is, in case of post-corroboration analysis and the whole of ethics so to say, does not imply that, therefore, anyone (ethicists and non-ethicists), who takes such holistic ethical interest, are chauvinists. This is so because *knowing* ethical theories for deconstructing ethical debates is not to be a chauvinist. To think that only this is application of ethics, which *only* ethicists need to do, is "chauvinism". To conclude, application of ethics understood in its complete sense includes certain things to be done where academic ethics plays a second fiddle. It may be conveniently said that the *pre-analytic stage* in application of ethics, when major focus is resolution of ethical crises in cooperation is major; whereas an *analytic* stage when academic ethics plays a major role with regard to discover normativity in ethical dialogues is what we call post-corroboration stage. In both cases, the non-ethicists and ethicists have many things to do but in the analytic stage, *ethics* comes to *our* rescue, that is, it becomes a major contributor to *ethics-trained people* (i.e., to both philosophers by training and non-philosophers adopting philosophical training).

We have also seen in the previous chapter what value-laden practical problems are, how to know that certain problems are ethically charged, who the concerned parties are, what people think about such problems and thus participate in moral debates and how to frame questions for debates that brings out the best of moral knowledge of the concerned parties. Yet, I refrained from giving details of dialogue, the way consensus were reached and the theories that were found active in moral debates. Many things like these were left to all interested in intersubjective corroboration. Now it is time that we take on the most crucial issue that has disturbed our ethicists, businessmen, managers and common public including the workers in India in the recent times, which in some sense overlaps the issue of mechanisation, computerisation, labour-related crises and even advertisements. We are now speaking about the broader ethical crises in globalisation, liberalisation, privatisation, free trade and disinvestment in Indian context because the general issues give way to more specific and troubling crises in culture-specific contexts. Hence, we should consider ways to resolve such ethical crises in India following the model of intersubjective corroboration. First step is to *learn about the value crises*.

Globalisation, liberalisation, free trade, privatisation, disinvestment of the public sector and outsourcing, for their family resemblance, may be put under the genus of *economic reforms*, which is distinctive of global economies in modern times. These have caught our imagination particularly owing to reformist economic policies adopted in the developing countries like India, since the last two decades of the twentieth century. Whether such reforms are based on an economic philosophy or cluster of such philosophies is not our immediate concern, what is most important to notice is that a number of reformist steps as mentioned above constructs what we now call a "reform of economy" in India, which is basic to a flurry of moral arguments because under the veil, it is said that imperialism and capitalism have been imported to nail down our decision-makers. Whereas the counter view is that economic reforms as urgent need in India has been shaped indigenously, nothing has been imported or imposed, we just went through certain processes which we were long avoiding and thus came in the main stream of a global economic phenomena, that is, "global participation in production, distribution and services". Hence, without losing the identity of a nation state in economic decision-making, the idea is to invite the *global* companies to contribute to non-strategic fields for their growth, thus having no apathy to encourage *private* players in this regard whether of one's own country or of another country showing courage in being *liberal* in setting an economy free from the clutches of both monopolistic government and/or private houses. This paves way to *freedom from trading* restrictions as well, thus enabling *multinational companies* to do relatively unrestricted trading and doing the same in other countries.

In doing all these, if the government needs to *disinvest* in any of its owned sectors to either dilute it completely or give them liberty for autonomy and privatisation, is welcome. Yet, if a nation is threatened with economic losses owing to malpractices or anti-national policies, they are free to put *embargoes* in trading and other practices. The stage is set for an ethical debate as supporters of reformism are sure about nation's well-being in this way, whereas those against it are sure about several pitfalls, most notorious being, human exploitation and environmental catastrophe. As in India we are already through the reformist agenda for quite some time now, the bitter pill is in or the sweetmeat has been consumed; anyway, there is no denial that we either support its ethical status with vengeance or we retreat gradually for gross unethicality with some shame and guilt for our past misdeeds. But where exactly do we fall? Are we in the horns of dilemma? May be we are in the horns of dilemma, but soon that has to be given up. But the moot question is how can we do that?

The genus, that is, "economic reform" covers multilevel reformist decisions or agendas regarding production, distribution, services, trade and commerce, thus extending to an extremely broad realm of affairs that becomes a matter of evaluation, that is, whether the agendas are defective, myopic, unpragmatic, non-beneficial or harmful, non-welfarist and so on. In view of the broad-based reformist need, there must be as expected a number of sub-classes or species of reformist processes under the genus, the most prominent being the process of "globalising of economy", which is further backed up or contributed by different other species or reformist processes like liberalisation, privatisation and free trade. This is not to say that liberalisation, privatisation, free trade as species are within an overreaching species of globalisation which in turns is covered by the genus of economic reforms. In fact, liberalisation, privatisation, free trade, disinvestment and globalisation as was hinted in the earlier passage, are different classes of economic reformist agenda or are different economic processes, though among other things they come together to constitute economic reforms. In many cases than not liberalisation and privatisation might be needed for globalisation of an economy and thus fulfil a holistic reformist agenda, because head on rush to globalise an economy may not be possible if the economy is not positive to privatisation and liberalisation processes to start with. In many cases than not, without an *open* vision about *market* there may not be any free trade, and if the vision about market is narrow or closed and restricted, where freedom in trade is ruled out as starters, the point of liberalising economy and making way to privatisation just do not match, and the mismatch (or contradiction) do not in any way fit in the scheme of a globalised economy. To be precise, these contradictions do not contribute to any reformist agenda; the state is in a *status quo* or if that is not an agreeable notion, the state is 'traditionalist'. Despite the intricate independence of and correlation among the cluster of species, it is always interesting to notice whether globalisation as a economic vision precedes liberalisation and other species of the whole, that is, whether bereft of globalisation of economy there is no possibility of liberalisation and other processes. Is there a causal nexus among the species, globalisation being the cause of liberalisation, privatisation and so on? Or, do we say that without liberalisation etc. there is no moving from a non-globalised to a globalised economy? Or, do we say that the causal nexus is pointless here to mention, what is important to notice is that the cluster of species of the whole are not related causally to each other, they nevertheless, are constituents of economic reforms, not causes of the same. In true sense, *economic reforms as genus or whole is the desired end of some economies, the pragmatic means of which are its said species or processes, each different but related non-causally*. Nevertheless, when we come to the point of a *desirable end* of the said desired end of reforms, we come to transcend an economy that wants to move from tradition to modernity and enter into *ethic of economy* that wants a change or transition. The moot point is thus the *desirability of reforms* to which we want to come, but after a while.

To be precise, as a non-economist I see liberalisation as a process in an economy of transition from hackneyed traditionality to modernity (a reformist move), in which private-sector organisations are allowed to participate in national market which were erstwhile open only for public sector organisations by virtue of the restrictive mechanisms of monopolistic market and licensing arrangements. It may well be that broad-based liberalisation frees the market from the monopoly of one or more national private organisation or organisations or private house or houses to allow foreign houses to compete in an open market that has relaxed the licensing arrangements and laid infrastructural facilities. Such broad-based liberalisation opens up for multinational companies to play in the market of a nation, which may be as a step forward to the ideal of a globalised economy. Privatisation as a process, unlike liberalisation is not merely opening up of a national market for private players; it is a step forward (or backward!) by the State to sell its assets which was owned directly or indirectly. The phenomenon of 'sell of assets' covers a selling offer to the public, to the private houses as a trade sale and a buy-out of the employees and/or management. In one sense, privatisation in a economy is a way to transfer State owned responsibilities in that economy to the public sector. This also means that the State might levy charges for the services its public-sector organisations provide and that for the effective services by the public sector contracts may be given to private players, notwithstanding their profits. In this way the State which was the major body acting as producer, distributor and service provider, now shares economic responsibilities, though that might amount to lesser free-lunch. The State thus does not show any apathy to interact and compete with private players in the market, neither does it show hesitation in selling any organ of its organisations which is sick or tends to be sick or is unmanageable. It may not hesitate in doing away with its managerial staff and the employees with adequate back-up compensatory arrangements. Both liberalisation and privatisation might go hand-in-hand in an economy that is gradually coming closer to the ideal of globalisation. Liberalising an economy is often motivated more when the State shows greater interests in the private sector participation in almost all the economic functions in a State, and for that the State is more courageous to shake off its early orthodoxy of ownership of assets to sell them to any competent private house. In fact, more extensively the State does it, the more likely is the speed of liberalisation process in an erstwhile closed economy. However, this does not mean that a State will be so courageous and so foolish overnight to be ready to transfer all and any of its responsibilities. The State might thus slow down liberalising trends through fine-tuned control of transfer of its key assets as well as responsibilities. In that case too, the relation between the processes is well-marked. Yet, the State might give a quantum fillip to liberalisation all of a sudden by virtue of greater political courage and consensus (encouraged by some urgent need), to liberalise more than what was the speed before, thus becoming free in a selling spree (that covers all the three cases)—if that be the case, the limits put to "key sectors" and "strategic areas" quickly change or they are pressed for an extension or a nearly fizzle-out. This may see the State privatising its defence sector, for instance. This in turn might encourage the private houses to the optimum and with it the trends in an economy's liberalisation is believed to have changed phenomenally. Nevertheless, it will be a little too much to think that the States around the world have by this time vigorously transferred most of its assets to the private owners because the State cannot and should not do so for all practical and ethical reasons. It is not difficult to understand why it is not practically possible for a State to give up all its activities to the private hands, but the moot point is, should it not do so for other than practical or ethical reasons? The point becomes more debatable when we come to consider whether it is ethically right and just for modern States to sell its assets at the will of some decision-makers to private hands in any case? This is a hard question, the question takes to the ethic of shaking off of the State responsibilities toward the people, managers, employees and so on. We shall come to them but it is interesting to note that processes of liberalisation and privatisation almost inexorably pushes us to ethical considerations because there is more often than not an ethical ought to a practical is. The discussion, however, must keep in mind the fact that privatisation as complementary to liberalisation does not bereft an erstwhile public monopolist of all its market power. Hence, if the privatisation is not radical and complete, which is difficult to imagine, I have said the State is still the same player in a economy, but it has changed its old ideologies or philosophy of economy and necessary methods and techniques in carrying on with its desirable role in and with the public, thus having assumed a new *private status*. Whether this private *avatār* of the State is practical is discussed in economies, but is the *avatār* ethical or just, is the key to economic ethics. As issues in privatisation and liberalisation takes us to issues in business, management (and also politics), the ethically relevant inquires of the same are key to business and management ethics (and to political ethics as well). The most troubling point in this regard is 'Should the State behave as a private player in a nation's economy?' To this may be added that a State to behave like a private player, should liberalise its economic conceptions, and for that reason, should the State have changed conception of economy, that is, against its monopoly? Or, is the State ethically right to give up its monopoly or to assume a competitive status of a company?

Coming to the process of globalisation, it would be said that though the term "globalisation", like "liberalisation" has a wide use and thus different meanings, here both the terms carry with them the sense of "economic", that is, they are used in the economic parlance to mean processes found in an economy. Hence, economic globalisation (like liberalisation) should be distinguished from non-economic globalisation such as globalisation of a political, religious, ethical, scientific and secular ideal. Ideological globalisations are different from economic globalisation in this sense. The point is that though non-economic and economic globalisation, both refer to the *genus* "globalisation" meaning thereby "a process of international integration", its differentiating property, which is "economic" (than political, ethical etc.), is marked by the "process of international integration of economic activities". Before moving into the clarification of what it means, I must stray a little farther to assert that the popular idea that a globalised conception of religion or metaphysics cannot be dragged into the realm of a conception of global economy. The point that both religious, metaphysical and economic globalisation being species of globalisation may not be *internally* related, that is, they do not share properties in a manner that a change in one marks a change in the other. Hence, even if Catholic Christianity, *Vedānta* and Buddhism have conceptions of globalising or integration of people of nations as an esteemed ideal in life because we are sons of God or because humanity has to be respected, both the conceptions of integration are not the same because both do not advocate economic integration or integration of international economic activities. Religious integration is in essence different from economic integration. This amounts to say that even if we are irreligious or non-religious or even anti-religious, as many tribes, Marxists and existentialists are, we can still participate in a process of economic globalisation. Nothing prevents religious persons to participate in economic globalisation either. The same must be true to a secular people, who co-exist with many religious people. Economic globalisation is a different category of globalisation because it is concerned with activities that are corporeal (belonging to the 'eco' or the household), and thus belongs to a category of material integration and not metaphysical or religious. It is also not the same as a political integration that democracy or autocracy or communism envisions because these are not integration through economical process. Even if political processes pertain to the physical world, they are nevertheless, not the same as the economic processes. Hence, even if there is no globalised polity, there may be still a globalisation of economies. Similarly, even if there is no globalised ethics, there can be economic globalisation though ethical questions may be raised about economic globalisation. It is clear that economic globalisation is not derived from or based on the conceptions of globalisation that transcends it; hence, to speak of economic globalisation as derived from religious or metaphysical theories of the *Vedānta* or Christianity or Buddhism is a confusion of categories, though remotely they may be related *externally* in so far as a matter of accidence *Vedānta* and economics both speak of need of integration of international community in some sense at least. But to think that religious integration (through a philosophy of its kind) is the basis of economic integration is pointless. Religions or metaphysics cannot be the basis of or cause of economic integration or economic globalisation. Hence, I do not buy the argument that Christian or *Vedāntic* thesis helps economic integration. Yet, we can argue at length whether economic integration showers any light on or can be *evaluated* in the light of Christianity or *Vedānta*. To evaluate economic globalisation as "good" or "right" or "just" or "bad" or "harmful" or "unjust" begs a number of criteria which truly can be both economic and non-economic as mentioned above, but non-economic criteria itself cannot be the basis of globalisation. Hence, we shall here "evaluate" economic globalisation on ethical grounds that we have, not surely on any religious or other grounds available to us, not even on purely economic grounds, but in any case we shall not argue that ethical philosophy of some kind or a kind can logically explain why there is economic globalisation. It is important to remember that it is one thing to argue that *Vedānta* has something in store its unique monistic metaphysics that evaluates economic integration as good or bad and another thing to argue that *Vedānta* has sufficient logical grounds to explain why there is economic globalisation or why was it needed or provides basis for economic globalisation. Similarly, we should keep in mind that if there is anything in *Vedānta* that deals with *economic affairs*, most of the time expected as conceptions of *artha* (wealth), *vyāpāra* (business) etc. there is no point in not listening to this philosophical grounds or the ethical grounds for *evaluating*. *Vedānta* does not make a point here if truly the conception in it are not economic integration rather than another thing. It will be thus extremely interesting to see what *Vedānta*, for instance, holds originally in the *proper context* of economic integration and then turn to its evaluation on grounds economic and non-economic that it has. Otherwise to say that *Vedānta* conceives of humanity at large as *one* on metaphysical grounds and therefore, it has an economic theory of globalisation is a futile talk. However, to argue that *Vedāntic* conception of oneness of humans contributes in integration as such or that it helps us to realise that economic integration is good, is equally interesting, with a qualification that this thesis cannot be necessary and sufficient ground to explain the process of economic integration. If Marxism and Capitalism are more clearly the cases of theories dealing with economic integration on purely economic terms and thus evaluates them on grounds both economic and non-economic, they are *stronger theses* about economic globalisation than Christianity or *Vedānta*, but even then we cannot say that either Marxism or Capitalism are necessary and sufficient to explain the process of economic globalisation, or that the idea is derived from them. Nevertheless, it is interesting to contest whether any of the two economic theories is logically sound to evaluate economic globalisation as good or bad on the economic and the ethical grounds they have. This clarification was needed because most of the time a philosopher's interests with economic issues are wrongly placed because they are interested in philosophising about economic affairs forgetting the truth that philosophical or metaphysical or religious thesis cannot be the exclusive basis for explaining an economic process.

We may now say that (economic) globalisation is a process in which the basic economic activities of production, distribution and services needs to be performed throughout the world in close regional and global association and not closely or isolatedly that may amount to a closed attitude towards regions or nations for some ideological and/or practical differences. Economic globalisation thus integrates the international community by means of economic functions, which keep off regionalism, provincialism, racism, sectarianism and narrow nationalism which champions that economic functions should be carried on by organisations without any alien cooperation, contributions, and thus sharing responsibilities and benefits. The idea is to flex the geographical boundaries to an optimum when it comes to economic good of a nation because world seen as a single space in economic matters is amenable to holistic material good of the political entities called nations. Economic globalisation thus shares the idea of 'equality' throughout the nations when economic benefits are concerned, which understandably comes not in isolation but in mutual trust and interdependence. Though in the midst of this pampered 'equality' of benefits to people there is no way to a unipolarity in business, trade and commerce and for that matter giving up competition for survival and gains. The idea of systematic globalised economy grew in proportion only with the advent of the last two decades of the twentieth century. This saw more and more inter-country relations in trade and commerce, investment, production, alliances of firms, collaborative ventures in research and development. The two world bodies emerged to address to the fresh set of needs of the international community engaged in economic activities, the World Trade Organisation (WTO) and the General Agreement of Tariff and Trade (GATT), though not all nations are the participants of these bodies.

We now come to the conceptions of *free trade* and *open market economy* as they are important features of economies tending to be liberalised, privatised and globalised more and more. It is expected that in an era of globalisation of economy, the markets where physically speaking, trading is taking place cannot be closed, that is, restrictive to the alien traders or those not belonging to one's own country. Similarly, it cannot be expected that private players in a country should not partake in any trading activity beyond its boundaries. Equally unbelievable is that within a country there will be an absolute absence of private players in even domestic market because the entire market is governed and controlled by the State machinery. Hence, in an extremely restrictive economy only the State owns markets and plays in it, that is, partake in trading practices. This might amount to restrictions in any imports though exports may be opened in dire necessities. If everything is fine in domestic front, there will be absolutely no traffic beyond the domestic market, thus trading will have a different definition altogether with a unique status for the market. An open market economy is the breaking up of such restrictiveness in trading practices in markets. It thus opens traffic to and fro, that is, exports with greater and greater liberty and imports with equal ease thus allowing broader participation of both the private players in the domestic front and those from abroad. The same must be the case when the state is a player in the market because it will with ease and force participate in competitive trading arenas globally and domestically thus interacting in intricate market practices in the state and abroad opening widely for both exports and imports, not merely for dire necessities but gain maximisation as is the case with any gain-seeking player in the market involved in trading. An open market economy thus allows trade relations among a number of national and international companies and states each going for maximisation of gains by providing goods and services. This, however, does not imply that the states do not or should not have any intervention in matters of trade because whatever degree of liberty may be given, the state for certain benefits and necessities of its people would like to impose taxes, duties and so on because it cannot be like a pure private player in a market to strive for its own good, as if it is a corporate body. It has to safeguard interests of common people by means of providing them necessities, infrastructure, welfare and so on. It also has to look into the infrastructural benefits of the players engaged in its markets whether they are private domestic players or the private international players. Hence, in an open economy the state can neither be restrictive in trading options nor can the state be a pure private profit maker having no checks for the private organisations as well as for the states abroad. In one sense, despite some gains from a market by trading, the state can gain indirectly from players in its market through certain economic interventions in an open market. If the state is, however, apathetic to the ideals of globalisation, liberalisation and privatisation, there is hardly any scope or even a need for an open economy or an open market economy.

Closely associated to this is the concept of *free trade*, which in reality is a *commercial policy* on the part of a state that imposes no restrictions on the exchange of goods and services among different states, thus showing no special favours to domestic commodities in relation to foreign commodities by putting certain burdens on the foreign commodities. Hence, free trade is a trading practice in which the state does not restrict foreign goods to enter in its market by imposing certain restrictive laws or checks and thus making it a loser or uncompetitive with the goods supplied by domestic companies. A free trade in essence is a pro-competitive market practice without discrimination on the basis of foreign goods as well as services in a truly open economy or open market economy that hopefully abides by trends in globalisation of economy. Yet, it is a little too much to believe that the state should have absolute non-control over the flow of foreign goods and services in terms of their quality, quantity, prices, profit margins, and most importantly in terms of the labour market. The absolute state non-control in a free trade should be with regard to flow of goods and services across the borders. These are arguments in favour of a truly free trade bereft of state impediments in the forms of tariffs, quotas, exchange controls, subsidies, taxes, and on production and consumption. Hence, in a free trade the protective measures of the state in favour of domestic market players including the state organisations, and in favour of domestic producers facing cheap imported items has to be seen off. This brings into focus the dilemmas of a otherwise protectionist developing state which is in the horns of dilemma of welfare of its people and its companies, and the crises of its erstwhile poor and slack economy which cannot in principle develop all by itself or by inviting people to trade across the border but not allowing them to make enough gains despite contributing to the gain of the economy in need. In any case, a country looking up for a globalised economy should nevertheless, be not puritan to free trade, and for that it should not be hesitant in liberalising its economy and go courageously for an open market economy either.

With this we come to a rough idea of what things are in value-consideration here. It is now that as a matter of proceeding along intersubjective corroboration we should see the ethical questions that the reformist steps have given us in particular. This way we come to know why the issues are value-charged and what are the pro and con views with regard to the value-questions. The best way to do so is not to go through books of ethics but through a process of learning in and with the public, that is, both by talking to people on these matters extensively and by reading what they express in articles and debates. This helps us further in the construction of questions which thus becomes non-structuralist set of inquiries about value issues like this. However, debating is our next step. We shall now concentrate on pro-con views in society that project value-laden dimension of the above mentioned economic issues. As usual we will proceed in the way we have done before, considering the value-issues that arise from economic reforms in general, and then to liberalisation and privatisation in India, which were natural outcomes of a reformist call. Further we will consider value-laden-ness of free trade in the Indian markets and finally the case of globalisation. The choice of moving from liberalisation to globalisation is not based on any particular philosophy, perhaps it is a matter of moving from the national to the international reformist scenario with value-crises added to them. The knowledge of value-crises and the pro-con views which helped me in the construction of questions for the debate is, as I have said before, based on interacting with economists, common men, workers, trade unionists, farmers, environmentalists, politicians, philosophers and so on. Some wisdom has been gathered from a number of articles published in newspapers and magazines.

One view about economic reforms in general in India is that the touted beneficial reforms in India is in fact not a deliberate conscientious choice of the people of the nation in general, it has been a compulsion of the government during 1991 to meet an acute crises in Indian economy that it had to succumb to the pressure of the external forces like the International Monetary Fund which is a money-lender in disguise pretending to be so good to countries in need. Hence, as a starter, the idea of opening up Indian economy was based on unconscientious grounds and thus unethical, says many. Following the well known story of June 1991, when Dr. Manmohan Singh convinced both the then President and the Prime Minister of India to borrow heavily from the IMF on their exploitative terms which only a capitalist agency can impose on a poor country in recession not surely for their welfare, the basic goal of economic reforms in India was to save from a complete ignominy of economic crisis, perhaps a result of our own foolish strategies in economy and polity. The con-arguments are thus based on the idea that neither was reforms in capitalists' terms publicly approved nor did it really help the public. The truth that even the members of the ruling party were not sure about the good of such exploitative loans in the name of reforms, made the reformist move shaky at its initiation. Still, changes could be seen, the most important being slashing subsidies and non-development expenditure, and the *liberalisation* of imports, financial and insurance sectors and the *privatisation* of public sector units. Stiff value questions were raised even by some ruling party members about the justification of pro-poor agendas like "*garibi hatao*" and the open invitation of the corporate empires across the borders, mostly known as the multinational companies to flourish in business when the *desi* companies were difficult managing the new onslaught. The unethicality charge thus lies in the anti-poor and anti-domestic economic policies. The main opposition at that time thus became saviours of the poor and the *desi* overnight because they thought that only such things can bring some ethical glory to the nation. Others said that the unethicality also lies in the "half-heartedness" of the reforms because people had enough of the *kitchery* in the form of "mixed economy" by that time and perhaps wanted one full way to go, either *desi* or *videsi* corporate, but did any one prefer the *desi* poor? Even the famous Dr. Singh was found to flounder, said many, because he urged at times to "liberalise" and "privatise", to put off all things that came "free" to the public, and at other times his Indian self cried for budgetary allocations for "subsidies" and that the corporate in markets cannot "rule" us. The result was that the unethical half-way reforms put the foreign masters in tenterhooks because in their ethical parlance, reforms must be complete, they must make corporate the masters with a belief that people will be better off when they first become good serfs. So this was how we opened up our economy for reforms to the global players, soon demanding ethical criticisms from our own people who were not ready for such a drastic step before their domestic market could see any sea change in terms of government encouraging the domestic private players more than before and that the State assumed any competitive status by virtue of keeping off monopolistic status in many sectors including the strategic ones. Hence, there was a lot of hue and cry that before any liberalist and privatising steps domestically we straightaway jumped to the mired idea of globalising our economy thus putting great pressures on a slack liberalising and privatising mechanisms. Hence, the lack of care taken for even our own investors and our own companies became a point for ethical attacks on reformist agenda. The point in the main is the deliberate disfavour to or discrimination against domestic companies in a competitive economy, which is at its worst encouraging the corporate imperialist of the West against whom we fought a long battle and for which the father of our nation advocated a pro-people economy, which is non-exploitative. These ethical criticisms thus gave up alternatives believed to be ethical on different grounds, which may be termed as the alternative of *swadeshi* or a variant of Gandhian conception of the market economy.

The proponents of the reforms were not mute people; they were vociferous too on ethical grounds because for them among other evils, the steps taken in reforms were ethically good mainly on two grounds. First, if left for some time to work, reforms are sure to bring a lot of purchase power to the State and the public who went poor, though remaining poor is not ethically desirable. Second, many orthodoxies including the economic ones have prevented us from being well-off if not affluent since a long time. We must have lost some economic wisdom that when the world demanded more and more economic interactions and cooperation, if we believed to be well-off, we must change our attitude towards the international players in the market. Third, if initially international lending were to stabilise our economy, putting it to steam depends on how much will do we have to open our markets. Hence, lendings were only a tentative means to a good to be visioned in the long run. This was backed up by data of growth in terms of GNP or GDP, foreign investment, foreign reserves and so on. The champions showed how physically the good results were already in view and that we were better off or did have some well-being is for sure. Well-being cannot be ethically bad; it is good, even if it is on pure physical terms. Further, the entire conception of reforms were ethically good in view of the modernisation, mechanisation and sophistication of our industries, farming and services when private houses produce more and serve better at competitive prices. The people were thus served with quantitative and qualitative goods and services which changed their lives from worse to better. We had access to what we needed at a competitive price, there was neither exploitation in term of quantity or quality or pricing. All these being pro-people, were ethically just.

Clearly, the main strength of economic reform being liberalising our economy, some people argued that it is an ethically desirable process in so far as it has made the ordinary Indians economically affordable in the market, it has made them a consumer of strength whose rights do we now champion though they were faceless and nameless entities in a places where state overwhelmed the economic functions and the markets, leaving them the meek creatures they were. The supporters of liberalisation thus argues that the ethical goodness of liberalisation could be realised almost after a decade when the power of affordability of common men increased which ended the idea that the Indians did not deserve modern (or western) products and services because they had no power to purchase. Hence, small amount of goods and services at exorbitant prices reached a few hands thus leaving the consumer market lacklustre and uncompetitive. As a result of reforms and impetus in liberalisation enabled the large multinationals to cater to the needs of the erstwhile ordinary Indian consumers, which is sign of the dignity of the Indian buyers. The self-esteem brought about by the trend is thus ethically commendable.

The ethical glorification of reforms and the process of liberalisation contributing to it were met with equal vengeance. The same conception of human well-being taken as ethically supreme in so far as economy is concerned, was shown to be a distant cry for two reasons. One is that the intrinsic worth or value lies in the end state of human good or well-being not necessarily in the touted *means* such as liberalisation and globalisation. The other is that an ethically noble means of liberalisation tending to promote well-being has replacement instances in domestic reforms in economy such as in *swadeshi* or in the Gandhian ideal of a market economy. These ethical alternatives need some explanation but before that let us have a look at certain news items that came up around late 1999 to early 2000 when a decade long reformist (liberalist) hullabaloo gained some steam. A particular data revealed that liberalising trends in the Indian market demanded great precaution as there has been a noticeable demand-supply imbalance observed in the market. The profit margins on sales produces of major industries dipped noticeably causing down-gradation of ratings of the industries. The crises cautioned about a steady recession with stagnation of demand of major products. The main reason being the failure to cope up with the corporate modernisation and upgrading capacities in view of phenomenal growth in demand in the market. If liberalisation continued with such speed, liquidity problems in the industries will be unmanageably acute. Certainly this was armour in the unethicality charges against liberalisation. Closely related to this was the news that a number of Indian ecologists and human rights champions saw a steep rise in the prices of vegetables and pulses (even to this date) owing to trade liberalisation because it has generated market fluctuations and volatile supply of these items. It was charged that the government in its new incarnation of a player in the open market has created an artificial food crisis by conniving with corporates involved in the agro-sector so that their monopolies on these essential items could be gradually established. More interesting is that the government wants to further favour the foreign producers and distributors of these items by opening for imports without any significant change in meeting the crises. The growing trends in the farming community of India, particularly the small farmer was to thus quit the perennial sector or to simply crash out of life. It is a matter of grave concern for the large Indian farming community that the public policy of the State with regard to food entitlement has been wayward. Such news may not be ethically strong for pro-liberalisation exponents. Again, the Indian trading community seems to have some ethical hunches against the liberalising strategies as it was reported that the Associated Chamber of Commerce and Industries (ASSOCHAM) constituted a task force to study the human face of reforms because it was completely impossible for the State to continue with its reforms that was anti-humans and anti-Indians. This was particularly in the face of the multinational onslaughts with government apathy to encourage them to displace poor men from their perennial abodes to erect industries. The environmental apartheid apart, the environmental refugees, their exploitation, non-compensation or inappropriate compensation added to the woes of the people. All these things again turned out to be ethically repugnant to many people. Similar outrages were heard from the opening up of the insurance sector for the international players when the Indian corporations were doing fairly well. It was urged that such liberalisation in the name of competition and qualitative service is dragging the mass-server to a class-server, which is again anti-people. More so ethically unjust was the news that within a decade of economic liberalisation in India, we have added more woes in the employment situation. The unemployment has risen sharply even though foreign investments in economy pledged employment phenomenally. In fact, the truth was that an army of unemployed rural Indians that spills over to the urban sector remain untraceable. The urban people, only some having technical knowledge and English educated have any chance to employment. The government now assuming the role of a spectator in public sector undertakings have added to the woes of the less educated or the rural masses. The public sectors are in fact offering golden handshake. The more glorified modernisation and mechanisation that liberalisation brings with it is a curse for a number of ordinary people who are not educationally empowered to a great extent. The point is whether in the midst of a high growth rate only a class is getting jobs in particular sectors? If this be true, it is anti-people.

Keeping these things in mind and many more, the ethical critics of liberalisation argue that GNP cannot be an indicator of human well-being on the whole because it is a referent of material good of the humans, which does not cover whole well-being of the humans. In fact, the misconceived implication of well-being from the growth of our GNP is owing to a complete philosophical confusion about what well-being or welfare means and what in reality or as a matter of fact is true. Human well-being depends on many things like an ethically charged way of life, social cohesion, family cohesion, and education that is not mere literacy or empowerment to earn a living and most importantly being responsive to the good of unempowered and downtrodden people as well as the care for the whole of ecological community as far as that is practicable. We can count many more of them; each refers to a non-material good for man that can be weighed by means of a quantitative calculus. The whole idea of quality-of-life and quality-of-work-life has changed dramatically in the face of the glare and glory of material advancement of human societies. The more the craving for GNP is acute, the less the welfare do we really have because that is a hedonic fallacy, which, when taken to the egoistic and grassroots level becomes unethical. Though remaining poor or ordinary is not ethical, even pleasure is not so bad for us, the idea is that to be well-off and to seek pleasure is not to have well-being. The critics argue that the measure or the quantitative calculus of GNP/GDP are also fallacies which economists themselves argue, and it is well known to us that statistical manipulations with data does not assure us of well-being because real life experiences tell us different truth. Another related misconception is that as GNP growth depends necessarily and sufficiently on growth in material production, which is possible through mechanisation, sophistication, industrialisation and many ways of modernisation, consequently all these means of growth are necessary and sufficient for human welfare. Even if it is partly true that GNP growth does depend on means of industrialisation, modernisation, and mechanisation and so on, it may not be wholly true that such things are *sufficient* for both GNP growth and subsequent welfare. In fact, heavy mechanisation has taken toll on our environment, social, cultural and political ways for which we now pay heavy price irreversibly—life as such has become trouble-trodden in such westernised conception of living a good life. Unethicality lies in the manifold value-degradation, the social, cultural, political and environmental value-degradation so to say. Loss of values in our life is to lose basic human face in the midst of economic growth; unethicality lies here. The modernisation (or westernised modernisation) in India is imported culture, an attack that corrodes the society from within in three ways of loss of our value-system. It carefully nurtures the evils of the past that has been passed on to us through modernisation; it plunders the reserved resources for the future and thus blind to the future generations and it makes us believe that all alien modernities given to us is to modernise us whether that changes the faces of our family, community, education and environment. It is interesting to note that those fixing the charges of unethicality argue that a modernisation that has been borrowed and not indigenous and innovative always keeps us behind because we are always worried about being at par with those who move ahead with their innovations in modernisation, and never strive ourselves to be modern in our ways. Hence, we depend more and more on the imperialist powers who move ahead of us and never catch them up. Unethicality lies in this dogmatic perception of modernisation that corrodes our will and power to modernise indigenously. The critics, many of them thus fall back on a Gandhian conception of self-reliance and indigenous modernisation or *swadeshi*, whereas others do not exactly use the same terms, but amounts to hold on to nearly the same idea by means of modernisation in and with the participation of our people, the State being the nodal agency. In any case, both the critics of imperialist modernisation argue that the unethicality of such modernisation in India also lies in the confusion of means and end of economic reforms because reformists do not realise that globalisation of economy and any step taken for that are mere *means* to the higher ideal or *end* of *human well-being*. As such globalisation is not an end itself; it does not have the intrinsic value of being an end of our economic life (what to speak of our life taken on the whole). The proponents of globalisation, liberalisation and free trade, all argue vociferously that the ethical end of these is to extend human welfare. The point is that even if it may be the case that human good is an intrinsically valuable ideal in life, globalisation etc. as means to it may not be valuable or good at all because in case of a limited economic good for man (which we have seen is not equivalent of whole of human well-being), these means have by now proved themselves to be good in some ways and evil in many other ways—the calculus does not show unambiguous results in favour of their value. Hence, all in all the government has to show interest in pro-people programmes for economic growth that cares for the wider innovations and involvement of our own people and companies. As such, the unethicality of government becoming a mute spectator who intervenes only when some harm is done to the private players is clear. Government cannot or ethically should not assume the status of a private player in its domestic market whether that amounts to its liberalisation or privatisation policies. Its reformist agendas should not therefore, make itself an exploiter of the people or to allow exploiters of its own people. The centrally planned economy just cannot collapse in India because that is an impetus to break alliance of the poor farmers, workers and even consumers. We must be careful to note that grave unethicality in liberalisation and privatisation lies in the systematic damage to our self-belief, free will, self-respect and sovereignty. However, all these do not amount to say that, therefore, India should raise an iron curtain of the era of fooldom yet again because self-reliance and centrally planned economy need not be foolish to allow balanced and pragmatic participation in most areas where growth has to be sped up in collaboration. It only encourages the idea that despite pragmatic opening up of economy, we should be careful about not being apathetic to our own capacities to develop.

An important aspect of Indian economy since the 90s is that the government is encouraging privatisation to the extent of wide ranging *disinvestment*. There is a lot of ethical debate about the process of disinvestment therefore, particularly in view of disinvestment in the core sectors including the profit making units in the sector, and the service sector including insurance, hotels and banking. The champions of privatisation in India are no less supporters of a half-way house. They are as tentative as in case of liberalisation and strangely their western *gurus* blame that they are unethical in being callous in inviting people to participate in their economic good but prevent them from doing so and to gain from the adventure by imposing taxes, tough licensing methods and bribes to be paid to *babus*. Moreover, the government is very unsure whether it should keep off from interventions, whether it should be aggressive in cases of acquisition, whether it should open strategic sectors and whether it should be a mere competitive player in the market. Naturally, the privatisation *gurus* across the world believe that the government should courageously disinvest in its holdings, even the strategic sectors partially, if that is enough. Surely, it is a gross unethicality to invite the fox for a dinner and serve soup in a long-neck jar, but the invitation cannot be a free-lunch either. Hence, the proponents of the half-way disinvestment is of the ethical opinion that the government of a developing country like India which was the major custodian of the assets for the people should not shock its people with drastic keeping-off policies that might pave way to rampant profiteering and exploitation by private players domestically and internationally. Hence, the ethical rightness lies in the partial participation of the government in business, though with greater spirit of economic Catholicism. The proponents of this view hold that disinvestment is ethically just in so far public sector units cannot run in heavy losses and thus bluff the tax payers of their money. The units cannot run smoothly even under unnecessary political interferences which was the case since long in the public sectors. Hence, the public holdings must be freed from such interferences and losses. The ethically desirable outcome is, therefore, government bringing its equity down to less that fifty per cent, taking challenges in business and meeting social sector needs and its assurances towards debts. All these ultimately free it from the indirect exploitation of the masses who paid dearly for the public sector units to nations' development. Disinvestment as going along with privatisation is, therefore, pro-people and conscientious act of the government. It has been argued that such disinvestment should not take place in the defence, railways and nuclear sectors. The ethicality of the decision lies in the safeguard of the population against any sabotage, loss of life and property, and any exploitation of the masses in terms of tariffs, convenience and sovereignty. The government will be thus ethically more responsible towards working better towards providing infrastructural and social needs of the people when it earns more by virtue of being in the business. Proponents of disinvestment also argue that the ethic of sparing profit-making public sector units and the service sector can be hardly contested as in a perfect monopoly in which they were functioning could hardly evaluate their value for the people. It may well be that they were lacklustre in performance and lackadaisical in services. This has to be removed by throwing them in an atmosphere of domestic and global competition through privatisation. Only with the advent of the private players in the market can their work culture develop and people are left with many options for they do enjoy the right to choose the best for the value they pay. Hence, there is no ethic of glorifying a profit making concern in the public sector if they really made pseudo-profits or they did not make any profit at all, which was noticed when some listed companies got no buyers. Equally true is that if privatisation is pro-people, pro-consumers, it is not ethically just to fix them up for only public buyers. There is every opportunity in the market that ensures a private buyer to buy a unit that has been disinvested because in any case that contributes to revival of the unit, workforce, management and population.

The ethical critics of privatisation, however, do not buy many of these arguments. To tell about those arguments we should first face some factual plain-truths. It was reported that G. V. Ramakrishna, the chairman of the Disinvestment Commission reported in a conference in 1999 that since the amount of Rs. 20,000 crore raised through disinvestment was not used for development project which refutes the idea that the process is ethical in meeting the essential economic and social commitments of the government. Instead a large amount was used to bridge the fiscal deficits. This was corroborated by the audit report of the Comptroller and Auditor General of India (CAG) which said that after first round of privatisation and disinvestment served fiscal and not the social sector. This must be a deliberate act of hiding objectives of a programme that has been touted to be pro-people in so far as they are served better than before at the levels of their social needs, which is an act of untruth and deceit, and thus unethical. Another deceit comes with the idea of *leasing* and *management* as in case of public sector hotels. May be, as was noticed, not all such units got buyers because they were losing units and private parties were uninterested. The truth cited was that though the buying opportunities were not all that gloomy, the bureaucrats and politicians wanted to continue with the lease-*cum*-management method thus delaying sales indefinitely for ulterior gains in expectation of heavy tourist arrivals by the end of the twentieth century. This must be a deceitful tact that bluffs both the private players and the public, but not those handpicked people to whom would be left lease and management. When we come to the privatisation of the insurance sector in particular, the critics hold that for the pro-people, pro-investor and mass-insurer, the shift in private insurance is pro-company and at best protection of interests of a class of investors and insurers. This shift is unethical in a number of ways, first being the diversion of the invested amounts to non-productive and non-social areas, in this way the end of invested amount for social use is defeated, which is ethically undesirable as being championing mercantile attitudes to make profits but not spend for social purposes or for welfare. Through the ages, it is argued that the nationalised insurance sectors have contributed handsomely to public good, without egoistic attitude which is therefore ethically more desirable. The plain truth is that after the decision of private entry in this business, the country was not flooded with funds because in the first five years their collection was a meagre Rs. 250 crores. Even to this date, they are not doing remarkably better than the nationalised sector. Moreover, one cannot buy the ethical view that a pro-customer insurance company can better its services than harassing the customers only when they are privatised or when private insurers enter the business. A government having goodwill can conveniently improve customer service and do away with corruption without entering into disinvestment in sectors bound to the social good. The ethical critics of disinvestment hold that the government has some such social commitments and duties which should never be given up in the greater national interest. It is not true that the government is bound by its duties in the strategic sectors but also in the infrastructural and social sectors demanding huge investments on the part of the government. Hence, ethically speaking, the government being a trustee to the public and a covenant that exists among them, is bound to its social responsibilities and welfarist duties. Private status of government and disinvestment of the assets of the public is thus going against a covenant of duty and responsibility and thus unethical. It is argued that even going private, the government can run a profitable business by taking several corrective measures in management. Hence, it is unethical to shift attention and energy of governance to profiteering than effective management of pro-people, pro-poor public sector units.

Let us now consider the ethical aspects of *free-trade* partially in view of the reformist trends in India. First, on the ground of India's economic self-confidence in trade liberalisation that it is able to push efficiently through the manufacturing trade liberalisation that has been in the rise of the domestic manufacturers and businessmen who thrive on it, and surely being part of the Indian Diaspora, their good is ethically commendable. Moreover, with this there has been no crunch in the domestic manufacturing units, their outputs and exports, all finding a nice headway. Thus, there is no threat empirically known in the market for the Indian manufacturers even though small and large international players are freely in the trade. The competition thus gives a fillip to the otherwise bogged down manufacturers owing to government interventions. Hence, the rise in the domestic trade and the esteem of the domestic traders shows the ethical justification of free trade, though undoubtedly in the final analysis the good is material but it has its own contributing value to overall human good. Free trade is also ethically just in so far as back-up funds for social safety in terms of aid-for-trade and other means takes care of any disruption owing to the structural changes that occurs with such process. Hence, free trade is not ignorant about any disparities in the Indian social security, particularly when it comes to the rural masses, who are pressed hard in the trends of a free trade regime. It will be thus a pro-people and pro-poor programme provided the back-up measures percolates to the rural workforce protection and to an overall social security. In any case, the fear that there will be rampant social disruption is a myth, and therefore, its chief criticism can be put off successfully. Only with more economic maturity on the part of the state that an opening up economy knows how to take care of social security. Extending the argument, the free trade proponent holds that in a developing country like India the effects of free trade are visibly so clear that one would hardly worry about the huge or considerable presence of foreign capitalists. Their presence and their caucus with domestic companies and the government in anyway do not amount to a neo-imperialist-growth in India that will take it up as a colony. The domestic players and government's polity being sound and equally large, and the market teeming in competitiveness, is good for the country's economy, not adverse to it. This is the ethical rightness of a market that is equanimous to presence of capital stocks hold by the foreigners because the presence does not outwit the capital stocks hold by the Indians. The care for equal opportunity in business with stronghold over polity is basic to a free market that is ethically just. Free trade is also ethically just in so far as it does away with the unilateral trading and gains by well-off countries that slowly finishes opportunities for not so well-off or poor countries. Equally untrue is that free trade with the advanced countries sees the inflow of poor products and unskilled people. There is also great opportunity for investments from developing and underdeveloped countries which empowers the people of those countries who erstwhile had no role in the international market. All in all equality of opportunity and making gains in trade, are signs of justice in free trade, it is thus ethically desirable. The ethical good of free trade also lies in the fact that it not only evolves a just and equitable global economy, it also evolves a system of values (ethical as well) that is not against any unique value system nurtured in different countries. The values of cooperation, camaraderie and well-being marks the value of a globalised economy of which free trade is an aspect and thus champions the global value. Still, our own values, culture and ethical domains are not forced to change. Free trade does not seek to change our own identities and thus ethical even though it does change our orthodox perceptions about alien values and cultures. Importantly, it changes our dogmas about national values as well. In fact, when there is trading at global level, one cannot expect that the *status quo* can be maintained in any country about its values. India as a multilingual, multi-religious and multi-cultural abode where secularism is constitutionally revered, the basic values (original as their identity) should not change. Free trade is not against preservation of such originality. It is, therefore, an ethical way to economic evolution—it encourages multiculturalism but not imposition of a culture or imperial acculturation.

The ethical critics of free trade are not so enthusiastic about what has been said above, and criticisms come from many angles. What Indian critics hold will be most important to see here as per our programme but it is not altogether unimportant to learn what a British think about it in an age where free trade is a way of life. Seabrook says: "When we consider the violence wrought by free markets in the early industrial and imperial era, it is difficult to imagine that an ideology which strewed both Britain and its overseas possessions with misery and impoverishment, and which afflicted humanity with famine, sickness and all the coercive uprooting and forced migrations, is now being imposed upon a whole planet as the sources of all hope, progress and prosperity"[1]. and coming to India he finds that the values of free market leaves it: "Strewn with the bones of weavers, leaves its freight of injured and damaged humanity to rot in the places where no one sees them, out of sight, out of mind of the global media, the fate of the women who give birth bestride a grave, of the infants whose eyes blink for a moment in the light before being eaten up by the dark from which they emerged just long enough to cry and expire"[2]. These are all reactions of rage against the free market economy, the exploitation and the devastation it has given us. Leaving them let us read this letter by one Mr. R. S. Sharma, must be an entrepreneur in the glorious communist ruled state of West Bengal, who must have big dreams when traders saw freedom. He writes: "Sir... In India, 80 per cent of the cost of any product is spent in financing the corrupt state and central government expenses—before and after starting a business.... The problems are so numerous that many people who want to start industries, drop out... if you happen to supply products to the government, you have to pay bribes to get orders.... Do you still expect Indian industry to compete?"[3]. Strangely, I have read and listened to many such reactions from the players from abroad. Many resident non-Indians are dismayed with the way things go here. Many multinationals stop after a fun-making MoU ceremony. Does free economy give us freedom to corruption? Is it becoming a global feature as well? Apart from what Seabrook thinks, is it really exploiting the masses? Let us see what ethical critics have to say. First ethical criticism is that free market as a means to globalisation rather than liberating us from poverty, and assurance of progress and well-being lulls us into abject exploitation and miseries. Therefore, it does not assure well-being, rather disparages it, and for that reason, immoral. The conception of free trade enables the mighty economies to *commodify* humans to an extent that humans are valued only on the basis of their use-value or value as means. This is clear by the perception of the capitalists in India, who are in the search of cheap intellectual and manual labourers. India as a free market is thus alluring in so far as it supplies cheap human workforce, skilled and unskilled, to them. Hence, the value perception of humans and a nation on its commodity value makes free trade the ethical rogue that it is. In fact, the perception of humans as commodities and the added cheap value, paves way for their physical, mental, cultural and financial exploitation, which is ethically unjust. Injustice begins with this perception in terms of payment for labour because clear discriminatory policies may be seen when companies abroad obtain double standards of payment for work in India and at their homeland to their natives. The unguarded labourers thus become vulnerable to abject exploitation when companies break unionism by all tricks, which are again an unethical way that acts against human rights, particularly right to non-exploitation and unionised protest to exploitation. Arguments go that franchisees of free market world over thrive on the glorious conception of global camaraderie, prosperity and liberty of the mankind but the inner story till date goes that only a few holding the capital, products, market and profits prosper and thus liberate from a less well-off status to a more well-off status *ad infinitum* till the gross unjust persons become Plato's chimera having numerous lion's head which eat each other and thus the chimera itself. Free market is unjust egoistic hedonist that still thrives on the conception of economic might is right. Hence, the unjust thesis of well-being as conceived in free market economy does not pave way to global prosperity. India at the present and many places alike are testimony to such blunt bluff of free market economy, Seabrook has nicely pictured—the poor are doomed to darkness when they are born. The parameters of human well-being is floundered in the forms of malnutrition, ill-health, mal-education, want of basic amenities and infrastructure, though free market played here for quite some time now. The unethicality lies in the several bluffs that it thrives on, the glory that never comes to the roots. One such blunt lie is that through market freedom, humans of all sections will attain freedom from their miseries. In reality, miseries stand where they were to the countless who never had a market to play with. Coming to a closer look at the developing countries like India and others, it was clear by the Seattle meet that the ethical value of the hyped international cooperation and integration and consequent gains owing to free trade came is a hoax. It was believed that in the name of free trade the rich world became a pole or a bloc in a non-polar world. Those in the other pole or powerful bloc connived to thrust their trading ambitions by closing their markets to the developing and underdeveloped countries by some excuses or the other so that all benefits of trade at cheap investment could be siphoned. This trend of power-tracking in trade by the rich, which was an expected course that free trade almost was sure to take in the face of crunch in rich man's resources and labour, is unethical because it is based on trading malpractice, groupism among power-trackers and discrimination in economic practices. The result of such groupism thus led rightly to counter with another group or bloc which was discriminated owing to a natural course of the free trade, but with a difference that this state of conflict was ethically just because it was grounded on the conception of using the exploitative techniques of the powerful. And truly power needs power to annul. The mistrust was growing more and more with instances of fall in total merchandise exports from developing countries to developed countries, and surely free market internationalism does not depend on mistrust. Most importantly now, for the underpowered and bluffed bloc, "non-trade" issues became the focus of unethicality, particularly the issue of exploitation of consumers, labour, resources and environment. It was believed that gross injustice and thus unethicality was rampant in the underdeveloped and developing countries as they were systematically plundered by the neo-mercantiles. Then we come to the closer look at the Indian way to free trade and the unethicality charges on the *raibahadurs* of our times. During the opening up of economy its staunch advocates, who were also vocal about the value of free-trade did so on two major grounds, both said to be ethically right. One is that it will banish over-protectionism prevalent in the Indian economy since long that made its market lacklustre and its consumers the most disadvantageous people. Hence, ethical value of protection of people's economic rights being supreme, the market and the consumer must be empowered. Another point is that the Indian employment opportunities were grim because there was a *status quo* in almost all major economic activities, nothing new was happening so that fresh educated as well as less educated workforces could be absorbed in any sector whether private or public. This is again against the good of educated people and detrimental to education as such. It was also ethically repugnant that many skilled and unskilled people migrated in flocks leaving India in the lack of proper services. The ethical critics hold that even if both things were at ground reality true and that the ethical ideals of overall good for the educated and the unemployed noble, there is no logical implication between these problems and an imperative to go for free trade inviting foreign competition. The critics argue that protectionism is an internal affair which should not be abruptly resolved through foreign interventions because that is on the one hand an undignified, unpragmatic and defeatist approach and on the other hand against the interest of domestic competitors who were never free to act in an atmosphere of strict public sector pressure and government interventions. Hence, many of them argue that it was ethically more just to have gradually strengthened domestic companies through domestic competition, releasing bindings on them in trade and then go for invitations to the foreign companies. Weakening our own entrepreneurs is against the holistic welfare of the nation and thus ethically unjust. Moreover, the critics argue that employment generation could begin with the wider area of absorption by means of expansion of domestic companies rather than inviting foreign companies who not only need time to settle, they have their own tricky ways to exploit cheap unskilled labour not employing them in the real sense of the term. The transfer of sophisticated technology and machineries to minimise workforce induction and borrow services of skilled people, even the CEOs from abroad was all against the good of the common man of India. The large companies (MNCs inclusive) being capital-intensive production units do not worry much about employment generation; they just exploit the resources and manpower to maximise gains. All these being basically anti-educated and anti-workers, in some sense anti-people, must be seen as ethically unjust. Further, it was believed that free trade would prevent large companies to exploit the market in a monopolistic way by extracting high profits in the name of quality. Hence, being a pro-consumer move, it was believed to be ethically right. The critics argue that in opposition to this popular conception, the MNCs always act as monopolistic players and necessarily aim at the maximisation of profits than any good to the consumers. Any good done (a small degree) is only accidental, not intended. The exploitative agenda is thus ethically wrong and not right. The crux of such ethical criticism is that rather than foreign capital investment, domestic private investment is good, and both liberalisation and privatisation should be at the domestic level well strengthened rather than jumping to free trade because these steps are more pragmatic and humane. Another group of critics, most of them Gandhians think that vociferous appeal to free trade as a complementary to the globalisation of economy is owing to the conception of growth of wealth by virtue of increment of division of labour facilitating mechanisation and technological advancements. To this should be added the growth of political power by virtue of using the same means to flourish an industry for modern wars because throughout history imperial powers succeeded when they were empowered monetarily, mechanically and as warriors. It is not true that in economy government has no role to play because they always have to cater some basic needs of people and to provide sufficient infrastructure to the corporate. The critics argue that the conception of free trade is based on some such ideas that are in essence arrogant and anti-human and for that matter ethically repugnant. The point is doubly asserted by the fact that if the champions of such ideal finds governments as sympathisers, they will soon convince the government that it should not have major role to play in non-material human goods like education and health and that it should not be in the rat race of war industries for the lurking threat it poses due to a liberal and flourishing economy. The psychopathic nurturing of modern wars and going for an unlimited arms buying spree never satisfies us in being modern because the more we do so, the least we catch up, a point noted earlier. The minimisation of government in economy and the nurturing of a war psyche and a war-like psyche in corporate competition are inhuman, it is thus unethical. The Gandhians gradually come to an important aspect of *sustainable economy*, which is advocated widely but hardly seen in reality. This is in the face of fast depleting non-renewable natural resources which can never sustain economies globally for a long time, apart from the fact that the extraction of these resources has caused great harm to the ecological community, people of nations and the future progenies. Free trade thus contributes phenomenally to the depletion of forests, causes ecological catastrophe, exploits people by displacing them, and devastates lives and culture of natives and many more. These are all against the well-being of the humans who live along with other beings and things, and therefore, unethical. The critics hold that the ideas inherent in free trade thus encourage a patriarchic model of economic expansion than a matriarchic model of care, ethicality and love. The patriarchic model being ruthless expansionism with disregard to human values, is unethical. The matriarchic model might thus replace the mainstream expansionism with more humane cottage industries, eco-oriented economic planning that is also oriented to strengthen the rural masses and the rural workforce who still constitutes a majority in India.

The discussion about free trade is not over yet because we have to still consider the case of *globalisation*, which is its close associate. In fact, we have reached the climax of our discussion feeling truly that the moves of liberalisation, privatisation, freeing trade or to say opening up economy is complete when the more overreaching means to complete reformist agenda, that is, globalisation is discussed. Let us now find out the ethical pros and cons of globalisation. Most of the champions of globalisation believe that the process is ethically desirable mainly owing to its disposition to create more opportunities to the people of nations and thus good for them. As against the conception of adverse effects of capital flow from abroad, the supporters hold that such a flow is good for both the domestic and the foreign investors. An Indian investor wanting to invest in a manufacturing unit for instance, was erstwhile unable to do so in the lack of funds, whereas others interested abroad failed to participate owing to restrictions. Globalisation is thus a way to express economic freedom as instantiated in to and fro capital flow among a number of countries thus benefiting them and largely their population. The inherent values of economic freedom and larger benefits to entrepreneurs and population hold the key to ethical desirability of globalisation. The same is true for trading as an important option in globalisation of economy. The champions of globalisation further argues that the much hated multinationals (MNCs) are in fact, basic to foreign direct investment which is the chief factor in industrial growth in the countries needing it, like India. The global companies not only give stiff competition to the domestic manufacturers to make them either more efficient and contributor to the market good or just drives them out, in any case protecting the consumers' benefits, which is ethically right and not wrong. Further, the global companies contribute to the growth of a number of domestic ancillary units. It is well known that a sound parent company always nurtures ancillaries mushrooming in its vicinity. With this growth, there is not only employment generation in countries opened up for a global participation, small and petty domestic entrepreneurs thrive, gain and contribute to the nation's economic growth. All in all they together contribute to a steady industrial growth, each of them further doing enormous good to the country's natural well-being, without which there can be no social and political stability. Hence, as having contributory values, globalisation is an ethically desirable process. If this be the case, the multinationals rather than doing any harm to our industries, have done a lot of good to them. Rather than championing monopolies, they have assimilated in the milieu of multifaceted competition not driving out anyone. Moreover, if there seems to be any threat of monopolistic chauvinism, the government is always free to curb it and look at the interests of small domestic players in the market. This must be true in case of any lurking threat from domestic companies. Globalisation thus thrives on the spirit of equal opportunities in business under the rightful vigil of the law of the land. It is thus civil and legal way of participating in global business, and thus ethically desirable. It all depends on the way the state acts in an atmosphere of international competition with its rules for anti-dumping, restrictions in imports and exports and so on. It is in this context that the proponents of globalisation argue against a "level-playing field theory" as touted in the *swadesi* because globalisation does thrive in an atmosphere of a "level playing field" for all the players in the market and nothing is imposed on any national policy, the civility of the thesis is thus clear. There is, however an interesting debate about whether a democratic government can at all play a level player with the benefit maximisation ploy of the multinationals. One opinion is that such things are possible only in a stable society which often a democracy and none other can provide us, whereas another opinion is that in democracy only the capitalists win (the most aggressive ones of course and no other); hence, autocracy is a reply to the expansionist ploy, only in it can there be a 'level playing field'. In fact, in democracy only autocrats and uncivil moves can thrive because there government gives minimal gratis to its people and act as safety valves to a mass rebellion or violent struggles though these are not uncommon or even improbable. In a reply to some questions put to eminent economist Kaushik Basu, he said: "Globalisation has a tendency to erode democracy... by virtue of globalisation, you can cut off financial flows, impede trade or use a variety of other economic mechanisms to influence livelihoods in other countries... as the world comes together, there will be more and more instruments for intervening in other countries"[4]. This must be put alongside the article by Dr. Bharat Jhunjhunwala, whose paper in a Hindi daily appeared sometime back, transliterate it: "Rich countries are keen to see democracies in poor countries because in democracy there is more stability; people do demand for education, health, roads and other amenities. The government has to invest its revenues in such heads and thus the democracy remains stable. Economic growth is static, but the people are pacified till they get minimal benefits. It is also easy to purchase the democratic governments, but difficult in an autocracy"[5]. Both assertions may be further put along the case of Iraq in the Saddam and post-Saddam era to evaluate what capitalists want in globalisation or what their custodian countries want. In any case the rogueness of the so-called rogues and the civility of the globalisation *gurus* make a case for the ethical evaluation of the advocated civility and honesty in the process of globalisation. Though enough has been said in different contexts by this time that contributes to an understanding of the ethicality of globalisation, we have two unique additions. Some people argue (we have a hint of it) that globalisation contributes to the uplift of the poor nations than the rich nations because as a natural course of strategy to maximise gains, the companies, whether domestic or foreign are in search of resource fertile lands, particularly the human resource fertile lands though they are poor because it is they who may be easily purchased for cheap labour. The companies thus profit in terms of cutting wages and extracting desired outputs thus enabling them in the atmosphere of competitive production. Hence, globalisation is ethically desirable as it is pro-poor. It is equally good in so far as it has benefited the rich because they had the courage to risk in international business. Another queer argument (more so than this one) is that globalisation brings with it an ethos of multiculturalism and secularism, which is in favour of broadening the otherwise dogmatic ways of thinking of people of many countries bogged down with religious and cultural fundamentalism that has given us worldwide violence and unrest. With free interaction among people of different cultures, our cultural prejudices break down. Religions assimilate nicely without their own chauvinistic ways pressed to change dramatically causing religious tolerance and secular attitudes. There is thus in the era of globalisation a post-modern conception of acculturation and religious assimilation, both good for the humanity at large, and hence, ethically desirable.

Let us now quickly move on to the ethical criticism of globalisation first with this report of the World Bank (1999-2000), which its president Mr. James Wolfenson says, "hammers the need for comprehensive view of people's lives and their well-being beyond the economic simplicism of growth". This may be read with reports that are coming up since 2005 to this date about the growing unrest in the West about outsourcing, unemployment and threat to the western companies with regard to the phoenix rise of India and China in particular. An important ethical charge against globalisation is the systematic minimalization of the pro-people, pro-welfarist public sector and national planning whose custodian being the government is thus minimalised. We have also seen that more often than not all this happens in the fertile ground of democracy, which is understood as 'for the people'. The dilution of the major public institutions and its economic machineries being essentially anti-unempowered and anti-welfare is thus, ethically repugnant. The role of the state government rather than being a major player turns out to be mute spectator of private flourishing and happiness for a few. It has nothing better to do but always pressed on the one hand to be pro-investors or on the other hand pro-poor. In the tenterhooks, the state dwells to satisfy none, thus reaches neither the goal of profiteering nor welfare. All this is aimless governance, unbeneficial and impractical, and for that matter unethical. The results, says its critiques, enable the corporate empire to be politically omnipotent as well, and again in meek democracies, particularly if there is weak opposition in terms of numbers and ideology (as in the case of India), or when there is near political-monopolism of a party, there is, what we have said the rise of neo-imperialism. The empire dictates terms in national policies, economic mechanisms and major social decision-making. This is done to favour a climate of exclusive private profits thus leaving the unempowered worse to worst. Such sabotage of governance and indirect socio-political and economic bondage owing to globalisation is attack on a free country, which is unethical. Globalisation thus causes colonisation of the weak countries where government act as shields to protect egoists; this is one way to the growth of neo-feudalism that exploits manpower and markets. Such egoism and blunt hedonic ways should be valued as unethical, say the critics because hedonic egoism is essentially against any form of act that sees distributive justice properly imbalanced, always favouring those having the capital. Globalisation is thus a political trap of the rich which assures systematic failure of human rights, workers' right, right to welfare and non-exploitation of domestic markets and resources. Such fine tuned anti-national acts are ethically wrong. It is even feared (or may be the signs of a genuine fear becoming more prominent day by day in India as in Orissa or West Bengal) that the corporate lobby has actually grabbed the developing democratic states to compel them to use force may be even military force in the near future to dominate its own more or less unorganised and affected people who have been plundered of assets and ways of life they led. This way the neo-feudal act as did the feudal and colonisers in all ages, which is sheer control over sovereignty. The grabbing of sovereignty must be thus seen as unethical. Hence, the global order that is seen as an example of global brotherhood and camaraderie has turned out to be global masters freely influencing the foreign policies of the governments and violating human rights. The issue of human rights is all the more important because it is against the ethic of the said brotherhood or a global order. A careful look at this issue, says thc critics that will reveal the rise of the corporate as a nation-state, that is, the non-stately institutions assuming the status of nation-states to infringe on human rights. The idea is that the state held some sovereignty over the protection of human rights through the political and legal powers that it enjoys, and it is the state who has held responsible for both upholding and violating human rights. Now the global companies, even the domestic companies act parallely as state do to influence policies and control workforce and people of a nation and major economic decision-making. Even they influence (or at least try to do so) to influence the judiciary to put any violation of rights in abeyance. The global companies in the name of business and economic development of countries are thus floundering with the state machinery and law to act as wished for their benefits to betray people and the workforce or to exploit them or just put them to an end if they raise voice too much. In fact, rights of humans are only violated when there are deliberate unlawful attacks on what is due to humans in terms of monetary or other material benefits; rights are violated even when the corporate attacks on human right to protest against exploitation and when people are imposed alien culture, uprooted from their perennial abodes and are left with an environmental disaster as mere refugees. All these things culminate to what we call human alienation, which is ethically repugnant. Disrespect to people's aspirations, environment and welfare priorities of the government by means of economic terrorism is essentially unethical. The terrorism is so threatening that global companies risk the law of the land believing that they will be protected in the name of development. Hence, gross disrespect is towards the whole system for interest fulfilment. It is not believed that economic growth in any case is not primary than human right, this is not only aggressive attitude, a kind of violence in thought, it is anti-human and unethical. The above points enable us to realise that there are at least four important aspects of globalisation bereft of value-based conception of economic development which is amenable to ethical criticism. First is classism or discrimination of a class of economic actors as favoured than others who are deprived as economic actors. Second are atrocities against workforce, particularly the unorganised and unskilled ones. Next are attacks on tribes and rural population owing to setting up of large production units. Finally, environment disaster without any subsequent green-management or green-obligation. The final one can be referred to as specism or discrimination against non-human beings and things on the one hand and on the other hand against the non-empowered or the non-capital holders. Classism is unethical as it alienates a section of economic producers or actors by means of division of labour and disparity in having right on the produced good. As globalisation favours those who are by virtue of division of labour investors and profit earners from the produced good whereas others are mere actors eking out wages that are disproportionately low, the former have first order rights in economic, political, social and legal affairs whereas others have nearly no such rights in practice, may be they exist in principle and on paper. Such favouritism towards a class is divisive; it cleaves the world from within causing serious class-struggle and violence. Hence, it is unethical. Globalisation being a systematic way to disintegrate workforce so that they cannot fight for rights and injustice, may be thus called an unethical act of social-terrorism. Further, globalisation alienating the aboriginals and their culture in the name of their developing and civilization may be called unethical perception of humans and their values in life and the value of life. Finally, specism is unethical as it is apartheid against the nature as such. This must be enough for the unethicality charges to be framed. In fact, if these aspects of globalisation and their ethical criticisms are not kept in mind, there can be hardly any talk about sustainable development. I will close this discussion now but let us ponder on what Pan Yue, the Vice-minister of China's State Environmental Protection and Administration writes. This is all the more important as China is said to be a more aggressive and successful globaliser than India and as a most surprising fact, it is a communist country. But let us read the passage: "This spring, the State Environmental Protection Administration produced the country's first official estimate of GDP adjusted downward for environmental losses... realistic estimates put environmental damage of 8-13 per cent of China's GDP growth each year, which means that China has lost almost everything it has gained since the last 1970s due to pollution"[6]. Further, he writes: "We believed that economic development would solve all our problems. In the reform period, this misreading of Marx morphed into an unrestrained pursuit of material gain devoid of morality. Traditional Chinese culture, with its emphasis on harmony between human beings and native, was thrown aside. As a result China's economy is dominated by resource-hungry and inefficient polluters"[7]. And then: "China is dangerously near a crisis point. The country's enormous environmental debt will have to be paid, one way or another"[8]. This must be extremely instigating for the Indian planners and economists. We are still not China, but we seriously tend to be so until we do not reach a climax of the glaring material rise by means of our dear globalisation. Should we repent after five or ten years? Or, are we repenting? Let us see what was found in the discussion I have arranged.

Thus far we were going through the first two stage of intersubjective corroboration in which we came to know what the problem in consideration amounts to, why it is ethically charged and what questions of value does it raise that initiates disagreements. Now we should move to frame a questionnaire and arrange for discussion with the concerned people thus coming to a consensus about this matter. As I have said before, the consensus does not amount to an absolute perception of the Indian Diaspora, but the ethical debate given above and the discussion to follow gives us ample idea about what *should* be decided in this regard. It is clear from the discussion above that moral controversies in the field of economic reforms associated by conceptions of liberalisation, privatisation, free trade and globalisation should be resolved through a dialogue among the economists, traders, administrators particularly those involved in human resource management, trade unionists, teachers in management schools, planners and others taking interest in the issue. I have said that this is not an easy task because it is extremely difficult to assemble people for a dialogue. However, as a starter and in no case as a paradigm, the debate among the following people crystallising consensus may be of some interest. It is a matter of common sense that what the participants said in the dialogue were not radically different from what has been explained above or that considerable addition to what has been already said is not possible. Those who participated in the dialogue were:

1. Dr. H. N. P. Suman, Head, Department of Economics, Ranchi University, Ranchi,

2. Fr. L. Franklin, S. J., Director, Xavier Institute of Social Science and Research, Ranchi,
3. Mr. Binod Kr. Prasad, Director, Prasad Group of Companies, Ranchi,
4. Mr. A. Prasad, G. M., H. R. D., Usha Martin Company, Ranchi
5. Mr. J. M. Sensharma, Secretary, LIC Staff Association, LIC Branch II, Ranchi, and
6. A number of students and teachers of Philosophy and Economics.

QUESTIONNAIRE

1. What in your opinion is human well-being? Is it an end in itself or a means towards a higher end?
2. Do you believe that GDP and GNP are the proper indicators of human well-being?
3. Do you think that free trade and globalisation in India are value-charged decisions under economic reforms?
4. Does free trade and globalisation contribute to the holistic human welfare?
5. Do you think that the economic reformist processes in India, like liberalisation, privatisation, free trade and globalisation amounts to:

(a) colonise our economy — Yes/No
(b) a modern form of feudalism — Yes/No
(c) political instability — Yes/No
(d) trade polarisation — Yes/No
(e) the fall of central economic planning — Yes/No
(f) destabilise central trade policies — Yes/No
(g) destabilise the public sector — Yes/No
(h) crushes the small and the very small domestic industries — Yes/No
(i) discourage domestic competition — Yes/No
(j) export-import imbalance — Yes/No
(k) market fluctuations and inflation — Yes/No
(l) exploitation of labourers — Yes/No
(m) rising unemployment — Yes/No
(n) family disintegration — Yes/No
(o) enhanced corruption — Yes/No

(p) cultural degradation — Yes/No
(q) ecological disaster — Yes/No

6. Are modernisation and westernisation of Indian economy as contributed through free trade and globalisation necessary?
7. Evaluate *swadesi vis-à-vis* free trade and globalisation. What are your suggestions for human well-being by means of economic mechanisms?

It is clear that the first question should be put to the participants to make sure about a more ethics-oriented discussion and not a purely economics-oriented one. It is also needed to evaluate the ethical conception of end and means of intentional economic decision and functions. The next three questions should be put to evaluate the conceptions of human well-being of the participants and the role of economic or material well-being in this regard. They also try to evaluate a participants' conception about steps in economic reforms in view of his or her basic ethical position. The fifth question tries to evaluate whether there are inconsistencies in replies to the value of reformist agendas and human well-being or is the participant logical and sure about what has been already maintained. Remaining two questions try to find out participants' idea about domestic economy, its good in the broader context of reforms as per the western ways or the so-called modern ways. The question try to bring out suggestions about the issue discussed thus far. The last question help us to know how far the participants have agreed to one another and what exactly are needed on ethical bases. In the final analysis we may find the ethical theories active in the discussion, but that is another part of the method of corroboration. Let me now supply the readers with the replies to these questions by the selected parties in the dialogue more or less exactly the way in which they put the things.

Replies of Dr. H. N. P. Suman

1. Human well-being means the satisfaction derived from the consumption of economic goods (exchangeable goods and services) as well as non-economic goods. Thus it is a subjective thing which consists in man's utilities or satisfaction or his feeling of happiness. It is an end unto itself.

2. No, because human well-being depends not only on generation of GNP and GDP, but also on the proper distribution of GNP and GDP among citizens of a country.
3. Yes, because they may lead to economic development and human well-being.
4. Yes, because they may increase the production of goods and services, national income, employment and per capita income of the people.
5. (a) No (b) No (c) No (d) No
   (e) No (f) No (g) Doubtful (h) No
   (i) No (j) No (k) No (l) Doubtful
   (m) Doubtful (n) No (o) No (p) Doubtful
   (q) Doubtful (r) Doubtful
6. Yes, modernisation and westernisation are now necessary to keep pace with economic and social progress of the various countries of the world.
7. Yes, free trade and globalisation are humane decisions depending on economic situations within and outside a country.

In spite of free trade and globalisation, '*swadesi*' has its special significance in rural as well as urban India and it is bound to stay and play important role in employment generation and eradication of poverty. So policies should be framed in such a way that '*swadesi*' survives even in face of free trade and globalisation.

Replies of Fr. L. Franklin

1. "Human well-being" is a means towards a higher end.
2. GNP and GDP are not appropriate indicators of human well-being because they do not indicate the inequality in income distribution.
3. Free trade and globalisation are up to some extent unavoidable in today's world economy.
4. Free trade and globalisation in them will not contribute to human well-being as they only take care of economic welfare and do not take care of the human aspects of development.
5. (a) Yes (b) No (c) Not necessarily
   (d) Yes (e) Not necessarily (f) Yes

(g) Yes	(h) Yes	(i) No
(j) Yes	(k) Yes	(l) Yes
(m) Yes	(n) Yes	(o) I do not know
(p) I do not know	(q) Yes	(r) I do not know

6. Free trade and globalisation are unavoidable; they involve some degree of modernisation and westernisation. Modernisation is ok if directed in the right way, i.e., respect for moral values should be maintained. Westernisation is not valuable and should be avoided.
7. *Swadesi* is valuable as it promotes self-respect and self-reliance.

Human well-being in India: what is required is:

- respect of human dignity and equality: caste system to be set aside
- child protection
- gender sensitivity and respect for women
- equal opportunities for all.

Replies of Mr. Binod Kumar Prasad

1. Human well-being means:

   (a) Better living conditions
   (b) Better economic conditions
   (c) Good human behaviour
   (d) Job for all
   (e) Better brotherhood with everyone
   (f) Maintaining the old cultural values of each creed
   (g) Discharge of rights and duties
2. No, because the farmers' well-being in India is not reflected in the calculation of GNP and GDP.
3. Free trade and globalisation are valuable decisions because:

   (a) In free trade all are equal thus no industry can claim special rights.
   (b) Free trade attracts foreign capitals which keep the national producer alive to their duties and to fight in the competitions.
   (c) The industrialists need not bribe the legislators for their

production freedom. Corruption is also reduced to minimum.

(d) Monopoly-profit earning is also removed.

(e) It also leads to fair distribution of wealth.

(f) It promotes division and specialisation.

4. Yes, because in free trade and globalisation, we can get the commodities at cheaper price. We can also get the more employment opportunities.

5. (a) No (b) No (c) No (d) No
(e) No (f) No (g) No (h) Yes
(i) No (j) No (k) No (l) No
(m) No (n) Yes (o) Yes (p) No
(q) Yes (r) No

   After analysing all the above points we can come to the conclusion and say that free trade and globalisation are humane decisions.

6. Yes, up to certain extent we can say that, in India, free trade and globalisation are the imperative steps for modernisation. It is valuable because in the 21st century; we cannot pull on without modernisation and globalisation as far as westernisation is concerned.

7. The term *swadesi* means the commodities produced in home industries within a set of policies framed to encourage the home industries whereas free trade and globalisation means a system of commercial policies which draws no distinction between domestic and foreign commodities.

With regard to human well-being in India, I can suggest that free trade and globalisation are more suitable.

Replies of Mr. A. Prasad

1. In my opinion 'human well-being' relates to human welfare and is an index of the overall satisfaction or level of development of the human civilisation. Human well-being is both an end unto itself whereby efforts are directed to improve the overall condition of human beings. It also becomes the building block for the growth of human civilisation or the nation at large.

2. GNP and GDP are an index of the material well-being which constitutes one part of human well-being. It does not give any indication about the social, moral or spiritual progress of a nation.
3. Free trade and globalisation is a step towards making the world one big market. But it also exposes the small fishes of the developing countries to the risk of being gobbled up by the much larger and stronger fish (multinationals). The companies/countries should be exposed to competition but slowly and with necessary coaching, guidance and support.
4. Free trade and globalisation leads to consumerism and certainly better quality products at fewer prices. But again this cannot account for human well-being *per se*.

5. (a) No (b) No (c) No (d) Yes
(e) No (f) Yes (g) Yes (h) Yes
(i) Yes (j) No (k) No (l) Yes
(m) No (n) Yes (o) No (p) No
(q) No (r) No

6. I personally think that we cannot keep away the winds of change in the form of free trade and globalisation from entering the country. It may come initially as a cyclone and cause much destruction. But since it is directed and welcomed by the individual customers and sharpens the competitive spirit, the country with its inherent strength will get over it. If technological advancement has taken place somewhere, there is no harm in adopting it to our benefit. It is better than re-inventing the wheel.
7. We should accept the strong points that have emerged in the West or even in the Far East. But we should know how to adopt it to our situation. We learnt computers from others but now we are one of the best brains in software. However, along with material development, we should preserve our culture. Look at how many Indian families living in US have kept their identity and culture and are still considered the best brains in the world.

Replies of Mr. J. M. Sensharma

1. Human well-being relates to the well-being of the people which

includes total population, rural and urban. It is not meant for a small section of human being. Socio-economic upliftment of the people comes under the purview of "Human well-being". It is not an end unto itself. It has a higher end because progress is a continuous process.

2. GNP and GDP cannot be an indicator of human well-being in the Capitalist System of Society where wealth is amassed in a few hands. GNP and GDP to be an indicator, distribution system has a great role to play.
3. No, for a developing country like India and other under-developed countries, free trade and globalisation do not allow self-reliant economy, and economic and political sovereignty is endangered. The nation has to be dependent on the dictates of the foreign finance capital.
4. If we consider the human being as a whole, free trade and globalisation cannot contribute to the human well-being. The MNCs and big industrial tycoons have the motive of super-profit, having no concern with the people's problems and social obligations. The agro-economy and small scale industries are the worst sufferers.
5. (a) Yes (b) Yes (c) Doubtful (d) Yes
(e) Yes (f) Yes (g) Yes (h) Yes
(i) Yes (j) Yes (k) Yes (l) Yes
(m) Yes (n) Yes (o) Yes (p) Yes
(q) Yes (r) Yes
6. Here two questions are raised; modernisation and westernisation. Westernisation is the fallout of globalisation. It can be done away with. So far the modernisation is concerned; in India free trade and globalisation are not the imperative steps. Modernisation of economy or society depends on its present level. It should be developed as per the imminent need of the society and economy. Nehruvian economy had a great urge for modernisation having self-reliant economy. The modern India started building in the fifties through one after another five year plans. For any society modernisation or development is desirable.
7. In a capitalist economy the new imperialism is bound to be intensified, and, therefore, so-called '*swadesi*' is meaningless and valueless.

The human well-being in India is a vast subject to be discussed. The latest Human Development Report brought out by the United Nations Development Programme presents a very dismal picture of India in terms of human development. It has place India at the 139th rank out of 174 countries for which Human Development index was prepared. According to the Report, about half of our adult population (48%) is still suffering from the scourge of illiteracy. The percentage of children not reaching Grade-V of schooling is 53 per cent; the percentage of population without any access to sanitation is 71 while the percentage of underweight children below five years is 53. The percentage of pregnant women with anaemia in the age group of 15 to 49 stands at 88 while infant mortality rate per thousand live births is 73 (All data of 1999).

This report is the indicator, how should we address to the human well-being. In a nutshell, following are the few areas which are to be taken care of by the nation:

— Egalitarian land reforms,
— A substantial step-up in public expenditure on education and health,
— Job-oriented growth, etc.

These can only be achieved through self-reliant and pro-people economy of India.

Inter-Subjective Corroboration and Post-Corroboration Analyses

We now come to the last stage of intersubjective corroboration to find out (a) what the debaters in general do not hesitate agreeing to when it comes to the issues in economic reforms; (b) which ethical theories are seen to be functional in the debate and (c) what most likely we would like to see in India with regard to reform. This is the analytic aspect of the method of ethical resolutions, which I have said, has a theoretical value in so far as it gives us an idea about the way application of ethics works at the social level without any artificial theory cooption though not without indication of our known and unknown normative theses in action. This is a strengthening instance of people's participation in ethical resolution without theoreticism by a class of intellectuals. A look at the replies to the first question gives us an idea about the conception of ethical value as well as ethical ideal of a participant. It is another matter whether the conception is taken seriously throughout the debate or it is contradicted as the debate enters into more stiff questions about value-laden practical matters. For Dr. Suman, it is clear that *the intrinsically valuable ideal is "human well being", the means of which are both consumption of economic and non-economic goods. Hence, both economic and non-economic goods are valuable as means to an end, and therefore, extrinsic goods.* Most interesting aspect is that he does not contest that "human welfare" and not "pleasure satisfaction" or "ego fulfilment" or "doing ones duty" and so on or any replaceable ideal is desirable end of consumption of economic and non-economic goods, though in a qualificatory assertion (in reply no. 1), he says that *the said highest good is something like "satisfaction" or "feeling of happiness"*, which he thinks, *is attained through subjective choice of either economic good at one instance or the choice of non-economic good at other instances or both.* In any case though the inherent ambiguity in the conception of "well being" has strayed best minds, it is by far clear that Dr. Suman does neither follow a pure hedonic line nor a pure egoistic line because as an Indian he must have something like "*ànanda*" or "bliss" or even "*kalyàna*" or "holistic flourishing of human being" in mind, which he says, can never be attained without means such as material or economic goods and services. This must be satisfying for any welfarist of the Aristotelian and even the Indian (excluding *Cārvāka*) tradition; in case of Indian ethical tradition, the discussion of *kàma* and *artha* as *purūṣārthas* enables us to say that non-hedonic/non-egoistic satisfaction of the corporal self is the desirable desire. Nevertheless, this is precisely contested by Father Franklin because he completes Dr. Suman's conception of the *÷reya* or the desirable highest good perfectly in tune with both the Christian (of which he is an advocate) and the Hindu ethical traditions that *even human well-being is a mere means to the higher purpose or teleos of attaining godhood or liberation or mokùa. Hence, is his idea that well-being is good as means, it is not intrinsically good, and by parity of reasoning all sub-means to well-being are extrinsically good, economic good must fall in this category.* There is nevertheless, a strong support to Dr. Suman's conception, which hopefully does not drag metaphysicalism and spiritualism in the discussion of ethical ideal of human welfare, and this must have its own strong grounds because ethics as different from spirituality need not necessarily fall back on an ideal that is spiritual. Hence, the contest is whether human well-being is a non-spiritual *teleos* in life or it has a spiritual *teleos* in life to achieve. Strongly none of the two participants enter into the debate at length because both are satisfied at least with the idea that in any sense human well-being has a value or is good, whether it be extrinsic, though our ethical knowledge tells us that nothing prevents human well-being to have both the values, intrinsic and extrinsic. In any case, Dr. Suman finds support from Mr. Binod Prasad. He is rather more specific in detailing with the *meaning* of well-being as economic and non-economic satisfaction as he points out things like, "living well", "economically strong" (must be monetarily so, as I got it), "job guarantee" or "guarantee to eke out an honest living" as well as "being behaviourally good", "sustenance of human brotherhood", "preserving cultural values" and most interestingly, "doing ones' institutional duties and claiming rights". The economic and non-economic goods are nicely balanced; in the latter class the incorporation of intended good behaviour, duties and rights and sustenance of brotherhood gives it a clear non-spiritual, ethical overtone. All in all for Mr. Binod, human well-being is sure to be as in Dr. Suman's case, intrinsically good end of life. It becomes all the more interesting when we come to the replies of Mr. A. Prasad and Mr. J. M. Sensharma. Mr. Prasad and Mr. Sensharma are clear about the *dual status of human well-being or welfare, that is, it is both good in itself and good as means*. This is different from the monistic status given by Dr. Suman and Mr. Binod and also by Fr. Franklin. This is unambiguously, but differently stated by Mr. Prasad as "whole improvement of our conditions causing satisfaction", which is a good itself when its economic feature or dimension is considered, and as contributing to "the growth of human civilisation", which is a means to the higher ideal of "flourishing of human civilisation". The first part is in agreement with Dr. Suman's and Mr. Binod's theses whereas the second part is not exactly in disagreement but an addition to the sense of "non-economic value aspect" of "well-being" as a means, which is nevertheless, in disagreement with a higher spiritual ideal in life (as implicit in Fr. Franklin's view). However, for Mr. Sensharma, the internal value of human well-being should be seen as "holistic socio-economic betterment of the humans", not much in disagreement with what Mr. Prasad or even what Dr. Suman and Mr. Binod have said, but his conception of human well-being as an external good is in variance with both Fr. Franklin and Mr. Prasad is that it is contributory to the "holistic social progress" as higher ideal. Again the non-economic feature of well-being is clearer when we speak about such things but it is neither a spiritual ideal nor the same as "flourishing of human civilisation". In fact, "social progress" as an ethical ideal of which welfare is a means cannot be the same as "flourishing of human civilisation" because the paradigm of "civilisation" is unclear for its meaning and significance. Surely, the most vocal westerners and champion of both modernism and modernity call themselves "civilised" rather than backward as the third world citizens or what is often the conception of the capitalists, but does that mean that they are civilised? The point is whether pure economic progress or spiritual progress or social progress or all of them constitute what we call, "human well-being". Equally true is, we must be clearer when societies have really "progressed". It appears from Mr. Sensharma's view that perhaps when we *continuously* strive for an equitable social, political and economic good of the "total population", there is a "social progress". This must be a glorious ethical ideal, often called, utopian because "equal" or even "just" or "nearly equal" good to "the total population" though it has been thus far elusive but ethics does not bother much about what *is* the case, it does care about what *should* be the case, and therefore, the 'utopia' sounds good. As we stand now, "human well-being" as *both good as means and end* comes out to be a valuable conception in ethics. This comes straight out of the common men who are non-ethicists.

Let us now see to what extent the analysis takes us in case of the actual issue of ethical reforms in India. First step is to analyse what are the values of economic goal for measuring GDP and GNP in the context of the ethically valuable human welfare. We shall then analyse the bearings of free trade and globalisation as chief means to economic reforms in the context of the ethical ideal of "human welfare". Economist Dr. Suman does not think that a rise in the GDP and GNP suffices necessarily to indicate that there is overall welfare of people of a nation. This is in tune with our age-old Aristotelian argument that economic justice is done when there is *distributive justice* as well. Hence, for Dr. Suman proper distribution of goods and services is of great value than an increment of GDP/GNP on paper. The point is, if there is any material increment on ground reality, it must reach the population equitably, which is of course not the same as mathematical equality because that is extremely difficult to conceive on ground levels of distribution; even its assurance is fraught with danger. This point is well-marked in the assertion of Fr. Franklin as well. What Mr. Binod tells us is not much different from these assertions though his point is not very clear. Mr. Prasad holds almost the same view with some addendum that welfare being a matter of non-economic evaluation as well, GDP and GNP are not necessary and sufficient measures of the same. However, his addendum is important in the context of clarification of the said non-economic bases of human well-being which Dr. Suman does not tell us now because he is stressing on more concrete economic reasons though he must not have much problem with this opinion either except for the idea of "spiritual progress" dragged by Mr. Prasad, which Fr. Franklin appreciates likely but not clearly and so is the case with Dr. Suman and Mr. Binod. Certainly the same idea is skipped by Mr. Sensharma as well though none must have any apathy to a non-economic indicator of being ethically just in a distribution system. It is good to notice that thus far there is hardly any logical disparity in the ethical positions maintained earlier and what has been said now about human well-being. As we stand here, human well-being whether good as means or end or both, is ethically good, but it does not necessarily and sufficiently depend on pure quantitative economic indicators such as an increment in nation's GDP and GNP. Nevertheless, stiff ethical disagreement could be seen in the context of human well-being when free trade and globalisation in an economy is discussed as means to it.

Most expectedly, Dr. Suman does not hesitate in accepting value of these reformist agendas in India in particular because he backs the idea with a reason in reply to question number four that in so far as a major aspect (the economic) of well-being is concerned, there must be minimal good in a society quantifiable in terms of employment enhancement, increase in per capita income and production of goods and services. Though these are not the only basis of human well-being, they are in part ethically good as means. This is again in tune with what Dr. Suman has maintained though his backup reasons as based on non-quantifiable goods, is still elusive. Fr. Franklin being an economist himself, is not under the influence of quantifiable aspects of human welfare because he is extremely clear in reply to the fourth question that though free trade and globalisation are partly good as means (as says Dr. Suman), it is not wholly good if some non-quantifiable or what we may now call, "qualitative aspects of human welfare", are not taken into consideration because it may well be that the qualitative aspects of reformist agendas add to its quantitative goodness. In that case, both participants cannot be said to be against free trade and globalisation as ethically bad though without qualitative considerations they might outweigh their goodness to turn out to be ethically bad. The difference is that Fr. Franklin has this specific ethical reason, which Dr. Suman does not have because his reasons tilt more in favour of the quantitative good of reforms. Mr. Binod again has more systematic reasons for us to justify that the reformist agendas are ethically commendable on two clear grounds—(a) on purely economic or what we now call, quantifiable or quantitative terms, which he mentions in the assertions (ii), (iv), (v), (vi) and in reply to the question number four; and (b) on non-quantifiable or qualitative terms such as "equality" and "rights" in assertion (i); partly in assertions (ii) in terms of "duties"; in assertion (v) in terms of "fairness" and in the assertion (iii) in terms of "freedom from corruption". We now have for us unambiguous ethical reasons such as the economic equality and the protection of the claim-rights of entrepreneurs as well as their concern or orientedness towards institutional duties linked to profits and professional commitment. More so, we have the reason based on distributive justice or justice as fairness in the reformist agenda and finally, the reason of abstaining from the malice of social and political corruption. This must be treated as threadbare ethical reasons in favour of reformism till each of these assertions are contested with success by arguments that deny what has been asserted on the grounds above. Mr. Binod's ethical reasons are different from Fr. Franklin as well because he does not have any spiritual/metaethical argument implicit in his argument. What is lacking in his reasons is whether the ethical conceptions of "equality" and "rights" are equally important for the general public and not only for the entrepreneurs. Mr. Binod's "producer oriented or industry oriented" argument, however, does not rule out the economic entrepreneurs of our nation and thus the Indian companies completely. The point is whether the industrialists and the producers (in a broader sense) have any care for equality and rights of the consumers or the public. Mr. Prasad thinks that it is good enough that free trade etc. will eradicate corruption to a great extent and industrialists will be helped by that, but does it really happen? Or, is the public helped in that respect? Again, the producer oriented argument brings in the idea of a monopolist breakdown but does not show its social impact. Wider assertions are found in (v) and (vi) when considering the social sphere, Mr. Binod speaks of benefits of "fairness" in distribution of wealth and division of work as per specialisation. Again the point is whether such fairness is truly visible and whether the latter is a boon or a bane. Similar problems may be faced in case of arguments from the "cheapness of price" and the "employment opportunities" caused by reforms. In any case, for Mr.

Binod, reforms do some good to some people at least, which must be therefore, good. When we come to the replies of Mr. Prasad, there are visible differences, as he too, nicely going along with his basic position of human welfare and the role of GDP and GNP in it, holds that the reformist agendas anywhere creates a field of economic competition which is unlevelled. The field thus creates an atmosphere of perform or perish with little scope for many small players in that field of market-competition to really perform well. As a few can in principle, perform well, so only they flourish and others do not flourish. The level field is lacking thus exposing the unethicality of disparity causing little or no human welfare. If "human" refers to both small players and the consumers as well, there is little level playing field in free markets. Hence, Mr. Binod slowly turns to the more ethical or humane possibility of domestic competition through liberalisation and privatisation (perhaps) and then prepare our own people or to empower them for a global onslaught. This must be his support to the qualitative ideal of well-being through economic performance, notwithstanding his quantitative conception as well when he rushes to remind us of both 'quality of products and consumer well-being' for which, free trade and globalisation are needed. Are these things possible through domestic and self-reliant market economy?

I have said before that replies to the cluster of questions in question number five is a way to check for discrepancy in arguments and to strengthen what has been said as value of economic reformist agendas. If we glance through Dr. Suman's replies, we find that he is emphatically *negative* in many cases as he does not buy the idea that free trade and globalisation is colonial, feudal, politically negative, polaristic, against central planning and trade policies, against small industries, against large domestic industries, against domestic competition, rises unemployment and breaks family structures. However, he is *indecisive* regarding whether reforms have any impact on public sector, inflation, labourers, corruption, culture and ecology. This amounts to say that Dr. Suman is not sure about these aspects of free trade and globalisation. However, more important is to notice why so many 'noes' are there and what they amount to the ethical position he has taken. This is all the more important when he concludes the clusters of replies saying emphatically that the reformist agendas are *humane*. We must remember that for him human well-being is not merely economic well-being because happiness does not come in that way alone, though it partly does come that way, is for sure. If this be the case, so many 'noes' are sure to follow. Even the "non-committals" sounds normal because taken together they mean that as means to human well-being free trade and globalisation *cannot* be or *most likely* not to be portrayed negatively as anti-human, anti-nation, anti-economic. On qualitative questions, he remained non-committal to questions (xvi) to (xviii) and to some extent to (xii), because he had to justify the *humane* status of reforms on the one hand and on the other hand the extrinsic value of these things. Strangely Fr. Franklin remains 'non-committal' or better said, ignorant about (xv), (xvi) and (xviii) but not about xiii, that is, about the exploitation of labourers, to which he responds positively (aye). This must be mainly owing to his earlier position that the reformist agendas are 'to some extent unavoidable' and 'good as means' to human welfare but not complete. Yet, in a complex blend of 'ayes' and 'noes' to other questions, he give us in two cases, "not necessarily" answer, which might imply "yes, no, and both", that is, in many cases free trade etc. might or might not cause political instability and instability in central planning. Other than this his "noes" and "ayes" to other questions along with his non-committals and indecisiveness amounts to a fine logical parity with his view that in any case no one can assure of an absolute ethical value of reforms as good. Any extrinsic good though a necessity at times, may not be necessarily good on all counts, economic and non-economic. Hence, it must be a blend of good and evil in modern times, and for that, it has to be never seen as contributing wholly to the human welfare. He says that it does not take care of the humane aspects of development, but this must have been unambiguously clear if his non-committals were not there. Coming to evaluate replies to the cluster of question by Mr. Binod Prasad we find that he has thorough "noes" for all questions except for three where he has "ayes" (xiv, xv and xvii), but no non-committals and indecisions. We have in mind Mr. Binod's position that free trade and globalisation are good as means to human welfare as they provide some economic and non-economic goods for man. Hence, for him, the *mixed value* of these reformist processes as we found in cases of Dr. Suman and Fr. Franklin are however, not the same. The point is why did Mr. Binod agree that reforms harm small industries and thus the people who run and depend on them, the unemployment they cause, families they disintegrate and the cultures they degenerate? And irrespective of such harmful consequences of the reformist processes, he concludes that reforms are humane and thus ethical! We have seen that Mr. Binod's earlier reasons, the ethical ones in particular, banks heavily on justifying the good that reforms does to large industries and the well-off industrialists. His "ayes" really does not appear to count anything against such organisations and entrepreneurs though they might count against small industries and petty entrepreneurs. Hence, he must be championing thoroughly the causes of free trade and globalisation as mixed good, but he does not spell it out clearly because the evil (as spoken in "ayes") does not count against his capitalist conception of ethical good of reforms. This view is certainly not championed by either Dr. Suman or Fr. Franklin because they find nothing so good in such processes in so far as people holding greater capital are in advantage though others may be left out or crash out of market. In fact, all these views agree on one major point, that is, reforms cannot be wholly good for all sections of people and society, still it makes a strong case for means to economic reforms at this epoch in India because (a) it does some good to most people, and (b) it does some good to some competitive people. Though reforms may be bad in many ways, they do not make enough ground for its elimination. Bad elements in reforms need to be minimised or nearly eliminated. A capitalist ethics thus does not rule out the badness of reforms, which takes it to a humane or ethical status—the world bodies worried to correct the maladies of reforms must be just for such correction though all do not buy this argument because the said evils are uneliminable, they are incorrigible fall out of a historical blunder in economics, called capitalist ethics based economics. We shall turn to this view as well but we might ask: What stuff is this 'capitalist's ethics'? It does not fall in what is there in ethics. Capitalist ethics is not another kind of normative ethical thesis; it is the specific construction of what is ethically good, right and just by the champions of capitalism, to justify the said tenets of economic theory so that they appear to be humane and not anti-human or unethical. For instance, capitalist ethics might champion the cases of norms of egoism and hedonism even egoistic hedonism for supporting reforms even if they have negative features. Still better, it might champion altruism, economic altruism inclusive, but not at the cost of the egoistic gains or pleasure. It might find out evils in egoism, egoistic hedonism and even in qualified altruism but that is for a revision in their thesis of egoism or hedonism or egoistic hedonism which makes it glossier to the sceptical. This is portrayed in altruistic hedonism or utilitarianism of Bentham who was testimony to the rise of capitalism in Britain. Bentham's capitalist approach was gross in terms of quantitative pleasure maximisation for maximum number of people to which adherence to principles of capitalist economy fitted nicely. Mill was a critic of such ethical conception of the capitalists because he propagated qualitative pleasure maximisation of people, and to add some human face to it noticed the value of ecological sustenance within the basic structures of a capitalist economy. Hence, for Mill many evils of a gross capitalist thesis may be revised by the system to a nobler thesis (with a human face so to say), which is nevertheless, not beyond capitalist conception of what is ethically right and just in economic decision-making. The modern day capitalist might thus have a revisionist ethics that moves *beyond utilitarianism* to *welfarism* along with the basic dogmas of capitalism to champion economic reforms even if they have evils which may not be pro-people wholly or may not be wholly pro-nature. Hence, there is no reason to believe that ethical welfarism is necessarily a non-capitalist revisionist thesis. It is perhaps due to this that a mixed good of reforms is well taken by the welfarists though their notion of "human well-being" must be severely twisted to suit the good of "a few humans". Is there something beyond the capitalist-structured ethical welfarism? Is there a welfarism which is not structured by the capitalists or by the followers of capitalist economy? The answer may be 'yes', but not the metaphysical/spiritual one because such theses might put us in a limbo of *nirvāṇic* thesis or theism or egalitarianism of a spiritual variety which stresses on the non-economic facets of "human welfare" in which "human" includes the "unempowered and uncompetitive humans" as well. It may be argued further that the *nirvāṇic* and the theistic conceptions of human well-being is out of the range of economic and ethical discussions, hence, they do not fit with cases of the reformist decision-making. For others, the *nirvāṇists* and the theists have their own structured thesis influenced by the capitalists because without *nirvāṇa* or the attainment of god we do not fare well in life. Hence, fresh set of arguments awaits us. The egalitarianism of Marx may not remain uncontested as a structured ethics of an economist yet again but claiming to be pro-people or a revision of "human well-being" where "human" is not limited to a few and, therefore, it is not the same as other types of egalitarian theses. More important is to find out how a broader human well-being is conceived here in economic and non-economic sense in the backdrop of the Marxist thesis. Do we notice an *implicit shift* or *revision* within the thesis adopting the capitalist features of both economics and ethics under its veil? If that be the case, it has to be evaluated for its own value and should not remain uncontested. We conclude that though human welfare is by far seen as mixed good by three of our participants, and hopefully by all of them and that most show signs of supporting a capitalist structured ethics of welfare, free trade and globalisation thus far did not turn out to be palpable anti-human and non-humane economic agendas of our times. Does Mr. A. Prasad fall in the same line? His replies to the cluster of questions and his conclusion is a shift no doubt from others in so far as not only is free trade and globalisation seen as doing good to some people, which is thus unambiguously *not* welfaristic, they are seen as *good for convenience* because they are things imposed on us at the present time and as a matter of convenience, we are going with it. This is clearer in the remaining replies to questions six and seven. In the midst of the confusion of taking reforms as a mixed good, may be more of an evil, Mr. Prasad thinks that it may not be pragmatically and practically avoidable; this is clear in his random "ayes" and "noes". This is much prominent in some of his "noes" which shows his favour towards a good that may not be wise to avoid even if such things are imposed on us or are structured as ethically noble by capitalists who mostly champion the cause. Here it must be added that when most of us show signs of getting along a mixed good of reforms knowing that they are given to us by a system not very close to the Indians by virtue of a *kitchery* economy since independence, is nevertheless, not taken as untouchable because there is no pertinent reasons found by these debaters to call capitalism and its structured ethics of reforms as rogue or essentially bad and not good in any case. Yes, there seems to be no logical relation between capitalism and ethical rogueness because its internal *revisionism* has tried to give it a humane character as far as possible by means of accepting its evil, inhuman and anti-poor aspects, and its tendencies to be anti-ecological. It is due to this that our participants could go along with a visibly upset capitalist thesis of reforms and its ethicality. The "noes" thus clearly sidesteps those which do not disparage reformist agenda completely, whereas "yeas" that draw fault lines do not pose serious threat to the same agenda. Now, if we quickly move on to the replies of all the four participants to the questions six and seven, things become clearer. We now find what the participants agree to broadly with respect to free trade and globalisation is that they are only *qualifiedly good as means*. Dr. Suman thus prefers modernisation and westernisation such as in the modern and western ways of production, distribution and services, but as said before, for mixed results, he does prefer "self-reliant" domestic good oriented economic reforms as well. Hence, he adopts the value of "*swadesi*" in the reformist agenda. Fr. Franklin supports the same. Mr. Binod does nearly the same but he prefers free trade and globalisation more than "*swadesi*" because the former for him is wider in opportunity. Mr. Prasad has hardly anything different to say.

Nevertheless, things are completely different when we come to the replies to questions five, six and seven as given by Mr. Sensharma. Barring a reply to the third part of the fifth question, where he is doubtful about reforms capable of destabilising central planning, Mr. Sensharma has emphatic "yeas" to all other parts, meaning thereby that he is confident about the *pure evil*, that is, inhuman, anti-environmental, anti-poor and unethical nature of the reformist processes such as the free trade and globalisation because without being a Marxist propagandist he hammers the point that human well-being is not achieved by *means* of such reforms in India because he adds that we need a self-reliant and free economy, an economy that does not endanger our economic and political sovereignty. The agro-based and small industries that champion the causes of the poor and the unprivileged arc truly closer to do economic welfare of people, which *ultimately* sees the ideal of *holistic human progress* fulfilled. However, when he comes to detail about the projects of modernisation and westernisation in Indian economy, he seems to accept a few things which supporters of the 'mixed good thesis' upheld. He says that benefits from the west and modern ways of planning, production and just distribution that grows our economy from within, that is, makes us self-reliant as epitomised in the five year plans and economic growth in India, are ethically desirable. Such modern ways and western methods are desirable in India if that benefits the poor, needy, unempowered and the entire populace.

Hence, *the point of corroboration is that human well being, if that amounts to the well being of all sections of people socially and economically through modernisation processes (may be western as well but not necessarily and exclusively) and those of free trade and globalisation, if they do not give exclusive powers in carrying on economic activities to the private parties is ethically good.* It may be seen that even the staunch supporter of reforms that perhaps Mr. Binod is and the more of less tentative ones that the three other participants are, could not completely shun either the good for all sections of our population or the modernisation of economy in other ways such as '*swadesi*', which is not in any case giving sole rights to private domestic parties. The nagging disagreement at the end, as I believe, is about agreeing as a *matter of convenience* that today in India, wisdom says that we accept free trade and globalisation as important ways to modernise our economy for some welfare at least. It may be said that signs are there in the domestic arena where leftist state governments are preparing reformist agendas as a matter of convenience that would *likely* be pro-people, can still not convince that there is scope of *revision* in basic egalitarian thinking even if that keeps strict vigil on certain things which the capitalists failed to do—the care for the poor, needy, unempowered small entrepreneurs and the environment. We can thus go on debating and strengthening our programme of intersubjective corroboration as basic to ethical resolution, which is a continuous process, humane but not absolute. Every other day through public debates like these we might find fresh sets of decision-making rules for our decision makers who are growingly in India blind to people's ethical conceptions or about practical impasses though they are for the people.

Intersubjective corroboration at the final stage of analysis turned out to be extremely useful for us to show how welfarist ethical theories either capitalist or egalitarian-structured, were active in the debate among non-ethicists. We found how without *structuralism of ethicists*, value issues may be debated and resolved to some extent at least. We came to know how egoism, hedonism, egoistic hedonism, altruistic hedonism, non-hedonic altruism and egalitarianism emerged in the dialogue each vying for supremacy though not all withstood in a corroboration of views which perhaps, in the final run defeated pure egoistic hedonism or even pure altruistic hedonism or the dogmatic welfarism structured by the capitalists. Decision-making rules need no special mention because replies to questions and decisions reached are unambiguous on this matter.

NOTES

1. Seabrook, Jeremy, "Free market no liberation agent" in *The Statesman*, Calcutta Edition, 08.07.2001.
2. *Ibid.*
3. Sharma, R. S., "Free Markets and Freer Bribery" in Letter to the Editor, *The Statesman*, Calcutta Edition, 10.04.2001.
4. Basu, Kaushik, "Trading Democracy" in an interview with Ronojoy Sen in

The Times of India, Patna Edition, 06.01.2002.

5. Jhunjhunwala, Dr. Bharat, "Loktaṅtra mein kathin hai ārthik vikās" in *The Prabhat Khabar*, Ranchi Edition, 11.10.2002.
6. Yue, Pan, "Tipping Point" in the Editorial Opinion of *The Times of India*, Patna Edition, 02.12.2006.
7. *Ibid.*
8. *Ibid.*

6

Afterword

Economic and Business Ethics, which includes ethics of administration and management as well, are vast fields of study. There are numerous issues needing ethical inquiry, which I was unable to include in this work for all practical reasons. Nevertheless, I think that I am successful to some extent in explaining how these fields of study which are essentially different from ethics, still makes cases for relevant ethical inquiries. In fact, the success of economic and business ethics depends much on justification of these fields of inquiry and the analysis of crucial value-laden issues therein and their resolution. In civil societies we do not prefer to live with value-crises, we need to resolve them urgently so that those concerned with the value laden practical problems have some positive ways to live a life of quality, and we know that a life that is led with some concern at least for basic values that humans as humans should have, is a life of quality. However, we came to know that value-crises in our economy, business, administration and management cannot or should not be resolved either in isolation or by taking the help of one or more expert ethicists as if they are consultants prescribing us absolute set of a value oriented decision-making cues so that we lead a life of value. Closely associated to this is the idea that the ethics consultants can make us moral persons by teaching ethics. I will turn to this aspect now because much has been said in the course of method of value resolution and the way it should be taken up. The issue of sophistical way to educate economists, businessmen, administrators and managers so that they become value-charged and thus noble people is a wayward project in ethics education. It has been noticed in our times, even in India that some schools of economics and business as well as administrative training institutes are seriously concerned about teaching ethics, business and management ethics (also administrative ethics, values and virtues and human values). What *should* be the aim of such teaching programmes and how it should be achieved? If we do not consider these questions we forget that teaching programmes have their own ethical objectives and methods. Hence, it is not important to discuss why something has to be taught, rather why something "should" be taught. A little care drags us to consider sophistical objectives and methods in teaching business ethics (to be precise), which is *ethically undesirable*. The sophistical objective of teaching ethics and business ethics, for instance, is to value-charge pupils, the prospective entrepreneurs and managers in particular so that they get important ethical lessons from ethics experts in their schools and going to the mainstream of their work-life they champion ethical entrepreneurs and managers, and that way they have become extremely noble persons assuming some moral authority to become ethics experts and consultants themselves. An ethics teaching project in business schools that go by such aims of the sophists to prepare unfaltering ethics *gurus* is not only a mired conception of teaching ethics, it is *unethical* as well because there is an inherent *classism* and *chauvinism* in such conceptions of teaching. One who has basic wisdom of philosophy comes to know that ethics do not prepare ethical beings because ethicists', 'programme in teaching' ethics has never been like the moralists who share moral ideas or teach them to pupils to prepare a flock of moralists though ethicists are not moralists, they do not and *should* not aim at producing morally noble people in society when 'moral nobility' is itself a matter of debate. In fact, a lot of ethics, almost the whole of it (a fantastic dose though), can never make us a noble person because nobility has no logically necessary dependence on teaching ethics—noble people exist among us by virtue of their common moral orientedness and not immoral orientedness in words, thoughts and acts. It is due to this that we should never include ethics or business ethics in business schools either with an idea that this is fashionable these days or with an idea that doing this the teachers in business schools who take interest in philosophy, finds new ways to earn a living, which is so lucrative in a division of labour as per expertise.

What has been said thus far is applicable in case of teaching values and virtues as well, human values and virtues in particular. The sophistical goal of such teaching prevalent in many schools to produce value and virtue oriented prospective businessmen and managers (or administrators), who thus assume a noble status in their work life to become consultants and rule from the top sitting in an edifice of glass is wayward and unethical. The idea must have crept in the business schools from the flurry of writings with the advent of neo-Aristotelianism in the name of virtue ethics and with the rise of neo-*śāstrism* in the name of Indian virtue ethics. In the midst of this it has been forgotten that any amount of teaching about virtues and values to our pupils do not produce virtuous and value-oriented persons in society who remain like that for long because there is again, no logical dependence on teaching a number of virtues and values and becoming virtuous and value-oriented. It is not difficult to find hundreds of virtuous people who have never received even formal education, what to speak of ethics and virtue-ethics. A lot more value-charged managers and workers are there who have never received such teaching in their schools. Many more are there who receive such teaching but do not remain so for long in the stress of perform or perish and in the paradox of egoism, hedonism, benefits and greed. Some people argue that just for these reasons constant orientation programmes are needed in our public and private sector companies and business units, administrative units and so that value and virtue charges are renewed when the inner spark fails or are discharged. Hence, the idea is continuous value-education/orientation by ethics experts or consultants of ethics, which strongly some business schools advertise that they are equipped with. Maybe this is another way to eke out a living by virtue of another modern division of labour. This is business-virtue-orientedness in business schools in teaching virtues and values, which is sophistical and unethical because the main aim is to earn and not to contribute to the society as philosophers. In fact, the value of virtues and values are relative in space and time; they change with respect to the changing social, economic and political conditions though certain objective values are conceivable. Many Aristotelian and *śāstric* virtues have great value, they are called, "eternal" and "universal", but the point is that though there are numerous virtues and values spread in many secular literatures or in non-*śāstric* literature, which are equally valuable, why at all *should* only those *śāstric* values be taught to the prospective managers, for instance? To enable them to see that only the said values and virtues needs to be *applied* by them in their *own* cases to become valuable individuals and in their work-fields to resolve crises is again wayward and unethical. It is wayward because by learning about the value of numerous values and virtues in life we just cannot artificially apply them in real life situations and it is unethical because an *artificial application* of a set of values or virtues taken as having great eternal and universal values by *an individual* in his or her work-life is mere predilection that disregard the relativism of values and virtues, and therefore, does not consider the case of rift in society about value and virtue perceptions, which is nothing but dogmatism and chauvinism. A manager dipped (or duped) in *śāstric* or any absolutist scheme of virtues and values when comes out in the society as moral expert and tries to act a moralist (not an ethicist), thus applying the so-called absolute set of values glorified as eternal and universal in the real life or the work-life situations as windowless monads shutting all value-disagreements among those who interact in society, may be colleagues, bosses or workers are having basic unethical way of life because artificiality on the part of the chauvinist value educated manager is itself a gross way in life. Is it difficult to find in India a number of Vedāntist manager who passed out of schools dipped in Vedāntic values and is in constant orientation programmes by the consultant *gurus* to remain like that but when it comes to work-life, the person turns out to be a great anti-worker or even anti-colleagues not trying anything to listen to the staunch *disbelievers* of values of Vedānta forgetting that in doing so Vedānta is forgotten? Let us try to be open-minded because the real life or the work-life is queer; it is a battle field of conflicting interests, opinions, dogmas, theses, ideologies, faiths, beliefs and notions of mortality. I have personally noticed and listened to the *śāstric* managers showing great apathy and antagonism to the workers who challenge their value-system. These people are even afraid of facing the petty workers who are up against their value-system. Is this the sign of a real Vedāntism? Any *śāstra*, whether it is *Vedānta* or *Koran* or *Bible* or *Das Kapital* when takes value-system to be dogmatically absolute and does not have courage to face the music of value-disagreements in the public life, which is the true picture in any society and work-life, is essentially chauvinistic, anti-people and thus unethical. A teaching project of ethics in our business schools "should" thus carefully avoid telling pupils that ethics, values and virtues are taught to them for making them moral chauvinists and to enable them to be experts or consultants in work-life remaining foolishly averse to ethical disagreements. Such ethics trained managers, even if they are constantly duped by a particular thesis in any training programme and workshops, which are very common in our schools, if they have minimum honesty left should realise and come out frankly to tell us that what they learnt could never be unilaterally applied in life whether in their own or in case of others because life is a queer phenomenon, it is a realm of two-way-traffic to know and to let others know. It is important to know that in real life some people commend and follow you, others do not. Importantly, if there is any substance in you *śāstric* ethics, you must courageously try to *assimilate* other ethics who do not commend you, and for this you need to know the basic ethics of acting, not in confrontation, bluff, trick and malice, but in association when acting is preceded by thorough *dialogues* not in every instance in life but more often when value-crises disturbs us urgently for resolution. It is only in this way that the inherent negative imports of "manager" as the one who "manages people by any means to get things done", might be eradicated. A manager 'should' be the one who thinks and acts to get things done in a most humane and efficient way, that is, when he goes by the system of doing things in a scientific way, always trying to find the *ideal* of doing and when in doing so, he orients his intentions to what is right, good and just not isolated but in and with the people who are most important for his duties or tasks to be fulfilled. If in doing so he is disliked by his peers and they do not participate in his ways of acting in camaraderie through dialogues with the concerned parties, the manager must be courageous to quit. A manager without being spiritual or damned by any *śāstra* whatsoever, must be thus an actor who performs his covenanted duties as a trustee to the *family* of his company and the consumers, always getting involved in knowing what is right and just when the 'family' is involved in speaking out to the collective. This takes us to the talk of method of ethical education in business schools, which I believe is clear, but it needs some clarification.

First, a note on why precisely *should* we teach ethics and business ethics in our business and administrative schools. What has been said thus far enables me to assert that these subjects should be taught to the prospective managers and administrators to empower them in life in some such ethical cues (not moral cues of the moralists), which helps them later on in work-life to become a professional who does things in the spirit of camaraderie, always being faithful to the large family of workers, peers and the general public, not trying to do a trick on them or disregard their opinion about what is a *desirable* course of decision-making and action. Then is it not true that contradicting my own position I have accepted that ethics teaching aims at making us a virtuous manager though virtuosity in this case has been equally dogmatically defined? Not so if we know basic logic because ethics and business ethics is *not a* gamut of virtues which are passed on to any generation through teaching. Our careful readers now come to know why at the very beginning I have enlisted the tasks of ethics and business ethics. What do we get from those tasks? Are they passing on virtues and values to us to make others virtuous in the way I now imagine? Certainly not, because normative ethics, business ethics and even virtue ethics as we know them are not bodies of virtues and values that aim us to be virtuous. Ethics or moral philosophy is simply a *philosophical inquiry* or *philosophical critique of the bases of moral evaluation, moral language, resolution of value-laden practical problems*, including those of the professionals who are in business as well and of a gamut of *values and virtues for their analyses of nature, meaning and significance*. Where is the noble programme of making us virtuous? If in doing these, we turn out to be equipped (or empowered) as I say, and thus hopefully turn out to be virtuous in someway, is a good enough consequence or derivation, but ethics is never taught for the said consequence (see vol. 4). A number of ethics-students do *not* turn out to be a desirable manager or whatsoever type of professional may be because that was never the aim of ethics because ethics is *not necessarily* capable of doing so. Then where lays the fallacy? Why is it that though performing tasks of ethics in our schools we are still "not necessarily" empowered as a virtuous manager, for instance? The reason is that an empowered ethicist becomes a non-chauvinist, manager when in work-life he, rather than applying any absolute thesis, acts as a de-classed, empathetic worker, a trustee who is always ready to work through *dialogue-based decision-making* that gives him in the milieu of disagreements, that which is right and good for the company, workers and the consumers. Hence, the project of ethics apart from other things should be to empower any *professional*, teachers, doctors, managers and others to be *pro-people* and *pro-discursive*, as well as to be a threadbare *analyst* of ethical views of participants so that the precious *corroborated points for decision-making* could be filtered.

Are we any far from knowing *how* and *what* should be done? Not to the least, because it is clear that in our professional schools, business schools inclusive, ethics teaching should be taken wholly, not partly because that does not prepare a complete ethics-empowered person who is pro-people, pro-dialogue and pro-analysis. Ethics teaching should not, therefore, be scrappy in our schools but things are enormous; even a careful selection might take two years for some satisfaction. My earnest request is to take care of all the *tasks* of ethics and not unnecessarily bank on values and virtues, and that too in a uncritical or most unphilosophical fashion, because philosophical ventures are essentially open and secular, nothing is true and false here, only certain things are logically stronger than other things. The *method* of teaching ethics should always take care of *interactions*, and *debates and dialogues* about issues which raise questions of ethical values. However, such things need not be done in an artificial atmosphere by taking a value-laden case and applying a normative theory or a virtue or a value for finding an answer to them. Often a classroom argument (not dialogue) in the context of a case does not take us to the desired objective. A preparation of a manager always involved in dialogue does not beg artificial manipulations as these. It may be much better if the prospective manager is thrown in the heat of interactions in a "family" conceived by me quite often while he is going through an academic course in ethics to see himself what ethics might take him to do. A manager should remember that *post-corroboration analysis* of any moral dialogue that gives him corroborated points and the knowledge of logical strength of norms is to be a strong learner of normative and metaethics as well. Ethics and business ethics needs care on our part, on the part of the teachers because it is them who either prepare chauvinists or de-classed managers.

Bibliography

Anscombe, G.E.M., *"Modern Moral Philosophy", Philosophy, Vol.* 33, Jan., 1958.

Aristotle, *The Nicomachean Ethics*, (English Trans.) Thomson, J.A.K., Penguin, Baltimore, 1966.

Austin, J. L., *How To Do Things With Words*, Harvard University Press, MA, 1962.

Basu, Kaushik, "Trading Democracy", *The Times of India*, Patna Edition, 06.01.2000.

Bayles, M. D., *Professional Ethics*, Wadsworth, Belmont, 1989.

Beauchamp, T. and Bowie, N., (eds.), *Ethical Theory and Business*, Prentice-Hall, NJ, 1979.

Bentham, Jeremy, *An Introduction to the Principles of Morals and Legislation*, Clarendon, Oxford, 1948.

Boatright, J. R., *Ethics and the Conduct of Business*, Prentice-Hall, NJ, 1997.

Boatright, J. R., *Ethics in Finance*, Blackwell, Oxford, 1999.

Bowie, N. E., *Business Ethics*, Prentice-Hall, NJ, 1982.

Bowie, N. E., "Post Modernism, Business Ethics and Solidarity," Morscher, E., Neumaier, O. and Simons, P. (Eds.), *Applied Ethics in a Troubled World*, Kluwer, London, 1998.

Brandt, R. B., *A Theory of the Good and the Right*, O.U.P., NY, 1979.

Brandt, R. B., *Ethical Theory*, Prentice-Hall, NJ, 1959.

Brennan, G., "The Economists' Approach to Ethics: A Late Twentieth Century View", Groenewegen, Peter (eds.), *Economics and Ethics?*, Routledge, London, 1996.

Buchnan, A., "Economics and Ethics", Werhane, P. H. and Freeman, R. E., (eds.), *The Blackwell Encyclopaedic Dictionary of Business Ethics*, Blackwell, 1997.

Bulgakov, Sergei, *Philosophy of Economy: The World as Household*, Yale University Press, New Haven, 2000.

Callahan, D. and Bok, S. (eds.), *The Teaching of Ethics in Higher Education*, Hastings Centre, NY, 1980.

Camenisch, P. F., "Marketing Ethics: Some Dimensions of the Challenge", Hartman, L. P. (eds.) *Perspectives in Business Ethics*, Tata McGraw-Hill Publishing Co. Ltd., New Delhi, 2003.

Carrit, E.F., *Theory of Morals*, O.U.P., London, 1928.

Carroll, A. B., "The Pyramid of Corporate Social Responsibility Towards the Moral Management of Organisational Stakeholders", *Business Horizon*, 34 (4), 1991.

Chakraborty, S. K. and Chatterjee, S. R. (eds.), *Applied Ethics in Management: Towards New Perspectives*, Springer, NY, 1999.

Chandler, A.D., *The Visible Hand: The Managerial Revolution in American Business,* Harvard University Press, MA, 1977.

Coats, A. W., "Value Judgements in Economics" *Yorkshire Bulletin of Economics and Social Science Research*, Vol. 16, 1964.

De George, R. T. and Pichler, J. A. (eds.), *Ethics, Free Enterprise and Public Policy*, O.U.P., NY, 1978.

De George, R. T., *Business Ethics*, Prentice-Hall, NJ, 1997.

De Marco, J. P. and Fox, R. M., (eds.), *New Directions in Ethics: The Challenge of Applied Ethics*, Routledge & Kegan Paul, NY, 1986.

Donagan, Alan, *The Theory of Morality*, University of Chicago Press, Chicago, 1977.

Donaldson, T., *The Ethics of International Business*, OUP, NY, 1989.

Drucker, P., *Management*, Heinemann, London, 1979.

Dunlop, Charles and Kling, Rob (eds.), *Computerization and Controversy: Value Conflicts and Social Changes*, Academic Press, NY, 1991.

Dunsire, R. S., *Roles and Values: An Introduction to Social Ethics*, Methuen, London, 1971.

Dworkin, R., *Taking Rights Seriously*, Harvard University Press, MA, 1978.

Enderle, G., "Business Ethics As A Goal-Right-System", Warner, Malcolm (ed.), *The International Encyclopaedia of Business Management*, Vol. 6, Thomson Learning, London, 2002.

Etzioni, A., *The Moral Dimension*, Free Press, NY, 1988.

Feinberg, Joel, *Essays On the Theory of Responsibility*, Princeton University Press, NJ, 1970.

Feinberg, Joel, *Rights, Justice and the Bounds of Liberty*, Princeton University Press, NJ, 1980.

Fischer, J. M. and Ravizza, M., *Perspectives on Moral Responsibility*, Cornell University Press, NY, 1993.

Frankena, W. K., *Ethics*, Prentice-Hall, New Delhi, 1989.

Frederick, W.C., *Values Nature and Culture in the American Corporation,* O.U.P., NY, 1995.

Freeman, R. E. and Gilbert, D., *Corporate Strategy and the Search for Ethics*, Prentice-Hall, NJ, 1988.

Freeman, R. E., *Strategic Management: A Stakeholder Approach*, Pitman, Boston, 1984.

French, P., *Collective Corporate Responsibility*, Columbia University Press, NY, 1984.

Friedman, A., "The Social Responsibility of Business Is to Increase Its Profits", *New York Times Magazine*, 13.09.1970.

Friedman, A., *Welfare Economics and Social Choice Theory*, Martinus Nijhoff, Boston, 1980.

Galbraithe, J. K., *The Affluent Society*, Houghton Griffin Co., Boston, 1958.

Garrett, T. M. and Kolonoski, R. J., *Business Ethics*, Prentice-Hall, NJ, 1986.

Gauthier, D., *Morals by Agreement*, OUP, Oxford, 1986.

Gill, Flora, "On Ethics and Economic Science", Groenewegen, Peter (ed.), *Economics and Ethics?*, Routledge, London, 1996.

Gilligan, C., *In a Different Voice: Psychological Theory and Women's Development*, Harvard University Press, MA, 1982.

Godlovitch, Stan, "Varieties of Progress: Commercial, Moral and Otherwise", Werhane, P. A. and Singer, A. E., (eds.), *Business Ethics in Theory and Practice: Contributions from Asia and New Zealand*, Kluwer, London, 1999.

Goodpaster, K. E., "Business Ethics", Werhane. P. H. and Freeman, R. E. (eds.), *The Blackwell Encyclopaedic Dictionary of Business Ethics*, Vol. XI, Blackwell, 1997.

Greene, D. M., *The Ethical Manager*, Macmillan, NY, 1994.

Groenewegen, Peter (ed.), *Economics and Ethics?* Routledge, London, 1996.

Hansman, D. M. and McPherson. M. S., "Taking Ethics Seriously: Economics and Contemporary Moral Philosophy", *Journal of Economic Literature*, 31 (2), 1993.

Hare, R. M., *Freedom and Reason*, OUP, NY, 1965.

Hare, R. M., *The Language of Morals*, Clarendon Press, Oxford, 1961.

Harsanyi, J. C., *Essays in Ethics, Social Behaviour and Scientific Explanation*, Riedel, Dordrecht, 1976.

Hartman, L. P., (ed.), *Perspectives in Business Ethics*, Tata McGraw-Hill Publishing Co. Ltd., New Delhi, 2003.

Hayek, F. A., *Studies in Philosophy, Politics and Economics*, Routledge, London, 1967.

Hodgkinson, Christopher, *Administrative Philosophy: Values and Motivations in Administrative Life,* Pergamon, Oxford, 1996.

Hosmer, L. T., *The Ethics of Management*, Irwin, Illinois, 1996.

Hume, David, *Enquiry Concerning the Principles of Morals*, OUP, Oxford, 1972.

Jackall, R., *Moral Mazes*, OUP, NY, 1988.

Jhunjhunwala, Dr. Bharat, "Loktańtra Mein Kathin Hai Ārthik Vikās", *Prabhat Khabar*, Patna Edition, 11.10.2002.

Kalpholz, Kurt, "Economics and Ethical Neutrality", Edward, Paul (ed.), *Encyclopaedia of Philosophy*, Vol. 2, Macmillan Publishing Co. & The Free Press, NY, 1964.

Kant, Immanuel, *Groundwork of the Metaphysic of Morals*, (Trans.), Paton H.J., Harper and Row, NY, 1964.

Kling, Rob, "When Organisations are Perpetrators: Assumptions About Computer Abuse and Computer Crime", Dunlop, Charles and Kling, Rob (eds.), *Computerization and Controversy: Value Conflicts and Social Change*, Academic Press, NY, 1991.

Koslovski, Peter (ed.), *The Social Market Economy: Theory and Ethics of the Economic Order*, Springer-Verlag, Berlin, 1992.

Ladd, John, "Computers and Moral Responsibility: A Framework for an Ethical Analysis", Dunlop, Charles and Kling, Rob (eds.), *Computerization and Controversy: Value Conflicts and Social Change*, Academic Press, NY, 1991.

LaCroix, W. L., *Principles for Ethics in Business*, University Press of America, Washington D. C., 1976.

Lawrence, Paul, R. and Lorsch, Jay W., *Organisation and Environment*, Harvard University Press, Cambridge, MA, 1967.

Liebig, James E. (ed.), *Merchants of Vision: People Bringing New Purpose and Values to Business*, Berrett-Koehler Publishers, San Francisco, 1994.

Little, I. M. D., *A Critique of Welfare Economics*, Clarendon Press, Oxford, 1957.

Locke, John, *Second Treatise of Government*, Cambridge University Press, Cambridge, 1988.

Lowe, Toby, "The Communitarian Critique of Market", Norman Richard (ed.), *Ethics and the Market*, Ashgate, Aldershot, 1999.

Mackie, J. L., *Ethics: Inventing Right and Wrong*, Penguin, Harmandsworth, 1978.

Mahoney, Jack, "Business Ethics", Malcolm, Warner (ed.), *The International Encyclopaedia of Business and Management*, Vol. 6. Thomson Learning, London, 2002.

Marx, Karl, *Capital: A Critical Analysis of Capitalist Production*, Sonneschein, London, 1887.

Mayer, R. N., *The Consumer Movement: Guardian of the Market Place*, Twayne Publishers, Boston, 1989.

Mayo, Elton, *The Human Problems of an Industrial Civilization*, Macmillan, NY, 1933.

McIntyre, A., *After Virtue*, University of Notre Dame, IN, 1984.

Michalos, A. C., *A Pragmatic Approach to Business Ethics*, Sage, California, 1995.

Mill, J. S., *Utilitarianism*, Fontana, London, 1962.

Moore, M. H., "How Difficult Is It To Construct Market Relation? A Commentary of Platteau", *Journal of Development Studies*, 30 (4), 1994.

Morscher, E., Neumaier, O. and Simons, P. (Eds.), *Applied Ethics in a Troubled World*, Kluwer, London, 1997.

Myrdal, Gunnar, *Value in Social Theory*, Routledge & Kegan Paul, London, 1958.

Nagel, T., *Moral Questions*, Cambridge University Press, Cambridge, 1979.

Nagel, T., *The Possibility of Altruism*, Clarendon Press, Oxford, 1970.

Noddings, N., *Caring: A Feminine Approach to Ethics and Moral Education*, University of California Press, Berkeley, 1984.

Norman, Richard, *Ethics and Market*, Ashgate, Vermont, 1999.

Nozick, Robert, *Anarchy, State and Utopia*, Basic Book, NY, 1974.

O' Neill, Onora, *Faces of Hunger*, Allen & Unwin, London, 1986.

Olson, M., *The Logic of Collective Action*, Harvard University Press, MA, 1965.

Ormerod, Paul, *The Death of Economics*, Faber, London, 1995.

Pastin, M., *The Hard Problem of Management Ethics*, Jossey–Bass, San Francisco, 1986.

Petrick, J. A. and Quinn, J. F., *Management Ethics: Integrity at Work*, Response Book, New Delhi, 1997.

Pigou, A. C., *The Economics of Welfare*, Macmillan, London, 1952.

Pitt, J. C. (ed.), *Philosophy of Economics*, Reidel, Dordrecht, 1981.

Plant, Raymond, "The Moral Boundaries of Markets", Norman, Richard (ed.), *Ethics and the Market*, Ashgate, Vermont, 1999.

Plato, *The Republic*, (Eng. Trans.) F. M. Cornford, OUP, NY, 1982.

Platteau, J. P., "Behind the Market Stage Where Real Societies Exist, I & II", *Journal of Development Studies*, 30 (3); 30 (4), 1994.

Quinn, R. E., Faerman, S. R., Thompson, M. P. and McGrath, M. R. (eds.), *Becoming a Master Manager*, John Wiley & Sons, NY, 1996.

Rachels, James, "The Challenge of Cultural Relativism", Cahn, S. M., and Markie, P. (eds.), *Ethics: History, Theory and Contemporary Issues*, OUP, NY, 1999.

Rawls, John, *A Theory of Good*, Harvard University Press, MA, 1971.

Regan, Tom, *New Introductory Essays in Business Ethics*, Random House, NY, 1984.

Robbins, L., *An Essay On The Nature and Significance of Economic Science*, Macmillan, London, 1935.

Rorty, Richard, *Contingent, Irony and Solidarity*, Cambridge University Press, Cambridge, 1989.

Ross, D., *Aristotle: The Nicomachean Ethics*, OUP, Oxford, 1980.

Ross, W. D., *The Right and the Good*, Clarendon Press, Oxford, 1930.

Rothschild, K. W., *Ethics and Economic Theory Ideas-Models-Dilemmas*, Cambridge, 1993.

Rowthorn, Robert, "Ethics and Economics: An Economists' Views", Groenewegen, Peter (ed.), *Economics and Ethics?* Routledge, London, 1996.

Samuelson, P. A., *Foundations of Economic Analysis*, Harvard University Press, MA, 1947.

Savage, Charles, M., "The Ethics of Teaching: The Key to the Knowledge Economy", Chakraborty, S. K. and Chatterjee, S. R. (eds.), *Applied Ethics in Management: Towards New Perspectives*, Springer, NY, 1993.

Seabrook, Jeremy, "Free Market no Liberation Agent", *The Statesman*, Kolkata Edition, Kolkata, 08.07.2001.

Searle, John R., *The Construction of Social Reality*, OUP, NY, 1995.

Sekhar, R. C., *Ethical Issues in Business*, Response Books, Sage, New Delhi, 2002.

Sen, A. and Williams, B. (eds.), *Utilitarianism and Beyond*, Cambridge University Press, Cambridge, 1982.

Sen, Amartya, *Choice, Welfare and Measurement*, MIT Press, Cambridge, 1982.

Sen, Amartya, *On Ethics and Economics*, OUP, Delhi, 1990.

Sharma, R. S., "Free Markets and Freer Bribery", *The Statesman*, Kolkata Edition, Kolkata, 10.04.2001.

Shaw, Patrick, "Markets and Moral Minimalism", Norman, Richard (ed.), *Ethics and the Market*, Ashgate, Aldershot, 1999.

Senge, P. M., *The Fifth Discipline: The Art and Practice of Learning Organisation,* Doubleday, NY, 1990.

Singer, Peter, *A Companion to Ethics*, OUP, Oxford, 1991.

Singer, Peter, *Practical Ethics*, Cambridge University Press, Cambridge, 1979.

Smith, Adam, *An Inquiry into the Nature and Cause of the Wealth of Nations*, Clarendon Press, Oxford, 1776.

Solomon, R. C., "Business Ethics", Singer, Peter (ed.), *A Companion to Ethics*, OUP, Oxford, 1991.

Solomon, R. C., "Is It Ever Right to Lie? (On Truth In Advertising)", Hartman, P. (ed.), *Perspectives in Business Ethics*, Tata McGraw-Hill Publishing Co. Ltd., New Delhi, 2003.

Stevenson, C. L., *Ethics and Language*, Yale University Press, New Haven, 1944.

Stone, C.D., *Where the Law Ends,* Harper and Row, NY, 1975.

Stonier, A. W. and Hague, D. C., *A Textbook of Economic Theory*, Pearson Education, Delhi, 2004.

Taylor, F., *The Principles of Scientific Management*, Harper, NY, 1911.

Velasquez, M.G., *Business Ethics: Concepts and Cases,* Prentice-Hall of India, New Delhi, 2002.

Velasquez, W. S., "An Exchange of Questions between Economics and Philosophy", Phelps, E. S. (ed.), *Economic Justice*, Penguin, Harmondsworth, 1953.

Walton, C. C., *The Moral Manager*, Harper Business, NY, 1988.

Waler, Michael, *Spheres of Justice*, Blackwell, Oxford, 1983.

Warner, Malcolm, *International Encyclopaedia of Business and Management*, Vols. 1–6, Thomson Learning, London, 2002.

Weber, Max, *Theory of Social and Economic Organisation*, OUP, Oxford, 1921.

Werhane, P. H., *Adam Smith and His Legacy for Modern Capitalism*, OUP, NY, 1991.

Werhane, P. H. and Freeman, R. E. (eds.), *The Blackwell Encyclopaedic Dictionary of Business Ethics*, Vol. X, Blackwell, Oxford, 1997.

Werhane, P. H. and Singer, A. E. (eds.), *Business Ethics in Theory and Practice: Contributions from Asia and New Zealand*, Kluwer, London, 1999.

Yue, Pan, "Tipping Point", *The Times of India*, Patna Edition, 02.12.2006.

Yuktananda, Swami, *Values and Ourselves*, Vivekananda Nidhi, Kolkata, 1989.

Index